This book is the product of a multiyear dialogue between leading human rights theorists and high-level representatives of international human rights nongovernmental organizations (INGOs) sponsored by the United Nations University, headquartered in Tokyo with centers around the world, and the City University of Hong Kong. It is divided into three parts that reflect the major ethical challenges discussed at a series of workshops: the ethical challenges associated with interaction between relatively rich and powerful Northern-based human rights INGOs and recipients of their aid in the South; whether and how to collaborate with governments that place severe restrictions on the activities of human rights INGOs; and the tension between expanding the organizations' mandate to address more fundamental social and economic problems and focusing on more immediate and clearly identifiable violations of civil and political rights. Each section contains contributions by both theorists and practitioners of human rights.

Daniel A. Bell is a professor in the Department of Philosophy at Tsinghua University in Beijing. He has held teaching posts at the City University of Hong Kong, the University of Hong Kong, and the National University of Singapore and research fellowships at Stanford's Center for Advanced Study in the Behavioral Sciences and Princeton's University Center of Human Values. His books include *Beyond Liberal Democracy: Political Thinking for an East Asian Context* (2006), *East Meets West: Human Rights and Democracy in East Asia* (2000), and *Communitarianism and Its Critics* (1993).

Jean-Marc Coicaud heads the United Nations University (UNU) Office at the United Nations in New York, prior to which he was senior academic officer in the UNU Peace and Governance Programme, Tokyo. He also served in the Executive Office of the United Nations Secretary-General as a speechwriter for Dr. Boutros Boutros-Ghali. A former Fellow at the Harvard University Department of Philosophy and Harvard Law School, the United States Institute of Peace, Washington, D.C., and New York University School of Law, Coicaud has held appointments with the French Ministry of Foreign Affairs, the European Parliament (Financial Committee), the University of Paris-I Sorbonne and the Ecole normale supérieure, Paris. His books include *Power in Transition: The Peaceful Change of International Order* (co-authored with Charles A. Kupchan, Emanuel Adler, and Yuen Foong Khong) (2001), *Legitimacy and Politics: A Contribution to the Study of Political Right and Political Responsibility* (Cambridge University Press, 2002), and *Beyond the National Interest* (2007).

The United Nations University is an organ of the United Nations established by the General Assembly in 1972 to be an international community of scholars engaged in research, advanced training, and the dissemination of knowledge related to the pressing global problems of human survival, development, and welfare. Its activities focus mainly on the areas of peace and governance, environment and sustainable development, and science and technology in relation to human welfare. The University operates through a worldwide network of research and postgraduate training centers, with its planning and coordinating headquarters in Tokyo.

Ethics in Action

THE ETHICAL CHALLENGES OF INTERNATIONAL HUMAN RIGHTS NONGOVERNMENTAL ORGANIZATIONS

Edited by

Daniel A. Bell
Tsinghua University, Beijing

Jean-Marc Coicaud
United Nations University

CAMBRIDGE UNIVERSITY PRESS
Cambridge, New York, Melbourne, Madrid, Cape Town, Singapore, São Paulo

Cambridge University Press
32 Avenue of the Americas, New York, NY 10013-2473, USA

www.cambridge.org
Information on this title: www.cambridge.org/9780521865661

First published 2007

Printed in the United States of America

A catalog record for this publication is available from the British Library.

Library of Congress Cataloging in Publication Data

Ethics in action : the ethical challenges of international human rights
nongovernmental organizations / edited by Daniel A. Bell, Jean-Marc Coicaud.
    p.   cm.
Includes bibliographical references and index.
ISBN-13: 978-0-521-86566-1 (hardback)
ISBN-10: 0-521-86566-2 (hardback)
ISBN-13: 978-0-521-68449-1 (pbk.)
ISBN-10: 0-521-68449-8 (pbk.)
1. Non-governmental organizations.   2. Human rights.   3. Political ethics.
I. Bell, Daniel (Daniel A.)   II. Coicaud, Jean-Marc.   III. Title.
JZ4850.E84   2006
323.06'01 – dc22   2006007800

ISBN-13   978-0-521-86566-1 hardback
ISBN-10   0-521-86566-2 hardback

ISBN-13   978-0-521-68449-1 paperback
ISBN-10   0-521-68449-8 paperback

From Daniel A. Bell

To my mother and Anthony

From Jean-Marc Coicaud

To Didier Louvel

Contents

Acknowledgments

This book emerged from a multiyear international project, Ethics in Action: The Successes, Compromises, and Setbacks of International Human Rights Non-governmental Organizations (INGOs), sponsored by the United Nations University, headquartered in Tokyo with centers around the world, and the City University of Hong Kong. The project took the form of dialogues between high-level representatives of INGOs and academic theorists who work on the subject of human rights. The editors are grateful to Geneviève Souillac, Joseph Carens, and Joanne Bauer, who helped to conceptualize the project in its early stages.

Project participants were asked to think about how INGOs deal with the ethical challenges they experience during the course of their work, how they ought to deal with those challenges and then to draw implications for human rights INGO work at the United Nations. We organized three workshops that dealt with those respective themes. The first workshop was held at the Carnegie Council on Ethics and International Affairs in New York (February 2002) and consisted of papers by high-level human rights INGO practitioners, with comments by theorists of human rights. The second, at the City University of Hong Kong (October 2003), consisted of papers by human rights theorists, with comments by practitioners. The third, at the United Nations University (UNU) in New York (August 2005), was a brainstorming session with human rights practitioners and theorists. We are indebted to the host organizations in New York and Hong Kong.

The chapters of this book were initially presented and discussed at these workshops. During the workshops, the papers were submitted to rigorous scrutiny and critical questioning by workshop participants. The editors encouraged further exchanges among participants, and most chapters were shaped by these exchanges. We are especially grateful to the human rights practitioners and theorists who participated in the workshops: John Ambler, Robert Arsenault, Michael Barnhart, Christian Barry, Joanne Bauer, Widney Brown, Joseph Carens, Neera Chandhoke, C. Y. Chong, Ci Jiwei, David Cingranelli, Allison Cohen, Larry Cox, Eric Dachy, Michael Davis, Michael Dowdle, Christopher Drake, Michael Edwards, Fan Ruiping, Basil Fernando, Andre Frankovits, Sakiko Fukuda-Parr,

Curt Goering, Jennifer Green, Hahm Chaibong, Niel Hicks, John Hirsh, Ian Holliday, Sharon Hom, Bonny Ihbawoh, Tatsuo Inoue, Lakshmi Jacota, Brian Joseph, Stephanie Kleine-Ahlbrandt, Shulamith Koenig, Will Kymlicka, Linda Li, Ram Mannikalingam, Julie Mertus, Ravi Nair, Ndubisi Obiorah, William Pace, Betty Plewes, Thomas Pogge, Ken Roth, Edward Rubin, Hans-Otto Sano, Joe Saunders, Rieky Stuart, Pisawat Sukonthapan, Kevin Sullivan, Sun Zhe, Lyal Sunga, Julia Tao, Hatla Thelle, Frank Upham, Alex de Waal, Steven Weir, Sophia Woodman, Mona Younis, and Zhang Qianfan. We are grateful that workshop participants showed willingess to go beyond traditional professional and disci-plinary boundaries. The theorists showed willingness to think in practical terms, and the practitioners showed willingness to think in theoretical terms. It is worth noting, however, that the distinction between *theorist* and *practitioner* is not always easy to make. Whatever their professional label, we found that most indi-viduals do both. The practitioners often think about normative issues, and the academics often think about implementation.

The project would not have been possible without the financial support of the United Nations University, the City University of Hong Kong (Faculty of Humanities and Social Sciences), and a generous grant from the Open Society Institute. We are grateful to Ramesh Thakur, Senior Vice-Rector of the UNU, and to Professor Matthew Chen, (then) dean of the Faculty of Humanities and Social Sciences and (then) head of the Department of Public and Social Administration, and Professor Ian Holliday at the City University of Hong Kong for helping to secure this funding. We express our appreciation to individuals who offered their time and effort to make the workshops possible. At the United Nations University, Tokyo, we would like to thank Yoshie Sawada, senior administrative assistant, in the UNU Peace and Governance Programme, and Geneviève Souillac, then academic programme associate in the Peace and Governance Programme. At the City University of Hong Kong, we would like to thank Louisa Lui as well as H. L. Chan, Mon Chin, Vivine Chow, Ivan Fong, Antony Ou, Cherry Tsang, and Kenneth Yu. At the Carnegie Council, we thank Joanne Bauer and Jess Messer.

We are grateful for the help and efficiency of our editor at Cambridge University Press, John Berger. Scott McQuade, head of UNU Press, was also very helpful in facilitating the cooperation between the two presses. The editors and authors are also very grateful to Jibecke Jönsson for her help in overseeing the editing process on the UNU side. We are also grateful for the insightful reports of three anonymous referees for Cambridge University Press.

Finally, we would like to thank our family members who kindly and patiently allowed us to work on this project. In particular, Daniel Bell would like to thank Bing and Julien.

List of Contributors

Daniel A. Bell is professor in the Department of Philosophy, Tsinghua University (Beijing). His latest book is *Beyond Liberal Democracy: Political Thinking for an East Asian Context* (Princeton University Press, 2006) and his coedited collections include (with Hahm Chaibong) *Confucianism for the Modern World* (Cambridge University Press, 2003) and (with Joanne R. Bauer) *The East Asian Challenge for Human Rights* (Cambridge University Press, 1999).

Joseph H. Carens is professor of Political Science at the University of Toronto. He is the author of *Culture, Citizenship and Community* (Oxford, 2000), three other books, and more than fifty journal articles or chapters in books. Carens is currently writing a book on the ethics of immigration.

Neera Chandhoke is professor in the Department of Political Science and the director of the Developing Countries Research Center at the University of Delhi. She is currently working on a book, *A State of One's Own: Secessionist Movements in India*, and is directing a Ford-funded project, Globalisation and the State in Media. Publications include *The Conceits of Civil Society* (Oxford University Press, 2003) and *Beyond Secularism: The Rights of Religious Minorities* (Oxford University Press, 1999).

Jean-Marc Coicaud heads the United Nations University (UNU) Office at the United Nations in New York. Coicaud's former positions include being a member of former UN Secretary-General Dr. Boutros Boutrous-Ghali's speech-writing team and fellowships at Harvard University, the United States Institute of Peace, and New York University School of Law. Sample publications include *Legitimacy and Politics: A Contribution to the Study of Political Right and Political Responsibility* (Cambridge University Press, 2002) and *Beyond the National Interest* (USIP Press, 2006).

Curt Goering is the senior deputy executive director and chief operating officer of Amnesty International USA (AI USA). Goering has a long background with AI USA, AI's world headquarters in London, and several field assignments worldwide. He has also been the delegate to seven International Council Meetings, Amnesty International's highest decision-making body.

Bonny Ibhawoh is assistant professor of history and social justice at Brock University in Canada. He was previously a Human Rights Fellow at the Danish Institute for Human Rights, Copenhagen, and the Carnegie Council for Ethics and International Affairs, New York. He is the author of the book *Imperialism and Human Rights* (State University of New York Press Human Rights Series, forthcoming).

Birgit Lindsnæs has been the deputy director general at the Danish Institute for Human Rights and the director of the International Department since 1991. She was previously with the Danish Red Cross, the Institute for Anthropology at the University of Copenhagen, and Danish Amnesty International. Lindsnæs is the chair of the Board for International Service for Human Rights in Geneva and chair of the work group on global public goods and human rights.

Betty Plewes is the former president-CEO of the Canadian Council for International Cooperation, the umbrella body for Canadian development nongovernmental organizations. She consults on development policy and organizational development and has a long-standing interest in policy issues.

Thomas Pogge has, since receiving his Ph.D. in philosophy from Harvard, been teaching moral and political philosophy and Kant at Columbia University. He is currently a Professorial Research Fellow at the Australian National University Centre for Applied Philosophy and Public Ethics.

Kenneth Roth has been the executive director of Human Rights Watch, the largest U.S.-based international human rights organization, since 1993. From 1987 to 1993, Roth served as deputy director of the organization. Previously, he was a federal prosecutor in New York and Washington, D.C., and a private litigator. He has written more than eighty articles and chapters on a wide range of human rights topics.

Hans-Otto Sano, director of research for the Danish Institute for Human Rights, Copenhagen, has a background in history and development studies. Sano holds a Ph.D. in economic history with the subject specialization in human rights and development. He is currently involved in research projects on rights-based development and global governance.

Rieky Stuart is the former executive director of Oxfam Canada. She consults on international development and is currently a Fellow at the Munk Centre for International Studies at the University of Toronto.

Sun Zhe received his doctorate from Columbia University and is now professor and deputy director of the Center for American Studies at Fudan University in Shanghai. Sun is the author or editor of several books on comparative politics and U.S.-China relations. He is considered one of the leading scholars in the field of American studies in China.

Lyal S. Sunga, currently senior lecturer and director of research at the Raoul Wallenberg Institute of Human Rights and Humanitarian Law, in Lund, Sweden, taught at the Hong Kong University Faculty of Law and served as director of the Master of Laws Programme in Human Rights from 2001 to 2005. From 1994 to 2001, he worked as human rights officer for the UN Office of the High Commissioner for Human Rights in Geneva, Switzerland. Sunga has lectured at academic institutes and conducted human rights training in some thirty countries.

Hatla Thelle has a Ph.D. in Chinese studies and is senior researcher at the Danish Institute for Human Rights (DIHR) in Copenhagen. Since 1980, she has taught modern Chinese history at the University of Copenhagen and has been working on human rights projects and research at the DIHR since 1997. She has specifically researched protection of social rights and social policy reform in China.

Steven Weir is Area Vice President, Asia Pacific, Habitat for Humanity International in Bangkok, Thailand, and is responsible for supporting affordable housing programs throughout Asia and the South Pacific. Weir is a registered architect and has been involved in community-based design and housing in the Pacific Rim for more than thirty years. Weir has written numerous papers on affordable urban housing, the most recent, which was presented at the 2006 United Nations World Urban Forum on "Community Based Disaster Response – Only One Component of an Effective Shelter Framework," reviewing the Asia tsunami response.

Sophia Woodman researches Chinese law, politics, and human rights at the University of Hong Kong and worked for many years in an international non-governmental organization. Recent publications include "Human Rights as

'Foreign Affairs': China's Reporting under Human Rights Treaties," *Hong Kong Law Journal* 35, pt. 1, 2005; and "Bilateral Aid to Improve Human Rights," *China Perspectives* no. 51 (January–February 2004).

Mona Younis is human rights program officer at the Mertz Gilmore Foundation in New York. From 2000 to 2005, she served as coordinator of the International Human Rights Funders Group. She is a founding board member of the Fund for Global Human Rights, Washington, D.C., and the Arab Human Rights Fund, Beirut. She received a Ph.D. in sociology from the University of California at Berkeley in 1996.

Reflections on Dialogues between Practitioners and Theorists of Human Rights[1]

Daniel A. Bell

International human rights and humanitarian nongovernmental organizations[2] (INGOs) are major players on the world stage. They fund human rights projects, actively participate in human rights and humanitarian work, and criticize human rights violations in foreign lands. They work in cooperative networks with each other, with local NGOs, and with international organizations. They consult and lobby governments and international organizations, sometimes participating in high-level negotiations and diplomacy for global policy development. They cooperate and negotiate with economic and political organizations in the field for the implementation of their projects, whether this be monitoring or assistance. In short, they are generating a new type of political power, the purpose of which is to secure the vital interests of human beings on an international scale, regardless of state boundaries.

---

[1] I thank Joe Carens, Jean-Marc Coicaud, Avner de-Shalit, Jibecke Jönsson, and Thomas Pogge for helpful comments.

[2] An INGO is defined here as an organization with substantial autonomy to decide on and carry out human rights and/or humanitarian projects in various regions around the world. According to this definition, the Danish Institute for Human Rights, for example, is an INGO because it has substantial autonomy to decide on and carry out projects in Asia, Africa, and elsewhere (although its funds come largely from the Danish Ministry of Foreign Affairs and most its staff is Danish). The core mission of a human rights INGO is to criticize human rights violations and/or promote human rights in various ways (in contrast, say, to religious organizations that may promote human rights as a by-product of missionary work). Humanitarian organizations may employ the normative language of human rights, but they are distinguished by what they do, that is, provide immediate assistance to those whose rights (especially the rights to food and decent health care) are being violated. These missions often overlap in practice and some organizations such as OXFAM do both. This book focuses largely on human rights INGOs that criticize human rights violations and/or engage in long-term development work. For a brief account of the ethical dilemmas of humanitarian INGOs, see Daniel A. Bell and Joseph H. Carens, "The Ethical Dilemmas of International Human Rights and Humanitarian NGOs: Reflections on a Dialogue between Practitioners and Theorists," *Human Rights Quarterly* 26, no. 2 (May 2004): 317–20.

Needless to say, good intentions are not always sufficient to produce desirable results. In an imperfect and unpredictable world, human rights INGOs often face ethical dilemmas that constrain their efforts to do good in foreign lands. How do people who want to do good behave when they meet obstacles? Is it justifiable to sacrifice some good in the short term for more good in the long term? And which human rights concerns should have priority? Like other organizations, INGOs are constrained by scarce time and resources and must choose between competing goods. Human rights practitioners experience hard choices, compromises, and prioritizing as ongoing features of their moral world. In such cases, long lists of fairly abstract desiderata such as the Universal Declaration of Human Rights (UDHR) that do not take real-world constraints into account do not help much.[3] So how do human rights INGOs set their moral priorities? On what basis do they choose how to do good and where to do it? How should their decisions be critically evaluated? Can their choices be improved? What role, if any, can theorizing about human rights contribute to these questions?

The purpose of this book is to discuss the ethical challenges that human rights INGOs encounter as they attempt to do good at home and abroad and to refine thinking on the relative merits and demerits of ways of dealing with those challenges. These organizations are often viewed as "good" counterweights to authoritarian state power and exploitative multinationals or "bad" agents of liberal capitalism and Western values. A more nuanced evaluation of human rights INGOs needs to delineate the typical constraints and dilemmas they face in their attempts to achieve their aims. The idea is to see what kinds of questions and problems emerge when one thinks of human rights from the perspective of people or organizations that have to make choices about how best to promote rights in concrete contexts rather than simply from the perspective of abstract theory or even general policy recommendations. Such knowledge is essential for minimizing the harm unintentionally done by lack of knowledge of how the world actually works. On the other hand, the conceptual resources, normative frameworks, and historical knowledge provided by academic theorists might help to guide moral prioritizing of human rights INGOs as they choose among various possible ways of doing good. Moral theorizing that is sensitive to the actual constraints of practitioners can perhaps provide a sounder basis for decision making than ad hoc adaptation to less-than-ideal circumstances. In short, both theorists and practitioners of human rights can benefit from engagement with each other.

In view of these considerations, we organized a multiyear dialogue on human rights between high-level representatives of human rights INGOs and prominent academics from various backgrounds and disciplines that work on the subject of

---

[3] None of the INGO representatives suggested that the UDHR and related human rights treaties could provide useful guidance for dealing with the ethical challenges discussed in this book. In Chapter 2, Mona Younis explicitly points out that the UDHR did not feature in the deliberations regarding her organization's funding priorities.

human rights. The overall project was coadministered and funded by the United Nations University (Tokyo) and the City University of Hong Kong and was also supported by a generous grant from the Open Society Institute. Workshops were held in New York (twice) and Hong Kong, and this book includes thirteen of the papers that were presented at these workshops. The first workshop, held at the Carnegie Council on Ethics and International Affairs in New York in February 2002, consisted of papers by representatives of international human rights INGOs. The second workshop, held at the City University of Hong Kong in October 2003, consisted of papers by academics. The third workshop, held at the United Nations University (New York branch) in August 2005, consisted of reflections on the papers by human rights INGOs and academics that were asked to draw implications for human rights work at the UN. The papers were subject to extensive critical commentary by workshop participants and were further refined through e-mail exchanges. Some of the disagreements could not be resolved, particularly regarding the question of how best to promote economic rights, and the sharpest exchanges are reproduced in this book.

The book is divided into three sections that correspond roughly to themes that generated the most debate at the aforementioned workshops: the ethical challenges associated with interaction between relatively rich and powerful Western-based human rights INGOs and recipients of their aid in the South; whether and how to collaborate with governments that place severe restrictions on the activities of human rights INGOs; and the tension between expanding the organization's mandate to address more fundamental social and economic problems and restricting it for the sake of focusing on more immediate and clearly identifiable violations of civil and political rights. Let us discuss each theme in turn, drawing on the papers as well as comments from the workshops and subsequent e-mail exchanges. Each section contains chapters by practitioners constituting reflections on the ethical challenges of their particular organizations, as well as by academics who aim to provide more explicit normative guidance.

SECTION I. NORTHERN INGOs AND SOUTHERN AID RECIPIENTS: THE CHALLENGE OF UNEQUAL POWER

Most human rights and humanitarian international nongovernmental organizations (INGOs) are based in the West.[4] With their executives and offices centralized in key Western cities, program officers and coordinators are then sent to the field.

---

[4] It is worth clarifying the potentially misleading terminology. The "North" refers to wealthy capitalist liberal democratic countries, most of which are based in the Northern Hemisphere (but not all, e.g., Australia would be considered part of the Northern camp). The "West" refers to Northern countries with a Judeo-Christian heritage (Japan would therefore not be part of the West on this account). The "South" refers to relatively poor countries that are largely based in the Southern Hemisphere (but not all; for example, China and India would be considered part of the Southern camp).

As Alex de Waal notes, "[i]n its basic structure, the ethics business is like many global businesses [with] its headquarters in a handful of Western centers, notably New York, Washington and London."[5] From a practical point of view, this may present a special challenge in foreign lands where detailed knowledge of different linguistic, social, cultural, and economic circumstances is more likely to ensure success. The history of aid projects in the developing world is littered with blunders that could have been avoided with more detailed local knowledge.[6] It is not merely a strategic matter of understanding and using "the other" for the purpose of promoting one's fixed moral agenda, however. INGO representatives must also grapple with ethical dilemmas that arise when they are trying to help people in poor Southern countries. There are different ways of dealing with these dilemmas, and the contributions to this section discuss some of the possible responses along with associated advantages and disadvantages.

The need to raise funds has generated ethical questions within human rights INGOs. Those reliant on public support must choose between dubious but effective fund-raising tactics that enhance their capacity to do work on behalf of human rights and "appropriate" methods that limit fund-raising success and constrain its ability to do good. In Chapter 1, Betty Plewes and Rieky Stuart (then) of Oxfam Canada condemn the "pornography of poverty," vivid images of helpless, passive, poor and starving Third World peoples that are used by Northern-based INGOs to raise money from the public for their development work. Emotional appeals of this sort based on notions of guilt and charity have been relatively effective at raising funds: "In 2004 in Canada the five largest NGOs (mainly child sponsorship organizations) raised about $300 (Canadian) million from private donations.... [Child sponsorship organizations] tell us that these images of misery and passive victimization generate much more in donations than alternatives they have tested and that it is vital to raise large amounts of money to be able to carry out relief and development world." Such images, however, convey other more destructive images.

Messages like these can undermine INGOs' efforts to create a broader understanding of the underlying structures causing poverty and injustice. These images portray people as helpless victims, dependent and unable to take action, and convey a sense that development problems can only be solved by Northern charity. They ignore Northern complicity in creating inequality. At the very least, they convey a limited picture of life in Southern countries. At their worst they reinforce racist stereotypes.

In view of the drawbacks associated with charity-based approaches, Oxfam Canada rejects pornography of poverty images and instead uses positive images

[5] Alex de Waal, "The Moral Solipsism of Global Ethics Inc.," *London Review of Books* 23, no. 16 (23 August 2001): 15.
[6] See, e.g., Michael Edwards, *Future Positive: International Cooperation in the 21st Century* (London: Earthscan, 1999).

of poor people improving their lives and clever or ironic images, such as its award-winning ad during the O. J. Simpson trial that used only text to compare the amount of media coverage of that event with the much smaller coverage of the Rwanda genocide taking place at the same time.

Workshop participant Andre Frankovits noted that similar debates took place at Amnesty International (AI) but with a different outcome. The national office of AI in Australia had heated debates within the organization and with the advertising agency commissioned to assist with fund-raising over whether to use pictures of torture victims for fund-raising. AI had refused to use such pictures because it was felt they exploit the victims (who probably did not agree to being used in such images) and that AI should appeal to people's better nature. Eventually AI reversed policy, and the ad agency (working pro bono, it should be said) did use such pictures in fund-raising activities. This likely had a positive effect on fund-raising (although it is difficult to disentangle cause and effect) and increased AI's capacity to do its work on behalf of human rights.

Human rights INGOs also disburse aid to relatively poor Southern hemisphere countries, and this gives rise to another source of tension. On the one hand, INGO grant makers need to set clear mandates and do their best to secure successful outcomes. On the other hand, human rights aid is often most effective if grantees play an important role in articulating and pursuing what they perceive to be the most pressing problems in their local (Southern) communities. These conflicting desiderata are discussed in Chapter 2 by Mona Younis, Program Officer for the Mertz Gilmore Foundation (MGF).

MGF, one of the leading U.S. human rights funders, has been known in the philanthropic community for its readiness to fund controversial issues that most grant makers had been reluctant to support. It prided itself on being field-driven, with program staff members taking their cues regarding needs and opportunities from the respective fields with which they were engaged. MGF also provided direct funding to grantees, which enabled them to be more autonomous and responsive to local concerns, as well as open-ended renewable funding that afforded grantees a certain amount of security.

Taking its cues from local human rights groups in the South, MGF recognized the value of focusing on economic, and social and cultural rights (ESCR) as well as the interconnection between ESCR and civil and political rights (CPR). In the beginning of 2003, it decided to focus grant making on economic, social and cultural rights, including work in the South where even a small amount of resources can make a substantial difference, in contrast to the traditional focus on civil and political liberties by U.S. human rights groups. One problem, however, is that it is difficult to apply Western-style monitoring of grants to organizations without Western forms of due diligence. As Younis noted, "few U.S. foundations are willing to support grassroots groups abroad because of the costs involved in administering such grants and concerns regarding due diligence. Faced with a chicken–egg predicament – local groups require funding to establish institutions

capable of meeting the standards of due diligence that funders require of groups
they fund – U.S. funders and foreign grant seekers may not meet and grant makers
may continue to prefer funding Northern intermediaries."[7] In the case of MGF,
its initial foray into economic, social, and cultural rights–focused funding and
direct support for NGOs in poor countries came to an abrupt end, partly because
the foundation's board doubted the effectiveness of scattered grants around the
world. Instead, MGF decided to focus entirely on social and economic justice
issues inside the United States.

Larger foundations, such as Ford and the Open Society Institute, do continue
to disburse human rights aid to grantees in the South. But these grantees often
need to change their organizational structure and conceptions of priorities to
obtain funding and support from wealthy Northern INGOs.[8] This pressure to
"institutionalize" and "professionalize" means that local NGOs can lose vital
linkages to their constituencies and ultimately limits their capacity to effect social
change. As Younis puts it, "Emulating human rights NGOs in the North, where
for decades human rights work has been treated as the preserve of lawyers and
legal experts, would discourage popular engagement and participation – a vital
resource in the global South. Given that, post-September 11, even U.S.-based
human rights groups lament their failure to establish solid constituency-based
support for human rights inside the United States, is it wise for U.S. funders to
promote the same model for groups in the South?"

Such dilemmas are further explored in Chapter 3 by Steven Weir, the Asia
and Pacific Director of Habitat for Humanity (HFH). HFH is an INGO founded
in the United States in 1976 with the goal of helping people acquire adequate
housing, which the organization sees as a basic human right and a prerequisite
for the effective enjoyment of many other rights. Its mission is to secure the right
to housing without discriminating against any ethnic group, religion, or sex. In
practice, however, trade-offs must be made. Weir notes that "[t]he contextual
reality for NGOs is characterized by trade-offs between competing human rights
and, more frequently, between human rights and cultural norms that stand in
opposition to human rights as they are defined in various UN texts." The drawbacks of imposing human rights norms on reluctant "benefactors" is illustrated
with HFH's experience in Fiji and Papua New Guinea. HFH insisted that its
projects be structured according to Western-style democratically elected rotating local boards, but this conflicted with the chiefly system that overseas local
matters. Because HFH's methodology insulted the local chief and was anathema
to the villagers, its projects were relatively ineffective. In response to such experiences, HFH has developed different ways of dealing with the conflict between
human rights and local cultural norms.

[7] Comment from the Carnegie Council on Ethics and International Affairs workshop in New York,
February 2002.
[8] See Clifford Bob, "Merchants of Morality," *Foreign Policy* (March–April 2002): 36.

One response is to distinguish between short- and long-term ways of challenging local cultural norms that conflict with human rights norms, with immediate focus on "errors of commission" and "errors of omission" being challenged later: "For example, affiliates who discriminate in favor of the relatives of local committee members or fellow church members are immediately put on probation, whereas an uneven distribution of homeowner ethnicity and religion is corrected in the long run by improving systems development and continued monitoring for conformance." Another strategy is to compromise on the human rights norm itself, assuming that some change is better than none. For example, HFH favors gender equity on local boards, but it compromises with local patriarchal norms by not insisting on more than 30 percent representation by women. A demand for full equality would not only be impractical, Weir comments, but it would also conflict with HFH's commitment to local participation and control over the process.[9] Perhaps the most culturally sensitive response is to allow for institutional learning in response to input from non-Western cultures. In the case of Fiji and Papua New Guinea, HFH created a broader regional organizational structure with a network of subcommittees or satellite branches that respect the local chiefly tradition, a strategy that seems to be resulting in increased cooperation and sustainability.

Chapter 4, by Bonny Ibhawoh of Brock University, draws on these dilemmas of North–South interaction and aims to provide constructive guidance to understanding and addressing them. Ibhawoh argues that the main problem does not lie in the geographic imbalance of the organizational structures of most human rights INGOs. Although based in the North, many INGOs have developed strong representations and networks in the South that keep them well connected with local situations. Moreover, Southern NGOs do not always welcome more INGO presence in their communities. In postauthoritarian African states such as South Africa and Nigeria, the influx of better-funded INGOs in the late 1990s was seen as undermining the local human rights NGOs and hampering their capacity-building efforts. In the competition for scarce donor funds, there was concern that the more influential INGOs would get funds for local projects that would otherwise had gone to them. Ibhawoh suggests a division of labor, with the larger and more established INGOs working with local NGOs to pursue domestic objectives.

The main challenge to the legitimacy of Northern-based INGOs lies in the ideological framework that underpins much of their work: "The first component is the hapless victim in distress, the second is the non-Western government whose action or inaction caused the violation, and the third component is the rescuer – the human rights INGO, the external aid agency, the international institution, or even the journalist covering the story – whose interests are seen as inseparable from those of the victim." This framework is problematic because it assumes

---

[9] Steven Weir, comment from the first workshop at the Carnegie Council on Ethics and International Affairs workshop in New York in February 2002.

that the primary responsibility for human rights abuses lie with Southern governments and consequently pays insufficient attention to how the structures of globalization negatively affect human rights conditions in the South. This tendency is linked to another problematic feature of INGO work – namely, the disproportionate concern with civil and political rights at the expense of social and economic rights. Ibhawoh points to studies that draw links between the operations of International Financial Institutions and Transnational Corporations and human rights abuses in Third World countries, and he argues that Northern INGOs should pay more attention to the negative impact of economic globalization on economic rights in the South.

Another challenge for Northern INGOs lies in the conflict between human rights norms and local cultural norms. "Culture talk" has been (mis)used by privileged elites in the Asian and African values debates for the purpose of holding on to power, but Ibhawoh notes that in some cases the deployment of culture talk to challenge the work of INGOs has deeper social roots. Workshop participant Ndubisi Obiorah raised the example of human rights workers in Nigeria who welcome the work of INGOs in the country but state that it would be difficult, given local cultural and religious beliefs, to press for gay and lesbian rights. In such cases, Ibhawoh suggests that the INGO need not alter its normative vision, but it can either opt for a gradualist approach to promote the contested right in the long term or it can confront the injustice head-on, similar to the uncompromising U.S. civil rights movement. Neither approach is ideal, however. The gradualist approach carries the cost of sending the message that the interests of vulnerable and marginalized minorities do not rank high as a priority, and the confrontational approach risks alienating local communities and partners in the South and undermining the rest of the work of the human rights INGO.

The chapters in Section I focus mainly on the ethical challenges arising from the unequal power relationship between Northern INGOs and Southern NGOs. Another set of challenges arise from the interaction between INGOs and governments, particularly states that place severe restrictions on the activities of INGOs. These challenges are discussed in Section II.

SECTION II. INGOs AND GOVERNMENTS: THE CHALLENGE OF DEALING WITH STATES THAT RESTRICT THE ACTIVITIES OF INGOs

Human rights international nongovernmental organizations often need to grapple with the question of whether to deal with governments to help remedy human rights violations. One important area of controversy is the issue of government funding for INGOs. Many INGOs do accept government funds, and the main advantage, of course, is that they can carry out their projects without wasting too much time and money on fund-raising efforts. This raises questions about their independence, however: "Many of the largest and most respectable INGOs of today (such as Save the Children and Oxfam) were born and raised in opposition to government policy and vested interests at the time. But can this role continue when Northern NGOs are becoming more and more dependent on government support?"[10]

The dilemmas of dependence on government funds are vividly illustrated in Chapter 5, by Lyal Sunga of the Raoul Wallenberg Institute of Human Rights and Humanitarian Law. Sunga discusses the acute dilemmas forced on INGOs working in coalition-occupied Iraq. Before the war, most INGOs vociferously denounced the Bush–Blair arguments for invading and occupying Iraq. Some representatives of INGOs did meet with U.S. government officials to clarify the extent to which they could operate freely inside Iraq, but these officials offered funds on the condition of a formation of a clear chain of command between U.S. authorities and INGOs.

The demise of the Saddam government flung the door wide open for INGOs to enter the country and set up their own operations, and the prewar fears over the independence, neutrality, and impartiality of INGOs proved to be well founded. In effect, the Bush administration forced NGOs either to disagree publicly with the U.S. government's policies or to accept quietly USAID funding for Iraq-related programs and surrender their prerogative to criticize U.S. policy, even if they felt that the use of military force worsened the humanitarian situation. Several INGOs, including the International Rescue Committee, CARE, and World Vision, made the difficult decision not to seek USAID funding under these conditions.

The independence of INGOs that chose to work in coalition-occupied Iraq was further curbed by being forced to rely on coalition authorities for security. The U.S. government linked the presence of INGOs in Iraq as an indicator of the coalition's success, which identified NGOs with U.S. policy and "thereby unnecessarily politicized NGO work throughout the country." Moreover, the White House policy to bring humanitarian aid to Iraq through the Department of Defense meant that soldiers were assigned to carry out humanitarian tasks in addition to their usual military duties, a policy that risked lending the erroneous impression among ordinary Iraqis that NGOs cooperating with coalition forces supported the coalition's invasion and occupation of Iraq. Many INGOs were concerned that their personnel would be indistinguishable from soldiers and thus be made the targets of attack, and they decided to leave the country.

Sunga draws implications for INGOs working in conflict zones. He argues that accepting funding from a belligerent in an armed conflict should not necessarily undermine an INGO's independence from government because not all governments have adopted the hard-line approach of USAID and the Bush administration. But when a government forces INGOs to toe the line, the kinds of

---

[10] David Hulme and Michael Edwards, "Too Close to the Powerful, Too Far from the Powerless," in *NGOs, States and Donors: Too Close for Comfort?*, eds. D. Hulme and M. Edwards (Basingstoke: Palgrave Macmillan, 1996): 280.

dilemmas experienced in Iraq are inevitable. Sunga therefore favors a division of labor between human rights INGOs whose calling is to draw attention in the most effective manner to human rights violations and humanitarian INGOs whose mission is to relieve suffering by extending assistance on a neutral basis and to refrain from political commentary.

Another important area of controversy regards the pros and cons of collaborating with less-than-democratic governments, such as that of China. INGOs such as the Ford Foundation and the Danish Institute for Human Rights focus on the necessity of collaborating with such governments to achieve any improvement in human rights or any success in pursuing humanitarian goals. It is obvious that such governments do not welcome critical perspectives from outside forces (not to mention inside forces), which puts human rights and humanitarian INGOs in a difficult position. Nonetheless, the INGO "engagers" argue that the advantages of collaboration outweigh the disadvantages.

The coauthors of Chapter 6, all from the Danish Institute for Human Rights (DIHR), outline the merits of the collaborative approach. The DIHR has been funding and supporting various human rights projects in China, including a program concerned with the prevention and use of torture and ill treatment by police in the pretrial phase, another program designed to train Chinese legal scholars and practitioners in European law and practice, a human rights center in a provincial capital, a project providing legal aid to women, and a death penalty study. These activities require active collaboration with the government sector: "In authoritarian states, where the local NGOs might be few or nonexistent within certain sectors, cooperation with governments might be the only option." It would be a mistake, the DIHR implies, to always view less-than-democratic governments as evil perpetrators of human rights abuses. Sometimes government officials are sincerely committed to improving the rights situation in selected areas. Where human rights violations do occur, this may be due to institutional inertia rather than to active state-willed perpetration of violations. It could also be due to lack of technical skills and know-how, and the government might welcome INGO aid in this respect. In sum, it is possible to obtain good results by collaborating with certain governmental agencies and personnel even in states that place severe constraints on political rights.

The DIHR recognizes that there are drawbacks associated with this partnership with less-than-democratic governments approach. The most obvious is that INGOs working in China often choose to "avoid politically sensitive places" such as Tibet and Xinjiang and "avoid politically sensitive issues" such as labor rights, press freedom, and the political rights of dissidents. Another disadvantage of collaboration was pointed out at the first New York workshop by Kenneth Roth of Human Rights Watch (HRW). The DIHR argues for an international division of labor, with organizations such as HRW adopting a confrontational approach while engagers such as DIHR cooperate with the governments on long-term projects. Roth pointed out, however, that there are trade-offs because less-than-democratic governments can use their cooperation with engagers as evidence that their policies on human rights are not so bad and are getting better, thus weakening the force of criticisms put forward by other organizations.

Chapter 7 by Sophia Woodman (formerly of Human Rights in China), points to further problems with the collaborative approach. Woodman looks at the experience of cooperation programs aimed at improving human rights in China through legal projects. Drawing on interviews with representatives of INGO donors as well as Chinese recipients of INGO aid, Woodman argues that there are several obstacles to successful implementation of these projects. First, hostility and suspicion in the Chinese bureaucracy to foreign cooperation regarding matters of human rights remain strong. Such problems can be avoided by dropping the language of human rights and democracy for more "politically correct" terms such as the *rule of law* and *governance,* but Western INGOs can face pressure from their own constituents and donors if they adopt this tactic. Second, the process of identifying human rights needs in China can be laborious, expensive, and time-consuming. Chinese partners often seem reluctant to identify their needs and take the initiative in proposing projects, partly because Chinese organizations seem unwilling to take the lead in a politically sensitive field. The slow cultivation of "good working relationships" with local Chinese partners can increase the likelihood of identifying projects aimed at improving specific human rights problems, but many donors are concerned with short to medium term outcomes and may not be willing to fund this costly and time-consuming process. Third, Chinese partners expressed frustration at the lack of in-depth knowledge of the China context, particularly the political context, which could make it hard for donors to understand the rationale of projects proposed by the Chinese side. This knowledge deficit can be remedied by more INGO reliance on people with in-depth country knowledge and language skills, but few donors have been willing to support such baseline empirical work.

Woodman offers some proposals for the future direction of human rights aid programs in China. Her Chinese informants were virtually unanimous in asserting that international pressure has played an important role in contributing to human rights concessions by the Chinese government, and consequently the engagers should be wary of collaborative projects that undermine international pressure. There is still an important role for collaborative projects, but INGOs should place more emphasis on the kinds of initiatives proposed by Chinese individuals and institutions without close ties to the government. A related issue is that INGOs should reconsider their focus on the formal apparatus of law as an entry point for human rights concerns in China, because people often demand their rights to be supported through such entities as community groups, bodies providing legal services to the poor, and media reporting of legal processes. These proposals require sufficient information about the conditions on the ground as well as a patient and long-term outlook.

Chapter 8 by Sun Zhe of Fudan University is a welcome reminder that rich and relatively peaceful countries also have serious human rights problems. The Chinese government has issued its White Paper on the American Human Rights Record that accuses the United States of turning a blind eye to its own human rights problems, such as the fact that it has the largest prison population in the world. In the international realm, the United States has frequently violated the human rights of other countries and has been highly selective in its condemnations of human rights violations. Thus, the U.S. government's critique of China's human rights record is not likely to have much moral authority in the Chinese context.

But because China condemns abuses of human rights in other countries, it cannot consistently refuse to engage with criticism from the international community, and this presents an opening for INGOs seeking to monitor human rights violations in China. Rather than invoking U.S. government-style, however, they should rely on international instruments and principles that would be accepted by Chinese in the normative sense. Sun suggests a two-step process that first compares accepted international standards of human rights as expressed in United Nations (UN) documents with national norms reflected in a state's constitution and then examines the relationship between the constitutionally guaranteed principles and reality.

Sun also proposes strategies for INGOs seeking to promote human rights in China through collaborative projects and international dialogues. First, INGOs should have a more long-term vision, such as a five- or ten-year outlook, and they should lengthen the time horizon in assessing human rights progress in China. Second, they should have a broader definition of human rights. Political rights should be considered in such areas as informing the Chinese government that the widespread use of administrative detention is not in conformity with international human rights standards, but economic and social rights should also be placed near the top of the agenda. Third, INGOs should consider establishing, through the UN channel, a comprehensive working body on human rights incorporating international and Chinese representatives. The prestige of the UN in China remains high, and cooperation with that organization can lead to concrete improvements in human rights.

One consistent theme of calls for the internationalization of the human rights discourse – as opposed to the U.S.-style prioritization of civil and political rights – is the demand for more focus on economic, social, and cultural rights, particularly economic rights. As things stand, however, Western governments still do not seem up to the task of promoting economic rights abroad. Even social welfare states in Scandinavia do not always take economic rights as seriously as they should: the authors from the DIHR report that their organization found it "necessary to refrain from a promising Chinese-proposed cooperation project on the protection of social and economic rights because the Danish Ministry of Foreign Affairs [the main funder of DIHR] did not perceive it to be a human rights project." As we will see in this section, INGOs have been grappling with the task of expanding their traditional focus on civil and political rights to place more emphasis on economic rights, although once again they are faced with certain inescapable dilemmas.

SECTION III. INGOs AND ECONOMIC RIGHTS: THE CHALLENGE OF DEALING WITH GLOBAL POVERTY

The two largest human rights international nongovernmental organizations – Amnesty International (AI) and Human Rights Watch (HRW) – traditionally focused exclusively on civil and political rights (CP) rights, but both organizations have decided to expand their concerns to include work in the area of economic, social, and cultural (ESC) rights. In the case of HRW, however, the organization has reason to limit its work on ESC rights, as Kenneth Roth, executive director of HRW, explains in Chapter 9.

The decision at HRW to include work on ESC rights dates from the early 1990s and can be attributed partly to the change of leadership at the organization. As Roth presents it, Aryeh Neier, the previous director of HRW, was opposed to ESC rights on philosophical grounds. When he left, Roth, as new director, put forward the view that HRW should rest its basic conception of human rights on the international covenants (that clearly include ESC rights) and should grad-ually expand its concerns to include work in the area of ESC rights when the organization could be effective in doing so. The board of HRW agreed to this proposal.[11]

Effectiveness is the key here. In Roth's view, human rights INGOs like HRW (as distinct from national and local ones) tend to be most effective when they employ the methodology he calls "shaming": investigating, documenting, and publicizing behavior by states (and some nonstate actors) that conflicts with international human rights norms. For the shaming methodology to work, Roth says, "clarity is needed about three issues: violation, violator, and remedy. That is, we must be able to show persuasively that a particular state of affairs amounts to a violation of human rights standards, that a particular violator is principally or significantly responsible, and that there is a widely accepted remedy for the violation." Roth argues that these requirements can often be met, even when dealing with ESC rights.

Roth argues that these three conditions for effective shaming usually coincide in the realm of CP rights but that they tend to operate independently in the realm of ESC rights. He suggests that the nature of the violation, violator, and remedy is clearest when it is possible to identify arbitrary or discriminatory governmental

---

[11] E-mail from Kenneth Roth to Daniel A. Bell (29 September 2002). According to Widney Brown (then at HRW) the impetus came from researchers because they found that human rights victims did not experience rights violations as discrete (comment from the third workshop in New York in August 2005).

conduct that causes or substantially contributes to an ESC violation but that these three dimensions are less clear when the ESC shortcoming is largely a problem of distributive justice. In those circumstances, human rights INGOs that employ a shaming methodology should refrain from intervention because they will not be able to have any significant impact on the problem. Roth is careful to point out that his argument applies only to INGOs working in countries away from their organizational base, not to local and national NGOs, which often employ methodologies besides shaming and have clearer standing to speak out about the proper direction of politically contested national policies in their own states. He also specifies that his argument does not apply to INGOs addressing the domestic or foreign policy of their "home" governments, where they have standing comparable to that of a local human rights group.

Still, Roth's views generated intense controversy at the workshops. The critics did not accept Roth's view that there is such a tight link between the effectiveness of human rights INGOs and the methodology of shaming. What Roth saw as pragmatic, they saw as unduly cautious and conservative. Bonny Ibhawoh (Chapter 4), for example, recognizes that INGOs will have difficulty promoting some economic rights using the naming and shaming method that has been employed for the promotion of civil and political rights, but he argues that INGOs should learn from organizations in the South that have successfully used new methodologies for advocacy of economic rights, such as education and mass mobilization: "rather than argue that ESC rights are 'not doable,' the focus should be on fashioning new tools for the task at hand." A related argument is that the focus on effectiveness might draw attention away from what is really important. If the most severe and extensive violations of human rights stem not from the misbehavior of authoritarian rulers but from the global maldistribution of wealth and power and from structural features of the international political and economic systems, then to limit the activities of the international human rights organizations to problems for which there are clear standards, a clear culprit, and a clear remedy may render the organizations irrelevant to the most important struggles for justice today.

In Chapter 10, Neera Chandhoke of the University of Delhi does not put forward such radical critiques of Roth's methodology. She argues that HRW can and should critique violations of economic rights in particular states, including violations stemming from an unfair distribution of resources, without abandoning its dual commitments to shaming and effectiveness. Her argument rests on the theoretical view that economic rights stand on their own conceptual ground as enabling rights and should have the same status as civil rights: "if rights are rights to the conditions that allow human beings to live lives that are of worth, social and economic rights are essential to human beings, for they enable them to access basic goods. It is true that civil rights protect the dignity of the human being, but this human being can be degraded and humiliated if she has to beg for the satisfaction of her basic needs." Civil rights do not do enough to substantiate our commitment to human rights because they do not challenge the unjust ways that societies can organize their collective resources or the way that people's lives can be degraded if they suffer from want or deprivation.

On this basis, Chandhoke argues that HRW limits the scope of its work on ESC rights by insisting that violations of rights are worth investigating only if they result from arbitrary behavior or will lead to the violation of the right to live without discrimination (which Chandhoke views as a civil right). In one example, Chandhoke cites the large quantities of food being stockpiled by the Indian government while millions of people are severely malnourished. The violation of people's right to food could be condemned without calling for redistribution of resources. In another example, Chandhoke notes that the right to health care can be violated by a government that fails to fulfill its obligations through an act of omission rather than open discrimination or arbitrary policy making. Such violations can lead to the same loss of human life as deliberate violations of rights – say, if health care is commercialized and poor people cannot afford to get treated for illness – and ought to fall under the purview of human rights INGOs. Chandhoke recognizes that remedying such violations may indeed require the redistribution of resources, but she responds to Roth's worry about effectiveness by noting that human rights INGOs may well have the power to effect change in such cases. Human rights movements based in the West "happen to exert an inordinate amount of influence on the way human rights movements based in the South do or do not privilege certain rights." An INGO that shames a government for failing to fulfill its obligations to secure economic rights and calls on it to redistribute resources to help remedy this problem can help to shape the agenda of local NGOs. It can also muster public opinion internationally and put moral pressure on the government in a way that relatively poorly funded and less visible local NGOs cannot. Roth, in other words, may be underestimating the power of his organization to effect change in foreign lands: "he just does not take cognizance of the power of INGOs to highlight some rights and underplay or even demote others."

In his written reply to Chandhoke's critique, Roth says that he agrees with the substance of Chandhoke's main theoretical propositions but that they fail to challenge HRW's existing methodology. He argues that HRW's work on ESC rights has been extensive and that its projects have all been pursued under its existing policy of focusing on arbitrary or discriminatory governmental action or inaction. Regarding the withholding of food surpluses, he argues that this would constitute arbitrary conduct and HRW could have intervened in this case using its current methodology. He does note that HRW could not have called for the redistribution of resources to help secure the right to health care in another country, but he reaffirms the empirical point that shaming organizations could not successfully press for redistribution in foreign lands.

In her "Final Response to Kenneth Roth," Chandhoke alludes to the importance of striking the right tone for productive debate. She argues that the process
of dialogue means that participants should always be open to change and mutual
learning without ever proclaiming one final truth. She concludes, "It is almost as
if HRW refuses to listen to persons located within the very constituency that the
organization works for and caters to. This saddens me, for it negates the notion
of dialogue, thereby rendering both the practitioner and the theorist of human
rights poorer in understanding and sympathy for each other."

Like HRW, Amnesty International recently expanded its mission to include
ESC rights. This decision followed lengthy internal debate, as discussed in
Chapter 11 by Curt Goering, deputy executive director of Amnesty International (AI) USA. AI members raised a number of objections to the change, many
of which were tied to its impact on the effectiveness of the organization. Some
feared that expanding the mandate to include ESC rights would cause the organization to lose its clear focus and makes its work too diffuse. They pointed out
that there was still a lot of work to be done in existing areas of concern. Some
worried that the inclusion of ESC rights in AI's mandate would blur what had
been a clear organizational identity and jeopardize its hard-won reputation for
consistency, credibility, and impartiality. Also, there was worry it could undermine the unity and cohesion of the movement because they felt that there was
not the same degree of consensus within the membership of AI and within the
wider public about the moral status of ESC rights as there was about the moral
status of CP rights, in part because it is often much harder to establish standards
for ESC rights or to determine what constitutes a violation of them. Still another
concern was that the organization did not have the expertise to address issues of
ESC rights and that, if AI attempted to acquire the necessary expertise, it would
lead to an undesirable shift in power away from the membership toward the
professional staff.

Despite these powerful objections, AI decided to expand its mission to include
ESC rights within its ambit of concern. According to Goering, three lines of
argument played a particularly important role in identifying the advantages of
an expanded mandate and in overcoming the objections to change. First, the
focus on CP rights had sometimes led to misguided priorities that implicitly
downplayed or ignored the sometimes more serious areas of human suffering.
One example frequently cited in internal debates was Sudan, "where in 1994 the
government engaged in massive displacement of local populations and destruction of their crops and food reserves. It was difficult to explain why AI researched
as human rights violations the shooting and torture of a few victims . . . while
the manufactured starvation of thousands of people was treated as background."
Second, there was strong support for an expansion of AI's mandate among its
branches in the South: "importantly to an organization that strived to be truly
international, the civil and political focus was also seen as a barrier to development of AI's structure and membership in the South." Third, AI responded to

the argument that its CP focus was biased toward male concerns: "Some noted that women's experience of human rights is often different from men's: property rights and reproductive rights and the rights to health, education, and nutrition were some of the areas mentioned."

In the end, the vast majority of AI members found the arguments for expanding the formal mission of the organization more persuasive than the arguments for the status quo. Moreover, this expansion was done without the same methodological limits as HRW. As Goering puts the point, "It is true, of course, that a substantial portion of our work is documenting abuses and campaigning to stop them, and public exposure plays an important role in such organizations. But AI is more than that. Our members around the world are active from within, helping to build a domestic human rights constituency and to strengthen civil society. Much energy at the local levels is aimed at promoting human rights education among the public [and] in the school system [and] working constructively with [and] training and lobbying home governments to incorporate human rights standards in penal codes and constitutions. There are also many situations where we engage with targets (governments and/or nonstate actors) behind the scenes and, as long as progress is being made, are content to conduct 'quiet diplomacy.'"[12]

As the world's largest human rights INGO with substantial grassroots support in the South and extensive cooperative links with Southern human rights NGOs, AI may have less of a need to prioritize rights and methodologies compared with smaller Western-based organizations. Still, it is worth asking whether AI is spreading itself out too thin. The problem may not be that it has incorporated ESC rights but rather that it does not prioritize them relative to other rights. In Chapter 12, Thomas Pogge of Columbia University argues that human rights INGOs should focus first and foremost on the elimination of severe poverty and concentrate their resources in places that offer the most favorable environments for the cost-effective reduction of severe poverty, rather than seek to spread their projects out across many countries.

Pogge begins his chapter with alarming statistics about the large numbers of people in severe poverty: "Some 850 million human beings are chronically undernourished, 1,037 million lack access to safe water and 2,747 million lack access to improved sanitation. About 2,000 million lack access to essential drugs ... Roughly one third of all human deaths, 18 million annually or 50,000 each day, are due to poverty-related causes, readily preventable through better nutrition, safe drinking water, cheap re-hydration packs, vaccines, antibiotics, and other medicines." Pogge reckons that a serious effort to eradicate severe poverty would initially cost about US $300 billion per year, vastly more than the US $13 billion the affluent countries and their citizens spend annually for this purpose. And so, "seeing how much deprivation there is, and how little money

---

[12] E-mail from Curt Goering to Daniel A. Bell (25 September 2002).

to reduce it, INGOs face difficult moral decisions about how to spend the funds they collect."

Pogge focuses on the case of INGOs that receive many small contributions meant to protect people abroad from serious harm. The ethical challenge is for them to decide how they should spend their funds: "This question points to an awesome responsibility because, in the world as it is, any decisions it makes are likely to affect many lives severely. To put it bluntly, an INGO must often make decisions that will certainly lead to many deaths because spending one's limited funds on trying to protect some is tantamount to leaving others to their fate." Contributors to INGOs also face awesome responsibilities because "[by] contributing to one rather than another, I am, then, indirectly deciding who will live and who will die." But because contributors lack the time and dedication to study carefully where their contributions are going, they place their trust in INGOs that are supposed to have carefully developed moral priorities governing how the collected money is spent. This saddles INGO staff with a second "awesome responsibility": to ensure that the INGO makes the contributions effective through morally important projects and does not set the wrong moral priorities or fund infeasible or counterproductive projects.

Pogge then turns to the question of how INGOs should develop moral priorities governing how the collected money should be spent. Relying on rigorous quantitative methods as well as the arguments of contemporary philosophers, he puts forward the following moral principle governing INGO conduct: "Other things being equal, an INGO should choose among candidate projects on the basis of the cost-effectiveness of each project, defined as its moral value divided by its cost. Here a project's moral value is the harm protection it achieves, that is, the sum of the moral values of the harm reductions (and increases) this project would bring about for the individual persons it affects." On this basis, he argues that INGOs have an obligation to concentrate their limited funds in places that allow for the cost-effective reduction of severe poverty. Because efficiency tends to be higher in countries with better government policies or a higher incidence of poverty, this would mean concentrating funds in a few countries; Pogge names Ethiopia, Uganda, India, and Bangladesh as likely worthy candidates of INGO aid. By implication, INGOs that seek to spread their aid over many developing countries out of some misguided ideal of distributive justice are making decisions that lead to large numbers of avoidable deaths. INGOs that spend lots of time and money cultivating relationships with government officials in China to promote civil rights in that country are using scarce resources that should have been spent saving lives elsewhere. INGOs that seek to promote dialogue with Southern NGOs in matters unrelated to the cost-effective allocation of funds designed to alleviate severe poverty are wasting precious time and resources. And INGOs that divert funds to help some badly off people in conflict zones where it is expensive to protect them are needlessly contributing to the deaths of (more) badly off people in peaceful countries who could have been cheaply protected from harm. Pogge does note that INGOs funded by citizens of rich countries might have a special responsibility to avert harms caused by the policies of their own governments, but he argues that the North is so deeply implicated in causing the South's predicament that it is impossible to distinguish between harms that rich countries are and are not materially involved in causing. In this context, INGOs need to direct their aid (only) toward the most cost-effective harm protection projects.

Not surprisingly, Pogge's views generated a storm of controversy at the workshops. In Chapter 13, Joseph Carens of the University of Toronto articulates some of these objections to Pogge's view. Carens begins his chapter by spelling out the benefits of bringing together moral theorists and representatives from INGOs. Both groups can potentially learn from engagement with each other. The moral theorist's abstract and systematic thinking about moral claims could help those in INGOs to reflect more deeply about the underlying moral principles that they want to guide their actions and about whether the courses pursued by their organizations really live up to those principles. Moral theorists might learn by paying attention to the kinds of ethical challenges INGOs face in trying to do good. The practices of INGOs might reveal moral problems and solutions that have been neglected in philosophical debates, and moral theorists might find ways to modify and improve their moral theories. Carens then draws on Pogge's chapter to show how philosophers could learn more from the experiences of those in INGOs and how those in INGOs could learn more from philosophers.

Carens observes that Pogge nowhere directly engages with the real world of INGOs as presented in this book's chapters and in the verbal contributions of participants at the first two workshops. Pogge's reluctance to turn his mind to the actual experiences of INGOs, Carens argues, leads to an important mistake in his moral analysis. Carens notes that few INGOs would disagree with Pogge's argument that INGOs have responsibilities to both the poor and oppressed abroad and to the contributors on whose behalf they set priorities. The problem is, "[w]hat if the contributors' own views of their moral responsibilities – the ones they want the INGOs to carry out – lead to different priorities from the ones that flow from Pogge's principle? Should the INGOs adopt Pogge's priorities or those of their contributors?" Carens responds that even if we assume (contrary to the experience at the workshops) that the INGOs are convinced by Pogge's argument, they could not (justifiably) override the views of contributors that cannot be so convinced. One reason is practical: "if an INGO were to pursue a course that its contributors regarded as significantly different from the one that they had given money to support, the INGO would lose its contributors and soon would have no funds to spend." The second reason is moral: "The people running the INGOs are not morally free to follow their own moral views (by hypothesis here, Pogge's principle) and to disregard those of their contributors, precisely because of the trustee relationship between INGOs and contributors to which Pogge has drawn our attention."

If Pogge had paid more attention to the actual workings of INGOs, he would not have assumed that contributors to INGOs do not have enough information to make any judgments about what the priorities of the INGOs ought to be. In the real world, there are many kinds of INGOs with different missions and priorities, and when they seek contributions, the INGOs describe their particular histories and commitments. Most contributors to INGOs would be able to learn enough from conventional fund-raising materials to distinguish among the basic orientations of the various INGOs, and they are likely to contribute only if they share the organization's basic moral views and established priorities.

It could be, of course, that both contributors and the organizations are wrong, that they should be using the moral standard put forward by Pogge for assessing INGO work. Carens, however, argues for an approach that incorporates a recognition of the plurality of moral views without succumbing to relativism. He notes that INGOs generally refrain from open criticism of each other and that this mutual forbearance lies (at least partly) in the recognition "that there are many ways of doing good in the world, and all of them deserve respect." Not all ways need to be viewed as equally morally valuable, but many pass a morally permissible standard "in the sense that it sets a minimum threshold for the justification of the activities of INGOs." Carens says that he personally agrees with Pogge's view that the most urgent moral task is to reduce harm caused by severe poverty along with the implication that INGOs focusing on severe poverty are doing the most morally valuable work, "this does not mean, however, that I see the work of human rights INGOs that do not focus on severe poverty as unimportant or, worse still, as morally unacceptable."

Even if we need to respect the basic organizational mission of INGOs that pass a morally permissible standard, Carens argues that Pogge's principle could still provide guidance to INGOs on how to set priorities in spending their money on specific projects. If an INGO must choose between two projects, it should choose the one that does more good. This might well lead INGOs to place less emphasis on geographic diversity of projects, but Carens notes that few, if any, INGO participants at the workshops really confronted the challenge that they should restrict the geographic scope of their projects to places where they can do the most good. In this sense, INGOs might benefit with deeper engagement with the views of a moral theorist.

Human rights work relies not just on the principles formulated by moral theorists. To an important extent, it also relies on the principles and mechanisms agreed on at the United Nations (UN). The final chapter, by Jean-Marc Coicaud of the United Nations University (UNU), focuses on INGO human rights work at the United Nations. Coicaud's conclusion draws on two themes that emerged at the third workshop in New York in August 2005 involving INGO representatives and academics that were asked to reflect on the book's findings and draw implications for INGO human rights work at the UN.

The first important theme is the need to specify what accounts for the grow-ing importance of INGOs in human rights work. Coicaud argues that INGO growth has to be understood in connection with the evolution of governance at the national and international levels. Traditionally, state institutions had a near-monopoly of voice and action on how society ought to be run, but forces below and above the state have called into question the state's authority and capacity to set the agenda on issues of public concern. Over the last three decades or so, the INGOs have stepped into the gap, and they have assumed a visible role in criti-cizing human rights violations, dealing with humanitarian crises, and helping to alleviate the conditions that lead to those crises. Moreover, Coicaud expects the growth of INGO activity to continue, particularly as they have come to replace trade unions as the main force for non-state collective mobilization. One might add that the proliferation of public causes and human rights issues – few progres-sive forces still endorse the traditional Marxist view that dealing with the condi-tion of the working class is the "magic bullet" for curing mankind's ills – leaves room for the diverse contributions of various kinds of human rights INGOs.

The second important theme is the need to specify the challenges that INGOs experience during the course of their human rights work at the UN. The UN is a sizeable and somewhat unwieldy bureaucracy, and it is composed of states with different and occasionally conflicting agendas. The UN setting leads to distinctive dilemmas for human rights INGOs working within the system. Coicaud discusses dilemmas of ends – the need occasionally to sacrifice short-term goals in the pursuit of long-term ones, and occasionally to prioritize human rights concerns that may not be viewed as priorities by the victims of human rights – and suggests possible ways of dealing with them. He also discusses dilemmas of means, such as whether to form coalitions with other INGOs to increase the likelihood of success, although coalition-building may entail compromising the INGO's ability to put forth its own agenda and speak out on sensitive issues. Notwithstanding the challenges of human rights work at the UN, most INGOs find it worthwhile to persist because the UN can perhaps most effectively highlight human rights on a global scale.

Coicaud's chapter ends by noting David Cingranelli's recommendation for annual report cards that would be more comprehensive than the traditional focus on civil and political rights. If such report cards are to be effective, however, they must be seen to have some sort of international legitimacy: report cards issued by, say, the U.S. State Department or even U.S.-based universities are likely to be viewed with some skepticism in the non-Western world. As things stand, the UN may be the only agency with the moral authority to confer international legitimacy. But the UN itself needs to distance itself from the political agendas of states with dubious human rights records. Such speculation points to the need for a truly independent, international agency sponsored by the UN to formulate and issue human rights report cards.

One common theme that emerged from all three workshops is that human rights INGOs always have to compromise to some extent. As William Pace of the World Federalist Movement put it at the UNU workshop, NGOs make constant priority calculations to be most effective in their actions. But normative values, as Pogge has shown, need to guide such priority calculations. It might not always be easy to compare such seemingly incommensurable goods as the freedom of religion and the right to food, but human rights theorists need to consider such questions and avoid utopian theorizing that is useless if not counterproductive in practice.

The benefits of engagement between theorists and practitioners still need to be explored, but to a certain extent, they are apparent in this book. The philosophers of human rights were compelled to think more explicitly about how their ideals might operate in the real world, and the practitioners were compelled to articulate the moral principles underpinning their work. At the very least, it can be said that the contributors, with one or two exceptions, clearly benefited from mutual dialogue in the sense that their essays were modified and improved following critical input by workshop participants who do not ordinarily engage in prolonged exchanges with each other. The reader can engage with these arguments to allow for further progress. By shedding light on the ethical challenges typically encountered by those trying to do good in the international arena and putting forward suggestions for better ways of dealing with those challenges, it is hoped that mistakes can be avoided, moral outlooks improved, and human rights more effectively implemented.

1 The Pornography of Poverty: A Cautionary Fundraising Tale

Betty Plewes and Rieky Stuart

Image: A Filipino child scavenges in a heap of garbage.

Image: A Sudanese mother stares at the camera while holding her emaciated and dying child.

Image: A Zimbabwean schoolchild sitting at a desk, pencil in hand smiles shyly; "Education Now" is emblazoned across the top of the picture.

These nongovernmental organization (NGO) ads implore you to help save these children. You can save them, the ads say, by sending money to the NGO for emergency food relief, to sponsor a child through monthly payments, or to help launch an education campaign.

PORNOGRAPHY OF POVERTY. This is a term used by development practitioners in the North and in the South to describe the worst of the images that exploit the poor for little more than voyeuristic ends and where people are portrayed as helpless, passive objects. It is a derogatory term, and it stimulated the ethicists involved in this project to request that we write to describe what we mean by the term, why it generates ethical debate, and what has been or can be done about it.

Most readers will know what it means – images of emaciated children with distended bellies or flies in their eyes, used to elicit a response from people who have never encountered this kind of suffering in their everyday lives.

These powerful images touch our hearts. They are used by NGOs in the North to raise money for their programs in the South. And they work. In 2004 in Canada the five largest NGOs (mainly childsponsorship organizations) raised about $300 (Canadian) million from private donations.

The fund-raising dimension, however, is only one part of the picture. For many years development practitioners in the South and the North have been concerned that these kinds of images convey other, more destructive messages.

These images portray people as helpless victims, dependent, and unable to take action; they convey a sense that development problems can only be solved by Northern charity. Messages like these can undermine NGOs' efforts to create a broader understanding of the underlying structures that cause poverty and injustice. They ignore Northern complicity in creating inequality. At the very least these images convey a limited picture of life in Southern countries. At their worst they reinforce racist stereotypes.

Several critics have described the negative implications of such images. According to Neville Gabriel from the Southern African Catholic Bishops' Conference, "There has been some concern amongst key African development practitioners and activists that the continent is portrayed exclusively as a hopeless case of endless wars, corruption, disease, and dictatorship. . . . This perception has a serious negative impact on Africa in many spheres." He thinks that one of the most serious consequences is the dismissal of real progress on the continent as "un-African" and a refusal to acknowledge the work of many Africans to overcome the legacy of destruction they inherited in a global context where global political economic and social odds are against them. He maintains that current relations with Africa "model colonial relations of paternalism on the one hand and the internalization of second class world citizenship by Africans on the other." For many Northern international development organizations this attitude translates into a way of working based more on a charitable model than on one of global justice. He emphasizes that justice for Africa will not come about as a result of charitable handouts even though "that may be easier to sell in campaigns and marketing of development organisations through sad pictures and tragic personal stories." This kind of approach often leads to a pattern of "extractive relationships" in which African organizations get funds and Northern organizations "extract" stories and information to sustain themselves. "The unfortunate impact is that this so easily falls into the pattern of reinforcing African people's negative self-image."[1]

Omega Bula of the United Church of Canada argues that negative images of Africa in the Canadian media not only shape the public's view of the continent but also have implications for Canadians of African descent. She says that this kind of negative stereotyping results in serious dysfunction for people of African ancestry, including immigrants, academics, businesspeople, students, and especially women in many areas of their lives.[2]

Bonny Ibhawoh, an assistant professor of history in Ontario and a contributor to this book, sees the impact of these media images on his students. He teaches African history and often begins his classes by asking students what image comes

---

[1] Personal communication to Rieky Stuart from Neville Gabriel, Southern African Catholic Bishops' Conference, October 2002.

[2] Omega Bula, "Images of Africa: Challenging negative stereotypes in media and society," *Making Waves* 2, no. 4 (September 2002), taken from AfricaFiles www.africafiles.org (2003).

to mind when they think about Africa. He writes that the answers he gets are always the same:

> Tarzan, (king of the jungle); famines and starving children; wars and conflicts; dictators and corrupt governments; slaves and slavery. Even when the responses are more benign (Nelson Mandela, Black people, safaris and deserts), they also come from media representations of Africa.[3]

Domestic charities (as well as news media) also use similar images to show poverty and catastrophe in their own society. The difference is that readers and viewers have a more complex picture of their own society to contextualize and assess such images and messages. This is seldom the case with images of Southern countries shown in Northern countries.

Why should we care about the impact in Northern countries if the images raise money? Is it not more important to have the funds to continue the work overseas than to be concerned about how this may influence the way Canadians think about Africa?

> When poverty is described in terms of individual victims and particular instances of hardship and context is ignored, the poor themselves are most often held responsible for their own plight. Yet when news items include background information about general trends and when poverty is expressed as a collective outcome, people tend to assign responsibility to societal factors.[4]

Promoting African development and the way Northerners think about Africa are related. Eliminating poverty and promoting social justice require more than supporting projects in African countries through voluntary organizations. Northern countries must have an enlightened foreign policy that promotes changes in unequal global power relationships. Influencing foreign policy calls for an informed and engaged public, and thus NGOs have developed public awareness programs to increase understanding of the underlying structures that cause poverty and injustice. Inconsistency in the messages conveyed through fundraising appeals and public education and awareness programs undermine efforts to build a constituency supportive of African development initiatives based on social, economic, and environmental justice.

This is why negative messages hidden in fund-raising images matter.

---

[3] Personal communication to Betty Plewes from Bonny Ibhawoh, assistant professor, Department of History, Brock University, St. Catharine's, Ontario, Canada, February 2004.

[4] Danielle Campbell, Stuart Carr, and Malcolm MacLachlan, "Attributing 'Third World Poverty' in Australia and Malawi: A Case for Donor Bias?" *Journal of Applied Social Psychology* 31, no. 2 (2001), quoted in *Images and Insights in Fundraising Advertising*, Janice Nathanson, April 2005, a presentation produced for the Canadian Council for International Cooperation (CCIC).

I. HISTORY OF THE DEBATE

The debate about the pornography of poverty and NGO fund-raising images has been going on for many years. In an April 1989 article titled "Pretty as a Picture" the author states, "The wide-eyed child, smiling or starving, is the most powerful fundraiser for aid agencies. But no matter how effective the image, the message can be very destructive." The article noted that one U.K. study found that 60 percent of fund-raising photographs in Great Britain were of women and children portrayed as "victims."[5] Following the famines in Ethiopia and Sudan in the mid-1980s, the issues of responsibility for the presentation of popular images and public understanding of disasters became prime concerns for NGOs in Europe and other parts of the world. NGOs found that "ideas about Africa became graphically stereotyped through the repetition of harrowing pictures from Ethiopia and Sudan."[6] A number of projects and training programs were organized on visual and verbal images and messages. As part of a multinational "Images of Africa Project" the European Community's Non Governmental Development Organisation (NGDO) network adopted a code of ethics outlining guidelines for the use of images and messages. The work originally focused on disaster assistance but came to include all NGO communications with the public.

Such codes were also developed in other countries. In Canada, for example, the Canadian Council for International Cooperation's (CCIC) *Code of Ethics*[7] has a section on fund-raising and communications. Following are the relevant sections.

CCIC Code of Ethics

Communications to the Public

- Fundraising solicitations shall be truthful, shall accurately describe the Organization's identity, purpose, programs and need, shall only make claims which the Organization can fulfill, and shall avoid using high-pressure tactics in soliciting donations. There shall be no misleading information (including material omissions or exaggerations of fact), no use of misleading photographs, nor any other communication which would tend to create a false impression or misunderstanding. Information in the Organization's appeals should give accurate balance to the actual programs for which the funds solicited will be used.

[5] Paddy Coulter, "Pretty as a Picture," *New Internationalist* 194 (April 1989), p.2, http://www.newint.org/issue194/pretty.htm (19 April 2006).

[6] NGDO-EC Liaison Committee, Development Education Group. "Development Education in the UK." http://www.c3.hu/~bocs/devedu/ecmem/uk.htm (27 April 2006).

[7] "Ethics." CCIC Web site. http://www.ccic.ca/e/002/ethics.shtml (8 March 2006).

- In all its fundraising activities, the Organization shall ensure that: its donors are informed of the Organization's mission, of the way the Organization intends to use donated resources, and of the Organization's capacity to use donations effectively for their intended purposes.
- Any and all communications to the public by the Organization shall respect the dignity, values, history, religion, and culture of the people supported by its programs. In particular, the Organization shall avoid the following:
  - messages which generalize and mask the diversity of situations;
  - messages which fuel prejudice;
  - messages which foster a sense of Northern superiority;
  - messages which show people as hopeless objects for our pity, rather than as equal partners in action and development.

Membership in CCIC is conditional upon compliance with the Code of Ethics.

II. HAS ALL THIS TALK LED TO ACTION?

The dialogue about NGO fund-raising messages has gone on for more than a decade. Two recent activities give us a sense of where we are today – one from VSO (formerly Voluntary Service Overseas), a volunteer sending agency based in England,[8] and the other from the Africa Canada Forum, a coalition of Canadian NGOs working in Africa or involved in issues concerning Africa.

In the United Kingdom

In 2001, VSO decided to look at the impact of Live Aid, the charity pop concert that raised $100 million for Ethiopian famine relief in the mid-1980s. Their research report, "Live Aid Legacy,"[9] was based on polling data and in-depth interviews. They found "stereotypical beliefs and outdated images hold a vice-like grip on British understanding of the developing world."[10]

- Eighty percent of the British public associates the developing world with doom-laden images of famine, disaster, and Western aid.
- The victims are seen as less than human.
- There is a false sense of superiority and inferiority – an image of the North as benevolent givers and Southerners as grateful receivers.

---

[8] VSO has national partners in Canada and the Netherlands.
[9] VSO. "Live Aid Legacy: The Developing World through British Eyes – A Research Report." 2002. http://www.vso.org.uk/Images/liveaid_legacy_tcm8-784.pdf (19 April 2006).
[10] Fiona Holland. "The Live Aid Legacy." *Orbit: Voices from the Developing World* (January 2002): Issue 82, 14.

- When people hear the term "development," they automatically think of Africa. Africa becomes the metaphor through which people understand development issues.
- Researchers remarked that people polled were very confident in their views.
- The images had a negative impact on how visible minority Britons were perceived by their neighbors.

Dr. David Keen, a lecturer at the Development Institute of the London School of Economics, says this is a concern because "If the only thing you get is negative stories, you become inured and people seem less human – they are either emaciated victims or violent and evil. This erodes our ability, willingness or interest in helping a place. It also gives the message that we have nothing to learn from them – which is unfortunate for us."[11]

There was an additional interesting component to the study. After the researchers elicited spontaneous reactions to the words "developing world," they presented a different view of developing countries to participants, using photos, facts, and the opportunity to talk with a VSO volunteer. In every case, the new information challenged the participants' views. Reactions to this new information were as follows:

- Feeling ignorant, even blinkered, due to their perceived lack of knowledge
- Confidence in their worldview was shaken
- Expressing intrigued interest and wanting to know more
- Expressing relief that there are positive stories as well as negative ones
- Expressing anger and looking for someone to blame[12]

In the VSO study, people who were interviewed identified the media as perhaps the most powerful influence in shaping their views but also identified charities' fund-raising materials for promoting "victim" images. A crucial finding from all the interviewees was that the key to breaking down the Live Aid Legacy. is information that promotes balance and to which they feel an emotional connection.

In Canada

In 2001, the NGOs of the Africa Canada Forum decided to look more systematically at the images they used in their fund-raising and promotional materials. About 100 images from twenty organizations were assembled in a display that was used as a basis for discussion with a group that included Canadian NGO workers and workers from organizations in several African countries.

The images were collected by asking the organizations to send examples of their fund-raising and promotional materials. A selection of these was then made and

---

[11] Ibid, 14.   [12] VSO, "The Live Aid Legacy."

organized in a series of categories (men, women, rural, urban, children) on large display boards.

There were a few pictures of famine victims and refugees, but the majority of the pictures were not in the "pornography of poverty" category. In fact, there seemed to be an effort to avoid negative images by using many shots of women and smiling children. Most photos were of rural life and primary producers with few pictures of urban areas, industrial production, artistic expression, or cultural life. There was almost no sense of context. The messages were simple: a few dollars can make a huge difference. Interestingly, there were few shots of men.

After viewing the display of photos, there was an opportunity to discuss the display in small groups, and participants made the following comments:

- Most images presented do not represent Africa but represent the roles of (Northern) organizations in Africa.
- Most photographs represent people in need and do not show obstacles that Africans and people all over the world are trying to surmount.
- Images should serve not only to raise funds but should also creatively link public education to fund-raising.
- Images should show a broader diversity of life in Africa.
- It is not necessary to stop using negative images (negative situations exist), but the context in which these images are used is important. Images should be used to demonstrate values such as solidarity and community rather than the loss of human dignity.

Based on this limited review, it is evident that there are still some agencies using pornography of poverty images especially for disaster relief and child sponsorship. On the other hand, many other agencies have made an effort to show more positive images and have replaced the pictures of desperate people with images of smiling women and children. In many cases, however, the people portrayed still seem passive – being "helped" by foreigners and not seen within a larger context. Some organizations have made considerable efforts to show a broader, more complex social-political context in their fund-raising. Others have developed the capacity to show, through image and text, people working in their communities to overcome serious barriers to social justice.

Pictures of desperate, starving people, especially children, have tremendous emotional and psychological impact that more positive pictures do not elicit. Also, agencies that use the more "pornographic" images are usually larger and have more resources to devote to television programs and newspaper ads; therefore, they have a deeper impact on public perceptions.

Although there has been a positive change in the decreasing number of agencies using the most extreme pornography of poverty images, current strategies still offer a decontextualized and partial image of the issues and societies that are the subject of their fund-raising. The overall impact of such images on Canadian audiences is unlikely to be different from the findings of the British public's perceptions in the VSO study.

III. DYNAMICS WITHIN AGENCIES

Why do development NGOs use pornography of poverty images? Have there been changes over time? Are all development NGOs alike in this? Although it is not possible to give complete answers to these questions, it is useful to give some overview and direction.

In most large NGOs, fund-raising from the public is done according to standard formulas tested over time and applied by fund-raising professionals. NGOs vary in their sources of funding: some raise little or no money from the public and depend on contracts and grants from bilateral or multilateral development agencies for the bulk of their funding. Some raise funds primarily from private foundations. Some raise the bulk of their funding from the public. Few raise all of their funds from a single source; most have a mix of strategies. Raising funds from the public is the most costly form of fund-raising, but it permits the greatest independence in programming.

In Canada and elsewhere, NGOs raising money for child sponsorship generate the most revenue from the public. For example, the three largest public fund-raising development NGOs in Canada are child-sponsorship organizations; they generate more than ten times as much money from the public as the three top nonsponsorship organizations do. Fund-raising for international development charities is still a small proportion of the total raised by domestic charities. In Canada, it is less than 5 percent.

Child-sponsorship organizations are demonstrably the biggest users of pornography of poverty images, whether for sponsorship or for fund-raising for humanitarian emergencies. They also have the means, because of their scale and fund-raising professionalism, to test alternative messaging. They tell us that these images of misery and passive victimization generate much more in donations than alternatives they have tested and that it is vital to raise large amounts of money to be able to carry out their relief and development work.

Among child-sponsorship agencies, it is possible to perceive a shift over time – at least in some of their sponsorship fund-raising – from miserable, starving children to "picking winners." Some ads show "after" pictures or "success stories" of children helped by their Northern sponsors; these demonstrate how the children were able to succeed with monthly support. Importantly, most child-sponsorship organizations now use a community development approach in their overseas programming and underline their commitment to sustainable development. They maintain the sponsorship approach in their fund-raising.

Other agencies such as Oxfam Canada, engaged in long-term development work, and committed to the "eradication of poverty" have a slightly different experience and perspective. They generally espouse a community development approach, which invests in a "hand-up" for community groups – of women, of farmers, or producer groups – rather than a "hand-out."

Another element that constrains the work of NGOs is the domestic legislation under which they operate. The legislation is imbued with a concept of charity as helping others who are less fortunate and also places serious constraints on a charity's ability to carry out education, policy, and advocacy work. Many agencies have long understood that there are major systemic and policy constraints that keep the poor poor and make the rich richer, and some, through their policy and campaigning initiatives, strive to change the attitudes and behavior that maintain and increase inequality and poverty. It is this type of work that is constrained by the legislation. Even without the legislative barriers, communicating systemic constraints to poverty eradication in a way that appeals to the public is far from easy. Such communication tends to focus on the head, not on the heart, and it is the heartstrings that traditionally open pocketbooks.

Environmental and human rights organizations have dealt with this dilemma of rational versus emotional approaches by developing a finely tuned victim–villain–remedy model that generates public support and funding by eliciting outrage rather than pity. This is a relatively new approach for development charities. A recent example is the effort of Oxfam and Médecins Sans Frontières and allies to target drug companies and World Trade Organization (WTO) negotiators about the scarcity and high prices of AIDS drugs available in Africa. This was a policy rather than a fund-raising campaign, which sought to entrench public health as an overriding priority for WTO policy related to generic drug availability. The campaign also targeted patent protection and profits by large drug conglomerates that prevent governments such as those of South Africa or Brazil from importing low-cost generics that can save millions of lives. Although such efforts do generate public support, their capacity to raise funds on the scale required for development NGOs is untested. This sometimes leads to clashing approaches – generating outrage for campaigning actions and images of suffering, at-risk humans (or animals) for fund-raising by the same agency.

Most human rights and environmental organizations expend their efforts in research, campaigning, education, and advocacy, whereas development NGOs still transfer the bulk of their funding to partners and communities overseas. For example, Greenpeace International and Oxfam International spend about the same amount on fund-raising, research, campaigning, education, and advocacy. This constitutes 100 percent of Greenpeace activities but only about 25 percent of Oxfam's – the remainder goes to fund partners and programs in developing countries. It is difficult to imagine established development agencies relinquishing their fund transfer role, although some, like Oxfam, are gradually increasing their policy, advocacy, and campaigning capacity. The debate about how best to accomplish our poverty eradication mission – with fund transfers for community-based programs targeting poor people or with research, policy and campaigning work – means that the ethics of resource allocation is increasingly coming into question.

Policy change without direct support for people living in poverty, the argument goes, is often window dressing. It is impossible to link policy and practice changes without strong roots in particular contexts to shape effective policy interventions and provide feedback loops. There are power inequalities – relationships of power embedded in the images of self and other that both the powerful and the powerless enact – that can only be challenged by different kinds of actions enabled by effective development interventions on the ground. If community development interventions, by themselves, are insufficient to eradicate poverty, so are policy interventions. What is needed is the interaction of the two processes.

Agencies such as Oxfam Canada have long since rejected pornography of poverty images and advertising and have created differing strategies as alternatives. One strategy has been to promote positive images – the smiling children, the women smiling as they operate their new village pump, the smiling nurse vaccinating plump healthy children.

Another has been to use "clever" or ironic images: a recent Oxfam ad for Ethiopian drought relief showed cracked dry earth with text stating that "Over 8 million people in Ethiopia could fall through the cracks." A campaign to promote fair trade used a poster with a large yellow banana with a fair trade sticker. During the O. J. Simpson trial, an award-winning Oxfam ad used only text to compare the amount of media coverage of that event with the much smaller coverage of the Rwanda genocide taking place at the same time. Other agencies use abstract art or traditional artistic patterns and forgo photographs of people entirely.

Although each of these strategies generates public support, it is fair to say that the level of public donations does not match by a long shot the level reached by child-sponsorship agencies, either in dollars raised or numbers of donors.[13] As a result, the comparatively small size of these charities means that it is difficult for them to invest in research to determine how best to scale up this type of advertising. Larger umbrella bodies, such as the CCIC, have also been unable to attract research funds or member agreement for such work.

Pressure to look at alternatives may come from the threat of decreasing financial returns. In an article reproduced in the *Mediasol* Web site, Ivan du Roy described a disastrous 35 percent decline in charitable donations in France in the first trimester of 2002.[14] Although the decline may have a number of sources, one hypothesis is that donors reject the exploitation of suffering and emotions generated by such images. Alain Wei of Wei Opinion, who undertook to interview a

---

[13] An unexplained exception is Oxfam Great Britain, which until recently was the largest public fund-raiser in Great Britain, including both domestic and international charities. It has just been overtaken by a consortium of domestic health charities.

[14] Ivan du Roy, "Rien ne va plus sur le 'marché de la générosité'" (20 June 2002). http://www. mediasol.org/xarticle.php3?id_article=2181&id_rubrique=11. This site is now unavailable.

sample of donors in some depth, was quoted as concluding that NGO appeals to emotion need to transform that emotion – and making a donation is insufficient for people to cope with the feelings generated by NGO images and advertising.

IV. MEDIA COVERAGE

Although NGO images do influence public perception, they are set in the context of the way the mass media cover developing countries and their cultures. If media coverage were providing balance and more background in the presentation of stories about developing countries, the public would have a broader context within which to understand the NGO images. Unfortunately, what coverage there is tends to focus on crises and problems and to create the image of Africans or Asians as helpless victims – and as remote and "other." Few Canadian journalists are assigned to "cover" Africa, Asia, or Latin America, and the number is smaller year by year. There is no systematic effort to build relationships with local media in these countries, so the coverage tends to be very Northern in orientation. A year after the 2001 floods in Mozambique, a CBC radio retrospective reflected on media coverage of that event, noting how the media focused on rescues by foreign helicopter pilots and on a woman, Sophia Tedro, giving birth in a tree. This was analyzed in the documentary as yet another example of choosing to portray a victim and a foreign "saviour" – rather than focusing on the indigenous Mozambican relief efforts that comprised the bulk of the crisis intervention. It is far easier for development charities to build on these stereotyped images – they are, after all, a reflection of the level of our collective societal consciousness – than to set out a deliberate agenda to counter these stereotypes of helplessness and inadequacy.

The Department for International Development (DFID) and BBC News commissioned a study,[15] published in October 2002, to increase understanding of public perceptions and attitudes toward television news coverage of the developing world with the longer-term goal of finding more effective ways to treat global issues in television coverage. They found that the greatest barrier to engaging viewers with news stories about the developing world was viewers' lack of knowledge about the subject. To engage viewers, news stories would require the following:

- An attention-grabbing introduction
- Background context and information
- Making the story relevant to people's lives
- A single story
- Providing a balanced view of the developing world

---

[15] Opinion Leader Research, "Making Sense of the World: A Joint BBC News–DFID Study of Public Perceptions of Television News Coverage of Developing Countries" (October 2002). http://www.dfid.gov.uk/Pubs/files/makingsense.pdf.

For both media coverage and NGO fund-raising, the key seems to be balance and context.

Make Poverty History/Global Call to Action Against Poverty

A recent example of innovation in this area is the Make Poverty History/Global Call to Action Against Poverty campaign. The main image of the television ads was of celebrities clicking their fingers every three seconds while Liam Neeson's voice called viewers to take action against needless (and immoral) death of children by providing more and better aid and through debt cancellation and trade justice. The ads received worldwide major media coverage, amplified by the Live8 concerts. They reached a much larger and more diverse audience than normal NGO ads and images. The fund-raising was indirect – asking citizens to press their government for use of tax money rather than to open their own wallets. The campaign message was one of hope and possibility – and moral outrage – rather than pity. The cost of the campaign, with its clever use of donated time and talent, was considerably less than the participating agencies spent on direct fund-raising in the same time period. Increased funding commitments and other policy changes, such as debt relief, generated by the campaign have the potential to save more lives than any individual NGO can even dream of achieving. Despite the widespread coverage and the substantial policy gains, there is still substantial critique about the degree to which the campaign reinforces current stereotypes of Africa.[16]

V. WHY IS IT TAKING SO LONG TO CHANGE?

There are many complex ethical dilemmas raised in this discussion: truthfulness, honesty, respect for people's dignity and privacy, racial stereotyping, balancing different needs, misleading by omission.[17] NGOs are aware of these debates and have made some changes. Nevertheless, there has been less change than one would have expected given the values base of many organizations. Why? Here in summary are some of the reasons.

1. NGOs raise substantial amounts of money using these techniques, and where they have tested other images, organizations say that they do not raise as much money. The bulk of their programming is funding overseas programs, and they do not want to jeopardize this work.

---

[16] See Madeleine Bunting's article "Humiliated Once More: The Recent Focus on Africa Reinforces Our Perception of It as Picturesque, Pitiful, Psychopathic and Passive," *The Guardian*, 4 July 2005, http://www.guardian.co.uk/comment/story/0,,1520640,00.html (19 April 2006).

[17] Anne Buchanan, "Beyond Stereotypes: Seeking New Images," *Au Courant* 11, no. 1 (spring 2001), 4–6.

2. Many NGOs still operate on a charitable model. Their fund-raising is consistent with the way they see the world. This is reinforced by the current law governing charities that uses a 400-year-old definition of poverty and severely limits the advocacy and policy work that can be carried out by organizations with a charitable designation.

3. Some NGOs operate inconsistently, using a charitable model in their fund-raising and a more political model in their advocacy and policy work. Some child-sponsorship organizations have changed their overseas programming from supporting individual children to community-based programs, but continue to use an individual approach in their fund-raising. The value of the advocacy or overseas work is used to justify or balance the fund-raising images and messages. Policy and advocacy work also raise ethical issues of accountability, however. Who do Northern NGOs speak for in their advocacy work? Are they being transparent in informing their donors about the policy work they are doing?

4. Government cutbacks have forced NGOs to raise more funds privately to maintain programs, and NGOs have cut back areas of public education that might have offered a broader context for the fund-raising activities.

5. NGOs do not have a lot of funds for experimentation with creative, alternative messaging. Because fund-raising is one of the most competitive areas within the NGO community, there has been little incentive to collaborate on joint initiatives and experiment with collective approaches.

6. There is a fundamental contradiction between an agency's need to raise funds by selling itself as an effective agent for poverty relief or eradication and the reality that positive change will come about primarily through a complex process of change led by citizens and governments of developing countries, along with changes in unjust global systems. In the former case, it is the NGO and its "beneficiaries" that occupy center stage in the fund-raising picture. A more accurate depiction of the latter reality would put the NGO in the background as "supporting cast" – and be ineffective in raising funds.

VI. IS NOT THE MONEY MORE IMPORTANT?

In this chapter, we have argued that many images, not only the so-called pornographic images used by NGOs in their communications to support fund-raising and other organizational activities, have negative consequences whether intentional or not. They can

- reinforce negative racial stereotypes in both the South and the North
- present a limited picture of life in Southern countries
- ignore the real progress that has been made in many areas
- ignore the substantial contributions made by many Southern actors

- reinforce perceptions that what is required is more charity rather than fundamental political and economic change
- generate a sense of hopelessness and helplessness (i.e., the problems are unsolvable and there is nothing we can do about it)

Taken together, these factors work against other efforts to create an engaged and active citizenry committed over the long term to effective strategies for poverty reduction and social justice. In Canada, despite more than thirty years of action, and some progress, the public still has little understanding of the issues, urgencies, and realities of international development, and many people have a sense of hopelessness about finding solutions.

Few people in the international sector would disagree that this kind of advertising has some unintended negative consequences. Their main counterargument is that these approaches raise more money and therefore allow more good work to be done by those agencies, and this counterbalances the negative consequences. If this is true, it raises the question of whether the benefits in fact do outweigh the consequences. This is a challenging issue. Our position in this chapter is that even if they do raise more money in the short term, the long-term negative consequences outweigh the short-term benefits. Creating a new and critical awareness among Northern citizens of the need to transform global political and economic relationships will be more effective in eliminating poverty than the additional funds raised through these methods.

A second question is whether these approaches raise more money. To explore these issues, the CCIC has created a working group of fund-raising practitioners. They are trying to increase the fund-raising capacity of development organizations by moving away from potentially damaging to more respectful images of people that also contribute to a long-term response.[18]

Several agencies participating in this group have noted that these kinds of emotional appeals may produce one-off contributions, but they are finding that they do not lead to long-term sustaining donors.[19] Creating sustaining donors is important because continued prospecting and development of new donors is expensive. The group is working with experienced consultants to look at ways to raise more money and create positive perceptions by changing the way they communicate. Some of the recent social marketing literature also suggests productive new approaches.

---

[18] For a useful document that covers many of these issues, see the presentation prepared for the CCIC Working Group on ethical fund-raising practices by Janice Nathanson, *Images and Insights in Fundraising Advertising*, April 2005. For more information on the results of the working group, contact CCIC at info@ccic.ca.

[19] In this chapter, we do not have time to explore the costs and benefits of various fund-raising approaches, but it is an important discussion because many of these fund-raising programs are costly.

Given that people are questioning the effectiveness of these kinds of approaches, NGOs need to explore new methods for fund-raising that are consistent with their other goals of creating a broader and deeper engagement on the part of Canadians. This involves having a better understanding of Canadian attitudes and effective social marketing strategies. More than thirty years of work have not produced the results we had hoped for, and new approaches are required. More of the same will not produce different results. By working more collaboratively, NGOs can pool scarce resources in exploring new approaches.

SOME DIRECTIONS FOR ACTION

In thinking how to take these issues forward, it is important to continue engaging with Southern partners and with immigrant communities in Canada.

1. In Canada, we could undertake an independent public review of images that are used and their impact on the public perception of development issues as a basis for creating a broader discussion.
2. We could encourage and disseminate an independent and professional review of new approaches being used and support some experimentation with alternative approaches.
3. We could explore with the Canadian International Development Agency the possibility of developing a more coherent and collective framework for public education in Canada on development issues.[20]
4. We could encourage boards of directors of development NGOs to review the images and messages the NGOs use and articulate the coherence among their organization's mission, fund-raising, public education, and policy advocacy images and messages.

Development practitioners deeply appreciate the cultural richness and variety of the countries where we work. We experience the richness of the noneconomic: of laughter and tears, of music and art. Most of us believe we learn more than we teach and see the value of our work in the mutual reflection of alternative possibility we are able to generate across difference. We struggle to articulate this perspective to Northern audiences and find the effort arduous and generally unsuccessful. It challenges the helper–victim, winner–loser images that pervade our culture and underpin our work, whether we think about poverty domestically or on a global scale. We need language and images that move beyond this mindset. We see the need and feel the possibility but have yet to unlock the words and images that will help us take the next step.

---

[20] Such frameworks have been in place for a number of years in Europe and have been seen to be particularly effective in shaping less paternalistic public attitudes in the Netherlands and in Nordic countries.

2 An Imperfect Process: Funding Human Rights – A Case Study

Mona Younis

U.S. foundations may well be guided by laudable values and visions. Legally, however, they are accountable to neither the public nor the community of groups that receive their funding, let alone the communities that those groups serve, with regard to *what* they fund. Given the prevailing political climate in the United States, the lack of program accountability to U.S. taxpayers and, indeed, the government may be a good thing; regrettably, international human rights norms do not appear to be at the top of either agenda. In fact, with only a minute percentage of the 68,000 registered U.S. foundations funding in this field in 2004, human rights is barely on the agenda of the philanthropic community itself.[1] Leaving aside who is responsible for this, it suggests that there is something unusual about foundations that fund in this area: a vision, a sense of responsibility or sense of the possible, perhaps? Regardless of the motivation or inspiration, the actual grant-making process is far less agreeable than the world human rights grant makers endeavor to make possible.

Those concerned with the ethics of transnational interventions can justifiably ask about the process by which funders in the United States determine what is to be funded around the world. At the most fundamental level, how ethical are funding programs that affect people with no voice in what is funded? Human rights grant makers, although even more removed from the site than the organizations they support, are no less responsible for the interventions they make possible. This dichotomy – money here, work there – frames the entire process, indeed the world, and suggests a number of important questions. Can this essentially undemocratic and nonparticipatory funding process effect good democratic change in the world? Can "trickle-down" funding counter the economic inequities between the global North and South, or does it merely replicate these in the civil societies that are being constructed? And what of the approach of

---

[1] Available data on human rights funding and funders, although flawed and incomplete, indicate that approximately 300 foundations made at least one human rights grant in 2003, and fewer than 100 U.S. foundations have entire programs explicitly devoted to human rights.

relying on professional nongovernmental organizations (NGOs) that are funded from abroad for achieving social and political change? The experience of the North, where neither external funding nor professional NGOs played a role in constructing its political democracies, indicates that it is social movements – "politics by other means" – that are key to meaningful political transformations. Is the relationship between NGOs and social movements a necessarily positive one? U.S. funders rarely tackle such large questions, operating as they do under the inexorable force of law that requires endowed foundations to give money away – at least 5 percent of their corpus – to "charitable" organizations every year like clockwork. They do, however, constantly grapple with "lesser" ethical dilemmas in the process of deciding which funding requests to support and which to turn down.

This chapter provides a window into one human rights funder's experience, the Mertz Gilmore Foundation (MGF),[2] over two decades of funding human rights organizations. Drawing on MGF's internal evaluation of fifteen years of grantmaking, I identify a number of successes that U.S. human rights funders can claim and the ethical dilemmas that accompanied those successes. I then turn to the elaborate process MGF undertook to establish a new funding direction for its international human rights program in 2002, the risks and challenges the new direction posed, and the surprise decision to end the program altogether the following year. Through this chapter, I share a glimpse into one foundation's experience as it developed, evaluated, revised, and then ended a funding program and discuss the ethical dilemmas posed at each juncture in the ever-imperfect process of funding. I conclude by returning to the questions raised earlier.

I. THE MERTZ GILMORE FOUNDATION

In 2001, with an annual human rights grants budget of approximately US $2.5 million, MGF[3] was the fifth largest human rights funder in the United States. In previous years, it had much more to spend on human rights – nearly US $8 million in 1994 – and soon would spend less, but a few years into the new millennium, MGF ranked as one of the leading U.S. human rights funders. On the face of it, that should have been a source of pride for the foundation. It was not; budgets of tens of millions of dollars separated MGF from the top three funders.[4] Indeed, the fact that MGF ranked fifth with only US $2.5 million in grants was a source of considerable concern as it reflected the limited involvement of U.S.

---

[2] I would like to thank Robert Crane, MGF's former president, and Jay Beckner, the Foundation's current executive director, for their valuable comments on an early draft of this chapter.

[3] The foundation was established as the Mertz Foundation in 1959. Its name was changed to the Joyce Mertz-Gilmore Foundation in 1976, then to the Mertz Gilmore Foundation in 2002.

[4] The top three human rights funders are the Ford Foundation, Open Society Institute, and the John D. and Catherine T. MacArthur Foundation.

foundations in human rights funding. As a result, MGF staff became particularly active in efforts to leverage more funds for the field. The objective was summed up nicely by the foundation's then new executive director, Jay Beckner, when he said, "We want to move our way down the list, working to become the fiftieth largest human rights funder." With no intention of reducing its human rights grant making, MGF looked forward to seeing many more funders supporting the field.

The foundation is known in the philanthropic community for a distinctive grant making style that includes a demonstrated readiness to fund controversial issues that most grant makers are reluctant to support. It was one of the first U.S. foundations to fund studies on global warming (1984) and work on lesbian and gay rights (1987) and immigrant rights (1987), and was the only foundation with a combined Israel and Palestine program (1997). Guided by the premise that grant makers that trust an organization enough to fund it should trust it to decide how it can best allocate its resources, MGF has been an important source of general operating support. Between 1989 and 1999, an average of nearly 70 percent of the foundation's grant dollars went to general operating support as compared with 13.7 percent for the foundation community as a whole in 1998.[5] A related feature of MGF's grant-making is multiyear support because most areas require both a long view and long-term investments to show results. Many of the foundation's grantees have received steady annual support for ten years or more. MGF recognizes that a variety of means are required at various times and so funds a broad range of approaches, including policy research, education of opinion makers, grassroots community organizing, and media work. Priding itself on being field-driven, program staff take their cues regarding needs and opportunities from the respective fields with which they are very much engaged. Finally, the foundation is committed to service NGOs and the philanthropic community to improve funding for the various fields. These general attributes of MGF's grantmaking equally characterized its human rights program. In the area of service to the field, for example, MGF has allocated substantial staff time and financial resources to the International Human Rights Funders Group – an international network of more than 400 individual grant makers – and would serve as its institutional home over 2000–2005.[6]

Evolution of a Human Rights Program

Originally one of five foundation programs, MGF's human rights program consisted of two components: U.S. Human Rights and International Human Rights.[7]

---

[5] Cited in an MGF report to the Board of Directors, May 11–12, 2000, 3.
[6] In July 2005, responsibility for the International Human Rights Funders Group transferred to Wellspring Advisors, the Group's new institutional home.
[7] In 2001, the foundation's other programs were Energy, New York City Human and Built Environment, Arts in New York City, and Israel and Palestine.

The U.S. program was devoted to supporting groups that worked with two particularly vulnerable populations – immigrants and lesbians and gays. From time to time, staff would discuss what it meant to fund the immigrant rights work and lesbian and gay rights groups under the rubric of Human Rights when none of the foundation's grantees in these two fields self-identified as human rights groups and, when asked about this, even questioned the relevance of international human rights law for their work in the United States. That would later change, but in the 1990s MGF staff and the board of directors left the question of what the U.S. Human Rights and International Human Rights programs shared beyond an amorphous commitment to improving the human condition, especially for marginalized communities, and focused on the funding guidelines that had been developed separately for each.

Launched in 1984, the foundation's international human rights grantmaking was driven by one family member and board members who shared his politics and Quaker principles. Initially, the relevant program combined funding for civil rights, human rights, democratic values, and peace and disarmament. One year later, a task force began exploring "civil and human rights" as a distinct area. Recognizing that the foundation's modest resources necessitated focused funding that "could provide some sense of cumulative accomplishments," the board spent considerable time and energy in developing a position paper and policy guidelines for the program in the two years that followed.[8] Among other things, they asserted an inextricable link between human rights and democracy, such that "one is not fully realizable without the other." Whereas human rights "focus attention on *what* an individual should be assured by a society," democratic values "focus attention on *how* societies organize to promote and assure those rights."[9] With regard to content of rights, the board committed itself to furthering "a set of principles" or "entitlements" that are "believed to be basic to human rights/democratic values," which included "a sense of security, welfare, equity, achievement and participation." As for form, they held that "each society must develop a structure and process appropriate for it, one which allows for the fullest exercise of the democratic rights of citizens. Whatever the model, the attainment of human rights is possible only in a democratic participatory structure."

Three categories of program interests were adopted: Community Development in Emerging Democracies, Protection and Support of Human Rights Worldwide, and Protection and Extension of Rights in the United States. Within these interest areas, a variety of approaches were supported: legal and social action, policy analysis and development, education and leadership development, and monitoring and exposure of rights violations. Following site visits and meetings with human rights experts, the board identified the Philippines, Haiti, and South Africa as primary candidates for funding because they were at critical junctures in their struggles for democracy. By 1988, however, the deteriorating political

---

[8] The quotes in this section were excerpted from internal MGF reports from various years.
[9] Emphasis added.

situation in all three countries made the determination of the value and effectiveness of proposed projects and their implementation difficult. Realizing that staff and resource limitations further constrained its ability to pursue direct country-specific funding, the foundation soon redirected its focus to U.S.-based international organizations active on the human rights front in many countries around the world.

Two aspects are noteworthy about the foundation's early approach to human rights funding and its evolution. At no point in the deliberations were there references to the actual texts, standards, or rights in the Universal Declaration of Human Rights (UDHR) or the human rights treaties to which it gave rise. Instead, and not unlike the majority of human rights funders today, MGF's board members were moved by an abstract notion of "human rights principles" that had little to do with states' obligations. Indeed, in the grantmaking rationales and guidelines they make public, human rights funders rarely link support for human rights organizations with the objective of securing governments' adherence to their legally binding obligations to respect, protect, and fulfill the rights enumerated in the two covenants and various conventions.

A second notable aspect of MGF's early attention to human rights is the board's anticipation of a number of later and important developments in the field; by invoking human rights in relation to work inside the United States, linking economic development with human rights, and funding groups in developing countries directly, MGF was relatively ahead of its time. Despite these noteworthy inclinations, with the exception of human rights in the United States, which the foundation maintained in the form of immigrant rights and lesbian and gay rights programs, the board eventually retreated to a focus on U.S.-based groups and civil and political rights for the most part. The question is why?

Foundations respond idiosyncratically, reflecting the varied proclivities of their board and staff members, attentiveness to developments in the field, level of comfort with new ideas and approaches, political outlook on the world, in-house expertise, and the amount of resources at their disposal. In MGF's case, although most of these internal factors favored directly supporting promising new human rights initiatives around the world, the foundation was influenced by external factors to pursue another route. Principal among the external factors that influence all foundation grantmaking is *what exists* in the way of fundable programs and organizations in the field. The following review of MGF's international human rights grantmaking reveals how foundations' funding both shapes and is shaped by the field.

International Human Rights Program, 1984–2003

Between 1989 and 1999, MGF contributed US $34 million through its U.S. and international human rights programs. In 1999, the international human rights grants budget of US $1.25 million was disbursed to twenty-seven NGOs with an average grant size of approximately US $50,000. Although not large, a general operating grant of this amount proved valuable to many groups. In 1999, more than two-thirds of the twenty international human rights grantees receiving operating support had been funded for eight years or more, and more than two-fifths had been supported for ten years or longer. Besides general operating support, project funding proved important in many cases, particularly in 1994 and 1995, which were exceptional years during which the foundation was able to make more than $5 million in capacity building grants above and beyond its regular budget. A $500,000 grant to Human Rights Watch, for example, made a major computer upgrade and full networking of its New York and Washington offices, and later other offices around the world, possible. The same amount to the Lawyers Committee for Human Rights (now Human Rights First) was applied toward an equipment upgrade, staff development, and a donor program. And the U.S. Committee for Refugees used a US $400,000 grant for institutional reorganization. In short, MGF contributed to the field-building efforts that resulted in a number of strong and effective human rights organizations – the early leaders of the field.

In supporting, along with other foundations, organizations that became leading NGOs in the international human rights movement, MGF's funding may be deemed to have been quite successful. Collectively, MGF grantees can claim a number of accomplishments over the course of the past two decades: they developed sophisticated techniques and training programs for monitoring and reporting human rights violations, creatively adopted and applied technologies from other fields such as forensic medicine, created a lasting record of human rights around the world by documenting and disseminating information in a variety of forms (publications, films, Internet, etc.), extended valuable assistance to their counterparts as they formed and developed in the global South, and are widely credited with the incorporation of human rights into the U.S. media and government discourse. These organizations' notable strengths and accomplishments notwithstanding, the field's development remains uneven. Through their funding priorities, U.S. foundations have contributed to the prevailing imbalance. MGF is no exception.

Funding Successes and Dilemmas, 1989–1999

Defining success is not easy for funders generally and human rights funders particularly. For one thing, policy and advocacy funders do not have the benefit of quantitative measurements available to funders of relief and services. For another, their focus on systemic problems requires them to adopt a long view, with most seeing themselves "in it for the long haul" – even a very long one. Although recognizing that "relief and services today" are vital, human rights funders focus on "prevention for tomorrow." Whether communities faced with this choice would choose similarly deserves to be explored. For the most part, however, human rights funders support groups that exist, that is, members of communities who themselves have chosen to focus on the long view via the realization of the human rights promise.

Extending support to established groups mitigates against the possibility that human rights funders are deciding for affected communities whether "assistance" in the immediate term or "rights" in the long term ought to be the priority. The decision to support human rights work, however, entails its own contentious questions: Which rights? Which organizations? Which activities? In which countries or communities? Therefore, the question remains: How do funders determine the "success" of their human rights programs? Because foundations do not do the actual work, they generally escape blame for unsuccessful projects, be they in Angola, Argentina, or Arizona, but often get credit for those that succeed. In any case, success and failure of individual projects may not be the best yardstick for funders. A more appropriate way to evaluate funders may be how well their programs respond to the needs of the field over time.

By most grant seekers' standards, MGF has done many right things. The foundation provided general operating support that permitted NGOs the flexibility they require, open-ended renewable funding that afforded grantees a certain amount of security, and capacity building grants that helped take organizations' institutional development to new levels. When resources permitted, MGF also contributed seed money to support new approaches and organizations. Combined, the foundation supported a broad range of organizations in terms of staff size (3–150), organizational budgets (US $64,000–$15.6 million), and year established (1958–1994). Although broad, the range of grant recipients did not, however, reflect the diversity that characterized the field as it was evolving.

Despite its openness to new efforts, approaches, and organizations, more than two-thirds of MGF's international human rights grantees were well-known organizations in their second or even third and fourth decade of work, and two-thirds were international NGOs (INGOs) based in the United States but focused on human rights abroad. In addition, the majority of grantees concentrated their efforts on the attainment and defense of civil and political rights. Although when the foundation began funding in the mid-1980s, pioneering human rights organizations located in the United States and focused on civil and political rights were "the field," a decade later, this was no longer the case. The end of the Cold War saw signs of a changing human rights community, one that might genuinely claim to be international, with human rights groups forming in virtually every country, collectively addressing the full spectrum of rights enumerated in the UDHR and subsequent treaties. Concomitantly, the field now presented countless new funding opportunities.

What foundations choose to fund is of consequence to the field directly by enabling and strengthening particular groups and work, and indirectly by signaling what is fundable and, by implication, deserving of support. Most U.S. foundation funding for human rights, and MGF's funding during 1989–1999, communicated that (a) already well-established U.S. and European INGOs that

(b) work on promoting the rights enshrined in the Covenant on Civil and Political Rights in (c) developing countries using (d) recognized human rights methods were the priority for funding. This message entailed a number of implications for the field.

WHO, NORTHERN OR SOUTHERN HUMAN RIGHTS GROUPS? Foundation support for human rights largely went into building and strengthening organizations based in the North, and principally a small number of prominent INGOs. The concentration of funding in Northern organizations replicated the resource-disparity between the North and South in the human rights NGO community that formed. Persistent concentration of funding in the larger and better-resourced groups, which reinforces the unevenness characterizing the human rights community internationally, has hampered efforts to advance human rights globally. Having discovered the limits of what can be accomplished through "naming and shaming" and external pressure on targeted governments, the INGOs came to recognize how vitally important it is that they have strong partners in the South capable of exerting pressure on governments internally. Groups in the global South, however, are not only competing for funding with institutionally more secure, better-funded Northern counterparts with greater and more direct access to U.S. funders, they are also competing with organizations that have resources to apply toward generating more resources. MGF's survey revealed that nearly half of its grantees had a full-time staff member devoted to fundraising already in 1999.[10]

WHICH, CP RIGHTS OR ESC RIGHTS? Through their funding, human rights funders have contributed to the disparity between attention and work on civil and political (CP) rights and that on economic, social, and cultural (ESC) rights. Whether the prevailing imbalance is primarily due to U.S. funders' inclinations or to U.S.-based human rights INGOs' partiality for CP rights over the course of several decades in which human rights was the captive of Cold War politics is unclear. Minimally, by continuing to fund work that privileged one set of rights over the other, human rights funders tacitly approved the focus and resulting imbalance.

MGF's relatively early readiness to support work on economic rights has been noted. Organizations that explicitly sought the realization of these rights, however, largely emerged in the 1990s. The timing is important. As a late arrival, ESC rights work has had to live up to standards of quality and clarity characterizing work on CP rights achieved over several decades. Criticisms regarding the viability of setting standards and identifying and then holding violators to account that were once leveled at CP rights advocates came to be directed at proponents

---

[10] The burden that fundraising places on NGOs is noted in the increasing professionalization of this role. Nearly half of the organizations surveyed had a full-time staff member devoted to fundraising, and in virtually every case, the first such hire occurred in the 1990s.

of ESC rights. The so-called problem of justiciability that plagued early efforts on CP rights is repeatedly invoked and hampers support for ESC rights work; the slowness of CP rights advocates to defend work on ESC rights has not helped. Yet increasing numbers of human rights groups around the world are carrying out the painstaking work required to bring ESC rights on par with CP rights. U.S. foundations have been slow to support these efforts. Their sluggishness can be attributed to their greater familiarity with CP rights work, greater comfort with the larger and well-established organizations that remained focused on CP rights, and, not insignificantly, the continued need for work on CP rights. Equally important, however, is funders' uneasiness about economic human rights specifically, which is attributable to the influence of U.S. human rights organizations that question the justiciability of ESC rights, the U.S. government's rejection of ESC rights, and/or the conservative world view of foundation board members and executives regarding "rights" in the economic realm. Still, even those organizations once devoted solely to the realization of CP rights have recognized the costs of doing so in a world in which gross violations of ESC rights directly threaten peoples' survival and undermine their receptiveness to CP rights.

HOW, PROFESSIONAL NGOs OR SOCIAL MOVEMENTS? The substantial outlay of resources for the better known organizations enabled them to grow significantly and professionalize in the 1990s; a testament to what organizations can accomplish when they enjoy steady renewable support. MGF's survey of its human rights grantees revealed that on average their budgets quadrupled and their staffs tripled between 1989 and 1999. Whereas the median budget was US $383,000 in 1989, ten years later the median was US $918,000. Similarly, median staff size grew from four to thirteen between 1989 and 1999, respectively. Accompanying this expansion has been the professionalization of human rights work.

External documenting and reporting and "naming and shaming" have contributed valuably to securing human rights protections and gains but clearly are not enough. The dominant INGO paradigm for human rights work is implicitly premised on open legal and political systems typical of the global North – an approach that U.S. funders can readily understand and comfortably support. Accompanying this is the association of human rights work with legal experts and the engagement of political elites, remote options for most NGOs around the world. Indeed, receptive judicial and political systems are part and parcel of what local human rights groups seek. For decades the practice of INGOs suggested that because open legal and political systems are necessary for political change, and these, by definition, were absent in targeted developing countries, external exposure and pressure would have to be the main means of achieving the desired change. U.S. foundations appeared to support this line of reasoning, perhaps because of a fear of what the alternative(s) might look like. However, by promoting the professionalization of human rights work that, for the majority of human rights organizations in the world, is financially not viable, funders may be dooming organizations in the South to remaining less developed versions of their counterparts in the North.

WHERE, AT HOME OR ABROAD? Interestingly enough, U.S. funders' historical preference for U.S.-based NGOs rarely included support for work to apply international human rights standards at home, in the United States, or to hold to account the U.S. government for its actions abroad. In the 1990s, INGOs remained focused on work outside the United States, in other countries, and foundations were content with this. INGO's neglect of the home front would eventually be regretted; post–September 11 developments would reveal that they had mistakenly taken the public's commitment to fundamental rights and liberties for granted. Moreover, while funders rarely questioned what a human rights organization did or contributed when it operated in or on behalf of countries outside the United States, many of the same grant makers would doubt its value and find difficulty conceiving "what it would look like" when applied to work on the United States. Implicitly, if not explicitly, they believed that human rights had been secured at home and now only needed to be achieved abroad, hence their support for INGOs focusing on other countries. The imbalance and the absence of a strong human rights constituency inside the United States would prove costly after September 11. At this point, however, neither human rights funders nor human rights NGOs could have predicted to what extent.

In short, when the foundation began funding, it supported what existed in the way of human rights groups – the pioneers in the field. U.S.- and Europe-based for the most part, these were the organizations that were also most accessible. The field, however, was changing, and the Internet daily brings new groups from every corner of the world in contact with U.S. foundations. Clearly the need for funding is growing on all fronts; both Northern and Southern groups, CP and ESC rights work, standard and novel approaches, and work at home and abroad require much greater support. Regrettably, although the needs of the human rights field grew, MGF's resources did not.

Funding Setbacks and Gains, 2000–2003

In 2000, facing new and unexpected resource constraints, the foundation made final two-year grants to its grantees and launched a year-and-a-half-long review of all its programs. MGF's review included an evaluation of fifteen (1989–99) of grantmaking, a survey, interviews with grantees, discussions with funders, and research on trends and priorities in the various fields in which it worked. The board explored a variety of scenarios that included spending out with a major infusion of funds for one or more programs over a short period of time, reducing the number of programs, and narrowing the focus within existing programs. A year and a half later, the board opted for a gradual (over five years) phasing out of those programs that have successfully attracted substantial funders; the international human rights program was not one of them. In fact, the board reaffirmed the foundation's commitment to this program. In keeping with the fundamental principle of taking its cue from the field and needing to identify a niche where focused funding could make a difference, however, the board approved a recommendation to support efforts aimed at bridging the gap between CP and ESC rights work.

The end of the Cold War had eliminated the biggest obstacle to combining efforts to secure both CP rights and ESC rights and presented the opportunity to treat the rights enumerated in the International Bill of Rights as "indivisible" and "interrelated" in practice as the original framers of the UDHR had intended. As noted, historically, human rights protected by the Covenant on Economic, Social and Cultural Rights received limited support from U.S. foundations in large part because of their greater experience and comfort with CP rights, which they had supported for decades; their dubiousness about economic human rights, which they viewed as merely aspirations at best and illegitimate at worst; the location of most ESC rights organizations outside the United States, where foundations have traditionally not funded; and the relative newness of work in this area. MGF's board determined that the confluence of need and opportunity made work on ESC rights particularly timely and necessary, and that the foundation could make a strategic contribution even within its resource constraints. Additionally, a focus on bridging work on CP and ESC rights would signal the foundation's endorsement of the full spectrum of human rights. Accordingly, the board decided that beginning in 2003, the foundation's international human rights program would support:

- Strategic planning and program capacity building for civil and political rights organizations that want to introduce ESC rights into their work;
- Capacity building for international NGOs focused on ESC rights;
- Capacity building for regional collaboratives in Africa, Asia, and Latin America that bring together human rights organizations working on CP rights with those working on ESC rights; and
- Efforts to develop and refine ESC rights standards and achieve implementation and enforcement comparable to that developed for CP rights. Eligible projects and programs include those devoted to advancing work on contents of rights and justiciability; developing a human rights approach for new areas such as health, housing, education, and other neglected rights; and demonstrating effective use of the courts, advocacy, constituency building, and other tools for the attainment of ESC rights.

Although the new funding direction had the potential to contribute valuably to the field, staff was aware of a number of drawbacks, some verging on ethical dilemmas.

Even before disbursing a single grant, funders can influence the field when they issue their funding guidelines; their decision to fund particular programs and not others signals to would-be grant seekers what grant makers deem worthy of support. Large foundations recognize this ability to influence the field; some even desire it. Through their funding choices, however, even "field-driven" foundations may inadvertently shape the field's direction. With its decision to focus on ESC rights, MGF risked signifying a preference for ESC rights or dismissal of CP rights despite the foundation's conviction that bridging the work on the two sets of rights was necessary for the advancement of work on either. Noting the indifference to CP rights, such as freedom of expression, the right to dissent, and the right to participate in government, of communities lacking food, housing, and health care, the foundation agreed with those who argued that moving ahead on CP rights was more likely to occur when communities' ESC rights are addressed in tandem. Likewise, however, to move forward on ESC rights requires the protections that CP rights provide. As communities call on their governments to meet obligations enshrined in the Covenant on Economic, Social and Cultural Rights, they will require CP rights protections such as freedom of information, freedom of association, and freedom from arbitrary arrest.

The foundation also risked that human rights organizations would interpret its new direction as suggesting that every human rights organization should address both CP and ESC rights. This would be regrettable because specialization has yielded many of the field's contributions and insights. Were organizations to rush into work on new rights merely because of their fundability, they would jeopardize the work they already do and that continues to be vital. As articulated by MGF's then president, Robert Crane, the foundation's hope in this regard was that "organizations will continue doing what they do best."

The possible effect on current MGF grantees of the foundation's new direction raised an ethical concern. Not surprisingly, the foundation's review found that, over time, as grantees became more successful in securing additional sources of support, MGF grants formed a smaller percentage of grantees' incomes. In fact, by 1999, most MGF grantees had "outgrown" the foundation's funding. Whereas a grant of US $50,000 may account for less than 1 percent of a mature organization's income, it may be invaluable to a new organization. The concern, however, was that although a currently well-funded organization can do without MGF's support, would these important human rights NGOs be able to withstand the cumulative effect if all medium-sized funders made the same decision to redirect their resources? Fortunately such a scenario is extremely unlikely because the vast majority of U.S. foundations will always feel more comfortable supporting organizations in the United States with a demonstrated record of accomplishments. Yet when a respected funder curtails its support for a particular institution, it may raise questions regarding that institution.

And what of the risks for the organizations that would now obtain MGF support? Through their funding, foundations influence the development of NGOs that become grantees. The cliché "good intentions are never enough" may well have been born in the world of philanthropy. Another apt cliché is that funding produces dependencies, and human rights NGOs, whether in the United States or abroad, are very dependent on the funding they currently receive. The extent and implications of that dependence is, however, uneven. When a funder withdraws from the field, U.S. groups can turn to readily identifiable potential alternatives in the United States, that is, internally, something that most groups in the South cannot do. By funding organizations around the world, U.S. foundations may be . contributing to creating dependencies on external resources that are not easily replaceable. Do funders have a responsibility to remain in the fields in which their funding is significant? With the exception of perhaps the Ford Foundation and the Open Society Institute, these questions are larger than any single foundation. Nevertheless, they should figure in all foundations' deliberations.

These and other concerns notwithstanding, MGF decided to pursue its new funding guidelines. In 2003, after a hiatus of a year and a half, MGF resumed making new grants and disbursed somewhat more than US $1 million to eighteen human rights NGOs based in nine countries. In all cases, grantees worked either regionally (in more than one country in the same region) or internationally (in more than one country in various regions). The projects and programs that received support addressed a range of rights and constituencies, including education, the environment, housing, sexual minorities, and people with disabilities, as well as a variety of methods such as, community organizing, budget analysis, litigation, capacity building, and monitoring and reporting. In September 2003, this initial foray into ESC-rights-focused funding and direct support for NGOs around the world came to an abrupt end when the board took a decision to phase out four of the foundation's programs, including international human rights, at the year's end.[11] The confluence of a reduced endowment, the desire of the new executive director and the board to concentrate on the United States, and their doubts about the effectiveness of scattered grants around the world were cited to explain the decision to end the international human rights program.

Program Ends, 2003
Given the foundation's long history of funding human rights, its standing as a leading human rights funder, and its prominent role in the International Human Rights Funders Group, the decision to close out the international human rights program surprised MGF staff as well as human rights organizations in the field. In hindsight, staff members realized that they had taken the board's commitment to a human rights program for granted. Once again, what the foundation would decide and do would entail implications well beyond its office.

The woefully limited U.S. foundation funding for human rights, especially for work carried out by the affected communities themselves, meant the decision to stop funding groups outside the United States would be felt. Indeed, although

---

[11] The Immigrant Rights, Lesbian and Gay Rights, and Israel and Palestine programs were eliminated. The foundation would continue to make grants in Dance in New York City, New York City Human and Built Environment, and Energy.

a grants budget of US $1 million was modest in comparison with both large foundations' budgets and the needs of the field, the amount made an enormous difference for the NGOs that received the funding, many of which were small or young groups that have difficulty attracting support from the large funders. Funding from a respected funder like MGF might have given these groups visibility in the philanthropic community, thereby improving their chances of securing additional funding. Moreover, the majority of the ESCR groups are located in the South where small and medium grants go a much longer way than in the United States or Europe.

The decision to turn back from international funding for ESCR could well be that proverbial "missed opportunity." For much of the 1980s and 1990s, MGF's annual giving of US $1.25 million for international human rights contributed to field building by supporting leaders in the field, or at least the CP rights portion of the field. The same amount over time might have potentially contributed valuably by supporting leaders in a long-neglected portion of the field – ESC rights – who are tackling new and controversial human rights and exploring new approaches. Indeed, over the same amount of years, MGF's ESCR grants might have helped relatively young groups prove themselves the way Human Rights Watch and Lawyers Committee for Human Rights (Human Rights First) did many years before.

Perhaps the biggest concern would be that the foundation's withdrawal from the field would be a blow to ongoing efforts to cultivate greater support for human rights. Other foundations might wonder whether MGF's decision reflected a diminished belief in the value of the work that human rights organizations do around the world; the loss of confidence in the attainability of the human rights vision; or a desire to avoid the mounting U.S. government pressures on funding overseas.

The foundation made its final international human rights grants in fall 2003 and would honor those already in the pipeline for 2004. In the meantime, MGF's board invited the executive director to develop a proposal for a program of his choice, as new foundation heads generally do. The board agreed to look at a program focused on social and economic justice issues inside the United States and to consider human rights as one component of such a program at its next meeting. Over the course of the following six months, staff researched, conducted site visits, and met with U.S. groups devoted to social and economic justice. In the spring 2004, the board approved a Human Rights in the United States program to support opportunities that would enable the foundation to evaluate the feasibility of applying the human rights framework in the United States. Rather than assume the viability of human rights as a vision and an approach for social change in the United States, the board opted to "test" this proposition and explore the "added value" of human rights via its grants program. Meanwhile, grant seekers that visited the foundation's Web site learned that, after two decades, MGF's funding for international human rights organizations had come to an end.

II. QUESTIONS FOR HUMAN RIGHTS PHILANTHROPY

Returning to the questions posed in the introduction, we may ask whether the essentially undemocratic and nonparticipatory process by which U.S. foundations make their funding decisions can effect genuine democratic change in the world. U.S. foundation support has enabled countless human rights groups to carry out their work, which includes conceptualizing and articulating the democratic forms of governance they seek. Through their funding decisions, however, foundations have wielded tremendous influence in determining the content and form these actually take. For example, the notion that economic democracy is a necessary underpinning to political democracy – a view that is common in the South, consistent with the human rights framework and virtually absent in Northern perspectives on democracy – has very little chance of receiving U.S. foundation support. Similarly, U.S. foundations generally eschew supporting movements, although history has shown that when responsive and accountable political structures are absent, communities have had to resort to "politics by other means," that is, social movements, to accomplish the political and social transformations they have sought and that popular pressure is essential for the democratization and then the preservation of democratic political systems.

What of the impact of "trickle-down" funding in addressing the prevailing inequities between the North and South? Given the history of the North's economic underdevelopment of the South and the persistent siphoning of natural and financial resources (through interest payments on debts) favoring the North, there is something to be said for resource transfers of all kinds to the global South.[12] Although foundations cannot be expected to remedy the prevailing inequities, do they do enough to redress them, or are they merely reproducing the inequalities in the civil societies they fund? All that the "some, but not enough" funding may be contributing to the global South is less developed versions of organizations that first appeared in the North. Clearly the resource scarcity in developing countries requires greater U.S. foundation engagement with Southern groups. But would the expansion of external funding for these groups along current lines necessarily be a good thing?

Indeed, what of the approach of externally funded professional NGOs for achieving social and political change? As they institutionalize and "professionalize" under the impetus of external funding, can local Southern organizations preserve strong and vital linkages to social movements and their constituencies? As noted, historically, efforts to achieve social and political change have been led by movements, not NGOs. Emulating human rights NGOs in the North, where for decades human rights work has been treated as the preserve of lawyers and legal experts, would discourage popular engagement and participation – a vital

---

[12] Moreover, the democracies of the global North formed under conditions of far less, and less damaging, external economic and political penetration than that to which most Southern countries are subjected.

resource in the global South. Given that, post-September 11, even U.S.-based human rights groups lament their failure to establish solid constituency-based support for human rights inside the United States, is it wise for U.S. funders to promote the same model for groups in the South? U.S. laws governing private foundations' grantmaking require that they confine their giving to entities that are the equivalents of U.S. 501(c)(3)s. Besides the obvious problem of requiring organizations to be registered, even with repressive governments, by promoting the institutionalization of social change efforts and requiring the professionalization of NGO staff, which is frequently accompanied by their disengagement from grassroots communities, funders may be inadvertently undermining the very sort of participation that is required to accomplish the social change necessary for the realization of human rights.

Finally, the review suggests an additional question. Given the above concerns, would it be better for U.S. foundations to cease funding human rights groups outside the United States and instead focus on work inside the country? After all, the U.S. government neither meets nor recognizes its ESC rights obligations and has demonstrated a readiness to ignore CP rights provisions it deems inconvenient or constraining. Moreover, although the focus of human rights work even by U.S.-based groups has been the global South, the political and economic powers that have propped up their despotic regimes, undermined vital subsidies to their poor, and decimated their self-sufficient communities reside in the North. Besides avoiding the pitfalls described earlier, people everywhere stand to benefit from the U.S. government's adherence to international human rights norms and laws domestically and internationally. Therefore, redirecting funding to the United States has much to recommend it. Fortunately, as the wealthiest philanthropic sector in the world, U.S. foundations can do both. The question is how well they do either.

Minimally, these and other questions call for greater communication and coordination among human rights grant makers and grant seekers beyond that which takes place between individual funders and their grantees. Regularly convened fora for this purpose can help human rights funders become better grant makers and more responsible contributors to the global human rights movement – something from which everyone stands to gain.

3 Transformational Development as the Key to Housing Rights

Steven Weir

I used to be a man without a permanent address. When I saw abuse and corruption at the school where I teach, I did not dare to speak out for fear of being transferred to a remote part of the country where I could not care for my family. With this house, my family and I have a permanent address, and we will never live in fear of speaking out again. In 1823, my forefather's family was forcibly relocated from southern India to Sri Lanka to work as laborers on the tea estates. After generations of savings, my grandfather purchased this small plot of land (approximately 5–10 m), but our family did not have the money to build a home and move out of the inhuman living conditions of company line housing. As a teacher, I should qualify for a government loan, but as a low caste Tamil, my application has never been processed. We have been refused help by the bank, our local Hindu temple, the school district and the government – we had nowhere to turn. Habitat for Humanity Hatton's assistance has changed the life of my family forever. We *are now* a family with a permanent address, and I will never be afraid to speak out again.

– Mr. S. Durairaj at the dedication celebration of their family's new home in April 1995.

Housing as the Basis for Human Rights Development

Transformational community development is central to broad-based human rights development, and secure housing is the cornerstone for a family's participation in that process. The UN Fact Sheet *The Right of Adequate Housing* expresses the connection and the scale of the need in this way:

> At first glance, it might seem unusual that a subject such as housing would constitute an issue of human rights. However a closer look at international and national laws, as well as at the significance of a secure place to live for human dignity, physical and mental health and overall quality of life, begins to reveal some of the human rights implications of housing. *Adequate housing is universally viewed as one of the most basic human needs.* [emphasis added]
>
> Yet as important as adequate housing is, ... 1 billion people live in inadequate housing, with in excess of 100 million people living in conditions classified as homelessness.

Access to drinking water and adequate sanitation facilities are additional needs directly associated with housing. According to figures released by the World health Organization, 1.2 billion people in developing countries do not have access to drinking water and 1.8 billion people live without access to adequate sanitation."[1]

Evidence that improved shelter, particularly using participatory methodology, serves as a catalyst for broad improvements in the quality of life as well as the development of civil society can be found in an interim report for a United States Agency for International Development (USAID) -funded Habitat for Humanity (Habitat) project, Measuring Transformation through Housing.[2] Although the results are still incomplete and causal links unclear, the consistency of the initial indicators is compelling:

Civil Society – improved participation by marginalized groups – 39%
Peace and Reconciliation – improved unity and positive relationship with different ethnic group – 71%
Education – improved school attendance by female children 32% and males 17%
Women – Improved self-confidence 87%
Health – fewer days of work missed – 46%
Economic – new economic activity 55%, increase in family income 76%, increase in clothing expenditure 55%, increase in furniture expenses 52%

Qualitative data drawn from homeowner interviews suggests that improved shelter leads to an increase in health, which in turn has catalytic effects on many aspects of family livelihood and security. The links between empowerment indicators and methodology is also based on qualitative data, and again the consistency is compelling.

Housing as a Human Right – A United Nations Perspective
The United Nations (UN) *Universal Declaration of Human Rights* (1948) named housing as an integral part of the right to an adequate standard of living.

Everyone has the right to a standard of living adequate for the health and well being of himself and of his family, including food, clothing, *housing* and medical care and necessary social services, and the right to security in the event of unemployment, sickness, disability, widowhood, old age or other lack of livelihood in circumstances beyond his control.[3]

[1] United Nations, Office of the High Commissioner for Human Rights, Fact Sheet No. 21.
[2] *Draft Community Impact Study*, MTTH project sponsored by USAID in Nepal and Sri Lanka, 2002.
[3] Nations, *Universal Declaration of Human Rights* (1948) Article 25.1.

A UN High Commissioner for Human Rights fact sheet adds that since the original 1948 declaration, "no less than 12 different texts adopted and proclaimed by the UN explicitly recognize the right to adequate housing."[4] Many of these instruments include specific language protecting distinct groups – women, children, migrant workers, workers in general, refugees, and indigenous people as well as discrimination based on ethnic group or national origin.[5]

The right to housing was not a legally binding treaty obligation until 1969, however, when the International Convention on the Elimination of All Forms of Racial Discrimination forbade racial discrimination in the realization of the right to housing. Since that time, several international treaties have created the right to housing as a binding obligation in international law. Interestingly, of these treaties the United States has ratified only one – the International Convention on the Elimination of All Forms of Racial Discrimination.[6]

Housing as a Moral Imperative – Habitat for Humanity Response

In 1996 at the UN Habitat II conference, leaders from 171 nations met in Istanbul to reaffirm and review the progress made on the right to housing. Habitat for Humanity founder Millard Fuller has on many occasions stated Habitat for Humanity's concurrence with the UN call to action: "Habitat for Humanity believes that it is politically, socially, morally and religiously unacceptable for people to live in substandard housing."[7] As a plenary speaker in Istanbul, Fuller affirmed the universal concern for housing and offered a way forward:

> The task at hand – namely to assure adequate shelter and livable, sustainable communities that nurture and enhance life rather than demeaning and destroying it – is too big, too daunting to leave any potential ally standing idly on the sidelines. Every such potential ally from whatever realm, government or otherwise, should be encouraged to make the maximum contribution possible to help alleviate the suffering of our fellow human beings who are languishing in miserable living conditions. We can ill afford the luxury of leaving any of them on the sidelines of our noble struggle to provide adequate shelter for all.[8]

It is clear from Fuller's statements that although the legal right to adequate housing may be globally recognized, our personal and corporate obligations are broader. What is needed is the political will or, more broadly, a social contract to eliminate subhuman living conditions in each of our communities.

Habitat for Humanity's approach to meeting this broader community obligation is direct personal engagement by community members through volunteer, grassroots participation. Unlike most nongovernmental organizations (NGOs) that limit their focus to the *community of need*, Habitat also engages those from

---

[4] United Nations, Office of the High Commissioner for Human Rights, Fact Sheet No. 21.
[5] Ibid.   [6] Fuller, *More than Houses*, 285.
[7] Ibid, xi.   [8] Ibid, 287.

the *community of influence and affluence* in personal action. Through Habitat's participatory methodology, individual personal engagement leads to a transformation of corporate community values and priorities.

This chapter discusses Habitat for Humanity's experience of how engaging citizens in direct community participation in areas more narrowly considered *economic, social, and cultural rights* issues, has led to a higher awareness and improvement in the community's norms in the area of civil and political rights. Like many international humanitarian aid organizations, Habitat's focus on broad, holistic, transformational development leads to broad, holistic human rights improvement.

Further, this chapter also describes specific challenges and the resulting compromises Habitat has chosen to make to its normative development framework in response to specific conflicts between cultural norms and the promotion of human rights.

I. NORMATIVE FRAMEWORK AND SUCCESSES

History and Evolution

Koinonia Farm

In 1942, twenty years before the civil rights movement, Clarence Jordan and Martin England started an experimental farm in rural Georgia. "Its purpose was two fold: to build a racially inclusive community in which (1) Christians would live in radical obedience to the teaching of Jesus; (2) in a way that that would help farmers – especially the poor."[9]

During the 1950s, Jordan was excommunicated from the Baptist church, and members of the KKK (Ku Klux Klan) sought to drive him out of the county. Koinonia Farm was boycotted and then bombed and their houses riddled with bullets. Insurance was canceled, and merchants feared to do business with them. In 1968, when survival seemed in doubt, Jordan teamed up with an entrepreneurial businessman, Millard Fuller, and started a new program called Koinonia Partners through which programs such as paralegal assistance, counseling, foster care, prison visitation, and a "Fund for Humanity" were begun.[10] This fund enabled land to be purchased and held in trust for cooperative farming, industry and housing. Jordan concluded that

> What the poor need is not charity but capital, not caseworkers but co-workers. And what the rich need is a wise honorable and just way of divesting themselves of their overabundance.[11]

---

[9] Henlee H. Barnette, *Clarence Jordan, Turning Dreams into Deeds,* vii–viii.
[10] Ibid.
[11] Dallas Lee, *The Cotton Patch Evidence* (New York: Harper & Row, 1971), 214–215.

Habitat for Humanity
The success of the Partnership Housing program as an agent for transformation among the rural poor in Georgia and a similar successful housing program in Zaire (the Democratic Republic of the Congo) begun in 1973[12] encouraged Fuller to incorporate Habitat for Humanity in 1976 as a global housing ministry.[13]

Koinonia Farm's radical vision of a racially integrated community predates the civil rights movement and is a clear antecedent to Habitat's strategy of holistic community engagement as the key to transformational change. This core principle continues to shape the normative intervention framework as well as Habitat's approach to human rights issues.

Normative Framework Success Story

The story of Mr. Durairaj, previously quoted, continues two years later with a dramatic transformation. During the construction itself, Mr. Durairaj's uphill neighbor demands that Mr. Durairaj's newly built adjoining wall be demolished and reconstructed away from their adjoining property line, 0.5 m to alleviate rainwater runoff onto his rather substantial lot. Although there is little room, Mr. Durairaj complies. When the monsoon rains come, the neighbor's house is severely damaged, and Mr. Durairaj offers a room in his home until his relatively affluent neighbor can rebuild his substantially larger home.

Impressed by the life changes in Mr. Durairaj, a private individual is convicted to sell two acres at a concessionary rate, and twenty poor families invest funds with Mr. Durairaj to purchase and subdivide these two acres into small plots. Because Mr. Durairaj organized the transaction on their behalf without remuneration, the community decided that each member would give Mr. Durairaj a small financial gift in appreciation of his efforts, which in aggregate amounts to nearly enough to pay off his Habitat home loan. Interestingly, rather than pay off his mortgage, Mr. Durairaj chooses instead to donate his windfall to Habitat and continue his monthly mortgage payments so that an additional family can immediately have the same transforming opportunity as his family.

Soon after this small community project, Mr. Durairaj helps a street sweeper widow with eleven children purchase and qualify for her own Habitat house.

[12] Fuller, Millard. *Bokotola*, 24–26.
[13] Fuller, Millard. *More than Houses*, 288. "Listening to Voice of America Broadcasts of the UN Habitat I conference in Vancouver, the word 'Habitat' and its inclusive and full-bodied meaning for human settlements intrigued Fuller. He combined the principles already successfully developed through the 'Fund for Humanity' with the holistic development concepts of the word 'Habitat,' and the movement had a name, 'Habitat for Humanity.'"

Human Rights Improvements

Several interesting observations on human rights improvements can be made from Mr. Durairaj's story. Interestingly, these are seldom understood or articulated in human rights language in part because neither the motivation nor the experiences originate from a human rights agenda.

- Motivated by faith-based obligations rather than human rights obligations, the local Habitat volunteer committee initiates a series of community improvements by helping a single family.
- Improvement in housing results in improvement in Mr. Durairaj's economic and social standing in the community. Cultural discrimination is overcome when neighbors of a different caste and ethnic background volunteer to assist Mr. Durairaj through their own labor. Mr. Durairaj's subsequent assistance to others further demonstrates the breaking down of cultural divisions. Civil and political improvements occur when a previously disenfranchised Mr. Durairaj organizes a small minority community and successfully negotiates municipal approvals for their development project.
- Through a participatory engagement methodology, improvements occur in the areas of economic, social, cultural, civil, and political human rights.
- The personal transformation by Mr. Durairaj and the individual participation by others in improving Mr. Durairaj's housing conditions result not only in holistic community development but also in transformed community motivation. Personal engagement is often the strongest motivation for continued change.

Although the improvement in Mr. Durairaj's physical comfort and security was surely dramatic, this level of personal transformation is typically not seen in the lives of the residents of government giveaway housing schemes who experience similar improvements in their human rights through improved housing conditions. An improvement in housing alone is generally insufficient to sustain the ongoing development in a community needed to affect its human rights. The plethora of failed government relocation and mass-housing schemes are evidence to the unique transformation experienced by Mr. Durairaj.

Perhaps more thought provoking is the efficacy of a methodology that combines personal engagement with faith-based motivation and seems to result in a transformation far beyond the notional human rights improvement.

Key to Transformation

The key indicator for transformation is *hope* – the perspective of what is possible is changed by what has been accomplished. The belief that the same opportunities can be given to others through your involvement reinforces the newfound hope in your own life and is the seed for broader community change.

What is the cause for this newfound hope or transformation? Reasons mentioned by Mr. Durairaj for his family's transformation can be grouped into three categories:

1. *Material Improvement* – Obvious improvements in shelter led to better health, sanitation, and general living conditions. Mr. Durairaj shares that now when it rains his family does not sit on their beds and watch the rain drip through the roof and run through their home. They now live literally in a different world.

2. *Dignity* – Mr. Durairaj used the word *dignity* repeatedly: the dignity gained from making your own blocks and building your own home; the dignity of being a donor to another family through your repayments, not just a beneficiary; the dignity of being a part of a local program run by local leaders, using funds raised, in part, locally; and the dignity of providing for your family without being made an object of charity.

3. *Perspective Shift* – The world's view of Mr. Durairaj and his family seemed to change from one of repeated discrimination to one in which consistent exceptions were made in their favor. From a Christian faith perspective, the term *grace* describes the condition of receiving something you have not or cannot earn – the grace of having dozens of school children volunteer to carry blocks on their heads to your home; the grace of middle-class community members unrelated by family, cast, religion, and ethnicity, volunteer time and participate in local fund-raising events to raise local resources to provide a loan to your family; the grace of participation and support given by a previously unconcerned local government through advocacy by others on your behalf; the grace of being selected when your family has been discriminated against for generations and others like you continue to suffer.

Some might argue that this is the restoration of basic human rights that have been withheld from the poor, not a gift or grace. Although this may be legally accurate, Habitat homeowners repeatedly describe their experience using the vocabulary of grace, and not satisfaction in securing their rights. How can the experience be otherwise when so many of their neighbors continue to languish in subhuman conditions?

Transformational Development Methodology
Transformational development is the key to long-term sustainability and civil society and by extension develops human rights awareness and advocacy. Clarence Jordan's original concepts of the poor needing *capital not charity* and *coworkers not caseworkers* are early antecedents to many of today's transformational development concepts.

In his book *Walking with the Poor; Principles and Practices of Transformational Development*, Bryant Meyers describes transformational development thus:

> I use the term *transformational development* to reflect my concern for seeking positive change in the whole of human life materially, socially and spiritually. . . . Transformational development is a lifelong journey. . . . In this book I suggest that the goals for this journey of transformation are to recover our true identity as human beings created in the image of God and to discover our true vocation as productive stewards, faithfully caring for the world and all the people in it.[14]

The Spiritual Component of Transformation

The inclusion of a spiritual factor in Meyer's definition is not unusual from an Asian perspective. In Asia, as with much of the non-Western world, the spiritual realm has not been dichotomized from the secular, and change is very much seen as happening in interconnected worlds. Both Hiebert and Newbigin offer compelling arguments for a development perspective that incorporates a spiritual reality.[15] Spiritual transformation is also an integral concept consistent with all of the major religions, and because of the importance of religion in most Asian cultures, spiritual development is inherently an important aspect of how lasting (transformational) change occurs and is understood by a family and their community.

An example from the Christian tradition of the importance of the spiritual component in transformation can be found in the biblical book of Romans in which the writer describes transformation to his readers as follows: "Do not be conformed any longer to this world, but be transformed by the renewing of your

---

[14] Bryant Meyers, *Walking with the Poor; Principles and Practices of Transformational Development*, 2. A more complete description of Meyer's definition follows; "I use the term *transformational development* to reflect my concern for seeking positive change in the whole of human life materially, socially and spiritually. The adjective *transformational* is used to remind us that human progress is not inevitable; it takes hard work, and there is an adversary who works against our desire to enhance life. True human development involves choices, setting aside that which is not for life in us and our community while actively seeking and supporting all that is for life. This requires that we say no to some things in order to say yes to what really matters. Transformation implies changing our choices.Transformational development is a lifelong journey. It never ends. There is always more before us. Everyone is on this journey: the poor, the non-poor, and the staff of the development agency. The transformational journey is about finding and enjoying life, as it should be, as it was intended to be. In this book I suggest that the goals for this journey of transformation are to recover our true identity as human beings created in the image of God and to discover our true vocation as productive stewards, faithfully caring for the world and all the people in it."

[15] Cf. Leslie Newbigin, *Foolishness to the Greeks: The Gospel and Western Culture*. Paul Hiebert, "The Flaw of the Excluded Middle," *Missiology* 10, 1 (1982): 35–47.

mind. Then you will be able to test and approve what God's will is – His good, pleasing and perfect will" (Rom. 12:2). Each of the other major religions would also describe transformation from a spiritual perspective.

Secular Development Perspective on Transformation – Participatory Approaches

A broadly accepted forerunner to many participatory development approaches used today is PRA (participatory rapid appraisal). In *Whose Reality Counts,* Robert Chambers describes the essence of PRA as an approach that "has been induced from practice and what has been found to work, not deduced from a priori principles. It has three foundational principles or pillars:

1. The behavior and attitudes of outsiders who facilitate, not dominate
2. The methods, which shift the normal balance from closed to open, from individual to group, from verbal to visual, and from measuring to comparing, and
3. Partnership and sharing of information, experience, food and training, between insiders and outsiders, and between organizations.

For many, PRA seeks to empower lowers – women minorities, the poor, the weak and the vulnerable – and to make power reversals real."[16]

Here again from a secular development perspective, a participatory "transformational" approach is used as a change strategy for community interventions whose broad outcomes are not limited to or even specifically targeted toward human rights. These participatory approaches consistently result in improvements in human rights, however.[17]

II. TRADE-OFFS AND COMPROMISES: HUMAN RIGHTS VERSUS CULTURAL NORMS

Not every Habitat homeowner is as successful in their ability to transform themselves and the community around them as Mr. Durairaj. The contextual reality for NGOs is characterized by trade-offs between competing human rights and, more frequently, between human rights and cultural norms that stand in opposition to human rights as they are defined in various UN texts.

Transformation occurs in an imperfect system often complicated by cultural conflicts that require compromise as INGOs seeks to implement their core philosophy and vision. This section outlines several such conflicts encountered by

---

[16] Robert Chambers, *Whose Reality Counts*, 104.
[17] While Habitat's methodology incorporates PRA and its sister participatory development approaches, we would argue along with Meyers that a more holistic perspective is needed to bring lasting transformational change.

Habitat and describes the compromises, the failures, and the long-term strategies that were eventually adopted.[18] They have been broadly grouped:

- Discrimination and Favoritism in Home Owner Selection
  A vision not a reality
- Right to Development and Cultural Governance Norms
  Human rights improvements in conflict with each other – choose one
- Media, Donors, and Human Rights in Complex Disasters
  Made for TV
- Related Human Rights Abuses
  The narrow view

Because Habitat for Humanity works through autonomous local partner organizations, it seldom forces change externally. This partnership approach, although consistent with Habitat's philosophy of developing civil society through ongoing constructive engagement with the community, limit's Habitat's ability to effect change directly.

Additional perspectives on how a cooperative approach is used by other INGOs as well as the institutional importance of many of the PRA principles to international human rights NGOs is well documented in Joseph Carens's chapter (Chapter 13) on ethical dilemmas and in other chapters throughout this book. Although the followings dilemmas are segregated for the purposes of analysis, as Carens rightly points out, ethical dilemmas are complex and typically overlap in practice.

Discrimination and Favoritism in Home Owner Selection: Human Rights Improvements – A Vision Not a Reality

Minority ethnic and religious populations are often discriminated against by the majority population – Indians in Fiji, Tamils in Sri Lanka, Christians in non-Christian countries, Aborigines, Maoris, and other indigenous tribal people in their native land. In many countries, including those in the developed North, antidiscrimination laws are unequally enforced.

Human right's principles can be easily compromised in a Habitat program when the local family selection process follows these traditional discrimination patterns. The following short case studies typify Habitat's response to societal discrimination.

---

[18] The conflicts described in this section are drawn from the author's experience with Habitat's work in more than twenty-five countries in Asia and the Pacific and in the United States since 1986. Interactions with colleagues from Africa and Latin America suggest that the principle concepts outlined in the section are consistent worldwide. The views expressed here are my own and do not reflect the position of Habitat for Humanity International.

Additionally, it can be argued that this approach is antithetical to the principle of distributive fairness and can result in less cost-efficient interventions by Habitat. In Thomas Pogge's chapter in this volume, "Moral Priorities for International Human Rights NGOs" (Chapter 12), however, he persuasively argues in favor of such exceptions in circumstances of moral culpability, extinction and diversity, aggregate harm protection, and, when harm reduction may be *smaller yet morally more valuable.*

Sri Lanka: Program Location Discrimination toward Ethnic Balance

Decisions on program location can have a dramatic impact on the distribution of families assisted. In the formative stages of Habitat for Humanity in Sri Lanka, the national board decided to expand its program equally and concurrently in Tamil and Singhalese areas, to avoid the appearance of favoritism. Initially little encouragement from Habitat's international representative was required, however as the program grew, internal politicking increased with each new program start-up.

Some from the majority Singhalese population argued that this ethnically balanced approach discriminated against those in greatest need and was disproportional to the relative populations – Pogge's argument of prioritization based on *greatest* harm reduction. The board, however, believed that the greater discrimination issues in Sri Lanka were ethnic-community focused rather than individual. They believed that their expansion strategy could contribute to the national ethnic reconciliation movement, fostering improved human rights among discriminated communities, and to the long-term cessation of a twenty-year civil war – consistent with Pogge's premise that exceptions should be made when *aggregate* harm reduction and moral culpability outweigh distributive fairness.

Although HFH Sri Lanka's vision for national reconciliation has guided a strategic – albeit discriminatory human rights strategy toward participant family selection – it has in fact enabled HFH Sri Lanka to be recognized as a leader in the national peace and reconciliation movement, resulting in a seat on the president's National Peace and Reconciliation task force. This strategy has as well given HFH Sri Lanka the credibility to serve as a facilitator for many interethnic and interreligious demonstration events affirming Pogge's premise.

Fiji: Program Location Discrimination toward Ethnic Imbalance

In contrast, Habitat for Humanity International was forced to step in and reconstitute the HFH Fiji national board, local governance, and staffing systems when cultural discrimination norms violated Habitat global policies. The Fiji national board initially developed programs largely in ethnically Fijian communities. Although Indo-Fijians make up nearly 50 percent of the national population, an Indo-Fijian did not receive assistance from HFH Fiji until the 100th home.

Discriminatory land entitlement laws that favor native Fijians, leaving most Indo-Fijians with few land entitlement options, limit Habitat's assistance due to the absence of secure tenure needed to create a legal mortgage.[19]

Habitat for Humanity International worked with limited success to encourage Indo-Fijian participation on the national board and among the national staff. Efforts also included funding for land acquisition targeted for Indo-Fijians, particularly those forced to relocate during the previous ethnically based coup. After the national director was found to have funneled all international funding into building programs in his own Fijian home village, Habitat was forced to step in and redirect the program.

Although the existing program was clearly cost-effective in its greater harm reduction strategy, it perpetuated a serious human rights prejudice.

Ghettoization: Homeowner Preference toward Discrimination

Urban slums throughout Asia's mega cities are characterized by ghettos of families connected by home village, religion, and often by income as a result of urban migration patterns. Recent communal violence between Muslim and Hindu communities in Gujarat led to the all too common outcome of further segregation as minority families in mixed communities abandon their homes in favor of communities where they would be among the majority. Any work done within these slum communities by a development agency will often necessitate a continuation of this urban segregation.

Habitat for Humanity has developed small-scale intentionally integrated communities of Muslims and Christians in both the Philippines and Sri Lanka but such efforts have been largely unsuccessful on a large scale, promoting desegregation and mixed-income development in either urban slum improvements or more complex, urban relocation projects. More common are the results of an ongoing integrated community project in Ireland. Initial attempts to build an integrated community of Catholics and Protestants in Belfast had to be abandoned when community pressure forced willing families to abandon their agreement to live in a mixed-faith community. Habitat's current strategy in Belfast is to have these segregated communities built by integrated volunteer teams. Habitat sees this as a transition strategy for a future that includes desegregated communities. This compromise in Habitat's nondiscrimination principle is a pragmatic reality if Habitat is to be engaged in the community at any level in Belfast.

Religious Favoritism and Discrimination

Although Habitat's normative nondiscriminatory methodology for participant family selection is consistent with UN human rights texts, they were derived from the teachings of Jesus, who stated that all human beings are created in the

---

[19] Cf. Joseph Carens, "Democracy and Respect for Differences; The Case of Fiji," chap. 9 in *Culture, Citizenship and Community*.

image of God; as such Habitat for Humanity believes that all deserve equal access to a simple, decent place to live. This concern for the poor is a religious belief common to each of the world's major monotheistic religions – Judaism, Islam, and Christianity – and is consistent with similar beliefs in the other major world religions. While Habitat often states that this philosophy is one that leaves no one out, this principle is often challenged by both Christians and non-Christians alike.

In Malaysia, Habitat is restricted from working with Muslim families through government concerns regarding conversion; this despite Habitat's clearly articulated policy against proselytization and Islam's principles for helping the poor. In other majority non-Christian countries such as India, Nepal, Sri Lanka, Bangladesh, and Indonesia, Habitat has chosen a strategy that discriminates in favor of selecting families that match the religious demographics of the poor. Again, this strategy may be inconsistent with the notion of providing the greatest good for the greatest number but is a political reality if Habitat is to continue operating in these countries.

Reverse discrimination can be a greater problem among the Christian minorities who believe that a Christian INGO has an obligation to support Christians who are traditionally discriminated against by the government and other social support institutions.

Nepal: New Program Discrimination

New programs like that of Nepal often engage in favoritism, selecting families they believe have a higher likelihood of loan repayment. This typically favors those at the top of the approved income range and those who are known personally to the board members. Habitat generally chooses not to intervene in these early selections unless the families do not qualify under the approved standards, in part because the local committee needs to "own" their selection decisions and in part because their motivation is often sustainability based. Typically committees quickly run through these early selections, and with Habitat's outside encouragement, committees gradually expand the areas where applications are advertised and new lower-cost construction methodology encourages lower-income family selections.

In Nepal, recent evaluations confirmed that homeowners who were above the income range were being selected. Through a participatory evaluation process, the local affiliate decided to change its house design to reach lower-income families and advertise to a broader community.[20] Habitat militates against the practice of long-term favoritism by asking national organizations to track homeowner profiles by local affiliate.[21]

---

[20] This is a good example of a successful implementation of the PRA principles described earlier.
[21] Of more than 10,000 homes in India built by Habitat for Humanity, the demographics of the homeowners closely track the demographics of poor Hindu, Muslim, Buddhist, and Christian households.

Lessons Learned: Discrimination

Over time Habitat has developed intervention strategies that focus in the short-run on errors of commission and in the long-run, on errors of omission. For example, affiliates who discriminate in favor of the relatives of local committee members or fellow church members are immediately put on probation, whereas an uneven distribution of homeowner ethnicity and religion is corrected in the long run by improving systems development and continued monitoring for conformance. Each of these exception strategies to the greatest harm reduction strategy are convincingly argued in Pogge's chapter.

In his critique of Pogge's thesis, Carens (see Chapter 13) rightly adds that INGOs are often faced with difficult choices between short-term efficacy in cost-per-beneficiary ratios (greatest harm reduction) and long-term impact – decisions where the risks and outcomes are often uncertain. As Carens suggests, balancing between the "many and the worst-offs" does not often lend itself neatly to the "analytical precision" suggested in Pogge's paper. Interventions that perpetuate clear human rights abuse in favor of any of Pogge's exceptions defy accurate quantitative postulation in the project design stage, and the efficacy becomes even more difficult to attribute over time as other factors influence change. Nevertheless, INGOs have a fiduciary responsibility to defend and evaluate these intervention strategies to both the donors who have given funds in trust and to the beneficiaries to whom they are incorporated to serve. To date this has not been publicly debated and often goes unexamined internally in many INGOs.

The Right to Development and Cultural Governance Norms: Human Rights Improvements in Conflict with Each Other – Choose One

In 1986, the Right to Development was made explicit under the UN's *Declaration on the Right to Development*. Article 1 states;

> The right to development is an inalienable human right by virtue of which every human person and all peoples are entitled to participate in, contribute to and enjoy economic, social, cultural, and political development, in which all human rights and fundamental freedoms can be fully realized.

The UN OHCHR states that "the right includes:

- full sovereignty over natural resources
- self determination
- popular participation in development
- equality of opportunity
- the creation of favorable conditions for the enjoyment of other civil, political, economic, social and cultural rights."[22]

---

[22] Human Rights in Development Web page: http\\www.unhchr.ch/development/right-01.html (January 2002).

Equality of Opportunity

Habitat's organizational ethic and philosophy of transformational development support the right to development described earlier. The following short case studies demonstrate how the right to development for women often clashes with local patriarchal norms. Determining when gender discrimination results in a greater harm than the loss of self-determination by the community is difficult to benchmark. Habitat's strategy typically favors increased community-based self-determination as a strategy to improve equality in ethnic and gender opportunity.

Homeowners and Full Participation by Women

A recent survey showed that women involved in a local Habitat program in Nepal and Sri Lanka increased their visits to local government offices by 35 percent and experienced an increase in overnight stays outside of their home village by 36 percent.[23] Clearly engaging women fully in the development process can have civil and political benefits.

In many Asian countries, wives are not traditionally included on the land title or loan documents. One strategy many Habitat affiliates use is to require that women's names be included on the land title as a condition for a Habitat loan. This is contrary to cultural norms and in some countries still carries no legal weight.

Increasingly, Habitat's Save and Build initiative[24] is engaging women participants from traditional microsavings programs. Although men typically support women's engagement in small family business microcredit programs, they often view family capital improvement decisions as being exclusively the male domain. Decisions relating to home improvements and the family's participation requirements for improved housing often receive the husband's close scrutiny when the wife initiates it. Even when inclusive community and family participation is structured by the NGO, women must often find indirect ways to participate in decisions related to the home.

As a result of these community norms, one area of pragmatic compromise for Habitat is often in equal participation in the community design and building process. In one community, the women's initial interest in situating the homes around a shared community space that facilitated communal child care was overridden by the village men, who favored a more traditional grid layout. Women often favor more cost-effective design features to lower monthly repayments but

[23] Draft Community Impact Study, MTTH project sponsored by USAID in Nepal and Sri Lanka, 2002.
[24] Save and Build is a housing micro-finance program used by Habitat that draws from MFI various principles including group savings, graduated loans, group cohesion, cross guarantees, and financial repayment incentives. Typically twelve families each save the equivalent of a cup of tea or two cigarettes (their disposable income) for a period of six months. This group savings is typically enough income to build a single one-room "core house." Habitat matches this savings – typically 2:1 – with a loan for additional homes. The cycle then repeats until each of the families has a core house. An additional two to three years of repayments is needed to retire the mortgage debt after the final savings cycle. Many groups then start a new savings program to build additional rooms.

are again overridden by their male counterparts who prefer the prestige of more traditional materials.

Local Boards and Full Participation by Women

To encourage good governance, Habitat's best practice standards require that local boards be diverse and representative of the community at large, including 30 percent representation by women. This has catalytic impacts on the implementation methodology, resulting in better gender equity and participation in civil society.

In most developing countries, reaching gender equity and full participation is a slow process and one in which Habitat has been forced to compromise in the initial stages. A typical local affiliate governing board in South Asia begins with the women serving tea, sitting quietly in the back, and evolves to their participation on the family selection and support subcommittees, finally developing into full participation on all committees, often including chairing the family selection and support committees. Some affiliates in traditionally male-dominated societies even eventually elect women as board presidents.

Another best practice standard that contributes to equity in gender participation is a board rotation policy. In addition to militating against board burn-out, this standard is designed to reduce the tendency toward the "good ol' boys club." Required rotation not only brings in new energy, but it is also an opportunity to broaden the number and breadth of community members that serve in a leadership capacity over time.

Lessons Learned: Equality of Opportunity

Equality of opportunity for men and women through the development process seems to have a particularly empowering effect on women but requires intentionality from the NGO. Habitat has been able to insist on legal improvements for women in the entitlement process but has been less consistently successful in ensuring that the voices of men and women are equally represented throughout the development process.

Habitat compromised full participation by women on the board from the beginning with the best practice standard for women's participation set at only 30 percent. The reality is often even lower, with the wives of male board members asked to attend to meet the required quota in the start-up phase. This has proven to be a reasonable start-up compromise. It has allowed affiliates to begin at a base level, with nearly universal improvement over time in the real participation by women as they slowly take over the real work of the committee.

Self-Determination

Volunteer Governance and Participation

Volunteer governance of local Habitat committees is a global requirement for affiliation and name use. Developing a local vision to eliminate poverty housing completely in their local geographic area has been key to developing broad community engagement. This broad engagement beyond the community of need improves access to government and community resources not available to a group comprising exclusively the economic poor. It also ensures long-term program development in lieu of a one-time project.

Challenges to a diverse and sustainable board include local cultural, ethnic, and religious discrimination; class suspicion; and adherence to traditional class participation and leadership structural norms. Initially members can be attracted to board membership for prestige, financial gain, and other reasons inconsistent with the mission and vision. As a grassroots movement, technical competence and previous board or governance experience is often limited in the start-up phase. With time and support, many of these start-up deficiencies can be overcome through strong volunteer support in the community.

Vietnam

An example of a compromise to this core principle exists in Vietnam. There, a volunteer board in the traditional sense is not possible because there are no legal provisions for local volunteer organizations separate from the government Peoples Committee structure. Because the government is "the people," self-determination is described very much in terms of societal good rather than individual rights. Habitat chose as a transition strategy, to develop a community volunteer-based program governed by a mix of Peoples Committee members and volunteers. The success of local volunteer engagement and sustainability has been mixed. Local party officials initially insisted on approving all volunteers participating on site as well as those on subcommittees. Through intensive ongoing negotiation, construction volunteers, although tracked, do not now require preapproval by the party to participate on site; however, subcommittee volunteers continue to require preapproval by the party.

In his chapter, "Normative Compliance and Hard Bargaining" (Chapter 8, this volume), Sun Zhe describes constructive engagement as the most pragmatic approach to working with the communist Chinese government. He notes that differences in priorities on human rights mainly refer to arguments over the "stability of the entire society rather than the welfare of the individual." Sun's suggestion of a five- to ten-year outlook for change is consistent with Habitat's strategy in communist Vietnam.

Political Parties and Politicization

There is often a fine line between engaging government as a partner and the perception of supporting a particular political party. Habitat has chosen to recruit volunteers from all political parties as a means to ensure ongoing self-determination but has sometimes been used by politicians as they seek to take credit for the program as well as for external funding.

It is common in developing countries for local politicians to favor and work through particular NGOs. This can cause a shift in the NGO's sustainability with a change in governing party. In one Eastern European country, a political benefactor forced from political power nearly caused organizational collapse for the local Habitat affiliate.

A political candidate with no connection to Habitat appeared on-site at a U.S. affiliate wearing a business suit and hardhat and accompanied by an entourage of reporters. After shaking the hands of all the volunteers, he struck a pose with a borrowed hammer and, smiling, asked, "Are the cameras ready?" To his surprise, the caption of the photo in the next day's paper was, "Are the cameras ready?"

The local affiliate's ability to rely on a free press for accurate reporting varies by country. The affiliate's willingness to take a public stand against strong politicians and their party when necessary and the ability to recruit volunteers from multiple parties also vary between countries and affiliates but is essential in maintaining self-determination.

Nationalization and Sustainability

From its inception in 1976 until 1993, Habitat for Humanity used predominately international staff to develop and manage local affiliates globally. To accelerate growth and increase local ownership through self-determination, the international board approved the Entebbe Initiative in 1993 creating National Boards that would govern affiliates in their respective country. The boards in economically developing countries were drawn from local affiliates and were largely unprepared to develop effective sustainable organizations and assume national level governance.

Although Habitat's implementation of core principles were universal, the organizational model and methodology was better suited to economically developed country norms. National organizations continued in less economically developed countries as long as Habitat for Humanity International supplied the majority of the funding and local boards concentrated on spending it effectively. This was clearly demonstrated when the first governance standards were developed and applied after ten years of national organization activity and 80 percent of those reviewed failed to meet even the minimum affiliation standards.

Habitat built 100,000 homes globally in the first twenty-five years and an additional 100,000 in less than five. Much of this was driven financially by funding from the United States, effectively rewarding non-U.S. affiliates with efficient construction programs often to the detriment of sustainable local development. This artificial acceleration has led to compromises in core principles such as nondiscriminatory selection, nepotism, board diversity, gender equity, and maintenance of a sustainable revolving fund when institutional development did not keep pace.

In this case, Pogge's recommendation for interventions that bring about the greatest harm reduction is complicated by the complexity and the uncertainty of long-term intervention decisions on sustainability and ultimately greatest harm reduction.

The Partnership Versus Confrontational Advocacy Trade-Off

Habitat's strategy for change is to work from within the system, constructively engaging the full range of stakeholders. Habitat does not employ the *name and shame strategy*[25] adopted by many human rights groups. One example of where this approach can require organizational compromise is in the area of land tenure, arguably the single largest impediment to adequate housing for the urban poor.

Habitat has chosen to advocate for land tenure through the development of specific joint venture development projects with government. This private–public partnership approach has enabled Habitat staff and board members to be selected to serve on presidential task forces working on housing and land tenure issues where they can advocate for policy development from within.

This approach, however, limits Habitat's ability to work in full partnership with some slum-dweller organizations that use radical confrontational advocacy tactics and squatter-settlement dwellers without land tenure. This has led Habitat for Humanity to make controversial internal decisions not to condemn publicly several well-publicized governmental housing abuses in a variety of countries.

Local Boards and Diverse Participation

In many cultures in the Asian Pacific region, family or clan favoritism is expected. This perspective is justified through a sense of duty and obligation as well as trust. This results in nepotism, nondiverse boards, family selection discrimination, and other nontransparent business arrangements that often lead to discrimination and favoritism.

Throughout the early decades, Habitat imposed a Western-style democratic organizational structure and predictably discovered repeated abuses to the system. In Fiji and Papua New Guinea, where highly structured chiefly systems still oversee all local village matters, Habitat originally insisted on a traditional democratically elected rotating local board and selection of the family in greatest need first. Although both development principles were consistent with Habitat's organizational ethics and accepted human rights principles of self-determination and nondiscrimination, they were an insult to the local chief and an anathema to the villagers. Low repayments and limited village cooperation were the results of the lack of respect Habitat's methodology showed the local chief. Because all land is held in common by the clan, ruled by the chief, Habitat had little recourse to collect repayments in default.[26]

---

[25] For a more thorough discussion on the efficacy of the name and shame strategy see the chapters by both Ken Roth on the experience of Human Rights Watch and by Curt Goering on the evolution of Amnesty International.

[26] It is interesting to note that in the recent military coup that held the democratically elected president and his cabinet hostage, it was the national council of chiefs who made the final determination on the legitimacy of the coup and ultimately brokered a resolution that ended the national crises.

Against a cultural norm that accords privilege to those with chiefly birthright over democratically elected institutions, Habitat's normative governing method-ology has proven highly ineffective. Bonny Ibhawoh in his chapter "Human Rights INGOs and the North–South Gap" (Chapter 4, this volume) provoca-tively characterizes Northern INGOs' narrow view of the actors in their South-ern projects as savages, victims, or saviors. Ibhawoh has this to say regarding the perspective of Northern human rights organizations: "Again, this stems from a framework that sees Southern societies from the simplistic perspective of polar extremes – passive victims and dangerous abusers. The complexity of the situa-tion is sometimes lost."

I believe his observations accurately characterize the perspective of many Northern humanitarian organizations on the governance breakdown among their Southern counterparts.

Government: Official Discrimination

One Southeast Asian government suggested that it would not issue expatriate technical visas or renew organizational registration for organizations working with particular border refugee populations. After limited debate, the local Habitat organization chose to address the housing need in less controversial areas first, in an attempt to build a strong track record that would allow possible development with these refugee groups at a later time.

Lessons Learned: Self-Determination

Self-determination is not only an important human right; it is a critical devel-opment principle.

In the case of Vietnam, after significant internal debate, Habitat chose a longer-term strategy of engagement, allowing violations in the its global standard for volunteer governance in the belief that the program and the government will change over time – perhaps in part through Habitat's successful demonstration that organized local volunteers could contribute collaboratively toward local government housing objectives.

Political parties and government partnerships continue to require difficult balancing, but the size of the need and the government resources and policy interventions required demand the risk of engagement. Habitat has chosen a strategy to advocate from within the system, effectively limiting some exter-nal partnership opportunities with local and foreign-based organizations that raise suspicions with local government officials. This must be done carefully and cautiously if INGOs are to remain aligned with their moral imperative both to advocate on behalf of and to represent the poor in national and global forums.

Regarding nationalization, Habitat's current strategy requires that a com-mensurate level of accountability accompany self-determination to ensure sustainability. Under the current nationalization strategy, Habitat has spent ten years building houses but not building sustainable national programs in many countries where this principle was not followed. One could argue this approach was consistent with many bilateral and INGO aid programs. More recently, Habitat has shifted to a model in which responsibility will be transferred consistent with demonstrated conformance to institutional development indicators. This, too, is a compromise from strict self-determination because national programs in developing countries are often willing to make organizational changes to continue to receive foreign funding. An alternative approach, in which Habitat provided a match to nationally raised funds, was never considered. This strategy, which may have resulted in accelerated self-determination, would certainly have resulted in fewer families assisted in the short run and was never seriously debated given Habitat's focus on number of families supported each fiscal year.

Habitat has realized that the principle of full participation in local governance can compromise the effectiveness and sustainability under conditions in which capacity and diversity are unavailable in the local community. In the case of Fiji and Papua New Guinea, creating a broader regional organizational structure with a network of subcommittees or satellite branches that respect local chiefly tradition is a compromise that seems to be resulting in increased cooperation and sustainability. As well, a regional board by definition is initially more diverse because of its larger geographic boundaries and a prejudice toward continued representation from each of the constituencies in this expanded area, which perpetuates diversity.

Media, Donors, and Human Rights in Complex Disasters: Made for TV

Time constraints imposed by critical human need and the "culture" of donor expectations drive human rights and organizational compromises to self-determination in complex disasters. The complexities of disaster relief in the relief-to-development continuum often compromise a development organization's normal methodology in areas of civil society, gender and ethnic rights, labor, housing, equity for the poor, and local participation in developing long-term solutions leading to cultural and social anomalies.

Gujarat

Partnering with another well-respected INGO in response to the 2001 Gujarat India earthquake has challenged many of Habitat India's traditional methodologies. Habitat's external INGO partner has both a relief and a development arm as well as an international and a national organization. There is much debate in the relief and development community about how the transition between these two activities should occur. The relief activities are often TV-media driven and rely on immediate public appeal for funding that demands a rapid response to ensure future credibility, whereas development activities are often slower in developing but more effective as a sustainable intervention. The decision to respond to a disaster often has more to do with the perceived media impact than the human impact – a necessary reality in an environment where competition for resources often dictate an INGO's response.[27]

Compromises to Habitat's organizational principles were made from the beginning when local Habitat India board members sided with the external partner's local NGO relief group, signing a Memorandum of Understanding (MOU) with local government officials promising in effect that the rebuilding effort would be done in the least sustainable way. The approach was a giveaway program that necessitated the employment of outside contractors to meet proposed deadlines. These needless expenditures resulted in many needy families not receiving assistance because of funding limitations. Distractions included an expedited staged-for-media construction of a home at the insistence of the partner INGO that the homeowner initially refused to occupy. Habitat and our INGO partner have been working on moving the program toward a more sustainable methodology with our respective local partners but continue to meet resistance.

Sri Lanka Tsunami

The enormous level of devastation across an entire region in the 2004 Asian Tsunami resulted in an unprecedented level of humanitarian relief funds raised by the global community. To the chagrin of experienced development-focused NGOs, many new players collected funds for reconstruction, resulting in a donor free-for-all in every country. Coupled with paralyzed governmental agencies, chaos ensued.

In an effort to demonstrate responsiveness to public pressure to spend funds in this largely unregulated and uncoordinated environment, one major global relief agency unfamiliar with reconstruction asked Habitat to build homes on their behalf at two to three times Habitat's current costs. When told that two to three times the number of families could be helped with that level of funding but that the final completion date would need to be extended to match the pace of the government land entitlement process, the agency asked whether we could just use more expensive materials or somehow spend more on each house so that they could report to their donors that all of their funding had been effectively used within the first six months.

Another well-known agency received so much dedicated funding in one country that it was surreptitiously approaching government officials and "outbidding" other NGOs to procure a priority position in land allocation.

[27] Betty Plewes and Rieky Stuart's compelling reference to *the Pornography of Poverty* (Chapter 1) is an apt description for the collateral damage in the race for disaster dollars.

Lessons Learned: Media and Complex Disasters

The response to complex disasters is often a trade-off between long-term development principles and the immediate response needed to alleviate human suffering that have significant human rights implications. In neither of these cases were the families affected by the disaster involved in the planning or decision making. In the case of all four countries affected by the tsunami, discrimination based on economic status and ethnic or political affiliation influenced the aid received. Some have even suggested that there was government-encouraged genocide in the immediate aftermath where government troops redirected aid bound for critically affected minority ethnic areas to lesser affected majority ethnic areas.

Much of the responsibility lies with the agencies themselves who, because of the nature of the fund-raising appeal process and the character of the personnel required in the immediate aftermath of a disaster, have segregated their disaster appeals and even their relief and development programs and staff.

To be successful, responsible agencies will need to expend efforts in public donor education. The funds are seldom enough in any disaster, but the tyranny of the urgent often militates against responsible spending. In cases like the tsunami, the impact will be measured in months on donor-required log frames but in generations by the families.

Related Human Rights Abuses – The Narrow View

Often related human rights abuses occur within the Habitat participant community, without directly involving the Habitat program. In India, a local female Habitat committee member was set on fire by her in-laws and burned to death in a tragic "accident" when her own family failed to make their promised dowry payments to the husband's family. The international Habitat staff representative encouraged the local committee members to assist the deceased's family in bringing legal charges, but in the end the local committee was unwilling to petition on the family's behalf. The committee's women members redoubled their efforts to advocate for stronger women's participation through the local committee but chose not to confront this all-too-common cultural phenomenon head on.

Lessons Learned: Related Human Rights Abuses

Habitat for Humanity International, like most INGOs and international funders, is legally unable to take direct action on behalf of a program participant when the abuses do not relate directly to their program, but it does encourage community intervention. Although this can result in inaction as in the case just described, it can also eventually lead to community empowerment when a local committee finally takes on discrimination issues on behalf of those in their group. Community action is one indicator of how successful an INGO has been in transformational development, but it is never required by donors to be measured and is rarely measured by the INGO as it is a secondary indicator of direct project impact.

CONCLUSION

Habitat for Humanity supports the UN human rights concerns surrounding adequate and decent shelter for the poor but believes that a rights-based approach alone is ineffective. Habitat believes that it is politically, socially, morally, and religiously unacceptable for people to live in substandard housing. It is only through constructive engagement of all of the constituents in the broad community that a common vision can be forged that is inclusive enough to eliminate subhuman living conditions. This vision must then be transformed into concrete action.

Housing as a single-sector intervention, using participatory methodology, can serve as a catalyst for broader human rights through its role in initiating and encouraging civil society and holistic community development. This approach must be holistic in nature to be transformational.

Transformational development is critical to the reversal of the power dynamics that allow human rights abuses to continue. This transformation is a journey that must include the economic poor and nonpoor as well as the staff of the development and government agencies involved. It must include material, social, and spiritual changes for the fullness of personal dignity and civil society to be developed. Both personal and community paradigm shifts are required.

Additionally, there must also be a shift in donor appreciation of the nature and complexities of the development process. Although action is required, transformation cannot always be measured by log frames, objectives, and crisp outputs or from the sound bites heard on the nightly news.

Despite the challenges, there is ample reason for hope. This hope is illustrated in the story of a man watching a little boy throwing starfish one at a time from the beach back into the sea. After some time the man approaches the boy and asks him whether he has any idea how many starfish there are on all of the beaches in the world and how little difference his efforts are making in the big picture. Without hesitation the boy picks up another starfish and tosses it safely back into the water and responds, "Made a difference to that one."

We draw hope and encouragement each time we hear of a Mr. Durairaj who has not only been transformed but is now transforming his community. If we are to be successful at eliminating human rights abuses, it must start with Mr. Durairaj and his neighbors, one family and one community at a time.

BIBLIOGRAPHY

Barnette, Henlee H. *Clarence Jordan, Turning Dreams into Deeds.* Smyth Helwys, 1992.
Carens, Joseph. "Democracy and Respect for Difference: The Case of Fiji", in *Culture, Citizenship, and Community.* Oxford: Oxford University Press, 2000, 200–261.

Chambers, Robert. *Whose Reality Counts.* Brichton, UK: Intermediate Technology Publications, 1997, 104.

Fuller, Millard. *Bokotola.* Association Press, Piscataway, NJ: New Century Publishers, 1977.

Fuller, Millard. *More than Houses.* Nashville: Word, 2000.

Government of India. *DEC Evaluation Report – Shelter and the Use of contractors.* Delhi: 2001

Hiebert, Paul. *The Flaw of the Excluded Middle. Missiology* 10, 1 (1982), 35–47.

Human Rights in Development Web page [http\\www.unhchr.ch/development/right-01.html] (January 2002)

Lee, Dallas. *The Cotton Patch Evidence.* New York: Harper & Row, 1971.

Meyers, Bryant. *Walking with the Poor; Principles and Practices of Transformational Development.* New York: Orbis Books, Maryknoll, 1999.

MTTH. *Draft Community Impact Study.* MTTH project sponsored by USAID in Nepal and Sri Lanka, 2002.

Newbigin, Leslie. *Foolishness to the Greeks: The Gospel and Western Culture.* Grand Rapids, MI: Eerdmans, 1986.

United Nations. *Universal Declaration of Human Rights.* Article 25.1. Geneva: Author, 1948. Available: http:/www.unhchr.ch (January 2002).

United Nations, Office of the High Commissioner for Human Rights. *The Human Rights to Adequate Housing.* Fact Sheet No. 21. Available: http:/www.unhchr.ch (January 2002).

4 Human Rights INGOs and the North–South Gap: The Challenge of Normative and Empirical Learning

Bonny Ibhawoh

The role of human rights International Nongovernmental Organizations (INGOs)[1] has become increasingly important in an age of globalization in which they are seen as heralding a global civil society and a new world order based on a universal human rights. INGOs have been at the forefront of the "human rights revolution" – a revolution of norms and values that has redefined our understanding of ethics and justice.[2] They have shaped the course of the human rights movement not only at the international level but also at regional and national levels. INGO involvements in global transnational networking, particularly in the 1980s and 1990s, have been crucial to the development of the universal human rights corpus as well as its enforcement and monitoring mechanisms.[3] One reason for the growing influence of INGOs within the human rights movement has been their ability to build transnational coalitions and mobilize global action on key human rights issues. This is evident in the role of INGOs in such human rights milestones as the 1992 Second World Conference on Human Rights in Vienna, the establishment of a United Nations (UN) High Commission for Human Rights, and the establishment of the International Criminal Court. If

---

[1] Human Rights INGOs as used here refers to organizations that have explicit mandates and agendas to promote human rights internationally. This includes organizations such as Amnesty International, Human Rights Watch, the International Human Rights Law Group, the International Commission of Jurists, and La Fédération internationale des ligues des droits de l'Homme (FIDH), among others.

[2] Michael Ignatieff, *Human Rights as Politics and Idolatry* (Princeton, NJ: Princeton University Press, 2001).

[3] Several studies have documented the role of NGOs in making human rights a major force in the agenda of international politics and diplomacy. See William Korey, *NGOs and the Universal Declaration of Human Rights: A Curious Grapevine* (New York: St. Martin Press, 1998); Claude E. Welch, *NGOs and Human Rights: Promise and Performance* (Philadelphia: University of Pennsylvania Press, 2001); and Ian Gary, *Human Rights in Africa: The Role of Donors and International Human Rights NGOs: A Survey* (New York: Ford Foundation, 1998).

the UN midwifed the postwar universal human rights movement, INGOs have weaned and nurtured it.

Despite these successes, however, the work of human rights INGOs (most of which are based in the West) is increasingly underscored by operational challenges and questions over their legitimacy in the global South where they do much of their work. Old arguments for cultural pluralism in the understanding and promotion of human rights have been reinforced by new questions over the relevance of INGO mandates and programs in non-Western societies. Although some of these issues are linked to the conflict between the "universal" human rights standards and local cultural norms, others stem from broader issues of political ideology, globalization, and the widening gap between the North and South, the rich and poor, the developed and less developed. The critique of INGO work in the South is normative and empirical, challenging both the moral priorities of these organizations and their modes of operation.

At a normative level, questions have been raised about the relevance of Western-oriented or "West-centric" human rights agendas and programs that INGOs promote to the peculiar sociocultural conditions in developing societies. INGOs have been accused of adopting homogenizing approaches to human rights that draw little from non-Western realities and yet focus disproportionately on Third World countries. Furthermore, the charge has been repeatedly made that despite its façade of neutrality, the human rights movement is neither nonideological nor postideological. Human rights INGOs as key players within the movement have since the Cold War era actively promoted a parochial Western liberal agenda – a deeply political agenda alongside the mantra of universal morality. One scholar recently argued that the human rights movement – and specifically the activities of human rights INGOs in the Third World – falls into the historical continuum of the Eurocentric colonial project that seeks to supplant all other traditions and casts actors into superior and subordinate positions.[4] Although few go this far, many human rights scholars and activists have raised normative questions about the moral priorities of human rights INGOs.

At a more empirical level, there is concern that the methodologies that INGOs adopt for doing their work draw too little from non-Western, Third World experiences and as such are not always well suited for the peculiar circumstances in these societies. INGOs have been unable or unwilling to go beyond their Western liberal roots to draw on eclectic Third World perspectives in formulating their agendas and methodologies. How do human rights INGOs deal with these complex questions of political bias, cultural engagement, and legitimacy?

There has been a tendency to cast these issues in the rather simplistic terms of the conflict between human rights principles and local cultural norms or, at an academic level, the tension between universalism versus cultural relativism. But

---

[4] Makau Mutua, *Human Rights: A Political and Cultural Critique* (Philadelphia: University of Pennsylvania Press, 2002).

the issues here are more complex. It is no longer enough to simply dismiss challenges to the work of INGOs in the South as opportunistic arguments by rulers and elites given their growing resonance beyond the narrow confines of privileged discourse. North–South tensions in the human rights movement go beyond the universalism-cultural relativism debate or manipulations by disingenuous elites in the South. Although elitist concerns have prompted some of the challenges to the universalist agendas of human rights INGOs, there are other voices of dissent that question the principles and methods of INGOs in the South. These are not the familiar cynical blanket criticisms of INGOs and their work in the South. Rather, these critics proceed from the premise that INGOs play an important role within a useful, even if flawed, human rights movement. The main concern is the gap between INGO idealism and the conditions they confront in the South. This chapter examines some of the normative and empirical challenges to the work of human rights INGOs that threaten to undermine their legitimacy in the global South. It argues the need for more constructive approaches to understanding and addressing them.

I. CONFRONTING THE GAP

Recent studies indicate that the human rights movement is divided in important ways along geographical lines.[5] Although united by the common principal goal of promoting human rights, the global human rights movement has been characterized by tensions between the large Northern-based INGOs and local NGOs in the South with national or regional mandates. On one hand, there is a level of cooperation and networking between NGOs in the North and South that is surprising for groups that are so geographically and culturally dispersed.[6] One example of this is the concerted international campaign against apartheid in South Africa in the 1980s, which has been described as one of "the two great human rights milestones of the latter part of the twentieth century."[7] The anti-apartheid milestone was partly the result of collaboration between human rights INGOs, the nascent NGO communities in the South, and political groups in South Africa. Amnesty International (AI) in particular played an important role in the anti-apartheid campaign and mobilizing international support for the domestic NGO sector.[8]

---

[5] Jackie Smith and Ron Pagnucco, "Globalizing Human Rights: The Work of Transnational Human Rights NGOs in the 1990s," *Human Rights Quarterly* 20, no. 2 (1998), 411.

[6] Ibid at 406.

[7] The other is the collapse of the Soviet Union. William Korey, *NGOs and the Universal Declaration of Human Rights: A Curious Grapevine* (New York: St. Martin Press, 1998), 180.

[8] Many of the local NGOs in South Africa in the apartheid era were not strictly human rights organizations. They were political movements, church groups and labour unions. However, they drew extensively from their universal human rights discourse for their advocacy work and human rights concerns were central to their anti-apartheid message.

On the other hand, however, the relationship between Northern and Southern human rights NGOs is increasingly underscored by tensions and a gulf that
threatens to undermine past gains. These tensions arise more from the socioeconomic realities of the North and South gap than from differences in the agendas of
Northern and Southern INGOs. Most human rights INGOs, like other transnational organizations, are based in Western Europe and North America. Although
a few are based in Asia, the least represented regions among international human
rights organizations according to a 1999 study are Africa, the Middle East, and
Eastern Europe.[9] The common explanation for this is that given the global scope
of their operations, INGOs need to be located in places where they have easy
access to the required manpower, communication facilities, and other support
structures. Besides, INGOs have made the valid argument that their work is better done in liberal democratic settings where they are free from state-imposed
restrictions. States in the North are more likely to offer these conditions.

This geographic imbalance is one aspect of the operation of human rights
INGOs that has raised concerns about their roles in Third World countries.
Another is the imbalance in the organizational structures of most human rights
INGOs. Although many INGOs have moved toward diversifying their organization, the norm had been leadership structures dominated by Westerners. For
these and other reasons that I examine later, human rights INGOs have sometimes been accused of pushing a predominantly Western agenda. The geographic
imbalance in the structure and operations of INGOs is often the first shot taken
by those who challenge their legitimacy in the South. Governments have sought
to ward off INGO's criticism of their human rights records on the grounds that
these "Western" organizations, even when they employ local staff, are not sufficiently engaged with the local community to understand or make judgments
about its human rights conditions.

Arguments like these, important as they are, do not pose a serious challenge
to the legitimacy of the work of INGOs in the South. Although based in the
North, many INGOs have developed strong representations and networks in the
South that keep them well connected with local situations. It is difficult to accept
the argument that NGOs can only be effective when they limit their activities to
the communities where they are based. In a perfect world, INGOs will be based
wherever they do most of their work, but ours is not a perfect world. At a practical
level, the reality of global economic inequalities makes it necessary for INGOs to
operate from bases in the North where, like other transnational actors, they can
benefit from the economic and technological advantages that make it easier for
them to pursue their global mandates.

Yet besides this, there is a prevailing assumption that INGOs would garner
more acceptance and support in the South if they had stronger representation
there. This is not always true. In 2000, I was part of a team that conducted a series

[9] Smith and Pagnucco, "Globalizing Human Rights," 387.

of interviews with officials of human rights NGOs across West Africa as part of an evaluative study of the human rights NGO community in Africa commissioned by the Danish Institute for Human Rights. What we quickly found was that contrary to our assumptions, local activists did not always welcome more INGO presence in their communities. They preferred an arrangement in which INGOs keep their focus global and collaborated with them on domestic projects. This was particularly true of postauthoritarian states such as South Africa, Malawi, and Nigeria where the influx of better-funded INGOs in the late 1990s was seen as undermining local human rights NGOs and giving the local human rights community a foreign character. In some cases, these INGOs were even accused of hampering the capacity-building efforts of local NGOs.[10]

Thus, although the concern about geographic or regional imbalance is a legitimate one, it may not be as problematic for the work of human rights INGOs as some have suggested. The imbalance borders of broader issues of global socioeconomic inequities that are not peculiar to INGO operations. Within Southern human rights communities, there are many who favor some form of human rights division of labor in which the larger and more established INGOs work with local NGOs to pursue domestic objectives. Many INGOs have also found that their programs and campaigns in the South have more impact when they collaborate with local activists and organizations to achieve common goals.

II. NORMATIVE LEARNING: POLITICAL IDEOLOGY AND INGOs AGENDAS

Concerns about organizational imbalance become more resonant when linked with political ideology and questions about the agendas of human rights INGOs. Although the ethical and humanistic ideals at the core of INGO work may be universally shared, they have not always been pursued with universal objectivity. In fact, the promotion of these ideals has been frequently undermined by political biases. These concerns are not new. During the Cold War, human rights became a battlefield on which the Western and Eastern blocs sought to legitimize opposing political ideologies. The Cold War deeply perverted the philosophy of states toward human rights as evident in the partisan debates over human rights at the United Nations. Caught in the middle of this ideological battle were human rights INGOs whose claim to neutrality was constantly challenged, particularly because

---

[10] In Nigeria, for instance, some within the local human rights INGO community were not pleased at the decision of the International Human Rights Law Group to open an office in the country soon after the establishment of democratic rule 1989. Because local NGOs and the big INGOs often seek donor funds for country projects from the same sources, they were concerned that the more influential INGOs would get funds for local projects that would otherwise have come to them. See Bonny Ibhawoh, *Human Rights Organisations in Nigeria: An Appraisal Report on the Human Rights NGO Community in Nigeria* (Copenhagen: The Danish Centre for Human Rights, 2001), 66.

many of their activities during this period focused mainly on human rights violations in the Soviet bloc. The oldest and most prestigious human rights INGOs – AI, the International Commission of Jurists (ICJ), and Human Rights Watch (HRW) – were established primarily to deal with human rights in Cold War–era Europe.[11] Indeed, one troubling trend in the work of human rights INGOs during this period was that they were caught up in the partisan international politics of the era. The "naming and shaming" seemed to focus quite disproportionately on countries of the Eastern bloc and a familiar group of "violators" in the South.[12]

Eastern bloc regimes responded to INGOs' criticism of their human rights record by challenging the legitimacy of these organizations – accusing them of pursuing a patently ideological agenda of propagating Western capitalism. The end of the Cold War in the 1990s changed the tone but not the substance of this challenge. The argument persists that the human rights movement and the role of key players like INGOs within it is neither nonideological nor postideological. The mantra of universal morality tends to mask its deeply political character. The human rights corpus has a philosophy that seeks the diffusion of liberalism and its primacy around the globe – a philosophy that is favorable to political and cultural homogenization and hostile to difference and diversity. Makau Mutua argues that

> [in] reality, INGOs have been highly partial: their work has historically concentrated on these countries that have not attained the stable and functioning democracies of the West, the standard of liberal democracy. Target states have included the Soviet bloc and virtually the entire South, where democratic or oppressive one-party state and military dictatorships have thrived.[13]

Mutua also makes the point that even though Western countries like the United States are notorious for their violation of the civil rights of minorities and the poor, they are rarely the focus of INGO reports. Although both HRW and AI have recently begun to bridge the advocacy barriers in these areas, such reports have been sparse and episodic and have given the impression of a public relations exercise designed to mute critics who charge NGO with a lopsided focus.[14] When in 2005, AI Secretary-General Irene Khan described the U.S. detention center at Guantanamo Bay as "the gulag of our times," it made headlines around the world partly because it was unusual for a powerful Western country to be at

---

[11] The Helsinki Accord of 1975, a Cold War agreement aimed at guaranteeing security and cooperation in Europe, typifies the link between the tensions of Cold War political ideology and the activities of human rights INGOs. The human rights provisions in the accord became part of the grounds on which Western-based INGOs criticized authoritarian regimes in the Eastern bloc. The accord also led to the emergence of a new generation of human rights NGOs in the West – notably, Helsinki Watch, which later became Human Rights Watch.

[12] "The Conscience of Mankind," *The Economist* (December 5, 1998), 5.

[13] Mutua, *Human Rights: A Political and Cultural Critique*, 53.

[14] Ibid at 20.

the receiving end of such strong INGO criticism of its human rights record.[15] Such uncompromising language had traditionally been reserved for communist and Third World nations. However, the widely reported human rights abuses associated with the U.S war on terror and in Iraq may well signal the beginning of a new era of change. Major INGOs, including AI and HRW, now acknowledge that human rights are in retreat worldwide and that the United States bears most responsibility for this.[16]

Until these recent trends, some observers sought to explain the lopsidedness and ideological predisposition of human rights INGOs in terms of the composition of their leadership and the Western liberal constituencies where they draw much of their moral and financial support. Henry Steiner argues that INGOs share a fundamental commitment to the proselytization of Western liberal values, particularly expressive of political rights.[17] Indeed for much of the 1980s and 1990s, most human rights INGOs stressed a narrow range of civil and political rights in their mandates and activities. They focused mainly on exposing civil and political rights violations in the Soviet bloc and the Third World. These were deemed "core" rights as opposed to "secondary" economic and social rights, which were emphasized in communist propaganda. With the collapse of the Soviet Union in the late 1990s, however, several INGOS began to talk more about the "indivisibility" of rights. After several decades of resistance, major INGOs like AI and HRW have moved to give economic and social rights more prominence in their mandates and activities. Yet although the end of the Cold War may have significantly affected the work of Northern INGOs, it has had a less dramatic impact on Southern NGOs. A recent survey of human rights NGOs in the North and South indicates that Northern NGOs were more likely to report that they had changed their mission statements, mandates, and organizational structures as a consequence of the end of the Cold War.[18]

Although the shift to broader mandates that include both civil and political (CP) and economic, social, and cultural (ESC) rights have been welcomed as engendering a more holistic human rights corpus, they also raise important questions about the ideological agenda of human rights INGOs and the human rights movement in general. Why have the "gatekeepers" of the human rights movement become better disposed to ESC rights advocacy in the post–Cold

---

[15] The secretary-general went further to compare the existence of "ghost detainees" who were being detained unregistered and incommunicado at the U.S base as being reminiscent of the "disappearances" common under the regimes of Latin American dictators in the past.

[16] See Foreword by the AI secretary-general in *Amnesty International Report 2005*, available at http://web.amnesty.org/report2005/index-eng and Human Rights Watch, *Getting Away with Torture? Command Responsibility for US Abuse of Detainees*, Human Rights Watch, April 2005 (18 March 2004).

[17] See Henry J. Steiner, *Diverse Partners: Non-Governmental Organizations in the Human Rights Movement* (Cambridge, MA: Harvard Law School Human Rights Program, 1991).

[18] Smith and Pagnucco, "Globalizing Human Rights," 391.

War era? Could it be because we no longer face the "risk" of communist states appropriating the economic and social rights discourse to challenge Western liberal norms? Have economic and social rights suddenly gained more prominence within the human rights movement only because it has become more politically and ideologically expedient for certain key players? If this is so, it throws into question all our assumptions about the objective moral foundations of the human rights movement.

Some within the INGO community have explained the shift toward ESC rights in terms of other factors that go beyond ideology and the end of the Cold War. The shift became necessary because, first, the disproportionate focus on CP rights resulted in misguided priorities that ignored serious threat to human suffering arising from economic and social rights issues; second, there was strong support for the expansion of INGOs mandates from activists and partners in the South; and third, CP rights tend to be biased toward male concerns, and this needed to be addressed.[19] These considerations may indeed have informed the shift toward broader mandates, but for many skeptics, the timing continues to pose the concern that beyond the simple mantra of promoting universal human rights, underlying political and ideological factors shape INGO's agendas and activities.

III. (UN)ETHICAL PARADIGMS: VIOLATORS, VICTIMS, AND SAVIORS

There is a uniquely Third Word dimension to the concern over the place of ideology in INGO mandates and the ethical challenges that these organizations confront in a post–Cold War world. With the collapse of the Soviet Union, the locus of the challenge to the legitimacy of human rights INGOs seems to have moved from the former Eastern bloc to an emerging "Third World bloc" loosely united against the totalizing values of the affluent West in what Rhoda Howard-Hassmann has termed the "international politics of distrust and resentment."[20] This challenge is clearly not peculiar to human rights INGOs. Yet although humanitarian and development-oriented INGOs also face these disputes over the relevance and legitimacy of their work, human rights INGOs particularly bear the brunt of it. The reason for this is obvious. The human rights movement has been defined by the tension between universalizing and localizing impulses. Unlike INGOs with purely humanitarian or development mandate, human rights INGOs overtly lay claim to a universalizing/globalizing mission that naturally pits them against forces of localization and cultural pluralism.

[19] See Chapter 11 (this volume) by Curt Goering (senior deputy executive director, Amnesty International USA), "Amnesty International and Economic, Social, and Cultural Rights."
[20] Rhoda Howard-Hassmann, "Moral Integrity and Reparations to Africa," in ed. John Torpey, *Politics and the Past: On Repairing Historical Injustices* (Lanham, MD: Rowman and Littlefield, 2002).

The challenge to the legitimacy of INGOs in the South centers mainly on the ideological framework on which INGO rights-based humanitarianism is founded – what David Chandler describes as "an ideological framework of the rationalism between Western institutions and the Third World."[21] In this framework, human rights, humanitarian, and development-oriented INGOs tend to portray the non-Western subject as needy, incapable of self-government, and in need of long-term external assistance. The framework creates the now familiar "moral fairy tale" of distress and rescue. Media editors now know in advance what a typical human rights intervention story looks like. The first component is the hapless victim in distress, the second is the non-Western government whose action or inaction caused the violation, and the third component is the rescuer – the human rights INGO, the external aid agency, the international institution, or even the journalist covering the story – whose interests are seen as inseparable from those of the victim.[22]

Mutua makes a similar point when he uses the metaphor of savages, victims, and saviors (SVS) to describe the guiding framework of the human rights movement and the role of human rights INGOs within it. The grand narrative of human rights, he argues, contains subtexts that depict an epochal contest pitting savages on one hand against saviors and victims on the other. This framework reinforces a dual stereotypical construct of Third World actors as either "savages" (despotic regimes or traditional authorities implementing patriarchal and repressive customs) or hapless "victims" (minority or other oppressed groups such as women). Certain key players in the West position themselves as the "gatekeepers" of human rights destined to save Third World "victims" from Third World "savages."[23] In this regard, the "modern human rights crusade" fits into the historical continuum of the violent Christian-colonial conquests in the South. The same methods are at work, and similar cultural dispossessions are taking place without dialogue or conversation.[24] Within this framework, INGOs position themselves as later day "abolitionists." They spotlight evils and demand their eradication. For them, there is no middle ground or moral dilemma.[25]

The campaigns against female genital mutilation (FGM) have been highlighted as an example of the poignancy of the imagery of savage, victim, and savior.

---

[21] David Chandler, "The Road to Military Humanitarianism: How the Human Right NGOs Shaped a New Humanitarian Agenda," *Human Rights Quarterly* 23, no. 3 (2001), 688.

[22] Chandler, "The Road to Military Humanitarianism," 688–9.

[23] These trends are not peculiar to human rights INGOs. Humanitarian- and development-oriented INGOs have come under stronger accusations of the searching for victims. Some of this also bears relevance to the "pornography of poverty" discussed in Chapter 1 of this volume, "The Pornography of Poverty: A Cautionary Fundraising Tale" by Betty Plewes and Rieky Stuart.

[24] Mutua, *Human Rights: A Political and Cultural Critique*, xi

[25] J. Oloka-Onyango, "Modern Day Missionaries or Misguided Miscreants? NGOs, the Women's Movements and the Promotion of Human Rights in Africa," in *Human Rights of Women: International Instruments and African Experiences*, ed. Wolfgang Benedek (London: Zed Books, 2002), 289.

INGOs are accused of picking up where European colonial missionaries left off. Objections to the methods employed in the campaign against FGM have come not only from those intent on maintaining the status quo for cultural reasons but also from local constituencies that reject FGM. The Association of African Women for Research and Development (AAWORD), while opposing "female circumcision," has consistently denounced the anti-FGM campaign by Western-based INGOs as being "insensitive to the dignity of the very women they want to 'save.'"[26] Others have questioned the language and tone of the campaign against FGM, the "false portrayal" and the "successful demonization of the practitioners."[27]

To draw parallels between the human rights movement and Christian-colonial conquests in the South may be going too far. There are, however, valid grounds for the argument that the activities of human rights INGOs have historically been driven more by interests in the North than in the South. The concerns about cultural dispossessions and the objectification of Third World actors within the human rights movement cannot simply be dismissed as elitist arguments for "cultural relativism" and against universal human rights. They speak to a growing concern about the mandates and agenda of human rights INGOs and other key players within the human rights movement – a concern that INGOs must take seriously. We need to seriously consider the influence of ideology, sectional interests, and preconceptions on the agendas and methods of INGOs, which can undermine their claims to universalism and objectivity. Human rights advocates need to be more self-critical and come to terms with the troubling rhetoric and history that has shaped, in part, the human rights movement. In the case of INGOs, this may require changes in some of the methods and frameworks that guide their work in the South. One first step in this direction will be to move away from the ideological frameworks that have become associated with INGO operations in the South.

IV. EMPIRICAL LEARNING: BEYOND DOMESTIC VIOLATORS

Preconceptions about human rights violator and victims are problematic for several reasons. For one, they preclude a deeper understanding of causes, courses, and consequences of human rights violations. The dominant framework for INGO operations in the South is based on the assumption that primary responsibility for human rights abuses lie with states and governments. This framework pays insufficient attention to how larger issues of global inequities, the role of international financial institutions (IFIs) and transnational corporations (TNCs) affect human rights conditions in the South. The contemporary human rights movement in which INGOs are key players sees violations in non-Western states

---

[26] AAWORD, "A Statement on Genital Mutilation," in *Third World-Second Sex: Women's Struggles and National Liberation,* ed. Miranda Davis (London: Zed Books, 1983), 217.

[27] Ifeyinwa Iweriebor, "Brief Reflections on Clitorodectomy," *Africa Update* (Spring 1996), 4.

as arising from a relationship of abuse. Indeed, most human rights violations stem from relationships of abuse, but these relationships are rooted not only in local cultures and domestic politics but also in the international political economy.

It has become widely accepted that the structures of globalization and the pressures they place on vulnerable Third World states contribute to conditions of political repression and human rights abuses therein. Several studies have drawn links among the operations of IFIs and TNCs, political repression, and human rights abuses in Third World countries.[28] Others have addressed the specific impacts of economic globalization on human rights in the South.[29] There is also a growing recognition of the link between economic globalization and human rights at the level of international policy making. In 2001, the United Nations Sub-commission on Human Rights passed a resolution, "Globalisation and Its Impact on the Full Enjoyment of Human Rights," that expressed concern about the impact of the liberalization of trade on agricultural products on the "promotion and protection of the right to food for members of vulnerable communities." The resolution drew particular attention to the human rights obligations of the World Bank, the International Monetary Fund, the Organization for Economic Cooperation and Development, and the World Trade Organization.[30]

Yet despite the ravages of globalization in the South, these international factors have received little attention from INGOs. Even where it is evident that domestic human rights conditions have been aggravated by international actors, INGOs have been reluctant to "name and shame" these actors in the same way as they have traditionally named and shamed states. For instance, following the devastating impact of the Asian financial crisis on Indonesia in the late 1990s, the international financial community promised the government a US $40 billion bailout on the condition that Indonesia restructure its economy and drastically cut subsidies on social programs. Under this pressure, the government increased fuel prices by 70 percent and started a program of massive layoffs of civil servants. The result was an outbreak of popular public protests, which the government of

[28] For instance, it has been argued that because International Monetary Fund and World Bank conditionalities are so stringent and unpopular, they predispose governments in Third World countries, many of which already have problems of legitimacy, to resort to the excessive use of repression and coercion to enforce them. See John Rusk, "Structures of Neo-Colonialism: The African Context of Human Rights," *Africa Today* 33, no. 4 (1986), 22–33; Peter Gibbon, Y. Bangura, and A. Ofstad, eds., *Authoritarianism, Democracy and Adjustment: The Politics of Economic Reform in Africa* (Uppsala: Scandinavian Institute of African Studies, 1992); and Eboe Hutchful, "The Crisis of the International Division of Labor: Authoritarianism and the Transition to Free Market Economies in Africa," *Africa Development* 12, no. 2 (1987), 14–25.

[29] Robert McCorquodale, with Richard Fairbrother, "Globalization and Human Rights," *Human Rights Quarterly* 21, no. 3 (1999), 35–76 and Alison Brysk, ed., *Globalization and Human Rights* (Berkeley: University of California Press, 2002).

[30] United Nations High Commission for Human Rights, "Globalization and Its Impact on the Full Enjoyment of All Human Rights," Sub-Commission on Human Rights resolution 2001/5, 2001," available: http://www.unhchr.ch (24 March 2004).

Haji Mohammad Suharto (already disposed to authoritarian tendencies) tried to suppress with armed force, arbitrary detentions, and press censorship. In the international outcry over these human rights abuses that followed, INGO campaigns and reports focused almost exclusively on state repression. Few went further to connect the dots among the role of IFIs, the international political economy, and human rights violations in Indonesia. Again, this stems from a framework that sees Southern societies from the simplistic perspective of polar extremes – passive victims and dangerous abusers. The complexity of the situation is sometimes lost. Domestic factors often play a major role in determining human rights conditions, but in an increasingly interconnected and globalizing world, we cannot ignore the roles of powerful "remote" factors. The tendency of human rights INGOs to focus on domestic causes of human rights abuses to the exclusion of broader international factors can be linked to another feature of INGO work – the disproportionate concern with CP rights at the expense of ESC rights.

V. TACKLING ESC RIGHTS: PRIORITIZATION AND METHODOLOGICAL LIMITATIONS

The prioritization of CP rights over ESC rights within the human rights movement has generated a familiar and long-standing debate that other chapters in this volume have adequately addressed. It is not necessary to go into the details of this debate here. It suffices to mention that the disinclination of INGOs to take up ESC rights advocacy with the same vigor that they have traditionally advocated CP rights is an important ground for criticism of their work in the South. Until recently, much of the work of INGOs focused only on certain aspects of political life, and they largely excluded the ESC rights issues that are of great concern to developing societies in the South. This approach also tended to overlook real issues of inequities in the global distribution of wealth.

One explanation for this is that INGOs see their agendas as mainly political. They seem committed to human rights and liberal democracy mainly as political projects. They stress the nature and frequency of political and civil rights violations, rather than exploring the socioeconomic and other factors that underlie them.[31] For this reason, INGO investigations and reports sometimes tend to address the symptoms rather than the source of the ailment and recommend cures that are at best superficial. Even the emphasis on political goals in the mandates of INGOs is sometimes further narrowed to the establishment of liberal democracy preceded by elections. There is less consideration for the social and economic conditions that are essential to the sustenance of liberal democracy. For instance, the Lawyers Committee for Human Rights seemed to have set the establishment of liberal democracy as the yardstick of the success of its human rights work when it closed its South Africa project soon after the 1994 elections.

---

[31] Steiner, *Diverse Partners*, 19.

INGOs have stressed the difficulty of promoting ESC rights in the same way as CP rights. Kenneth Roth, the executive director of Human Rights Watch, clearly and persuasively articulates the difficulty associated with promoting ESC rights in the same way that INGOs that they have traditionally promoted CP rights. First, because ESC rights are "costly" and have to do with the allocation of scarce resources in Third World countries, INGOs as outsiders can only play a limited role. Such decisions about resource allocation must reside with local voices. Second, there are difficulties in applying the human rights movement's time-tested methodologies of investigating, exposing, and shaming on issues of ECR rights. Third, there is still a lot of fuzziness over the mechanisms for enforcing ECR rights. There is no clarity around the issues of violation, violator, and remedy that have been the basis of the movement's traditional methodology.[32]

Few would disagree that promoting ECR rights poses peculiar challenge to INGOs, especially on matters that bother on distributive justice rather than clear-cut civil and political entitlements. The methods that the human rights movement have traditionally employed to promote CP rights may indeed be inadequate for ESC rights. What this shows, however, is not that we cannot promote ESC rights as vigorously and successfully as we have promoted CP rights. It simply shows that we need new tools – new methodologies. Thus, rather than argue that ESC rights are "not doable," the focus should be on fashioning new tools for the task at hand. The human rights movement should be open to adopting new tools to meet the challenges of ESC rights advocacy. To do this, they may need to look more to the South.

Countries in the South that may have achieved notoriety for human rights abuses can also be important sources of new methodologies for human rights advocacy. As others have pointed out, many organizations in the South have successfully used the methods of education and mass mobilization to promote ESC rights.[33] One of the main constraints that INGOs face in promoting ESC rights is the lack of clarity over ESC rights jurisprudence and litigation. That clarity is beginning to emerge and some of the progress has come from the South. In such landmark cases as *Soobramoney v. Minister of Health*[34] and *Government of RSA*

---

[32] See Chapter 9, "Defending Economic, Social, and Cultural Rights: Practical Issues Faced by an International Human Rights Organization," this volume, by Kenneth Roth.

[33] See Chapter 1 of this volume by Betty Plewes and Rieky Stuart.

[34] This case dealt with the rights of a diabetic man who was denied admission into the dialysis program of a state hospital because he did not qualify for admission under the hospital priority policy. The man then applied to the Durban High Court claiming that he had a right to receive dialysis treatment on the grounds of his constitutional right to life and the provision that no one may be refused emergency medical treatment. Although the application was dismissed on technical grounds, the case demonstrated the possibilities of legally enforcing constitutionally guaranteed economic and social rights in South Africa. See Constitutional Court of South Africa, Case CCT 32/97, 27 November 1997.

v. Grootboom,[35] the South African constitutional courts has tacked problematic issues of "distributive justice" and provided useful directions for developing the jurisprudence on economic and social rights. The first case addressed the possibilities of legally enforcing the right to health care guaranteed in the South African constitution, and the latter dealt with the state's constitutional obligations to provide adequate housing for its citizens. These important initiatives in South Africa and elsewhere in the South can provide useful directions for INGO work in ESC rights advocacy. INGOs must recognize that their engagement in Southern Third World societies need not be a one-way street of rescuers and violators or victims. Their work need not be limited to tackling human rights violations in these societies with agendas and programs developed in head offices in London, Paris, and New York. Rather, they should recognize that these societies, too, can make important contributions to their methodology.

Apart from concerns about prioritization and lopsidedness, there are other issues arising from the work of INGOs in the South that deserve close attention. One of this is what may be termed the "sociocultural challenge" – the task of promoting internationalism and universal human rights in a way that is responsive to the reality of sociocultural difference and diversity.

VI. THE SOCIOCULTURAL CHALLENGE

The conflict between human rights principles and local cultural norms is one of the crucial ethical dilemmas that face the INGO community generally, but for human rights INGOs the conflict has particular resonance. The conflict often manifests in the form of challenges from local authorities seeking to maintain practices that are antithetical to universal human rights on the grounds of culture. Whether in the form of Asian or African values debate, culture talk in the human rights discourse has largely been deployed by the privileged and those who seek to maintain the status quo. In some cases, however, the deployment of culture talk to challenge the work INGOs in the South goes beyond the realm of privileged discourse. One particularly controversial example of this is the issue of gay and lesbian rights – an issue over which INGOs have frequently encountered differences with human rights movements in the South. In Egypt, for instance, local NGOs have consistently refused to campaign against the persecution of gays in that country despite international concern and pressure from Western funders and partner INGOs. During the 2001 trial for homosexual activity of fifty-two men, the largest human rights organization in the country, the Egyptian

---

[35] This case addressed the state's obligations under section 26 of the South African Constitution, which gives everyone the right of access to adequate housing, and section 28(1)(c), which affords children the right to shelter. The judgment addressed jurisprudential questions about the enforceability of social and economic rights. See *Government of Republic of South Africa and others v. Grootboom and others*, Case CCT11/00, 4 October 2000.

Organisation for Human Rights (EOHR), refused to be drawn into the debate. Given the prevailing cultural and religious attitudes toward homosexuality, local activists found the issue simply too hot to handle. They argued that Egyptians would simply not stand for gay rights. Under increasing pressure from those who thought his organization should be doing more to protect gay and lesbian rights, EOHR's director responded:

> What could we do? Nothing. If we were to uphold this issue, this would be the end of what remains of the concept of human rights in Egypt. . . . We let them [homosexuals] down, but I don't have a mandate from the people, and I don't want the West to set the pace for the human rights movement in Egypt.[36]

The situation is the same in Nigeria where human rights workers have welcomed the work of human rights INGOs in the country but state that it would be impossible, given local cultural beliefs, for them to press for gay and lesbian rights.[37]

How do INGOs respond when the deployment of culture talk to challenge universal human rights agendas comes, not from rulers and privileged elites but from within their own constituencies in the South? There are two possible routes that INGOs can take. They may adopt a gradualist approach and acquiesce to the position of local activists (if not totally agree with it) that these societies are currently not ready for gay and lesbian rights advocacy. They may therefore modify their gay and lesbian rights advocacy programs to suit local realities rather than risk undermining their legitimacy within these communities. As one Southern activist put it, to promote gay rights in the South with the same methods used in the North is to risk undoing the modest success achieved in two decades of human rights advocacy work.[38] Advocates of the gradualist approach point to the West where there has been a gradual but growing public acceptance of gay and lesbian rights over time.

The other route INGOs may take is to insist on an uncompromising campaign for gay and lesbian rights even at the risk of alienating local communities and partners in the South. The strongest argument for this option is that INGOs cannot abandon legitimate human rights issues simply because they are unpopular or "too hot to handle." To do so would be to negate the very essence of human rights, which is counter-majoritarian – the protection of vulnerable and marginalized minorities. Commitment to human rights is not about getting mandates from dominant groups to protect the oppressed and persecuted; it is about protecting

---

[36] Interview with Hisham Kassem, director of the Egyptian Organisation for Human Rights by the British Broadcasting Corporation, http://news.bbc.co.uk/2/hi/middle_east/1813926.stm.

[37] Comments by Ndubisi Obiorah (senior legal officer at HURILAWS) at the conference, "Ethics in Action: The Successes, Compromises, and Setbacks of Transnational Human Rights and Humanitarian NGOs" organized by the United Nations University and the City University of Hong Kong, New York, February 2002.

[38] Personal communication with Raul Erinieo of the Philippine NGO, Project Protect, 26 June 2001.

the persecuted despite prevalent attitudes. A comparison can be made with the civil rights movement against racial segregation in the United States. Segregation was an established social, if not cultural, norm accepted and supported by a privileged majority. Its eventual breakdown came not by accommodationist strategies and the hope for gradual social reform but through a concerted and uncompromising civil rights movement that confronted head-on the inherent injustice of the system.

There are no easy responses to this dilemma. In cases in which INGOs have chosen the route of tackling gay and lesbian rights issues despite objections from local human rights groups, they have faced the familiar accusations of cultural arrogance and insensitivity. In Egypt, INGOs have been accused of leading "an international homosexual campaign" against the country.[39] In Malaysia, criticism of the role of INGOs during the trial of Anwar Ibrahim for homosexuality by the Mahathir Mohahmad government came not only from official sources but also from the local human rights community. This was particularly so when Human Rights Watch issued a press release listing ten human rights violations it observed in the course of the trial. Although most of these concerns were about due process and the right to counsel, HRW also condemned Malaysian sodomy laws and its selective application by the Mahathir government. When the HRW statement made the headlines of the leading Malay newspaper the next morning, it read: "Foreign Human Rights Group Supports Sodomy in Malaysia." As would be expected, the news caused public outrage in Malaysia's conservative society. But perhaps more important, the sodomy angle completely overshadowed the other nine substantive issues about due process that HRW has made about the trial itself. Malaysian gay and lesbian rights activists faulted the tone and timing of the HRW statement. Given the backlash generated by the statement, HRWs officials later acknowledged that they should have done more consultation with local activists before issuing the press release.[40] This underscores the need for INGOs to move away from the "West-centric" considerations that have traditionally shaped their methodologies and recognize the importance of local knowledge and values for their human rights work.

What is at issue here is not necessarily a conflict between HRW's objectives and those of local human rights activists. If anything, there is agreement on the core objectives of promoting human rights. The differences arise over how best to achieve these objectives. In Malaysia as elsewhere in South, HRW has done much to raise awareness about human rights and mobilize international support for local activists. Few will fault the organization's commitment to promoting human rights in these societies. However, its statement on Malaysian sodomy

[39] Editorial of the *Rose El-Youssef* weekly quoted on the British Broadcasting Corporation News Online, http://news.bbc.co.uk/2/hi/middle_east/1813926.stm.
[40] Personal communication with Joe Sunders, former HRW program officer for Malaysia, New York, 28 October 2002.

laws at the height of a politically charged trial was bound to be used by a regime, intent on deflecting criticism of its human rights record, to discredit opposition and human rights groups. It also played well into the hands of those eager to present the situation as a conflict between Malaysian and Western cultural values. Under these circumstances, would it have been more expedient for HRW to tone down its statement on sodomy? Perhaps. Would this have meant that HRW had compromised its human rights mandate? I think not. The larger point here is that INGOs do not necessarily compromise their broad human rights objective when they mediate their methods with local extenuating circumstances. Even in the quest to promote a universal rights agenda, INGOs need to consider the peculiarities of the sociocultural context in which they work and adopt strategies that will achieve the best results under such circumstances.

VII. ALTERNATIVE VISIONS

Human rights INGOs need to review and modify their mandates and strategies continually to meet the peculiar challenges they confront in the South. Their methods must respond to concerns about ideology, paternalism, and lopsidedness that have been raised in the South. They must do more to convince the skeptics who continue to challenge the legitimacy of their work and partners in the South who question their methods. To command more legitimacy in the South, INGOs must be seen as even-handed in their work – promoting ESC rights with as much vigor as they have traditionally promoted CP rights, addressing more seriously factors of globalization that affect human rights conditions in the South and balancing individual and communal rights advocacy. This latter point is important because the international human rights corpus from which INGOs take their cue tends to emphasize the individual at the expense of the community. There is need for a human rights approach that comprehensively unites the conflicting notions of individual and communal rights.

INGOs particularly need to do more to address human rights issues arising from globalization and underdevelopment in the South from broader international perspectives. They have not given enough attention to the rights of communities and states within the context of the international political economy. There issues are of particular importance to Third World societies where there is serious concern about such collective rights issues as the right of states and communities to "freely dispose of their wealth and natural resources" and their right to "economic, social and cultural development."[41] For instance, INGOs have not, in my view, adequately addressed the question of the rights of people in the South to the use and ownership of their natural resources. Recent attempts by Western transnational corporations to claim legal control and ownership of plants through patents, thereby limiting traditional uses of these natural resources, is a

---

[41] African Charter on Human and People's Rights, 1986 (see Articles 21 and 22).

vexed issue in many parts of the Third World. Governments and activists in the South have raised concerns about the West-centric character of the international patent system and its implications for the rights of peoples in the South to natural resources.

The commercial orientation and West-centric character of the patent system and international copyright regulations are factors that facilitate the appropriation and privatization of natural resources and their traditional uses, from the South by the North. This has significant implications not only for economic and cultural rights of Third World peoples but more broadly, their overall development. In deciding whether inventions relating to plants should be granted patent protection, there has been little consideration for the environmental safety and broader human rights implications of such inventions on developing societies, such as the "right" to food and a safe and sustainable environment.[42] This important issue, which is of growing concern to many advocacy groups in the South, has unfortunately taken a backseat on the agenda of human rights INGOs. Human rights INGOs have clearly not done enough to tackle this important issue, which affects the economic and social rights of many ordinary people in the South. Environmental groups such as Greenpeace, the World Wildlife Federation, and development oriented INGOs such as Médecins sans Frontières (MSF) and OXFAM have done significantly more than human rights INGOs in this regard. OXFAM, for instance, has been actively involved in campaigning for access to medicines in developing countries and against an international pharmaceutical patents regime that restricts the production of generic versions of vital life saving drugs. Because of the implications for development and living conditions in the South, INGOs need to do more to take up these issues on a human rights platform.

CONCLUSION

Advocacy across cultural barriers is often complex, particularly on the issue of human rights. Even at this, there is no evidence of a fundamental disconnect between the goals of Northern-based human rights INGOs and those of activists in the South. Within the global human rights movement, there appears to be broad agreement on the normative value of the universal human rights corpus. In most international advocacy platforms, Southern NGOs, from minority groups and environmental campaigners to human rights activists, have been the most frequent users of the rights language. These groups are often eager to work with Northern INGOs to achieve common objectives. For instance, despite the challenges to the universal human rights corpus at the 1992 World Conference on Human Rights in Vienna, NGOs from the North and South worked together

---

[42] See Ikechi Mgbeoji, "Patents and Traditional Knowledge of the Use of Plants: Is a Communal Patent Regime Part of the Solution to the Scourge of Bio Piracy?" *Indiana Journal of Global Legal Studies* (Vol. 9, No. 1, Fall 2001), 163–186.

on several lobby coalitions. The indication is that there is a sense of common understanding of the values, goals, and policies expressed by human rights activist from both the North and South.[43] Thus, although NGOs and activists within the human rights movement disagree on specific issues, they do so in a context of intensive interaction and debates.[44]

The argument here is that even within this context, INGOs continue to face challenges to their legitimacy from both hostile and supportive constituencies in the South. These challenges cannot simply be seen in terms of the tensions between universal human rights and local cultural norms. They run much deeper. To address them, INGOs need to be more responsive to the sociocultural peculiarities of the Southern communities in which they work by accommodating diversity in their agendas and methods. Human rights INGOs do not need to compromise their mandate of promoting universal human rights, but they do need to actively seek and offer non-Western political or moral foundations for them. They do not need to be apologetic about their work in the face of accusations of cultural imperialism from authoritarian rulers and privileged groups, but they need to take more seriously normative and empirical questions about lopsidedness in their work that have come from within their own constituencies in the South. INGOs can do more to avoid being seen as pushing a parochial liberal agenda alongside the mantra of universal human rights. They can do more to respect and represent local perspectives in their agendas and methodologies. INGOs and the message of human rights that they preach can draw legitimacy from both universal and local appeal. Only by localizing their methods and drawing more from the sociocultural experiences of local peoples can human rights INGOs address the continued challenges of relevance and legitimacy that they confront in the South.

---

[43] Kelvin Boyle, "Stocktaking on Human Rights: The World Conference on Human Rights, Vienna 1993," *Political Studies*, no. 43 (1995), 91.

[44] Clark and Friedman have rightly argued that the tensions within the human rights movement have not always been a question of geographic, economic, or sociocultural divides. The North–South divide partly overlaps with more persistent divisions between newer generations of small grassroots organizations focused on local action and the more professional and often larger INGOs. See Ann Marie Clark and Elisabeth J. Friedman, "The Sovereign Limits of Global Civil Society: A Comparison of NGO Participation in UN World Conferences on the Environment, Human Rights and Women," *World Politics* 51, no. 1 (1998), 34.

5 Dilemmas Facing NGOs in Coalition-Occupied Iraq

Lyal S. Sunga

Governments genuinely concerned about improving human rights and humanitarian conditions around the world have generally recognized the enormous
contribution of international nongovernmental organizations (NGOs) in reliev-
ing human suffering in time of armed conflict and natural disaster. Such governments have welcomed the rising influence of humanitarian NGOs and have
respected their independence, neutrality, and impartiality – attributes essential
for effective humanitarian NGO action.

Recently, however, certain Bush administration policies have forced humanitarian NGOs working in coalition-occupied Iraq to confront a number of vexing
ethical, political, theoretical, and practical dilemmas. The invasion of Iraq polar-
ized international public opinion and placed many traditional U.S. allies in clear
opposition to Bush administration policy. The coalition partners failed to convince the international community at large of the need to go to war or of the
genuineness of their war aims. By taking military action against Iraq without
clear approval from the United Nations (UN) Security Council, the Bush administration marginalized the UN and steered the course of U.S. foreign policy and
military operations toward a heavily unilateralist agenda that alienated the international community at large, including many international NGOs. As part of the
U.S. president's "you are either with us or against us" policy, the Bush administration tried to force international NGOs in Iraq to work almost as an arm of the
U.S. government, forcing them either to refrain completely from any criticism
of U.S. policy on Iraq, or risk being cut off from U.S. government funding and
support.

The present enquiry explores dilemmas relating to international humanitarian
NGO involvement in coalition-occupied Iraq as well as possible future implications for humanitarian NGOs working in other conflict zones under occupation. First, I review the contentious political atmosphere surrounding the U.S.-
led invasion of Iraq that involved vocal opposition from many international
humanitarian NGOs. I take note of early humanitarian NGO concern, registered

with the U.S. government even before the commencement of hostilities, to establish clear procedures for NGO cooperation with coalition forces so as to facilitate effective humanitarian assistance. Next, I consider the dilemmas NGOs had to face in connection with the U.S.-led occupation of Iraq. Finally, I consider the possible implications of the Iraq experience on the relationship of humanitarian NGOs with an occupying Power in future conflict zones.

I. THE HIGHLY CONTROVERSIAL INVASION AND OCCUPATION

Unconvincing Grounds for War

To understand the contentious relationship that developed between NGOs working in Iraq and the coalition subsequently occupying the country, it is essential to recall the United States and United Kingdom governments' stated reasons for attacking Iraq in the first place and the international reaction to it.

President Bush argued that armed force had to be deployed not only against Afghanistan, where the Taliban government had provided safe haven for Osama bin Laden, his Al Qaeda leadership and training camps, but also against Iraq to stem the threat of possible further attacks on the United States.[1] In his State of the Union Address of 29 January 2002, the president called Iraq, Iran, and North Korea "evil countries" that had to be forced to stop sponsoring terrorism. He resolved to prevent Iran, Iraq, and North Korea from acquiring chemical, biological, or nuclear weapons and then said that "States like these, and their terrorist allies, constitute an axis of evil, arming to threaten the peace of the world."[2]

---

[1] The 9/11 Commission noted that Richard Clarke, President Bush's National Counterterrorism Coordinator of the National Security Council, had "written that on the evening of September 12, President Bush told him and some of his staff to explore possible Iraqi links to 9/11. 'See if Saddam did this,' Clarke recalls the President telling them. 'See if he's linked in any way.' While he believed the details of Clarke's account to be incorrect, President Bush acknowledged that he might well have spoken to Clarke at some point, asking him about Iraq." In response, on 18 September 2001, Clarke sent a memo to Condoleeza Rice. The 9/11 Commission Report recounts, "Arguing that the case for links between Iraq and Al Qaeda was weak, the memo pointed out that Bin Laden resented the securalism of Saddam Hussein's regime. Finally, the memo said, there was no confirmed reporting on Saddam cooperating with Bin Ladin on unconventional weapons." See "The 9/11 Report: National Commission on Terrorist Attacks upon the United States: Authorized Edition," released on 22 July 2004, p. 334.

[2] See "President Delivers State of the Union Address: The United States Capitol Washington, DC," Office of the White House Press Secretary, 29 January 2002. The characterization of Iraq, Iran, and North Korea as an "axis of evil" drew ridicule from many at the time, including former U.S. Secretary of State Madeleine Albright who called the president's comments "a big mistake." NATO Secretary General Lord Robertson and Russian Prime Minister Mikhail Kasyanov expressed their doubts as to whether there existed any evidence to back up such a claim.

Many people in the human rights and humanitarian NGO community wondered from the outset whether the Bush administration's stated reasons for going to war against Iraq were little more than prevarications. Some of Bush's own advisors have claimed that, even prior to the 11 September 2001 terrorists attacks on the United States ("9/11"), Bush had intended to invade Iraq.[3] In any case, immediately after 9/11, Iraq found itself in the crosshairs of U.S. military attack planners.

It soon became clear that President Bush and Prime Minister Tony Blair had overstated both the likelihood of an active Iraqi chemical and biological weapons program as well as of any link between the government of Iraq and the 9/11 attacks on the other. Despite three weeks of intense lobbying from the White House, from the third week of February until mid-March 2003, even close U.S. allies remained unconvinced of a need to invade Iraq, particularly before UN weapons inspectors could determine whether Iraq really had an ongoing chemical or biological weapons program. The result was that the United States and United Kingdom failed to win UN Security Council approval for the use of military force against Iraq, but they decided to go ahead regardless.[4] The coalition's announcement that it would shortly commence aerial bombardment of Iraq forced UN weapons inspectors to leave Iraq on 18 March 2003.

Despite trenchant criticism from the international community at large, the United States launched Operation Iraqi Freedom on 19 March 2003 with heavy aerial bombardment of Baghdad and other major cities in Iraq, followed by the entry of ground troops into Iraqi territory the next day. By 9 April, Baghdad as well as Kirkuk and Tikrit fell to coalition forces, and in a 1 May 2003 publicity stunt, Bush co-piloted a U.S. Navy – S-3B Viking jet; landing aboard the aircraft carrier *USS Abraham Lincoln,* he announced "an end to major combat operations" in Iraq, in effect proclaiming U.S. victory.

From the beginning, however, even top military and intelligence officials had expressed their deep skepticism over the Bush–Blair justifications for war. In

---

[3] In "Bush Superficial and Lacking in Intellect, Claims O'Neill," *Reuters,* 15 January 2003, it was reported that in his new book titled *The Price of Loyalty,* Bush's former secretary of the U.S. Treasury Paul O'Neill claimed Bush began planning for an invasion of Iraq right after taking office – months before 9/11.

[4] "Bush Defends Quality of Intelligence Data Information for Speeches as 'Darn Good'," *Associated Press,* 15 July 2003. Because only Bulgaria and Spain indicated that they would vote for a UN Security Council resolution authorizing the use of military force against Iraq, the United States withdrew its draft resolution rather than face clear defeat in the Council on a vote. The coalition attack on Iraq could not be considered an act of self-defense, anticipatory or otherwise, because the Bush and Blair governments had failed to meet the minimum international law requirements as set out in the famous *Caroline Case.* In the *Caroline Case,* the governments of the United States and Great Britain agreed that the burden of proof was on the British government "to show a necessity of self-defence, instant, overwhelming, leaving no choice of means, and no moment for deliberation." See 29 *The British and Foreign State Papers* 1137–8; and 30 *The British and Foreign State Papers* 195–6 (1837).

July 2003, former director of the Central Intelligence Agency John Deutsch warned a congressional committee that if the coalition failed to find chemical or biological weapons in Iraq, this would constitute an intelligence failure of "massive proportions" because it would mean that the U.S. government attacked Iraq "on an incorrect intelligence judgment."[5] Similarly, Prime Minister Blair was called to appear before the Foreign Affairs Committee to discover whether the British government had disregarded the warnings of its own intelligence services not to exaggerate the Iraqi missile threat against neighboring countries and Israel.[6]

The coalition was never able to uncover any indications of an Iraqi program to produce chemical or biological weapons, much less weapons capable of posing any threat to the United States or United Kingdom. Unfortunately, the U.S. administration did not seem to appreciate at the time that forcing UN weapons inspectors out of Iraq would naturally degrade information gathering since the United States had become reliant over several years on imagery collection and mapping with the aid of spy satellites, electronic intercepts, and signals intelligence generally, rather than firsthand human intelligence collection and analysis.[7] Despite all this, U.S. Vice-President Dick Cheney and U.S. Attorney General John Ashcroft continued to insist for months that Iraq had possessed biological, chemical, or nuclear weapons capability shortly before the coalition's March 2003 invasion,[8] despite a lack of any reliable evidence to support this

[5]   See Brian Knowlton, "Bush Aide Defends 'Murky Intelligence' on Terror as Norm," *International Herald Tribune,* 28 July 2003. By the beginning of February 2004, Bush was forced to promise to call an independent inquiry into intelligence failures on Iraq, and Blair had to face the same music. See "Sources: Bush to Order WMD Intelligence Inquiry: Independent Probe Has Bipartisan Support," *CNN,* 2 February 2004; and "Blair to Hold Inquiry on War Intelligence," *Agence France-Presse,* 4 February 2004.

[6]   Top civil servants had to explain why they relied on a graduate thesis they found on the Internet that contained outdated information gathered from 1991 Operation Desert Storm to support the government's claims that Iraq had an ongoing chemical and biological weapons program. "Top Aide Admits UK Erred in Crafting Case against Iraq," *Associated Press,* 26 June 2003. Not only that, Blair's former foreign secretary, Robin Cook, submitted his resignation over the British government's decision to attack Iraq and disclosed publicly that Blair had stated to him just two weeks before the coalition attack on Iraq that he knew Iraq posed no immediate threat to the United Kingdom. See Warren Hoge, "Cook Diary Casts Doubt on Blair," *International Herald Tribune,* 6 October 2003. Hoge reports that "An intelligence dossier published last September argued that Iraq had unconventional weapons that could be used within 45 minutes of an order being given. Cook said that he had no reason to doubt that Blair believed the claim at the time it was made, but that in their conversation on March 5, Blair told him the weapons were only battlefield munitions and could not be assembled by Saddam for quick use because of 'all the effort he has put into concealment.' "

[7]   The 9/11 Commission has recommended, among other things, the restructuring of U.S. national intelligence agencies, the rebuilding of CIA human intelligence collection and analysis capabilities, and transformation of the clandestine service. See "The 9/11 Report: National Commission on Terrorist Attacks upon the United States: Authorized Edition," released on 22 July 2004, p. 415.

[8]   See Brian Knowlton, "In Rebuttal, US Insists War Was Justified," *International Herald Tribune,* 27 January 2004; and "Cheney's Myopia," *International Herald Tribune,* 28 January 2004.

hypothesis. Even the chief of the U.S. government's own weapons inspections team, David Kay,[9] stated publicly that he did not believe Iraq possessed such capability in the period leading up to the coalition's March 2003 invasion of Iraq or that such weapons could possibly have been shunted to Syria during that time.[10] On 13 January 2005, a U.S. government spokesperson announced that U.S. weapons inspectors were ending their search for weapons of mass destruction, while President Bush continued to defend the coalition's use of military force in Iraq.[11]

U.S. and coalition casualties continued to mount in Iraq such that by the end of August 2003, more soldiers had died since Bush had declared an end to major combat operations on 1 May 2003 than during the declared war itself.[12] On 17 January 2004, the number of U.S. soldiers killed during Operation Iraqi Freedom reached 500 when three soldiers died in a roadside bombing near Baghdad.[13] A little more than a year later, the highest number of U.S. soldiers killed in a single incident since the start of the war transpired with the death of thirty-seven soldiers in a helicopter crash near the Iraq–Jordan border, which brought the number of dead U.S. soldiers to 1,418 out of which 1,085 were attributed to hostile action.[14] In the first week of August 2005 alone, twenty seven U.S. soldiers were killed, bringing the total of U.S. troops by 5 August 2005 to 1,825.

To put things into better perspective, one has to take account also of civilian casualties in Iraq, which U.S. military authorities, as a matter of official policy, do not count.[15] Extensive research carried out by Iraq Body Count – an NGO based in London that has been analyzing a wide range of media accounts on civilian casualties in Iraq since the war began in March 2003, reported in July

---

[9] David Kay was director of the U.S. government's Iraq Survey Group, run jointly by the Central Intelligence Agency and the Pentagon.

[10] "Kay: No Evidence Iraq Stockpiled WMDs: Former Chief US Inspector Faults Intelligence Agencies," *CNN*, 26 January 2004.

[11] "Official: U.S. Calls Off Search for Iraqi WMDs, Bush Stands by Decision to Go to War, Spokesman Says," *CNN*, 13 January 2005.

[12] The *Washington Post* reported that "Since the war began on March 19, a total of 470 service members have died in Iraq: 325 were killed in action, and 145 died in non-hostile circumstances involving accidents and suicides. The number killed in action in the war's counterinsurgency phase, 210, is nearly twice the 115 battlefield fatalities during major combat operations. . . . The number of soldiers wounded in action totaled 2,333, with an additional 370 injured in non-hostile circumstances. The total wounded in action in counterinsurgency operations, 1,783, is now more than three times the 550 wounded in action during major combat operations." See Vernon Loeb, "In Iraq, Pace of US Casualties Has Accelerated," *Washington Post*, 28 December 2003, p. A01.

[13] "US Death Toll in Iraq Tops 500: Blast North of Baghdad Kills 3 American Soldiers, 2 Iraqis," *CNN*, 19 January 2004.

[14] "Deadliest Day for US in Iraq War," *CNN*, 27 January 2005.

[15] U.S. General Tommy Franks declared at a press conference in April 2003 on Afghanistan that "We don't do body counts." See "Casualties in the Iraq War," *CBC News On-Line*, 27 July 2005 (updated); and also Derrick Z. Jackson, "US Stays Blind to Iraqi Casualties," *Boston Globe*, 14 November 2003.

2005 that by March 2005, almost 25,000 civilians in Iraq had been killed.[16] A year later, in a 19 March 2006 interview with the British Broadcasting Corporation, former Prime Minister of Iraq Mr. Iyad Allawi characterized the situation in Iraq as one of civil war, rather than of mere instability, criminality or sporadic violence: "It is unfortunate that we are in civil war. We are losing each day as an average 50 to 60 people throughout the country, if not more. If this is not civil war, then God knows what civil war is."[17] By April 2006, Iraq Body Count estimated that civilian deaths in Iraq had reached somewhere between 34,511 and 38,660.[18]

NGOs Criticize the Decision to Go to War

Returning to the period leading up to the launch of the war, it is important to recall that the Bush–Blair arguments for invading and occupying Iraq were vociferously denounced by the international NGO community at large. Months before the start of the Iraq war, many human rights and humanitarian NGOs lined up against the Bush administration's bellicose policy.[19] For example, CARE International embarked on a lengthy political campaign opposing the use of force against Iraq that involved the lobbying of Security Council members in February 2003 not to authorize the planned U.S. invasion, testimony to the British House of Commons' International Development Committee, a million-strong march in London, adoption of joint policy positions with Save the Children and Christian Aid, and, in July 2003, representations to the relevant U.S. congressional committee.[20] Other NGOs banded together in a concerted "stop the war" effort that included Islamic Relief, Christian Aid, Tearfund, Amnesty International, and Oxfam.[21]

A few days before the war began, a broad coalition of NGOs urged the Security Council to prevent the unlawful use of force against a UN member State[22] and

---

[16] In its report "A Dossier of Civilian Casualties: 2003–2005" (2005, p. 10), Iraq Body Count reports that "US-led forces were sole killers of 37% of civilian victims; Criminals killed 36% of all civilians; Anti-occupation forces were sole killers of 9% of civilian victims; and US military forces accounted for 98.5% of 'coalition' killings."

[17] "Iraq in civil war, says former PM," BBC, 19 March 2006.

[18] See the Internet Web site of Iraq Body Count at http://www.iraqbodycount.net/ (27 April 2006).

[19] See, for example, press release of the North-South Institute, "Canadian NGOs Underscore Centrality of the United Nations in Dispute over Iraq," 19 September 2002.

[20] The full name of the committee is the United States Congressional Committee on Government Reform, Subcommittee on National Security, Emerging Threats and International Relations, Humanitarian Assistance following Military Operations.

[21] See, for example, "Statement on Iraq by CARE International Secretary General Denis Caillaux," 21 February 2003, http://www.careinternational.org.uk (last accessed 4 February 2005, using the CARE Web site search engine).

[22] International Progress Organization, "Call by International NGOs for Invoking Uniting for Peace Resolution," Press Release /P/RE/18121c-is (Vienna) 27 March 2003. The International Progress Organization is a Vienna-based NGO with ECOSOC consultative status.

called on UN member states to invoke the Uniting for Peace resolution. Adoption of this resolution would have allowed the General Assembly to convene an emergency session on the grounds that the Security Council was unable to discharge its responsibilities to maintain international peace and security.[23]

Prior to the commencement of armed hostilities, American-based NGOs met with U.S. government officials on several occasions to clarify the extent to which NGOs could operate freely inside Iraq, whether the UN would be free to assist in NGO coordination, and whether NGOs would be required to deal with the Pentagon instead of the U.S. State Department. According to NGO representatives who participated in these negotiations, U.S. government officials offered funds to NGOs at this juncture but insisted on the formation of a clear chain of command between U.S. authorities and NGOs – an early bad omen for NGOs intending to work in Iraq.[24]

Humanitarian NGOs Stream into Iraq

The overthrow of the government of Iraq swept away its restrictive procedures for NGO access and flung the door wide open for peace activists and NGOs of every kind and description to enter the country and set up operations. It is therefore difficult to get an accurate picture either of the precise number of NGOs or their representatives that streamed into Iraq as the coalition took over or of their degree of seriousness. A quick look at the list of NGOs that registered with the UN Assistance Mission in Iraq (UNAMI) gives an idea of the range and diversity of humanitarian NGOs working in coalition-occupied Iraq and the need for their effective coordination.[25]

---

[23] Thalif Deen, "Iraq: NGOs Decry 'Bribes' and 'Threats' Behind UN Vote," Inter Press Service News Agency, 22 May 2003.

[24] Larry Minear, "A Moment of Truth for the Humanitarian Enterprise," *The Progressive Response* 7, no. 21 (16 July 2003).

[25] By 15 January 2004, UNAMI listed the following international NGOs working in Iraq registered with it: ACTED; Action Contre la Faim; Aide Médicale International; Amnesty International; arche noVa – initiative for people in need; Architects for People in Need; Atlas Logistique; CAFOD; Cap Anamur; CARE International; Caritas International; Cesvi – World Aid from Italy; Christian Aid; Cooperazione e Sviluppo; Counterpart International; DanChurchAid; Danish Refugee Committee; Dortmunden Helfen Kurden; Dutch Consortium; Enfants du Monde – Droits de l'Homme; Food for the Hungry International; France Libertés; Fundação Assistência Médica Internacional; Global Hope Network; GOAL; Handicap International; Help from Germany; HelpAge International; Human Rights Watch; IKNN; International Medical Corps; International Rescue Committee; InterSOS; Islamic International Relief Organisation; Islamic Kurdish League; Islamic Relief; Islamic Relief Agency; Islamic Relief Worldwide; Italian Consortium of Solidarity; Japan Emergency NGOs; Johanniter-International Germany; Korea Peace Team; Kurdish Human Rights Watch; Kurdish Life Aid; Life for Relief and Development; Makkalmukarrama Charity Trust; Malteser; Medair; Médecins du Monde Belgium; Médecins du Monde Canada; Médecins du Monde Espagne; Médecins du Monde France; Médecins du Monde Greece; Médecins sans Frontières Belgium; Médecins sans Frontières France; Médecins sans Frontières Holland; Mercy

II. COALITION AUTHORITIES MARGINALIZE NGOs WORKING IN IRAQ

The Pentagon versus Humanitarian NGOs

The prewar concerns of humanitarian NGOs over their independence, neutrality, and impartiality quickly proved well founded as the White House ran Operation Iraqi Freedom through the Pentagon rather than the State Department. The Pentagon adopted a hard-line approach to humanitarian NGOs and showed little interest in cooperating with them. By 1 April 2003, a coalition of NGOs working in Iraq complained bitterly that the U.S. government was seriously marginalizing humanitarian NGOs:

> In an unusually tough statement, InterAction – which with 160 members is the largest US alliance of non-governmental relief groups – expressed deep concern about military-driven plans for bringing humanitarian aid to Iraq. . . . "The Department of Defence's efforts to marginalize the State Department and force non-governmental organizations to operate under DOD jurisdiction complicates our ability to help the Iraqi people and multiplies the dangers faced by relief workers in the field," said InterAction CEO Mary McClymont. She said relief professionals at the State Department and the US Agency for International Development, not the Pentagon's military establishment, know best how to conduct emergency assistance operations. "Having been deeply involved for decades with non-governmental organizations that provide humanitarian assistance around the world, USAID and [the] State [Department] are familiar with the principles of independence and impartiality under which we must operate," she said.[26]

The White House policy to bring humanitarian aid to Iraq through the Department of Defense meant that soldiers were assigned to carry out humanitarian tasks in addition to their usual military duties. This policy mixed prosecution of war aims with humanitarian objectives, and it may well have lent the erroneous impression to the Iraqi public that NGOs cooperating with coalition forces supported the invasion and occupation. The problem was exacerbated at the logistical level by strict U.S. Army rules on NGO liaison and cooperation:

> "People are upset. They do not want to report to the military," one agency official said. . . . One problem involves Pentagon plans to require aid workers to wear military-issued identification tags. "We said we won't do it," the official said. "The military needs to have confidence that people are genuine aid workers but the answer is not to slap a military ID on them," he added.[27]

Corps; Mercy International; Merlin; Middle East Council of Churches; Middle East Development Service; Mines Advisory Group; Mission Enfance; North West Medical Teams; Norwegian Church Aid; Norwegian Peoples' Aid; Oxfam; Peace Winds Japan; Premiere Urgence; Qandil; REACH; Response, Relief, Resettlement & Rehabilitation; Save the Children (US/UK); Save the Children UK; Solidarités; STEP; Telecoms sans Frontières; Terre des Hommes; Turk ve Ortadogu Dayanisma Vakfi; Turkmeneli Cooperation & Cultural Fdn.; Un Ponte Per; War Child; Washington Kurdish Institute; World Assembly of Muslim Youth; and World Vision.

[26] Carol Giacomo, "Aid Groups Oppose Pentagon Control of Aid Effort," *Alertnet*, 1 April 2003.
[27] Ibid.

However, if humanitarian NGOs thought that they were going to get better treatment from USAID than from the Pentagon, they were in for a rude surprise.

USAID's Ultimatum to NGOs

On 21 May 2003, USAID administrator Andrew Natsios indicated that NGOs receiving USAID funding had to "agree to clear any and all publicity or media-related matters tied to their funded-activities through USAID first and to repeatedly and consistently publicize the US government's funding of their efforts throughout each phase of their on-the-ground service delivery, *reflecting the Administration's belief that recipients of federal grants are agents of the US government and its policies.*"[28] On 27 May 2003, five major U.S.-based NGOs, namely, Agricultural Cooperative Development International and Volunteers in Overseas Cooperative Assistance (ACDI/VOCA), Cooperative Housing Foundation International, International Relief and Development, Mercy Corps, and Save the Children (U.S.), that had received US $7 million each in initial funding from USAID[29] were pressured to agree to a clause that reportedly read "Contact with the news media, in the United States or overseas, shall be notified to and coordinated with" USAID press officers.[30] USAID's policy to co-opt humanitarian NGOs was emphatically restated by the USAID administrator in the InterAction forum as the *Financial Times* reported:

> According to notes taken by InterAction officials, Mr Natsios described NGOs and private contractors fulfilling US government contracts as 'an arm of the US government'. Unless they improved their performance and did a better job of promoting their contacts to the US administration, the government would cut off funding, he warned.[31]

The conditions on USAID-funded NGOs formed part of the Bush administration's overall strategy of political favoritism in reconstruction and assistance[32] to Iraq as a foreign policy tool to shift the balance of power in the Middle East. A clear pattern emerged in the selection of businesses almost exclusively from European

---

[28] Jonathan Wright, "NGOs Feel the Squeeze from Bush Administration," *Reuters*, 24 June 2003 [emphasis added].

[29] See "USAID Awards Grants for Iraq Community Action Program," USAID Press Release, 27 May 2003.

[30] See Richard Read, "Aid Agencies Reject Money Due to Strings," *Oregonian*, 6 June 2003.

[31] Alan Beattie, "NGOs Under Pressure on Relief Funds," *Financial Times*, 13 June 2003.

[32] The major part of the lucrative reconstruction contracts were allocated to the American conglomerate Bechtel, which the U.S. government awarded around US $680 million in contracts, along with certain British companies. Egypt lobbied the U.S. government insistently for a share. U.S. officials assured close allies Kuwait and Saudi Arabia that they would receive a good share of the contracts to be handed out. In contrast, Syria stood little chance to gain from any contracts owing to its strained relations with Washington. "Citing Past Work in Iraq, Arab Nations Vie for Contracts," *Associated Press*, 10 September 2003.

countries that supported the Iraq invasion.[33] Corporations in European countries where governments had opposed coalition intervention in Iraq worried that the U.S. government would prevent them from cashing in on an estimated US $1 billion at stake in potential business in Iraq.[34]

The Bush administration's divisive attitude to the rebuilding of Iraq forced NGOs either to disagree publicly with those U.S. government policies or to accept USAID funding quietly for Iraq-related activities and surrender their prerogative to criticize U.S. policy. Not all NGOs could agree to such restrictions. Several NGOs, including International Rescue Committee, CARE, and World Vision, made the difficult decision not to seek USAID funding under these conditions.[35]

The dilemma over government funding and NGO independence split the NGO community and could be seen clearly in the example of disagreement over the issue between Save the Children (U.S.) and Save the Children (UK). *The Guardian* reported that

> One of Britain's most high-profile charities was ordered to end criticism of military action in Iraq by its powerful US wing to avoid jeopardising financial support from Washington and corporate donors, a *Guardian* investigation has discovered. Internal emails reveal how Save the Children UK came under enormous pressure after it accused coalition forces of breaching the Geneva convention by blocking humanitarian aid. Senior figures at Save the Children US, based in Westport, Connecticut, demanded the withdrawal of the criticism and an effective veto on any future statements blaming the invasion for the plight of Iraqi civilians suffering malnourishment and shortages of medical supplies. Uncovered documents expose tensions within an alliance that describes itself as 'the world's largest independent global organisation for children' but which is heavily reliant on governments and big business for cash. Save the Children UK, which had an income of £122 m in 2002–03, boasts the Queen as patron and Princess Anne as president, plus a phalanx of the great and the good lending their titles and time. The row over Iraq erupted in April when the London statement said coalition forces had gone back on an earlier agreement to allow a relief plane, packed with emergency food and medical supplies for 40,000 people, to land in northern Iraq.[36]

Almost two-thirds of the Save the Children (US) budget came from grants and contracts with the U.S. government.[37]

---

[33] Some experts estimated that the award of contracts to rebuild Iraq could double the projected increase in the GNP for Poland – a country that supported the coalition's war policies – from 1.3% to almost 3%. See Brian Whitmore, "Poland Hopes Rebuilding Iraq Will Aid Economy," *Boston Globe*, 11 June 2003.

[34] Joseph Fitchett, "Rewards and Punishments in the Rebuilding of Postwar Iraq," *International Herald Tribune*, 3 April 2003.

[35] Richard Read, "Aid Agencies Reject Money Due to Strings," *Oregonian*, 6 June 2003.

[36] Kevin Maguire, "How British Charity Was Silenced on Iraq," *Guardian*, 28 November 2003.

[37] To respond to the damaging *Guardian* article, Save the Children (UK) proclaimed its commitment to impartiality and independence from government in an official response posted on its Web site. *See* "Save the Children UK Not Silenced on Iraq," *Press Release*, 28 November 2003, posted

NGO Watch Watches NGOs

In a parallel development, it could not go unnoticed that in June 2003, a conservative institute with close ties to the Bush administration created a new organization called NGO Watch. Many influential senior officials in the Bush administration's Departments of State and Justice had been recruited from the American Enterprise Institute and the Federalist, which together founded NGO Watch.[38] It was reported that

> Having led the charge to war in Iraq, an influential think tank close to the Bush administration has added a new target: international non-governmental organizations (NGOs). The American Enterprise Institute (AEI) is setting its sights on those groups with a progressive or liberal agenda that favors global governance and other notions that are also promoted by the United Nations and other multilateral agencies. AEI and another right-wing group, the Federalist Society for Law and Public Policy Studies, announced Wednesday they are launching a new website (http://www.NGOWatch.org) to expose the funding, operations and agendas of international NGOs, and particularly their alleged efforts to constrain US freedom of action in international affairs and influence the behaviour of corporations abroad.[39]

Significantly, NGO Watch's Web site states its concern that:

> NGO officials and their activities are widely cited in the media and relied upon in congressional testimony; corporations regularly consult with NGOs prior to major investments. Many groups have strayed beyond their original mandates and have assumed quasi-governmental roles. Increasingly, non-governmental organizations are not just accredited observers at international organizations, they are full-fledged decision-makers. . . . Throughout much of the world, non-governmental organizations are unregulated, and are spared any requirement to account for expenditures, to disclose activities or sources of funding, or even to declare their officers. That is not the case in the United States, where the tax code affords the public some transparency about its NGOs. But where is the rest of the story? Do NGOs influence international organizations like the World Trade Organization? What are their agendas? Who runs these groups? Who funds them? And to whom are they accountable?[40]

Some journalists wondered whether NGO Watch might be a wolf in sheep's clothing whose list of NGOs might in fact be a "McCarthyite blacklist, telling tales on any NGO that dares speak against Bush administration policies or in support of international treaties opposed by the White House."[41]

---

at http://www.savethechildren.org.uk, last accessed 4 February 2005, using the CARE Web site search engine.

[38] See also "Holding NGOs to Account," *Christian Science Monitor*, 15 January 2004.

[39] Jim Lobe, "Think Tank Turns Wrath on NGOs," *Inter-Press Service*, 12 June 2003.

[40] *See* "Information Page" of NGO Watch's Web site at www.NGOWatch.org, last accessed 4 February 2005.

[41] Naomi Klein, "Bush to NGOs: Watch Your Mouths," *Globe and Mail*, 24 June 2003.

III. DILEMMAS OF NGO INVOLVEMENT
IN COALITION-OCCUPIED IRAQ

The Bush–Blair military action against Iraq marginalized the UN and the humanitarian NGO community in the process. The strong-arm tactics of the Pentagon and USAID together with the establishment of NGO Watch amount to a concerted attempt to muzzle humanitarian NGOs working in the country.

The dilemmas for NGOs basically arose as follows: political advocacy or neutral humanitarian assistance; independent NGO action or dependency on UN coordination; and neutral access or coalition security. Behind each of these dilemmas, explored subsequently, lurks menacingly the tension between NGO acceptance of substantial government funding and the risk that NGOs cannot maintain their independence from government under these conditions.

Political Advocacy or Neutral Humanitarian Assistance?

Not to speak out against the launch of war – an event that inevitably causes or worsens humanitarian situations – or to refrain from criticizing violations during armed conflict that cause human suffering, in many cases would seem blatantly unethical. However, an NGO's denunciation of a government's violations can undercut the NGO's provision of humanitarian assistance on a politically neutral and impartial basis at ground level.

This ethical dilemma involves also difficult political and practical dilemmas for NGOs. Humanitarian NGOs can work much more effectively where they form part of an overall, integrated approach to reconstruction and relief efforts so as to avoid duplication and maximize the effective use of scarce resources in their totality.[42] For example, it makes little sense for NGOs to expend their time and energy trying to extend humanitarian assistance where the destruction of roads and bridges have rendered access impossible or where other logistical preconditions have not been met. At the practical level, coordination and integration in relief efforts requires cooperation among UN agencies, bodies, and programs, country authorities, and humanitarian NGOs. However, highly critical NGO political advocacy can jeopardize such coordination and cooperation, particularly when NGOs have to rely on occupation Powers for security and other forms of logistical support to gain access to people in need of humanitarian assistance.

---

[42] The problem of coordination among humanitarian NGOs arises in many other major relief operations, for example, those dealing with the aftermath of the Indian Ocean tsunami that claimed the lives of perhaps a quarter of a million people on 26 December 2004. See Stephanie Strom, "Asia's Deadly Waves: Coordination amid Good Intentions, Aid Workers Try to Bring Order to the Generosity," *New York Times*, 3 January 2005.

Putting it another way, the dilemma between speaking out against the use of violence to solve international disputes can conflict with effective NGO provision of humanitarian assistance once war has started. If humanitarian assistance should be politically neutral and impartial, then, arguably, opposing the onset of hostilities itself involves humanitarian NGOs in a political dispute with the occupying Power. If NGOs are seen as opponents of the war, they risk being shut out of occupying Power operational strategy and planning, as NGOs in fact have been in coalition-occupied Iraq, and this can severely hamper the aid effort. Access under security provided by armed forces almost always comes at a price, and that price can be the image if not the fact of neutrality and impartiality, as discussed later in this chapter.

One way to solve this dilemma could be to adopt the approach taken by the International Committee of the Red Cross (ICRC), which, although neither an intergovernmental organization nor an NGO, exemplifies a strictly neutral and impartial approach to humanitarian relief operations in war zones. The ICRC refuses to take any side in hostilities or engage at any time in any political, racial, religious, or ideological controversy whatsoever. On this basis, the ICRC has been more successful than any intergovernmental or nongovernmental body in gaining the confidence and respect of all sides to an armed conflict. This in turn has afforded ICRC delegates an unrivalled degree of access to detainees, prisoners of war, refugees, internally displaced persons, and other persons protected by the Geneva Conventions of 1949.[43] The ICRC's unique history, image, and role make it difficult for humanitarian NGOs to emulate its example, however.

Would humanitarian NGOs be willing to give up political advocacy to guard their neutrality and impartiality in the field? Probably not. Political advocacy forms an essential activity for many NGOs. Aside from its obvious value as an instrument to influence decision making on the part of governments and intergovernmental organizations, it also enhances public visibility, helps to generate funds, and increases membership. Moreover, many humanitarian NGOs might consider that, in any case, armed conflict zones inevitably involve NGOs in politically controversial issues. For any NGO wishing to speak out on political issues, the ICRC's approach of strict neutrality again would be difficult to follow.

Independent NGO Action or Dependency on UN Coordination?

As discussed earlier, an important component of effective humanitarian NGO action lies in good coordination and a certain minimum level of basic logistical support including security. Because of strained relations between coalition authorities and the humanitarian community, NGOs had to rely more heavily on

---

[43] Geneva Conventions, *adopted* 12 August 1949, *entered into force* 21 October 1950.

the presence of the UN to facilitate their work. When security conditions forced the UN to reduce its presence in Iraq, humanitarian NGOs again had to depend on coalition authorities for security, which raised fresh dilemmas.

In his report of 15 July 2003, UN Secretary General Kofi Annan expressed his concerns over the deteriorating security situation in Iraq,[44] noting that three of eighteen governates were deemed "off-limits" to UN personnel and that

> [t]he work of the United Nations humanitarian agencies is further impeded by the massive presence of explosive ordnance, mines and unexploded ordnance, which pose an immediate humanitarian threat to the local population. A sharp increase has been recorded in the number of casualties, as a result of people tampering with stockpiles and caches of munitions. Freshly laid landmines, and submunitions used during the recent conflict, have exacerbated a serious existing problem of landmine and unexploded ordnance contamination.[45]

Significantly, the Secretary General also recounted that although UN personnel had not yet come under direct attack, "One exception to this was an incident in Basra on 17 June when a crowd trapped two United Nations vehicles, apparently not distinguishing the United Nations from the [coalition] Authority."[46]

In mid-August 2003, the UN Security Council, concerned about the deteriorating security conditions, adopted resolution 1500[47] establishing UNAMI from 1 September 2003.

On 19 August 2003, a truck bomb was exploded at the UN Headquarters in Baghdad, claiming the lives of twenty-two persons, including that of Sergio Vieira de Mello, who served as both the Secretary General's Special Representative for Iraq and the UN High Commissioner for Human Rights. Another 130 others were injured, many severely. On 22 September, the UN compound suffered another bombing that took the life of an Iraqi policeman and left a further nineteen wounded.[48] These horrendous attacks forced the UN to reduce drastically its presence in Iraq, severely hampering the ongoing humanitarian relief efforts of intergovernmental agencies and NGOs.[49]

---

[44] See Report of the Secretary-General Pursuant to Paragraph 24 of Security Council resolution 1483 (2003); S/2003/715 of 17 July 2003.

[45] Ibid, paragraph 31.

[46] Ibid, paragraph 32.

[47] S/Res/1500(2003) of 14 August 2003, was adopted following the UN Secretary General's report of 15 July 2003 on the situation in Iraq (S/2003/715). The resolution recalls all the Council's previous relevant resolutions, in particular resolution 1483 (2003) of 22 May 2003 in which the Council, acting under Chapter VII of the Charter of the United Nations, *inter alia*, appealed to all member States and concerned organizations to assist the people of Iraq to rebuild their country.

[48] "UN Cuts Iraq Staff after Second Bombing," *Associated Press*, 26 September 2003.

[49] Brian Knowlton, "More UN Workers Told to Quit Iraq: But Annan Stops Short of Full Pullout: Reductions Hinder US Efforts to Get Aid," *International Herald Tribune*, 26 September 2003.

Once the United Nations evacuated its staff from Iraq, many NGO personnel felt demoralized and decided they also had to leave. Agence France Presse
reported that

> Many of the humanitarian NGOs operating in Iraq also cut back, or even closed
> down, following the August 19 attack on the UN offices at the Canal Hotel. But
> according to officials of those still operating here, housed in discrete hotels, protected
> by local security guards, NGO personnel are being subjected to violence on the roads,
> are being threatened by unknown extremists and even having grenades thrown at
> their offices.[50]

Given the radically scaled down UN presence in Iraq, and the coalition's failure to
secure general conditions of security throughout Iraq, international NGOs could
not realistically take their own chances, which in many cases meant they could not
continue with their humanitarian assistance missions without coalition security.
Yet, as discussed in the next section, NGO reliance on the coalition for security
pitted this reality against the ideal of neutral access.

Neutral Access or Coalition Security?

Humanitarian NGOs have had to choose whether to speak out against coalition action in Iraq at a time when they also have to rely on coalition authorities for security. Once the image of NGO neutrality has been weakened, it can
be difficult or impossible to restore, and the taint of partiality can make all
humanitarian NGOs direct targets of armed hostilities. At the same time, governments waging war have themselves increasingly mixed politics with humanitarian
assistance.

This point was further driven home with the bombing of the ICRC Headquarters in Baghdad on 27 October 2003. Médecins sans Frontières (MSF) issued
an angry statement that declared that humanitarian NGOs in Iraq were not
participants in the war against terrorism and blamed the U.S. government for
worsening the confusion.[51] MSF complained in particular that U.S. Secretary
of State Colin Powell had linked the continuing presence of NGOs in Iraq as

---

[50] Beatriz Lecumberri, "As UN Pulls Out of Iraq, NGOs Lose Heart," *Agence France-Presse*, 26
September 2003.
[51] "MSF Statement on Independent Humanitarian Aid in Iraq: We Are Not Actors in the War on
Terrorism," Médecins sans Frontières Press Release, 31 October 2003. MSF reiterated that "We
are not part of the US-led Coalition in Iraq nor actors in the war on terrorism or any other war.
Those responsible for the attack on the ICRC have made it even more difficult than before for
independent aid organizations to continue providing assistance to the Iraqi people.... And, each
time politicians describe humanitarian aid as an instrument of foreign policy or ask humanitarian organizations to take sides in a conflict, our independence – upon which the safety of
our staff and the future of our ability to offer assistance to those in need depends – is further
eroded."

an indicator of the coalition's supposed success in establishing normal conditions, which identified NGOs with U.S. policy and thereby unnecessarily politicized NGO work throughout the country. MSF felt obliged to distance itself
from the coalition as far as possible to preserve its neutrality and independence
from it:

> Actions and statements made by Western officials, however, have only contributed
> to the vulnerability of humanitarian organizations to attacks. Western officials con-
> stantly attempt to include humanitarian action as part of their "good" political inten-
> tions in intervening in other people's countries.... Whether dropping "humani-
> tarian" food packets while simultaneously unloading bombs from warplanes over
> Afghanistan or deploying military personnel in vehicles marked "humanitarian
> assistance" in Iraq, the US's attempt to partially justify its military goals as "human-
> itarian" has seriously undermined the very principle of true humanitarian action:
> unconditional provision of assistance to those in need without taking sides in a
> conflict.[52]

Even before the attack on the ICRC headquarters, other international NGOs had
registered their concern that the deployment of armed forces from their own
countries could render humanitarian NGO workers more difficult to distinguish
from military personnel and could make NGOs more likely targets of attack.[53]
Ultimately, many NGOs considered that they could no longer work under such
conditions and left the country.[54]

Terrorists have shown no qualms about attacking any target of opportunity,
regardless of whether it kills or maims civilian men, women, or children, including Arabs and Muslims. The impact of the indiscriminate character of terrorism
on the humanitarian NGO community in Iraq was graphically illustrated with
the abduction of Margaret Hassan on 19 October 2004 and her probable mur-
der some three weeks later.[55] Hassan, a British–Iraqi national, had dedicated
almost thirty years of her life to providing humanitarian assistance to the Iraqi
people as director of CARE (Iraq). She had converted to Islam, spoke fluent
Arabic, and was noted for her staunch criticism of UN sanctions against Iraq.[56]
Terrorist attacks are easier to carry out where there is support from the general
public, however, and this support depends very much on perceptions of legitimacy, which brings us back to the issue of NGO independence, neutrality, and
impartiality.

---

[52] Ibid.
[53] Shinya Ajima, "Japanese NGOs in Iraq Worried about SDF Dispatch," *Kyodo News*, 5 July 2003.
[54] "Stay or Go: The Question for NGOs in Iraq," *Deutsche Welle*, 28 October 2003, available at
http://www.dw-world.de (last accessed 4 February 2005 under "Current Affairs").
[55] As of April 2006, Margaret Hassan's body had still not been recovered.
[56] See Jason Burke, "Margaret Hassan: 1944–2004," *The Guardian*, 17 November 2004.

CONCLUSION: FUTURE IMPLICATIONS FOR INTERNATIONAL HUMANITARIAN NGOs WORKING IN CONFLICT ZONES

The choice between political advocacy and politically neutral humanitarian assistance does not always have to take the form of a serious dilemma for humanitarian NGOs. Effective humanitarian assistance frequently does require NGOs to draw international attention to the plight of persons in need of urgent care. NGO advocacy on behalf of victims of starvation, flood, war, or other disaster, hardly seems political in the sense that no moral person could seriously dispute the goodness of the humanitarian cause at stake, even if one could disagree about means and approach. More difficult issues arise where NGOs criticize governments for the use of military force that worsens the humanitarian situation or involves the occupying Power in such violations of human rights and humanitarian law as those perpetrated in Abu Ghraib prison,[57] while at the same time remaining reliant on the same governments for funding, security, access to certain zones in the territory, and basic logistical support.

Wherever governments expect NGOs to behave as their agents, the horns of the dilemmas for NGOs become dangerously sharp. The more that governments resort to the use of force on highly controversial grounds, the more we can expect to see them invoke humanitarian action and language to gloss over unpopular bombardment campaigns and legally questionable invasion and occupation. The muddier the waters, the more opaque will be the search for possible solutions to the vexing ethical, political, theoretical, and practical dilemmas likely to plague NGOs in future conflict zones.

The crisis between Save the Children (U.S.) and Save the Children (UK) is only one example of the soul-searching that humanitarian NGOs have had to undergo in reexamining their aims, objectives, and modus operandi. In principle, accepting funding from a belligerent to an armed conflict should not necessarily undermine an NGO's neutrality and impartiality and independence, because not all governments have adopted the hard-line approach of USAID and the Bush administration. Perhaps NGOs have to choose whether they wish to maintain high political visibility on contentious issues, or, rather, work more quietly to avoid becoming politicized at ground level. Perhaps a certain specialization is inevitable between human rights NGOs on the one hand, whose calling is to draw attention in the most effective manner possible to human rights violations and even to denounce governments, and humanitarian NGOs on the other hand, whose missions focus more on relief operations. Humanitarian NGOs might have to recognize that denouncing violations will likely undercut the effective extension of humanitarian assistance on a neutral basis.

---

[57] See Seymour Hersch, "The Gray Zone: How a Secret Pentagon Program Came to Abu Ghraib," *New Yorker*, 24 May 2004.

Of course, the ideal solution would be that the U.S. government return to its previous policies, which were to foster, encourage, and support NGOs as an invaluable element of the international community's social fabric and to tolerate gracefully disagreement from the nongovernmental sector. One can only hope that the Bush administration's approach to NGOs will not be adopted by other countries and that the U.S. government itself will return to its previous attitude of showing genuine respect for the immense contribution of humanitarian NGOs.

6 Human Rights in Action: Supporting Human Rights Work in Authoritarian Countries

Birgit Lindsnæs, Hans-Otto Sano, and Hatla Thelle

The Danish Institute for Human Rights (DIHR) has been involved in human rights implementation in transitional countries in Europe and in the South since the beginning of the 1990s. Not all work is restricted to countries in transition, however. Cooperation also takes place in authoritarian contexts, where activities are typically implemented in close contact with branches of the state. It is a common feature that civil society tends to be weak in these countries. Yet even if civil society has developed, there is a need for interaction between the authoritarian state and external agencies supporting human rights. The degree of state control is typically high and necessitates that avenues are explored to establish trust between donors and relevant branches of the state – even in cases where donors support civil society development. This chapter looks into the dilemmas of engaging in human rights projects in authoritarian countries. It seeks to explore the strategies and choices that are made in these countries on the basis of two cases, namely, China and Rwanda. More specifically, the purpose of the chapter is to examine whether and, if so, how it is possible to secure the consolidation of human rights in such countries. A second concern is whether it is possible to cooperate on human rights ground with oppressive states without legitimizing continued oppression by state forces.

The chapter is divided into three main parts. First, the strategy for DIHR international programs is introduced and then the principles of implementation are discussed. Part II discusses the case of China, and Part III examines the Rwandan case.

I. DIHR STRATEGY[1]

DIHR was established in 1987 by an act of Parliament. It is primarily funded by the Danish government but also receives funding from international organizations

[1] Strategic Plan for DIHR Partnership Programmes: 2001–2003. Drafting group: Birgit Lindsnæs (ed), Karin Poulsen, Lone Lindholt, and Benita Bertram. Coach: Bent Vase. With substantial input from the International Programmes/DIHR staff.

and private donors. The institute employs a staff of about eighty people. In 2001, the total turnover was DKK 87.6 million (approximately US $11.5 million). The institute is based in Copenhagen and works almost exclusively without local field offices or local technical assistance staff.[2]

One of the objectives of the DIHR is to promote human rights nationally and internationally and to contribute to human rights implementation abroad as well as domestically. Whereas in Denmark the institute is mandated to monitor human rights compliance and to provide advisory services on Danish legislation, the international mandate encompasses support to human rights implementation abroad. The particular focus of implementation strategies is on institution- and capacity-building measures.

The strategy for DIHR's international programs is rooted in a set of ambitions, principles, and policies. The partnership concept is at the core of the strategy, but the emphasis on partnership has recently been made more explicit. Key concepts are dialogue, mutual understanding, and respect.

A partnership is defined as a contractual relationship, which (as a minimum) involves a definition of common goals and outputs, a time frame, and DIHR assistance in providing funding for the agreed activities. A precondition for entering into a partnership is the mutual commitment to the long-term goal of fulfilling human rights standards. The type of government in the specific country always influences the attainable goals. Likewise, a government's commitment or lack thereof to human rights affects partners; for example, they may have different interpretations of human rights articles.[3] In those situations, independent institutions and NGOs have to choose among monitoring, having a dialogue, or collaborating with the executive on how to implement human rights standards. Governments of one-party states may not be committed to human rights at all, or they may not be committed to political rights but may show an interest in dialogue on civil and social rights. Similarly, NGOs may not be willing to promote all types of human rights standards. An example hereof is the abolition of the death

---

[2] DIHR has established two field offices supporting the international programs. The first was established in 1996 in Malawi. It is now registered as a local NGO, run by a Malawian board, local management, and staff. A legal aid training and support office was established in 1997 in Rwanda. A success criterion is that the office will be taken over by a local professional Corps de Judicial Defenders in the near future. The Rwandan Ministry of Justice has so far requested that DIHR continue to manage the program.

[3] It could be argued that the ideal commitment to human rights standards per se is a fiction. Human rights are constantly at debate in ongoing economic, political, and ideological power struggles between various interest groups seeking to promote or restrict human rights. The picture of commitment is complex, and various governments may be committed to different types of rights. To take one example, although the right to due process is a human rights standard, in practice, interpretations differ substantively with regard to the time within which a suspect shall be brought before a judge – twenty-four hours in Denmark but five days in Nepal because of the distance, lack of quick means of transportation, and so on. Few human rights standards are absolute like, for example, the prohibition against torture.

penalty, which NGOs in emerging democracies are often hesitant to promote.[4] As a consequence, DIHR's strategic short-term goals may be quite differentiated and, without a close scrutiny, may appear not to be sufficiently ambitious. Goals may vary from dealing with government agendas with significant human rights reforms to government agendas with a few – and in the short-term perspective, insignificant – human rights improvements. At one end of the scale, this gives DIHR the possibility to enter into partnerships with institutions that can contribute to making a significant difference in this area;[5] at the other end of the scale, DIHR may engage in a limited partnership with institutions controlled by one-party governments.

The DIHR strategic goal will then be to find the key to a human rights dialogue from within. Such a dialogue will often be restricted to academic circles (universities and civil servants), with little or no public outreach or participation in democratic discussions. Thus, the success or failure of partnerships in countries with a low level of human rights commitment is highly dependent on the DIHR perception of and trust in the commitment of the partner. The experience is, however, that such a dialogue may, from a long-term perspective, prove to be significant[6] in setting the stage for a more focused approach.

A second precondition for entering into a partnership is that the respective partners are committed to developing its human resources and institutional capacity. This sounds simple but is in fact rather difficult because partners, particularly NGOs and independent institutions in new democracies and poor countries, are often far better at promoting human rights than at establishing methods and mechanisms to cater for the actual implementation of these rights. Building institutional capacity to promote the implementation of human rights therefore constitutes a real challenge in terms of mainstreaming human rights in the development sphere.

Third, the partner must accept DIHR's mode of operation characterized by the Swedish International Development Cooperation Agency (SIDA) evaluation as the "Danish model." This model implies a high degree of DIHR involvement and coaching without DIHR taking charge of the process or the results.[7] DIHR in its strategy strives to be perceived as a facilitator, coach, and advisor on possibilities,

---

[4] In the beginning of the 1990s, a DIHR partner, an NGO in Lithuania, would not campaign for the abolition of the death penalty. The justification was that it would be too risky and that it, as a newly established NGO, would lose credibility in the population because the majority of people, according to public opinion polls, were for the death penalty.
[5] This was the case after the abolishment of apartheid in South Africa and today in Serbia.
[6] The Helsinki and Organization for Security and Cooperation in Europe processes started with dialogue at the political level in 1975. The dialogue probably had a decisive influence on Gorbachev's glasnost policy; Mikhail Gorbachev, *Perestrojka – New Thinking for Our Country and the World* (New York: Harper & Row, 1987).
[7] Evaluation, The African Commission on Human and Peoples' Rights, The Danish Centre for Human Rights, Commissioned by SIDA, Stockholm and Nordiska Afrikainstitutet, Uppsala, 1998, http://www.humanrights.dk/upload/application/cdf466a6/afr.commmanus.pdf (2 May 2006).

challenges, pitfalls, and risks. It aims to hold up a mirror to local partners for them to analyze their strategies, methods, organization, and activities in the context in which they operate. Coupled with the lack of local offices, DIHR may be perceived as an invisible partner in the local context, while at the same time other partners may perceive it as being insistent or, at times, as putting strong pressure on partner institutions.[8]

The Context of Implementation

DIHR works within a framework in which one donor, the Danish Ministry of Foreign Affairs (MFA), plays a predominant role.[9] To a certain degree, this reality defines parameters of cooperation with partners. Human rights are on the Danish government's agenda in bilateral negotiations with recipient governments. Even though a general policy paper for project assistance exists, the Ministry of Foreign Affairs (MFA) has not yet developed a strategy for mainstreaming human rights into development cooperation. In general, the experimental and open character of Danish human rights assistance has left Danish embassies, country desks in the ministry, and DIHR with space for carrying out pilot projects that may involve some risks. The ambiguity of policy directions has, however, also allowed experimentation and sometimes courageous efforts that, in some cases, have placed Denmark at the forefront of human rights assistance.

Partner cooperation therefore takes place within a triangular or quadrilateral relationship of interdependence. The triangular relationship is between the donor, the DIHR, and the partner – be it the government, an independent institution, or an NGO. The quadrilateral relationship is between the donor, DIHR, an independent institution or NGO partner, and the national government in the country of the partner.

In its relationship with the donor, DIHR can, in some cases, be regarded as an intermediary between the donor and the partner, particularly if the donor is pursuing a particular human rights agenda that the donor does not wish to communicate directly with the local government or to support civil society openly. This pattern is common when the donor targets one-party states or authoritarian regimes through DIHR or countries of strategic political or economic importance to Denmark or its allies.[10]

In relation to local partners, the executive authorities such as ministries of justice and interior and independent institutions such as national human rights

[8] Danida capacity assessment of DIHR: Malawi country study, Ole Stage (ed), T &B Consult, Final reports June 2002.

[9] MFA funds more than 75 percent of the DIHR's international programs, half of these through a Cooperation Agreement. DIHR collaborates with many sections in the MFA, the main ones being Danida, Fresta, and the Secretariat for Support to Eastern Europe (SSEE). Support channeled through Danida is aimed at ten program countries selected from among the poorest in the world; Fresta programs and SSEE target Europe, regions in conflict, and, to some degree, the European Union integration process and do not include poverty alleviation assistance.

[10] For example, neighbors such as the Baltic countries or big powers such as China.

institutions and universities often have a strong hand in regard to policy making and setting human rights priorities.

In some cases, the relationship with local NGO partners can be described as asymmetrical, or as a kind of David-Goliath relationship. The donor and DIHR together control financial as well as human resources and may, contrary to the partner, have access to the executive in the partner's country. In the beginning of a partnership, the NGO partner may therefore seem to be vulnerable and without much leverage. In addition, at times the executive plays a strong political role in trying to influence the donor and its government, the DIHR, and the NGO partner. This risk is particularly high when an NGO partner monitors its government by dealing with controversial human rights issues.

The balance of power between DIHR and its partners depends on a number of factors that are equally important for all. These comprise factors such as the strength of the power base, political alliances, professional human rights skills, organizational capacity, ability to pursue goals, communication skills, and managing of criticism, conflict, and financial resources. Strengths and weaknesses of partners can vary considerably: a partner such as a ministry often has a strong power base; high, middle, or low professional standards; and good communication skills at the ministerial level, but lacks a clear strategy in relation to human rights goals. In this context, DIHR is politically and financially weak but has strong professional human rights skills, the capacity to deliver the requested output, and the ability to pursue human rights goals.

In relation to NGOs, the situation may be quite the opposite: the partner has no real power base but a few NGO allies, a weak organizational capacity, and almost no financial resources. Most NGO partners, however, have some very strong assets: human rights and communication skills and, most important, an almost extraordinary will to pursue human rights goals. In this case, partners who at an early stage may appear to be unequal allies may at a later stage constitute genuine and strong professional partners – particularly when in the process a weak NGO succeeds in strengthening its professional and organizational skills and not least its ability to navigate in a political environment.[11] This might also happen in authoritarian systems in which experience shows that politically weak NGOs can have an important influence on affecting policy development and put rights issues on the public agenda, as illustrated in the China and Rwanda cases that follow.

Country Selection

A number of strategy discussions about the type of countries on which DIHR should ideally concentrate its efforts has been undertaken in recent years. In this

---

[11] International experience from many countries shows that NGOs with strong human rights and leadership commitment can develop in half a decade into impressive and respected NGOs. The key is strategic and locally adopted human rights international programs.

debate, conflicting concerns have been raised, namely, whether DIHR should concentrate (1) on states committing themselves strongly to human rights (e.g., new democracies); (2) on states strategically placed within a region (e.g., in Africa, South Africa, Nigeria, Kenya, and Congo; in the Middle East, Israel/Palestine and Egypt; (3) on states in which Denmark has key strategic interests in terms of peace and security (e.g., in Europe); (4) on the poorest states; or (5) on states characterized by gross human rights violations.

In the first half of the 1990s, DIHR's strategy was to concentrate its efforts on the new democracies. Upon entering into a cooperation agreement with the Danish, MFA, DIHR changed its strategy in 1997, focusing instead on three of the five categories mentioned earlier: (1) transitional states with intermediary or high human rights commitment, (2) European states of security concern, and (3) the poorest states.

Another choice that has to be made with respect to country selection is the choice of concentration versus dispersed engagement. The general acceptance of human rights as a normative framework for politics and development spread globally during the 1990s. Most developing states have now ratified the main human rights covenants and have even integrated the bill of rights as part of their constitutional framework.[12]

This positive development has created a strong demand for assistance in the field of human rights implementation. Although the normative framework has been accepted and incorporated into national bills of rights, the challenge of many developing as well as developed countries is to put human rights into practice – that is, to make rights valid even in local contexts. The demand for DIHR support was increasing, with the result that at the end of the 1990s it appeared necessary for the institute to reconsider to what degree the support should be dispersed among countries in Europe and in the South. The current choice is to concentrate and deepen human rights work, perhaps by engaging in country programming rather than in country projects.

The Choice of Partners

The DIHR strategy envisages work with both governments and civil society. Whereas other Northern human rights groups emphasize civil society and NGOs as their main partner, being an independent national human rights institution, DIHR has decided to opt for collaboration with governments as well as with domestic human rights institutions and local NGOs. In authoritarian states, where local NGOs may be few or nonexistent within certain sectors, cooperation with governments might be the only option. In other authoritarian countries where civil society does exist, it might still be a priority to work with state institutions. This is the case, for instance, in a number of states with a far from

---

[12] Hans-Otto Sano and Lone Lindholt, *Human Rights Indicators 2000. Country Data and Methodology,* Copenhagen: DIHR, 2001; see also http://www.humanrights.dk.

promising human rights record, where cooperation with the police has been initiated for the simple reason that governments and police forces have expressed their commitment to change. In most of these cases, the cooperation is formed as a triangle – state, NGO, and DIHR – to ensure that improved collaboration between state agencies and civil groups is realized as part of the project.

In other situations, as, for instance, in the case of justice sector reforms in new democracies, collaboration with state authorities is initiated, for example, ministries of justice or interior, to institute sectorwide reform processes from above and with collaboration ensured from the top.

Windows of Opportunity

Even in states that place severe constraints on political rights it is possible to obtain good results by collaborating with state agencies according to a "windows of opportunity" strategy. This happens particularly when human rights violations are perpetrated as a result of a failure of the state to respond to such violations because of, for example, institutional incapacity and inertia. Torture and ill treatment by law enforcement agencies may be committed because of a perpetuation of practices and a failure to learn new ones or because of a particular state-endorsed strategy of violence. In cases in which human rights violations are committed as part of a controlled strategy of the branches of state, it is more difficult to create positive and measurable results. Hence, it is important to distinguish between violations prompted by weak state control or violations rooted in a political strategy on behalf of the state apparatus.

The concept windows of opportunity refers to openings in the authoritarian patterns. In concrete terms, it refers to an invitation to cooperate and an acceptance of cooperation by a partner in an unexpected or unfamiliar area. The experience is that such openings exist in most authoritarian countries, partly because of globalization processes through which trade and civil society interaction may contribute to establishing new political commitment, but also because prevailing poverty forces the state to interact with donor agencies and international NGOs.

Pursuing windows of opportunity may take place at various levels, depending on the context; these levels include dialogues, research cooperation, and project implementation. In authoritarian contexts, the initial pattern of cooperation may take the following forms:

- Training of key high-level authorities
- University and research cooperation
- Institutional cooperation including governance support within key sectors (e.g., justice or policing)
- Legal aid projects

These types of support have all proven to be useful in the building of trust in authoritarian structures of governance. Institutional cooperation on governance dimensions such as the independent role of the judiciary or the interaction between the police and civil society has proven to be important not only because of the training and capacity building embarked on with the particular services but also because of the wider institutional linkages that may be created as a result of specific capacity-building efforts. Thus, training of the police may lead to new relations with civil groups or to procedural changes in the treatment of detainees. Legal aid projects may provide a needed service to marginalized populations, but they may also entail institutional changes in the system of justice itself. The point to be made in these observations is to retain a longer and wider perspective than the immediate goals of the project itself.

II. THE CASE OF CHINA

The case of China is not only illustrative of some of the specific choices made from working in an authoritarian context, but it also demonstrates some of the implications of working with governments as partners. Given the special characteristics of the relationship between the Chinese government and the international human rights community, human rights work in China can provide useful input to the discussion of trade-offs and compromises in promoting implementation of human rights worldwide. As in a prism, the question of China and human rights reflects the tension between the political arena of international negotiations and power balancing on one hand and the objective of finding a solution to people's real problems on the other. Although DIHR experience in China is still minor and of a more recent date, it makes sense to ponder the choices and strategies pursued by the almost five-year cooperation with Chinese authorities on human rights implementation.

It can be argued that China belongs to the category of states of strategic and economic importance within a region. China may also be placed in the group of regimes where gross human rights violations occur. The character of the political system in China necessitates strong government support for human rights engagements. Nonstate organizations exist and are allowed to operate within fairly clear restrictions. They are especially active and maneuver within such fields as poverty alleviation, protection of women and children, and environmental protection. Within certain political and bureaucratic limits, their role in these areas is assessed by scholars and international donors to be instrumental not only in obtaining their immediate specific goals but also in promoting legal awareness and rights consciousness in the population at large. Given this situation, DIHR projects on human rights in China must be defined as being implemented through a primarily triangular relationship between the donor (Danida), DIHR, and the Chinese government.

The overall special feature of the Chinese case is the highly politicized character of the human rights issue, created by both the international community and the Chinese counterpart. Since the tragic outcome of student protests in Beijing in

June 1989, international organizations and the public in many Western countries have been on high alert concerning human rights violations in China.

The DIHR engagement in China began in 1998 at the first round of the European Union (EU)–China human rights dialogue, initiated by China in February. The first contacts resulted in agreement on a joint research project on "Protection of the rights of suspects and detainees," meaning prevention of the use of torture and ill treatment by the police in the pretrial phase. The project was completed in December 2001. Half a year later, DIHR was enrolled in the EU–China Legal and Judicial Programme, a four-year project training Chinese legal scholars and practitioners in European law and legal practice. The next engagement was an individual research project on social rights in China, funded by the Danish Development Research Council and conducted by a researcher in DIHR. Recently, a Danida-funded program (2000 to 2003) involved a death penalty study, support for a human rights center in a provincial capital, and legal aid to women channeled through the Women's Federation in two provinces, Hunan and Guangxi. DIHR activities thus involved joint research and training on the specific areas of torture prevention, establishment of social security systems, and legal aid to women, primarily concerning divorce cases and domestic violence. Partners comprised "NGOs" according to the Chinese use of the term, whereas we would call them universities and mass organizations, affiliated with the party-state.

The strategy has for the most part been a windows of opportunity approach, within the framework of certain principles, that crystallized in the beginning of the process. These principles can be summarized as follows:

- Avoid politically sensitive issues. Such issues might have included torture or the death penalty, but these themes have been subject to the explicit wishes of the partner. Other themes could be freedom of association, especially in the area of labor reform, or freedom of the press, two topics that in our view urgently need to be addressed. Recently they have both become the subject of international cooperation.
- Avoid politically sensitive places, such as Tibet or Xinjiang. The costs surrounding the political nature of the Tibetan or the Muslim questions can be too high to ensure a substantive effect.
- Establish lasting relationship with a few partners.
- Find a focus point outside the capital; partners in Beijing are efficient and competent but overloaded with work.
- Avoid conflicts over "formalities," for example, whether to call a seminar "prevention of torture" or "administration of justice." The difference between using the term "human rights" or "citizens' rights" can be vital to obtaining the necessary support from national or local authorities.

The windows of opportunity approach has been a necessary method both with regard to China and in relation to securing funding from the Danish side. These two considerations are explained in the following discussion of the triangular structure that made project implementation possible, although not necessarily successful. In short the process must be said to have been both donor- and partner-driven, as well as shaped by the partner needs perceived by DIHR on the basis of prior knowledge of China.

At the donor end, Denmark was one of few Western countries not to resume development assistance to China after 1989. Politicians, the media, and the public tended to support a boycott-like approach, strengthened by the proposal for a resolution criticizing Chinese human rights violations put forward by the Danish government in April 1997. The formal reaction of China – freezing trade contracts, postponing official visits, and the like – added to the anti-Chinese atmosphere in Denmark. In 1998, however, the climate changed, and small amounts of funding were allocated to human rights and democracy projects in China. The priorities from the Foreign Ministry were threefold: (1) legal reform, (2) local elections, and (3) strengthening of the knowledge of human rights in civil society. Thus, from the outset DIHR had a restricted mandate and a limited budget within which cooperation activities were to be defined.

At the DIHR, the opinion was that death penalty and treatment of political prisoners as well as prisoners in general were important concerns for human rights cooperation. The expectations in terms of actually getting to work with these issues were not too high in the beginning, however, and the aim was first simply to get started with a project within our mandate from which we could create a base for further exploration of possibilities and assessing needs. There was not a fixed area within which the institute insisted on working. There was a strong awareness of the fragile and political nature of any China cooperation necessitating caution in choosing areas and partners.

At the partner end, there are few organizations in China that have been approved by the government to work with human rights issues. Those few cases are universities or social science academies concentrated in Beijing and in a few provincial capitals. Furthermore, the areas of cooperation projects are closely monitored by both the central government and the foreign affairs bureaus of the institutions themselves. Consequently, local officials may be reluctant to approve projects not because of interference from above but because of ignorance or lack of interest in human rights concerns. Despite the alleged autocratic nature of the Chinese political system, local authorities are quite capable of pursuing their own agendas to some degree, including in relation to international cooperation. Given the framework outlined earlier, DIHR has made the following assessments and trade-offs.

It has been necessary to refrain from a promising Chinese-proposed cooperation project on protection of social and economic rights because the Danish Ministry of Foreign Affairs did not perceive it to be a human rights project. In fact, the ministry did not even respond to the proposal, while at the same time claiming it wanted to support implementation of human rights in China. The project received funding from elsewhere, but for the DIHR as a whole, the ministry's interpretation of human rights as civil and political rights might prompt the organization to focus more on the latter, although external influence is not the only reason for that priority.

It has been necessary to maneuver between the wish of the Danish donor to see a strong human rights profile and the wish of the Chinese side to downplay the human rights discourse and instead speak of citizens' rights or rights of special groups such as suspects, women, retired persons, and so on. To speak of someone's legal rights is not controversial in China, whereas the topic of human rights is tinged with power politics and colonial exploitation and often prompts a nationalistic response. The problem is more technical than substantial, and we have not had any strong confrontations from either side, but the tension between the two interests creates a dilemma that could influence choices and strategies in some areas.

Another choice DIHR has been asked by the donor to make was also based on internal political concerns. Work with torture and ill treatment would naturally include the prison administration, but the institute received clear signs from Danida that it was not to go into prisons, to train prison guards, or undertake other such tasks. This reaction can partly be explained by a Swedish experience in which a newly released political dissident was touring Sweden some years ago telling how Swedish human rights training helped prison guards to improve their surveillance of political prisoners! That he later claimed to have been misquoted did not alleviate the fear, especially among Danish media, of how human rights training can be abused.

The DIHR engagement in China at large is often met with the criticism of legitimizing human rights violations by cooperating with the same authorities that perpetrate these violations.

The position DIHR has taken is to give high priority to professional contact and try to avoid misuse, as well as to explore the possibility of engaging bilateral dialogue and multilateral pressure simultaneously. The institute has, for example, invited representatives from exiled dissident organizations to talks and conferences. At some point, however, it can be necessary to choose between cooperation and a confrontational approach; both may have to be used, but perhaps not by the same organizations at the same time. On the issue of China, DIHR adheres to a kind of international "division of labor" in which Amnesty International and Human Rights Watch take on the task of documenting violations and lobbying for international criticism; national human rights institutions can choose to do this as well – which DIHR is not designed to – or these institutions can choose the option of pursuing academic and project cooperation on a long-term basis.

III. THE CASE OF RWANDA

Internationally, cooperation in Rwanda has not attracted the same kind of attention as that in China. Cooperation in Rwanda does not seem to be controversial on the same scale, yet human rights violations similar to those in China have prevailed in Rwanda.[13] This reluctance to wage an internationally coordinated criticism against the state in Rwanda seems to relate partly to the plight of the nation during and after the genocide and partly to the fact that Rwanda is a small state. Yet Rwanda continues to play an important role regionally beyond its borders, and not necessarily a role that can be justified by the need for self-defense. The choice of supporting the authoritarian regime in Rwanda may therefore pose just as many challenges as the one in China.

DIHR has supported the education and deployment of judicial defenders in relation to Rwandan genocide trials since 1997. The project was originally initiated as a result of a contact among a Réseau citoyen, a Belgian NGO, and DIHR. However, the specific project contents was defined in a dialogue with the Rwandan state proposing to use auxiliary legal professionals in defending the vast number of persons accused for crimes of genocide and crimes against humanity in the aftermath of the atrocities during 1994. DIHR and Danida responded positively to this request because it was recognized that the forty-seven educated lawyers in Rwanda who had survived the genocide could not come close to providing the legal services needed for the defense of more than 120,000 people in pretrial detention and an even larger number of victims and survivors. DIHR involvement was therefore built on the prospect of contributing to the improvement of the rule of law in a situation in which both state authorities and societal forces were committed to fundamental change.

DIHR's cooperation in Rwanda was started as a judicial defender project under the authority of the Rwandan Ministry of Justice. At the time of writing, the project had been running for four years. Although initially under the aegis of the ministry, the project reached a level and size necessitating partnership with an independent body. Hence, a Bureau of the Corps of Judicial Defenders is currently the main institutional link of the project; that is, administration of the project has been transferred from the state to civil society. This process of change from a government-based contact to one within civil society is the result of specific DIHR efforts to contribute to the reinforcement of civil society in Rwanda.

Project performance has been good in terms of achieving the goals of training paralegals and integrating them into judicial processes in Rwanda. The judicial defenders have served in the defense of 662 accused under the genocide law. They have held information meetings in prisons and in communities concerning the rights and procedures of the law. Moreover, the eighty-four trained judicial defenders have represented 1,825 civil claimants before the twelve first instance courts.

---

[13] According to DIHR indicators on violations of civil and political rights, both states committed violations on a broad range of rights; ibid. The index compares systematic, not single-case, violations in eight dimensions of civil and political rights. Whereas sources confirmed violations in China in seven of eight dimensions, they confirmed violations in Rwanda in six dimensions.

It would be wrong to argue that the process of training and employing the paralegals has been a smooth one, however. The difficulties have arisen in part as a result of the deep social cleavages in the Rwandan society and the watchfulness that surrounds any new institution. The context of implementation in Rwanda is therefore as much one of an embedded conflict as one of an authoritarian government.

Other difficulties have been caused by the problems involved in creating a system of justice in a society where injustice has been the norm. The backlog of trying 120,000 odd genocide cases in fair trials represents the most important constraint, but the lack of trust in institutions and structures prevailing at all levels of society represents another difficulty. It goes without saying that capacity deficits within state institutions as well as in civil society add to these problems.

DIHR policies in Rwanda have been founded on at least three criteria:

1. Deal with politically sensitive issues only when they significantly affect the project; for instance, one endeavor was to persist in the needs of instituting fair trial values and rights. As a corollary, a strong focus on project priorities is necessary.
2. Dimensions of governance are crucial and time-consuming; values of accountability, transparency, participation, and efficiency are largely unknown territory within institutions, yet they have to form part of the capacity-building effort.
3. Creation of trust is vital; and a short-term presence is not conducive to reaching this goal. Long-term commitment is crucial, because of not only the immensity of problems but also the importance of trust in the formation of institutional relations. Building trust at the highest levels of governance is a priority even in a project that has moved outside the aegis of the state administration. For this reason, transparency is needed in dealing with both authorities and civil groups.

Although the Rwandan judicial defenders project has been a success in terms of the output indicators, the question remains whether development goals of consolidating fair trial rights and the rule of law have been realized. Or, alternatively, a more general question persists: is it possible to achieve progress on the human rights front in such a society, or are such activities serving only to maintain an acceptable front for an authoritarian state where democratization seems still far away?

Three methods of assessment maybe useful in answering these questions:

1. There must be tangible indications that the windows of opportunity strategy is transformed into institutional achievements in society, that is, that institutional (and value) change are in progress. In the Rwandan case, this seems to be the case as far as some elements of fair trial rights are concerned.

There is now a growing acceptance of and respect for the rights of the accused in Rwanda as measured by the fact that genocide cases increasingly involve defense lawyers or auxiliary paralegals. Also, the relatively high number of acquittals in genocide cases (approximately 80 percent) is evidence of such a process. The experience of progress is not unambiguous, however, because government has chosen to disregard some fair trial rights in the *gacaca* cases, that is, a revival of customary court procedures in the less serious genocide cases. In any case, institutional changes are necessary to document and reinforce a strategy of benchmarking so that assessment is not just based on perception.

2. A second method of assessment also seems relevant: there can be tangible social benefits deriving from the project, especially to marginalized or poorer groups, although this is not a requirement. Such benefits should become sustainable in the sense that they do not vanish at the end of the project. In the Rwandan case, these benefits are partly available to prison populations and communities because the judicial defenders are becoming a resource employed in society. The employment of paralegals may still be attached too strongly to the donor, however.

3. A third method relates to the linking between human rights activities and processes of democratization and better governance. In Rwanda, it would be difficult to argue thus far that the DIHR project has had wide impact in this sense. This is partly because other donors, especially those of powerful states like the United States and the United Kingdom, and even some of smaller powers, have been complacent about progress in this field. In such a context, it remains impossible for a small donor like DIHR to achieve results in terms of general governance and democratization.

CONCLUSION

The Danish Institute for Human Rights has entered into partnership arrangements in mostly low-income or lower middle-income countries with regimes described as authoritarian as well as in countries in a process of economic or political transition. The DIHR does not institute formulated conditionalities, which makes human rights support possible even in regimes with strong violations of such tenets. What counts is a "window of opportunity" or sign of commitment on part of authorities or NGOs in these countries. This does not mean that DIHR works in every context, however. What is important is that local human rights defenders endorse a positive strategy of cooperation. What is also important is that the human rights assistance offered is not used to legitimize further suppression. The fact that human rights assistance is not based on specific conditionalities does not mean that assistance is given without mutual obligations. The partnership remains a contractual relationship preconditioned on mutual trust, common goals, agreed-on methods of implementation, and predefined resource contributions. Thus, the nature of a political system is not an obstacle to engagement.

The cooperation in the two cases described here builds on certain shared principles that were not fully worked out from the beginning but that crystallized as the projects got under way. The starting point was the perception of windows of opportunity and the institute's mandate to support implementation of human rights in local contexts. The basic principles grew out of a practice of working together but were also ready-made plans conceived at a desk, not in the field. Certain commonalities can be identified in the way strategies of implementation have been pursued in the Rwandan and Chinese cases:

- A selective and cautious approach regarding the issues taken up in sensitive dialogues with government authorities.
- A selective and adaptive approach regarding the specific focus of human rights interventions, adaptive in the sense that recipient partners play a crucial role in deciding general priorities of intervention.
- A progressive, step-by-step method of implementation in which the aim during the first phases is to create a foundation of cooperation and trust within what is sometimes a limited scope of activities. Then, during subsequent phases, more emphasis is placed on broadening the scope of interaction, thus creating a foundation for more far-reaching institutional changes and more demanding dialogues. In the latter context, benchmarking goals within rights-based changes might be an important option.

What seems important in the short-term perspective is therefore the establishment of trust and successful cooperative ventures. Such ventures may involve research and university institutions; training of high-level officials, police, or judges; and pilot legal aid projects. In the longer-term perspective, however, the prospect of cooperation may involve a stronger focus on institutional change, be it within the police, the judiciary, or within legal aid schemes, to arrive at more sustainable changes based on human rights values. With an institutional focus, dimensions of governance become increasingly important in tandem with human rights.

This incremental approach through which the human rights focus becomes an increasingly strong dimension of dialogue and cooperation has only been partially tested to date, in part because DIHR has worked for limited periods in authoritarian contexts. Nonetheless, our experience thus far in the two case countries points to the efficacy of such an approach. A final assessment of human rights improvements that the limited support DIHR can provide and will achieve has yet to be made.

7 Driving without a Map: Implementing Legal Projects in China Aimed at Improving Human Rights

Sophia Woodman

The idea that Western countries should combine a principled stand against abuses of human rights with "positive" measures to bring about change in the circumstances that cause those abuses is one that many countries have firmly embraced, especially those that commit the most resources to human rights endeavors. Inevitably, there is significant tension between the more traditional approach to human rights of "naming and shaming" and such positive measures, often provoking debate among various actors about the appropriate balance between the two approaches in particular cases.

Debate has been particularly heated over the way to deal with China in the period after the 1989 Beijing Massacre. Around 1997, the policy of most Western governments on China's human rights situation shifted toward greater engagement, including through positive measures,[1] while in the face of reports of extensive violations of human rights in China, human rights organizations continued to insist that a more critical approach should be adopted. The Chinese government initiated the shift toward engagement, arguing strongly that any shortcomings in its rights record were due to the country's level of development, as well as historical and cultural factors, and thus the best approach would be one that would assist the country in its efforts to develop.[2]

This chapter looks at the experience of the cooperation programs aimed at improving human rights in China through legal projects that have emerged

---

[1] These have become a centerpiece of many Western countries' policies toward China's human rights situation, as part of a package of bilateral "dialogue and cooperation" that replaced the annual effort to pass resolutions at the session of the United Nations Commission on Human Rights. The approach combines regular human rights "dialogues" between diplomats and Western-funded "cooperation" programs in China to address human rights concerns.

[2] For accounts of the policy shift and its origins, see Human Rights in China, *From Principle to Pragmatism: Can "Dialogue" Improve China's Human Rights Situation* (New York: HRIC, June 1998); and Ann Kent, "Human Rights: From Sanctions to Delegations to Dialogue," in *Re-Orienting Australia-China Relations: 1972 to the Present,* ed. Nicholas Thomas (Aldershot, England: Ashgate, 2004), 147–262.

from the post-1997 policy shift, with a focus on the work of a particular subset of international nongovernmental organizations (INGOs) that implement such projects.[3] Largely based in and identified with the donor countries, these INGOs act as intermediaries between donor governments, the Chinese government, and Chinese partners and face various dilemmas arising from divergences between donor priorities, objectives, and operating practices on the one hand and those of their Chinese partners and realities on the ground in China on the other. The implications of the INGOs own varying institutional mandates and personnel serve to further complicate this picture, as does the fact that their projects are linked to high-profile policy positions taken by their home governments. Following some brief background on the aid programs for which these INGOs are the implementers, the chapter concentrates on three main areas in which dilemmas manifest themselves: commitment levels, the process of identifying needs, and knowledge gaps.

I. BACKGROUND

The activities covered here form part of the donor programs of bilateral aid to legal reform and law-related projects in China of six countries (Australia, Canada, Denmark, Norway, Sweden, and the United Kingdom [UK])[4] and one regional institution, the European Union (EU). At the outset, "legal exchange" was chosen by China and its partners as an acceptably neutral entry point for their cooperation.

In most cases, although governments and their official aid agencies provide funding and are involved to varying degrees in selecting projects and thematic focuses, the task of implementing projects is given to academic institutions,

---

[3] The material discussed emerges from a research project on strategies employed in bilateral aid programs that support legal projects in China aimed at improving human rights conditions there. My research was supported by a fellowship from the Global Security and Cooperation Program of the Social Science Research Council. The Centre for Comparative and Public Law at the University of Hong Kong hosted me during the project. I am profoundly grateful to both these institutions and to Jill Cottrell, Fu Hualing, Yash Ghai, and Carole Petersen for inspiration and guidance. I also thank many interviewees who were generous with their time. None of them are responsible for any errors or omissions in my work.

[4] The choice of countries was determined by two main criteria: programs are part of a "human rights dialogue and cooperation" package that has been underway in most cases for five or more years and a substantial program of aid to legal projects has been established during this period that is more or less explicitly linked to the human rights dialogues and thus to achieving human rights objectives. Although the United States now has a substantial program of aid to rule of law projects in China, these were not included in the study because U.S. policy has not exclusively followed the dialogue and cooperation route. In addition, a number of articles on U.S. aid to legal projects have already appeared, whereas to my knowledge nothing has been written in English about the programs under study here. For more information, see Sophia Woodman, "Bilateral aid to improve human rights," *China Perspectives*, no. 51 (January–February 2004), 28–49.

specialized NGOs, national human rights institutions of donor countries, temporary consortia of interested parties in the donor country set up for the purpose, or, in the case of the EU, specially formed project management teams composed of representatives from both sides.

The principal implementers covered in this chapter are three national human rights institutions:[5] the Australian Human Rights and Equal Opportunities Commission (HREOC), the Danish Institute for Human Rights (DIHR), and the Norwegian Centre for Human Rights (NCHR); two professional bodies focusing on international law with a strong academic element: Sweden's Raoul Wallenberg Institute of Human Rights and Humanitarian Law (RWI) and Canada's International Centre for Criminal Law Reform and Criminal Justice Policy (ICCLR); the cultural and educational arm of the UK Foreign Office, the British Council; the Great Britain China Centre (GBCC), a body set up to promote exchanges between the two countries; the Rights Practice, a UK nonprofit organization set up to implement human rights projects; a consortium of Canadian universities that ran a judges' training project in China; and the Association of Canadian Community Colleges, which has implemented a number of projects in China over the years.

The main activities in the projects these INGOs implement include study tours, arranging input from international experts, joint research projects and training inside and outside of China, ranging from a few days to studying for academic degrees. Some donors and implementers focus on long-term collaboration with one or several Chinese partners, and others operate more on a project basis, supporting discrete activities for one or two years, with HREOC being an exception in mostly supporting onetime exchanges with government agencies. Chinese partners include universities, think tanks, government agencies, and semigovernmental organizations, such as the All-China Women's Federation and the China Law Society.

In terms of substantive content, the programs can essentially be divided into two main categories: those based on comparative law "modeling" and those focusing on international human rights law. Most are in the first category, presenting Western practice as a model for China to follow. Canada, the UK, and the EU put the bulk of their funding into generalized legal programs, while providing some support for work in the area of criminal justice and a few specifically human rights focused projects. Australia has concentrated its funding on projects relating to the criminal justice system, working almost exclusively with government agencies. The programs of the Nordic countries are mainly in the second category: for Denmark, Norway, and Sweden, international human rights law has been the main entry point, with efforts mainly directed at building up education

---

[5] These institutions are generally responsible for monitoring implementation of human rights standards on a domestic level and sometimes for dealing with complaints from people who claim their rights have been violated.

in the field. This approach emerges from the specific expertise that the Nordic countries have to offer to a country like China and thus does incorporate some degree of modeling and comparative work.

Where the donor programs address human rights directly, the focus tends to be on civil and political rights plus concern for the rights of minorities, women, and children, as is usually the case in aid programs globally.[6] Virtually without exception, the legal cooperation programs do not address economic, social and cultural rights, as donors assume that traditional development programs take care of this area.[7] As mentioned in the chapter by Lindsnæs, Sano, and Thelle (Chapter 6, this volume), the Danish Foreign Ministry decided not to fund a rare research project exploring attitudes to economic and social rights among populations of several Chinese cities that teamed up DIHR and Chinese academics. This seems like a missed opportunity, given that the Chinese government has stated that its priority is "the right to subsistence."

Information on the programs has been collected from a variety of sources, including documentation provided by governments and implementing agencies and interviews with representatives of donors, implementing agencies, and Chinese legal professionals, most of whom were scholars involved in one way or another with donor-funded legal projects.[8]

II. COOPERATION BASED ON WEAK FOUNDATIONS

In terms of joint commitment to a common set of objectives, the programs under study began on a weak basis with little in the way of specific agreement between the two sides as to what the cooperation would entail in practice. A minimalist platform of "legal exchanges" was agreed on in bilateral human rights dialogues or other diplomatic interactions. Although donors generally called these "rule of law programs," this was not a formulation that China accepted, preferring to describe what is being done as "legal cooperation" or "legal exchange" and rejecting the "rule of law" label.[9]

---

[6] See, for example, Gordon Crawford, *Foreign Aid and Political Reform: A Comparative Analysis of Democracy Assistance and Political Conditionality* (Basingstoke: Palgrave, 2001).

[7] This is hardly surprising, given the fact that most donors have not incorporated human rights into aid policy but have more often tacked rights as an addition to existing programs and have failed to go beyond rhetorical commitment to economic, social, and cultural rights. See ibid. In recent years, however, the Nordic human rights institutes have incorporated economic and social rights issues into their training of Chinese university teachers who are teaching or will teach human rights.

[8] Among forty-seven interviews for my research, thirteen were with Chinese legal professionals. Nine of these had involvement with the type of donor-funded projects covered here, ranging from being the main representative of the Chinese partner to participation in some donor-funded activities. All interviews were conducted in 2002 and 2003.

[9] See, for example, Paul Gewirtz, "The US–China Rule of Law Initiative," *William and Mary Bill of Rights Journal*, no. 11 (February 2003), 609, describing negotiations over this program.

While the Chinese government was evidently aware that "rule of law" programs were infused with a liberal color, it should be stressed that the motives for donors in concentrating on this area are decidedly mixed. Western multinationals have a strong interest in China developing a legal system that can protect their investments, and this concern is a major reason why Western governments are keen to contribute to China developing its legal system. The rule of law approach is part of a broader strategy among aid donors globally to concentrate on "strengthening" this aspect of "governance," linking it to both economic development and democratization.[10] There is a deep-seated – and possibly erroneous – assumption that the kind of changes advocated under the rubric of "governance reforms" will inevitably lead to improvements in protections for human rights.[11]

In the China context, the rule of law is usually a key element of the broader bilateral aid programs of the countries under consideration, many of which make supporting the development of a market economy in China through economic reform a principal focus. Considered in purely financial terms, the relative priority accorded to law and rights programming in China does not match the rhetorical weight many of China's dialogue partners give to this cooperation. For the majority of donors covered here, projects in this area represented well below 5 percent of their overall aid program in China, although Denmark and Sweden were above this level.[12] In China, as elsewhere, much more money is spent on aid to legal projects relating to the economy, commerce, and finance than on human rights-related projects.[13]

An official of the Australian Human Rights and Equal Opportunities Commission (HREOC) linked Australia's human rights cooperation with China to constructing a legal system in China that would facilitate trade, saying that China's commitment to this objective made cooperation easier.[14] Australia's possible interest in legal reform for the same reasons was not mentioned.

[10] Thomas Carothers, "Promoting the Rule of Law Abroad: The Problem of Knowledge," Carnegie Endowment for International Peace Working Papers No. 34 (January 2003), 7.
[11] The point made by Peter Burnell is worth noting here: "Governance reforms that create a more hospitable climate for private enterprise and capital accumulation can also lead to great social and economic inequalities. These engender inequalities of political opportunity and, potentially, of political power too." P. Burnell, "Democracy Assistance: The State of the Discourse," in *Democracy Assistance: International Cooperation for Democratization*, ed. Burnell (London/Portland, OR: Frank Cass, 2000), 22.
[12] Canada could possibly be included in this list, but most of the projects in its "human rights, democratic development and good governance" category do not have a specific human rights focus.
[13] A comprehensive list of legal projects supported by different donors is available in Office of the General Council, *Law and Policy Reform Bulletin*, 2001 edition, Asian Development Bank. Some of the major projects in economic law are also described briefly in Donald C. Clarke, "Empirical Research in Chinese Law," in *Beyond Common Knowledge: Empirical Approaches to the Rule of Law*, eds. Erik Jensen and Thomas Heller (Stanford, CA: Stanford University Press, 2003), 164–192.
[14] Caroline Fleay, "The Australia–China Human Rights Technical Cooperation Programme," unpublished paper, May 2003, citing interview with legal and human rights consultant to HREOC.

Donor governments have generally put much more effort into negotiations with China on trade-related matters than on human rights, including on the cooperation programs. Thus, implementing agencies have been left to find ways to address specific human rights concerns through practical projects when the willingness of the Chinese side to do so is often questionable.[15]

A 1999 assessment of Swedish human rights training programs in China run by RWI identified a lack of shared objectives as problematic and called for more frank and open discussion between the Chinese and Swedish sides about the nature and aims of the program.[16] Currently, the Australia–China bilateral dialogue is the only one in which specific cooperation programs are regularly discussed at all. Some representatives of donors and implementing agencies thought that it was better this way because the dialogues were overly politicized events and involved people who knew little or nothing about the practicalities of cooperation.[17]

The lack of political will on the Chinese side is evident in the difficult environment for human rights projects. Even after the agreement to cooperate, most Chinese officials remained allergic to mention of human rights as a focus of the cooperation, and to some extent this continues to date. For example, HREOC staff said that while initially Chinese officials did not accept that they had any human rights problems that could be dealt with through the cooperation, they now acknowledge that Australian assistance may help resolve certain deficiencies in their legal system. But these are not framed in terms of human rights, and therefore HREOC "rarely use[d] the human rights term in response."[18] According to RWI, if the term human rights is mentioned in descriptions of projects that involve foreign participation, the organizers may run the risk of cancellation.[19]

The continuing sensitivity of the term is highlighted by the fact that the Canadian International Development Agency (CIDA) had originally planned to drop the term "human rights and democratic development" from the new country development policy framework then under preparation and refer only to "good governance," the goal of which would be to "support Chinese efforts to increase rule of law as a means to uphold the rights of its women and men."[20] After the proposed change met with an outcry from Canadian NGOs, CIDA backed down.[21]

---

[15] For further exploration of this point, see Woodman, "Bilateral Aid to Improve Human Rights."

[16] Anders Mellbourn and Marina Svensson, "Swedish Human Rights Training in China: An Assessment," SIDA Studies in Democracy and Human Rights (February 1999), 14.

[17] Interviews UK Foreign Office; NCHR; ICCLR; communication from DIHR.

[18] Fleay, citing interview with HREOC official.   [19] RWI, "Plan of Operations, 2002–23."

[20] Paul Knox, "Human Rights Cut in Canada's China Plan," Globe and Mail (17 December 2002): A1.

[21] Paul Knox, "Ottawa Reserves Stand on China Plan," Globe and Mail (18 December 2002), A18. The new programming document was finally released in 2004 and is available at: http://www.acdi-cida.gc.ca/CIDAWEB/webcountry.nsf/VLUDocEn/China-ProgrammingFramework.

More important than terminology, in the Chinese bureaucracy hostility and suspicion to some kinds of foreign cooperation remains strong. For example, the proceedings of a 2001 three-week Nordic workshop in Jilin Province for Chinese law teachers on international human rights law were videotaped.[22] "Anything involving international elements and human rights in China is still very sensitive," said one Chinese informant, and another said foreign involvement in law per se remained sensitive. Foreign funding was less of a problem than foreign participation, especially if the project involved examination of conditions on the ground.[23]

A statement by an official in charge of INGOs in China in a rare article on foreign aid in China published in a popular Chinese magazine presented a paranoid view of donor engagement with academics:

> There is no free lunch in this world. If the other side needs to find out something, they support your experts to do a study, to do some research, and when it is done, they take all the material away. Some of these things the government doesn't even know about.... The origins of the figures some scholars use are problematic, they are not very accurate; some should really be considered estimates, but they don't even check them and just put them out. This can have a really bad effect, and can become a human rights bomb that is used against you.[24]

While the climate for human rights research and education in universities has certainly improved in recent years – and now human rights centers in universities are proliferating, with five set up in 2003 alone[25] – the field remains hemmed in by political restrictions and lack of domestic funding. Teachers who lecture on international human rights law have to be aware of the fact that students may be reporting on what they say in class to the authorities, and this can get them in trouble.[26] A university lecturer prefaces his human rights course with an admonition to students not to choose to specialize in this field, because "it is morally embarrassing, economically unprofitable, politically dangerous and academically difficult."[27]

However, according to one implementer, lack of shared objectives is less of a problem than it might appear. In this view, the divergence is greatest at the level of the two governments involved, while at the level of project implementation, Danish and Chinese project managers agree on aims for projects.[28] Such a view assumes, however, that communication between the two sides is entirely frank,

[22] RWI, "Plan of Operations, 2002–23."   [23] Chinese scholar interviews.

[24] Zhang Gang, "Free Money? Foreign Non-Profit Funds Seek to Influence China Through Grant Aid" (Bai gei de qian: feiyinglixing waiguo jijin tongguo wuchang yuanzhu yingxiang Zhongguo), *News Weekly (xinwen zhoukan)*, 10 June 2002, p. 25, quoting Li Yong, director of the Ministry of Civil Affairs Department of Registration and Management of Social Organizations with a Foreign Element.

[25] Interview, RWI.   [26] Chinese scholar interviews.

[27] Cited in RWI, "Plan of Operations, 2002–23."   [28] Communication with DIHR.

which may be unlikely given the inherently unequal relationship between donor[29] and recipient.

III. IDENTIFICATION OF NEEDS

Given the lack of agreement between donors and the Chinese government on what the objectives of cooperation should be, the process of identifying projects in China generally meant a lot of legwork by implementing agencies to find appropriate projects to support. Some staff members of implementing agencies acknowledge that it has often been difficult to engage Chinese partners in identifying their needs and encouraging them to take the initiative in proposing projects. One UK implementer described the difficulty as follows:

> Having spent many years in discussion with Chinese organizations from universities to government departments asking them to identify their needs or what projects they'd like I have usually found this to be a frustrating exercise. Either the Chinese partner identifies a project which does not meet the interests of the funding agency – too big, inappropriate methodology (perhaps too many overseas trips, large conferences, etc.) or too general – or they just respond positively to any suggestion you make perhaps assuming, often rightly, that this way at least there will be some funding. I think this situation is beginning to change as more Chinese partners travel and gain experience in developing projects. It is also improved by being able to discuss directly with the personnel involved rather than via foreign affairs officers etc. Our approach now is to try and build on research interests to develop more practical projects.[30]

The staple of development cooperation, formal needs assessments, was not part of preparation for initial projects. To start with, at least, Chinese partners appear to have been unwilling to identify gaps in knowledge or deficiencies in practice that cooperation programs could help to address. Although the situation has been improving, to some extent, this remains a problem today.

In the initial stages, implementing agencies tended to draw on their standard list of activities, such as RWI's launch of short training programs on international human rights law for a range of Chinese government agencies; to replicate models that others had already pioneered, as NCHR did in beginning with similar trainings to those RWI had been putting on; to support organizations previously funded by private foundations, particularly the Ford Foundation; or to employ the favored method of reciprocal "study visits" by officials from legal institutions during which projects might be worked out, the approach adopted by HREOC.[31]

---

[29] Although the implementing agency is not the direct donor of the funds, in this relationship it is the one that controls the purse strings.

[30] Communication from the Rights Practice.

[31] Chinese partners have consistently seen "study visits" to the donor country as a major element of the cooperation, reflecting in part the role of foreign affairs departments in negotiating projects. For an exploration of the importance of foreign study and foreign trips in the interaction between

Until recently, when RWI asked academics what they would like to do in terms of cooperation in the human rights field, they would turn the question around and ask what RWI would like to do. Officials in the Shanghai procuratorate were bemused by RWI's insistence that the focus of the training materials being prepared as part of the cooperation should be on Chinese problems, as they wanted to do a book series on Swedish law.[32]

In 1999, RWI launched a yearlong project identification mission, a commendable initiative.[33] In the course of this, RWI held a number of project planning workshops with academics and procurators (and some with both together) to identify aims, focuses, and means of cooperation. At the conclusion of the mission, none of the six academic institutions that had sent representatives to several exercises was willing to take the lead in committing themselves to being RWI's main partner for the development of international human rights law education projects in China. In RWI's assessment, "A number of reasons can be discerned, such as the unwillingness to take the forefront in a politically sensitive field; the tendency of Chinese organizations to assume a passive role; and the habitual international cooperation strategy where the donor country provides a lot of input."[34]

Following the project identification mission, RWI launched two three-year-long projects, the first with academics to "build capacity" in the teaching of international human rights law and the second, with the procuracy in Shanghai and elsewhere, to support the institution's reform plan[35] through management training[36] and knowledge about human rights issues. Both projects aimed to promote networking among those RWI worked with, as well as between officials and academics, and set as a long-term goal "that the concept of human rights will be incorporated in[to] the values and traditions of the cooperating institutions."[37] But it is not at all clear from the report on the project identification mission that this was really the goal of the Chinese partners to the projects.

People involved in British-funded projects in all the implementing agencies contacted for this study mentioned the difficulty of getting down to projects that were specific enough to have an impact on conditions on the ground. Often years of working together on more general topics were necessary before a Chinese

Chinese and foreign institutions in the context of donor programs and university exchanges, see David Zweig, *Internationalizing China: Domestic Interests and Global Linkages* (Ithaca, NY: Cornell University Press, 2002).

[32] Interview, RWI.

[33] This followed on the release of the critical assessment by Mellbourn and Svensson commissioned by the funder, the Swedish International Development Agency (SIDA), mentioned earlier.

[34] Jonas Grimheden, "RWI China Human Rights Project Identification Report III, Final Report" (November 14, 2000), 18.

[35] Supreme People's Procuratorate, "Opinions Concerning the Implementation of the Three Year Reform of Procuratorial Work," 10 January 2000.

[36] The management training component is provided by the Swedish Institute for Public Administration (SIPU International). RWI, "Plan of Operations 2002–23."

[37] Grimheden, "RWI Project Identification Report," 1–2, quote p. 4.

partner would be willing (or able) to engage in a project focused on achieving a practical result. To reach this point, the necessary ingredients, one person said, were a "good working relationship" with a Chinese partner built up over several years; "a process oriented and participatory approach moving from awareness raising of rights issues and alternative models of law and practice to the identification of a project to address a specific and defined problem"; and strong contextual knowledge on the part of the implementer.[38]

Results of such an approach are apparent in two juvenile justice pilot projects in Shanghai, funded by the UK Human Rights Project Fund[39] and the EU Human Rights Small Project Facility.[40] These are among the most practical of any projects surveyed in this study. The first pilot is aimed at ensuring children accused of a crime access to an adult who can represent their interests and the second at pretrial release on bail for children facing criminal charges. These projects, which are under the auspices of the GBCC but managed by the Rights Practice, were proposed by the implementers following consultation with the Chinese partner, the East China University of Politics and Law, after years of "get to know you" type work.[41] The project depends in particular on one academic at ECUPL who has worked with the implementer on various projects for more than ten years. "Although initially we took the lead in setting objectives for our cooperation we are now impressed by the sense of local ownership of the appropriate adult project," wrote the UK implementer.[42]

According to a European Commission official, since governance and human rights are not China's priority, the EU has to take the initiative in cooperation in these areas and "kind of impose" projects on the Chinese side. At the same time, he recognized that without Chinese ownership, such projects would not work.[43] This dilemma has clearly dogged the EC's entire cooperation program and has meant long delays in project implementation as the practicalities of doing something that has been identified as a priority by the EC are worked out with the Chinese side. An example is the Human Rights Small Project Facility, launched by the EU in 2001. Because no arrangement had been made in advance on what role the Chinese side would play in selecting projects for funding, there were long delays while this was worked out, and eventually some projects that had been chosen were vetoed by the Chinese authorities.[44]

---

[38] Communication from the Rights Practice.
[39] This global fund is administered by the UK Foreign Office and was operational between 1998 and 2004. It is now being replaced by a grant-making facility to be called the Global Opportunities Fund.
[40] This is a onetime fund that provided grants to eighteen projects in China between 2001 and 2002.
[41] Communication from the Rights Practice.   [42] Ibid.
[43] Interview EC.
[44] This experience does not bode well for the efficient disbursal of the €20 million allocated in the EC's current program of aid to China to support the development of civil society in China. Again, no arrangements appear to have been worked out with the Chinese side on how this will be done, and what the grant-making criteria should be.

Working primarily with one partner that has a clear objective shared by the donor side obviously makes the whole process of needs identification and project planning much easier. An example is the ICCLR's work with two research centers at the Chinese University of Politics and Law focusing respectively on criminal law and criminal procedure. According to the director of ICCLR's China projects, the main modus operandi for the cooperation between the two sides has been the Chinese side requesting expert input on a particular aspect of law reform that it is working on, and ICCLR seeking to provide experts familiar with international law and Canadian practice in the relevant areas.[45]

Thus a range of issues contribute to difficulties in identifying needs that fit with the human rights objectives the programs under study are committed to, as well as to planning specific projects to address them. Several implementers mentioned the problem of project negotiations not involving the people doing the substantive work but being conducted by foreign affairs department officials, who have other agendas.[46] Other issues include the sensitivity of the subject matter and the lack of commitment to specific human rights improvements on the part of the Chinese authorities; some Chinese partners evidently feel that while they know cooperation is acceptable, they are not sure what its scope should be. Also, if most of the budget for a particular project is spent outside China, this understandably diminishes the commitment of Chinese partners.[47] Another element may be how Chinese partners see cooperation: not as aid, but as exchange, in which the fact of working together is more important than what gets done.[48] A further element may be a certain passivity built into aid relationships, where the recipient side does not feel in a position to take the initiative.[49]

Because donors tend to be concerned mainly with "outcomes," they may not be willing to fund the kind of slow identification process that is often necessary to begin to engage on a practical level with specific human rights problems.[50] The case of Sweden and RWI is a notable exception, and generally the Nordic institutes are virtually assured of long-term support for approaches that assume building up working relationships takes time. It is more of a problem for those implementers receiving funds from donors for projects lasting one or two years at a time. As one UK implementer put it, "With regard to funding I think our interest is in the transparency of funding criteria and for short-term funding a

---

[45] Interview with ICCLR.   [46] See Zweig, *Internationalizing China.*
[47] An example is the Canada–China Senior Judges Training Project.
[48] The limited literature in China on aid shows a realist view of the motives for aid, with the assumption being that the donor interests are the most important factor in shaping topics and styles of cooperation. See, for example, "Summary report on conference to announce results of research project 'Foreign Aid and International Relations'" ("*duiwai yuanzhu yu guoji guanxi*" *chengguo fabuhui ji yantaohui zongshu*), *Europe* (*Ouzhou*), No. 2, 2002, as well as cited article from *News Weekly.*
[49] In my personal experience working in an INGO, recipients of donor funds are generally unwilling to reject donors' ideas for projects even when they privately admit that they are unworkable.
[50] Communication from The Rights Practice; interview with ICCLR.

degree of predictability over several years."[51] Constantly shifting donor priorities are part of the problem; as a representative of GBCC put it, the areas of concern donors identify for funding do not necessarily match the needs in China, which often call for "groundwork," rather than "fancy" projects. [52]

Most Chinese informants were concerned that donors had insufficient understanding of the needs their programs were supposed to be addressing. Said one, "The country needs to change itself and needs help with this. But this should be based on needs identified by people in China – not telling them what to do, or doing it for them." Donors should not come with preconceptions about what would be useful based on their own system and values, and should use more Chinese consultants. In their planning, donors should have more discussion with Chinese academics and officials to identify the real problems that need addressing.[53]

A number of Chinese informants were concerned about donors' interests in overly "political" projects. Certain donors want too much specific involvement, both in terms of substance and administration, said one. To be successful, projects needed to combine clear objectives, cooperation of relevant government agencies, and commitment on the part of the person running the project on the Chinese side.[54]

Chinese informants identified various specific areas – both geographic and substantive – in which donor programs should broaden their scope to address real needs for cooperation. Scholars and practitioners outside Beijing and Shanghai felt that donors concentrate far too much of their attention on those cities, to the exclusion of other areas.[55] Not only were these cities not representative of the country as a whole – thus solutions worked out there might not be feasible elsewhere – but also the concentration of donor attention made recipients blasé about it, and thus they might not put in as much energy and commitment to the projects as people in other, less favored, areas.[56] Questions can certainly be asked about the relative need for foreign funds of some of the institutions being given money; for example, while many donors are supporting high-level training of judges, Shanghai pays to bring in American teachers to teach judges and sends its judges to the United States for a study program.[57] There is a tendency for donors to work only with people who can speak English because this saves time and money. These may be the people who *least* need the kind of exposure that is an important part of such cooperation programs.

Perhaps the central dilemma for the implementing agencies emerging from the experience of identifying needs is the fact that, with a handful of exceptions,

---

[51] Communication from The Rights Practice.   [52] Interview, GBCC.
[53] Chinese scholar interviews.   [54] Chinese scholar interviews.
[55] Chinese scholar interview, Chinese legal practitioner interview.
[56] Chinese scholar interview.
[57] Conversation with John Ohnesorge, University of Wisconsin, which is providing such training for Shanghai judges.

they have been pushed into the position of creating the field.[58] The more honest among them acknowledge this problem, which runs contrary to the trend of what is considered good practice in aid policy. To some extent, with the passage of time this may be changing, but it is hard to distinguish between changes in the climate and greater familiarity on the part of Chinese institutions with how to negotiate the parameters of donor priorities. Thus, the spread of university-based human rights centers can be interpreted either as indicating a growing demand for education and research in international human rights law or as a sign that universities have realized that this is a good way of bringing money into their institutions and giving faculty coveted opportunities to travel abroad. The reality is that it is probably a bit of both.

IV. IMPORTANCE OF KNOWLEDGE

In a situation in which Chinese partners have been unwilling to propose specific projects, as described earlier, implementers may need a formidable array of competences to make cooperation meaningful, including knowledge of international human rights standards, of expertise in their own countries on specific rights-related legal issues, and of best practice in key areas of human rights implementation.

Most important, they need contextual knowledge.[59] On the donor side, the aid process generally often suffers from a lack of people with in-depth country knowledge and language skills working on project design and management, and this tends to be a particular problem in bilateral programs.[60] Developing such understanding is no easy task in the China context, where there is a serious shortage of accurate information about the functioning of the legal system and where most information that is available is in Chinese.[61] Several of the more knowledgeable people working in implementing agencies complained about the lack of time and money devoted to the learning necessary for their jobs. Some

---

[58] For an examination of the role of private foundations in this process globally, see Mona Younis, "An Imperfect Process: Funding Human Rights – A Case Study," Chapter 2 in this volume.

[59] The lack of such knowledge, as well as failure to make best use of information that is available in donor programs, is certainly not a problem that is unique to China, as even a cursory review of some of the literature on the field of "rule of law" aid makes clear. See Carothers, "Promoting the Rule of Law Abroad," 14.

[60] Chinese scholar interview; comments from Titi Liu and Yash Ghai; "Project Report on the Role of Foreign Aid for Legal Reform Programs in the Russian Federation," Woodrow Wilson School of Public and International Affairs, Graduate Policy Workshop on Legal Reform Projects After Communism, January 1999, 80.

[61] It is one thing to expect Chinese language communication skills from donors and implementers but another for them to be able to obtain and digest scholarly literature in the language. Although there are a number of scholars of Chinese law in the United States whose expertise is often invaluable for donors in bringing this gap, there are few such scholars in most of the countries with China programs under study here.

Chinese informants expressed frustration at the lack of knowledge of the Chinese context, particularly the political context, among people working for some donor agencies, which they said could make it difficult for them to understand the rationale of proposed projects.[62]

With the exception of ICCLR, many Canadian projects in particular appeared to suffer from a knowledge deficit, which at times appeared almost to amount to willful ignorance. According to one person familiar with the project planning process, Chinese partners get tired of repeatedly answering the same questions asked by Canadians, as for each new project, the people involved want to learn from scratch, apparently without relying on experts to inform them.[63] An example of the effects of this is the Canada–China Women's Law Project. Implemented by the Association of Canadian Community Colleges[64] working with the All-China Women's Federation (ACWF), it was originally scheduled to run from 1998 to 2003.[65] The project aimed to help promote and implement China's 1992 Law on the Protection of Women's Rights and Interests.

The ACWF has been tasked with promoting women's legal rights since 1983 and was the main drafter of this 1992 law, which had been a principal subject of its second five-year plan of legal education for women launched the same year.[66] Thus, the ACWF had a wealth of experience relevant to this project, yet it appears to have allowed the Canadians to assume that it was a tabula rasa to which Canadian experts could bring a wealth of experience.[67] The Canadian side does not seem to have studied the nature of the law in question, as an assessment conducted during the fourth year of the project indicates that the Canadians had little idea that it lacked enforcement mechanisms. Plans for media training by Canadian experts had not taken into account government controls on the Chinese media, and evidently there was little understanding of the ACWF's previous work in this area. A recommendation in the assessment states: "Future project appraisal and design missions should ensure Chinese and Canadian recognized sectoral experts be teamed up and collaborate on findings to ensure optimal

---

[62] Chinese scholar interviews.   [63] Interview with academic.

[64] ACCC has been involved in implementing a number of China projects, as described in David Zweig, "Foreign Aid, Domestic Institutions and Entrepreneurship: Fashioning Management Training Centers in China," *Pacific Affairs* 73, no. 2 (summer 2000), 209–31.

[65] The project was due to conclude in 2003 but was extended for a year. Communication from ACCC.

[66] Jonathan Hecht, "Women's Rights, State Law: The Role of Law in Women's Rights Policy in China," in *Human Rights: Positive Policies in Asia and the Pacific Rim*, ed. John D. Montgomery (Hollis, NH: Hollis, 1998), 71–96; and Xu Weihua, "The Women's Federation and Its Role in Protecting Women's Rights and Interests," in *Human Rights: Chinese and Canadian Perspectives*, eds. Errol P. Mendes and Anne-Marie Traeholt (Ottawa: Human Rights Research and Education Centre, 1997), 473–487. The latter paper appeared in a book published with CIDA funding the year prior to the launch of the CCWLP.

[67] The ACWF and women's rights issues have been the subject of an extensive scholarly literature in English in recent years.

goodness of fit with the Chinese context."[68] The project also failed to incorporate any information on the UN Convention on the Elimination of Discrimination Against Women, a treaty to which both states have acceded.[69]

Given the size and complexity of China, there is a serious shortage of information on the functioning of legal institutions and on human rights violations that could be a suitable guide for these programs. Little empirical work has been done, although more is available now than a few years ago.[70] For example, so little research has been done on the actual situation of the judiciary that even unambiguous information on the level of training of judges is still unavailable.[71]

Research is also lacking on how and for what people really use the legal system. Such information is crucial to framing strategies that seek to assist those who are attempting to assert their rights.[72] What little information is available raises serious questions for the aid programs covered here about the relative importance of lawyers in assisting people seeking to pursue complaints or assert rights claims. "Legal workers" and legal activists who are not actually qualified as lawyers may be playing a more important role in this regard than lawyers.[73]

But few donors have been willing to support baseline empirical work, which is costly and time-consuming, and only a handful have supported human rights monitoring work, with almost all excluding the work of groups and individuals working outside China from funding.[74] Sometimes empirical studies are vital in deciding on strategy for particular projects, yet donors and implementers have not insisted that even preliminary work be done. An example is the Canada–China Senior Judges Training Project, which appears to have been launched without the Canadian implementing consortium really having an idea of the level of training of judges in the country or the needs of the particular partner, the National Judges College.[75]

---

[68] "Canada–China Women's Law Project: Assessment Mission Report," April 2002. Kindly supplied by ACCC, on file with the author.

[69] The ACCC staff member responsible for the project had not even heard of the treaty.

[70] Randall Peerenboom, *China's Long March Toward Rule of Law* (Cambridge, England: Cambridge University Press, 2002): 155, gives a number of examples of studies in areas ranging from administrative law to the implementation of the Criminal Procedure Law.

[71] See Clarke, "Empirical Research in Chinese Law," 175–177.

[72] As Michelson points out, empirical work on how people resolve their disputes in China today has hardly begun, as scholarly work done so far has relied on small sets of interviews, official information, or surveys based on hypothetical questions ("what would you do if...?"). Ethan Michelson, "How Much Does Law Matter in Beijing?" paper presented at the Law and Society Association Annual Meeting, 2002, 1–2.

[73] Comments from Ethan Michelson, Benjamin Liebman, and Tai Xuesen.

[74] The only known exception among the donors covered here is the UK Human Rights Project Fund, which provided two grants to the Hong Kong office of the organization Human Rights in China in the early years of the fund's operation.

[75] While Alain Bissonnette, "La formation des juges en Chine et le dialogue portant sur l'etat de droit," *Bulletin de liaison du Laboratoire d'anthropologie juridique de* Paris, No. 25, September 2000, p. 75, asserts that all judges in China have the equivalent of an LLB in law and was told

Another important part of the accumulation of knowledge is evaluating work that has been done. But in this field, few evaluations have been done,[76] and some donors mentioned that Chinese partners did not like evaluations of projects.[77] In some cases, evaluations are now underway.[78] In many cases, there has not been sufficient follow-up on donor projects to see what has happened as a result, or whether outputs are being used.[79]

A major reason for this lack of learning is the strong pressure for success in law and rights work in China. The linkage of these cooperation projects to donor government policies means that assessments of projects are often overly optimistic. The strong interest of implementing agencies in continuing to receive funding[80] also militates against dispassionate assessment, and may not encourage adventurous or creative programming. Another reason people lack information is that there has been insufficient attention to the circulation of donor-supported research, a point made by both implementers and some Chinese informants.

CONCLUSION

When representatives of the implementing agencies for the kind of legal projects covered in this chapter discuss their work in China, most are relatively candid about the difficulties they face in dealing with the dilemmas emerging from their intermediary role.[81] They generally present a modest assessment of the potential

---

this by the National Judges College, a group of Chinese legal academics told Clarke ("Empirical Research in Chinese Law") they estimated that less than 10 percent of judges had the equivalent of an LLB degree. Yet the Canadian judges training program was apparently based on the assumption that the basic training of Chinese judges was in place and thus it was justified to focus on more specialized in-service training on complex and novel areas of law.

[76] Notable exceptions are the Mellbourn and Svensson assessment and the participatory assessment of the Canada–China Women and Law Project, both mentioned earlier. HREOC does annual internal evaluations, but these are not publicly available. A UK Foreign Office evaluation of Human Rights Project Fund projects in China was said to be "classified."

[77] Fleay, "The Australia–China HRTC."

[78] RWI's China program is currently undergoing an evaluation, and an evaluation of the EU–China Legal and Judicial Project is being planned.

[79] An example in Randy Peerenboom, "The Ford Foundation and Legal Reform in China," unpublished paper, 2001, is that there have been a number of projects supporting production of manuals for judges, but no follow-up to see how or if they are being used.

[80] To give just a few examples, from 1996 to 1999, the Canadian ICCLR received more than a third of its budget for its China program, see ICCLR annual reports 1996–2, 1997–2, 1998–2, available at: http://www.icclr.law.ubc.ca/Site%20Map/Publications%20Page/Annual_Reports.htm. For the Australian HREOC, China projects meant not only an infusion of funds but also a way of proving its usefulness to a government that had imposed a 42 percent overall budget cut on the agency; see Oxfam Community Aid Abroad, "Australian Federal Election Report: Human Rights," on 2001 election, at http://www.caa.org.au/current/election/humanrights.html. Finally, both the NCHR and the DIHR are almost entirely dependent on their respective foreign ministries for funding.

[81] The degree of candor varies, however, depending on the attitude of the government involved, with the Nordics being the most willing to discuss difficulties openly.

impact of the work in which they are engaged, acknowledging its limited scope in comparison to the enormity of the issues it seeks to address.[82]

Representatives of donors, however – whether government aid agencies or diplomats – are more likely to downplay the problems and express confidence that a great deal is being achieved through their support for legal projects in China.[83] This contrast highlights the pressure for success created by the projects' linkage to the foreign policy positions taken by donor governments.

The INGOs have generally chosen to ignore the inflation of the importance of their work by donors, believing that the openings represented by the work they are able to do with Chinese partners are worth pursuing, even when it means they are pushed into roles replicating aid relationships that have been found to be unproductive elsewhere.[84] The choice seems to be less a question of a considered strategy on the part of most of these INGOs (as Lindsnæs, Sano, and Thelle claim for DIHR in Chapter 6) but of finding virtue in necessity.

This is not to say that the projects these INGOs are running in China are not useful or beneficial on some level. Some undoubtedly are, some probably are not, and a few may even be harmful; generally too little information is available at present to judge. What is clear is that the INGOs have almost no time to consider questions of strategy or to assess what they have been doing in a critical light. This is a common problem of aid programs, because funds are allocated according to political priorities of donors and then have to be spent within a limited period of time.

Although conditions for the implementation of legal projects with a human rights focus in China may have improved, a thoughtful review comparable to that undertaken by the Mertz-Gilmore Foundation and described by Younis (Chapter 2) in this volume would be invaluable if this kind of work is to have more impact in the future. In addition, these INGOs may need to be more willing to challenge unhelpful donor policies and unworkable priorities, and donors to listen and respond to such critiques.

A number of questions for the future direction of the aid programs in China arise from the dilemmas faced by these INGOs. First is whether donors' overall approach to China's human rights situation has helped to create the best

[82] This is not always the case: some implementers exaggerate their own contributions and also inflate the impact of changes in China to which their work may have contributed. Many examples can be seen in the annual reports of ICCLR, particularly in relation to the 1996 revisions of the Criminal Procedure Law. See ICCLR annual reports cited earlier.

[83] In fact, many diplomats privately say that although the human rights dialogues achieve little and return repeatedly to the same points, the associated cooperation programs are the real benefit of the overall policy approach.

[84] See, for example, Carothers, "Promoting the Rule of Law Abroad," the International Council on Human Rights Policy, *Local Perspectives: Foreign Aid to the Justice Sector* (Versoix, Switzerland, 2000); and Carothers, *Aiding Democracy Abroad: The Learning Curve* (Washington, DC: Carnegie Endowment for International Peace, 1999).

environment for human rights positive measures. To deal with the commitment deficit, donors need to do more to address the political environment in which the programs take place, acknowledging the synergy between cooperation and pressure. Chinese informants for this study were virtually unanimous in asserting that international pressure has played an important role in contributing to human rights concessions by the Chinese government, and if there is a trade-off between the donor programs covered here and continuing to exert such pressure, this is something they would not find acceptable.

Second is whether the elite-focused approach adopted by these programs has neglected partners who might be able to achieve more with donor cooperation than those actually chosen. Could the way INGOs have had to take the initiative rather than following the lead of their Chinese partners mean that they have been concentrating their attention on the wrong type of people and groups? What if they had begun by looking at what type of initiatives Chinese individuals and institutions were taking that could have an impact on various human rights problems and tried to support such efforts, both financially and through opening up international channels of communication and expertise to them? There are interesting examples to cite of domestically initiated work on domestic violence and HIV/AIDS that are now receiving foreign support. In addition, donors could support work on human rights being conducted outside China, by exile groups and others, but have generally refused to do so. Chinese informants indicate that donors need to go beyond safe circles of people and places and make more effort to support people who are really engaged in work on human rights and law on the ground.

A related issue is the appropriateness of the focus on the formal apparatus of law as an entry point for human rights concerns in China. After a frustrating experience of failure in U.S. programs on "administration of justice" aimed at improving legal institutions in many Latin American countries, the need to pay attention to the "demand side" is now being discussed.[85] In other words, if people do not demand that their rights be protected through the legal system, practices will not change. But to do this one needs to go beyond legal institutions to support such entities as community groups, bodies providing legal services to the poor, media reporting of legal processes, and so on.

Third is the problem of having sufficient information about conditions on the ground to make projects meaningful. Donors can help by supporting more empirical work and by insisting on serious needs assessments that allow for a clearer picture of where intervention can be most useful. As much as possible, such exercises should use Chinese consultants and encourage an open discussion about needs and priorities.

---

[85] See, for example, Linn Hammergren, "Political Will, Constituency Building and Public Support in Rule of Law Programs," Center for Democracy and Governance, USAID, August 1998.

There is certainly a need for foreign support for human rights-related legal programs in China, and in recent years, the political space has expanded for programs that can have an important positive effect in encouraging and supporting individuals and groups that are committed to bringing about improvements in respect for human rights. This makes it all the more important that the limited resources devoted to such work should be used effectively.

8 Normative Compliance and Hard Bargaining: INGOs and China's Response to International Human Rights Criticism

Sun Zhe

In this chapter, I argue that as international affairs focus on a balance of ideologies and the battle for social supremacy,[1] the structure of human associations is determined, to a great extent, by shared ideas rather than material forces.[2] For example, struggles over human rights pose opportunities and threats to political stability, economic development, and international peace. Human rights ideals, in other words, can play an important role in shaping social reality.

This argument has policy relevance and practical implications for human rights organizations and practitioners. As discussed in the introduction to this book, international nongovernmental organizations (INGOs) often face ethical challenges that constrain their efforts to do good in foreign lands, and they need to choose ways that allow them to promote human rights most effectively. This chapter focuses on the dilemma of whether to collaborate with governments who are themselves responsible for human rights violations. It begins with an examination of current INGO activities and dilemmas in China and explores China's counterarguments on human rights to identify forces that shape the complex relationship between China and INGOs. China has been engaging in the international debate on human rights and has adopted tactical adjustments by signing some important international documents on human rights.[3] What are the implications for INGOs in their future work in China? And what, in a more general sense, should be done in making a fundamental change to China's basic

---

[1] See Joseph S. Nye, Jr., "Propaganda Isn't the Way: Soft Power," *The International Herald Tribune*, January 10, 2003, internet resource http://www.ksg.harvard.edu/news/opeds/2003/nye_soft_power_iht_011003.htm (June 2003); *The Paradox of American Power – Why the World's Only Superpower Can't Go It Alone* (New York: Oxford University Press, 2003).

[2] Alexander Wendt, *Social Theory of International Politics* (Cambridge, England: Cambridge University Press, 1999), 1.

[3] Ernest Hass, "Collective Learning: Some Theoretical Speculations," in *Learning in U.S. and Soviet Foreign Policy*, eds. George W. Breslauer and Philip E. Tetlock (Boulder, CO: Westview Press, 1991), 62–9.

values and the foreign policies of Western countries? The author concludes that INGOs need to explore new strategies in fighting for international human rights and seek a more comprehensive framework in dealing with individual cases and systemic protections or abuses of human rights, drawing implications for INGO human rights work in China.

I. INGOs IN CHINA: TWO POLITICAL RISKS

INGOs in China have faced two unexpected political risks: first, they must decide how to obtain and maintain their legal status in China, because until June 2004 there was no specific law or regulation addressing the management of INGOs' operations in China. Second, they must make strategic choices regarding which programs they want to pursue in China in view of normative and political controversies. This has also led to difficulties because INGOs face the need to prioritize their tasks in ways that may not correspond to their own political missions and moral priorities.

The first risk is that related to the political barriers encountered by INGOs. Looking back, one finds that INGOs have long had difficulties entering China, and the process of entry has been gradual. In the early 1980s, some INGOs (World Vision, Oxfam International, Salvation Army, and Save the Children of Great Britain) tried to operate in Yunnan and other provinces in China. Beginning in the 1990s, some environmental protection groups (Greenpeace, American Environmental Protection Fund, Green Earth Network of Japan, etc.) initiated their China programs. In the late 1990s, political INGOs such as the Carter Foundation had initiated and supported political and local programs in China.[4]

At present, there are about 250 to 300 INGOs operating in China. Given that there were an estimated 37,281 INGOs in the world by 2000,[5] this low number reflects the political difficulties that INGOs have had in trying to establish a presence in China. Moreover, the total amount of INGO funds dedicated to China is about 10 percent of that for India.[6] It is estimated that the annual amount is about US $200 million.[7]

Because China lacked laws to regulate INGO activities before 2004, INGOs usually adopted three strategies in entering China: (1) some were "pressured" to report and register at government agencies, (2) some avoided official channels but registered under personal or business names for the purpose of opening accounts or offices in China, and (3) some registered as commercial or business

---

[4] Guo Gaozhong, "Legal Landing of INGOs in China," *Oriental Outlook* (June 15, 2004).

[5] See the 2002 United Nations Development Report.

[6] "The 250 NGOs in China," in *Newsletters of China's Development*, State Council, Center for Developmental Research, 2002; Guo Gaozhong, "Legal Landing of INGOs in China," *Oriental Outlook* (June 15, 2004).

[7] Ibid.

associations.[8] Those practices created a dilemma for both sides: on the one hand, the Chinese government took an attitude of "no registration, no hassle," for example, it allowed de facto existence and operation of INGOs in China as long as they did not act against Chinese norms and political rules. On the other hand, most INGOs registered under personal or business names found it difficult to be officially recognized by the Chinese government, let alone to obtain legal status or an "identity" in China.

On June 1, 2004, China issued the "Regulations on Foundation Management" (Ji jin hui guan li tiao li). This was a significant step toward a more open environment for INGOs. International Red Cross, Amnesty International, World Vision, and many other well-known but "sensitive" INGOs tried to establish a presence in China.[9]

The second risk that INGOs encountered is perhaps more substantial: it has been difficult for INGOs to establish noncontroversial evaluative criteria for measuring the rights of people in China. Without such criteria, it is impossible to understand the real evolution of the Chinese system, not to mention working out right strategies for addressing human right issues in China in a more efficient fashion.

Although some scholars have questioned China's readiness for a democratic government, a general consensus exists among INGOs that China is experiencing an awakening of individuals and a restructuring of private and public domains. As China experiences a gradual transformation toward a more open, market-oriented economy, the formal Marxist–Leninist system is eroding under the impact of society's increasing complexity. It is said that "formally the country was marching toward socialism," but in China today, "people are marching in all sorts of directions, many of which could not by any stretch of the imagination be called socialist."[10]

Although most INGOs recognize that substantial liberalization has occurred in China, they also believe that the "right of citizenship" has yet to be improved.[11]

---

[8] World Vision planned to enter China in 1982 but had to register in Hong Kong. The International Red Cross has more than seventy offices worldwide but none in China.

[9] The Regulations for the Management of Foundations (Ji jin hui guan li tiao li) were passed by the Chinese State Council on March 8, 2004, and enforced on June 1, 2004. See Xin Hua News, Beijing, March 18, 2004. Also, "China Development Brief" has full context of regulation. See, internet resource: http://www.chinadevelopmentbrief.com/node/301 (April 2004).

[10] Thomas P. Bernstein, "China: Change in a Marxist–Leninist State," in *Driven by Growth: Political Development in the Asian-Pacific Region*, ed. James W. Morley (New York: M. E. Sharpe, 1993), 66.

[11] The right of citizenship "involves both the right to be treated by fellow human beings as equal with respect to the making of collective choices and the obligation of those implementing such choices to be equally accountable and accessible to all members of the polity. Inversely, this principle imposes obligations on the ruled, that is, to respect the legitimacy of choices made by deliberation among equals." See Philippe C. Schmitter and Guillermo A. O'Donnell, *Transitions*

They are aware that the gradual development of China's legal system toward
affording greater protection for persons and property, the growing independence
and educational levels of members of the National People's Congress (NPC), and
the recent experiments with self-government at the grassroots level will help
China moving toward a more open and democratic society. Nonetheless, the
complex relationship between the regime and its people has created much confusion for INGOs in prioritizing their tasks. For example, the Chinese ruling
party counts on improving livelihoods to maintain political support. So it has
put forward the theory of "Three Representatives"[12] in the party's constitution, thus forming a new alliance with intellectuals and business elites to ensure
a political consensus. Ordinary people now try to limit their appeals to economic issues and avoid making political requests. INGOs might be surprised
that as long as the regime has both the intention and the capability to satisfy
the economic demands of protesters, those protesters are willing to package
their social and political demands into economic ones. It is even more difficult
for them to understand that the majority of organized collective acts in China
may remain "regime-confirming" rather than "regime-challenging" activities.
Unlawful demonstrations for human rights protections might be considered as
a form of negotiation with the regime, which confirm rather than challenge its
legitimacy.

The underlying issue that the Chinese case raises here is the following: by what
standard should we evaluate human rights development in China? There are,
of course, many ways to do this. One method is to apply a model of human
rights based on the Universal Declaration of Human Rights and its covenants to
China's actual human rights situation. This is the approach adopted by a number
of Western countries and by most INGOs. Perhaps the most useful methodology is a two-step process that first compares accepted international standards of
human rights and national norms, reflected in a state's constitution, and then
second examines the relationship between the constitutionally guaranteed principles and reality.[13] This approach has yet to be adopted by INGOs in entering
China.

from *Authoritarian Rule: Tentative Conclusions about Uncertain Democracies* (Johns Hopkins
University Press, 1986), 7–8.

[12] The idea was put forward by the former Chinese president, Jiang Zemin, in February 2000
during his working trip to the Guangdong province, China. Jiang further elaborated this idea
and published a book which is entitled *Jiang Zemin on the "Three Representatives"* (Beijing: the
Foreign Languages Press, 2002). Also, see Jiang Zemin: *On Socialism with Chinese Characteristics*,
Beijing: the Party Literature Research Center of the Communist Party of China (CPC) Central
Committee, 2002.

[13] For example, Randle R. Edwards, Louis Henkin, and Andrew Nathan took this two-step approach
in their *Human Rights in Contemporary China* (New York: Columbia University Press, 1985),
introduction.

II. INTERACTION: THE PRESENCE OF INGOs IN CHINA
AND THEIR INFLUENCE

China claimed in its annual "White Paper on Human Rights"[14] that "in the past fifty years the Chinese people have made a great historic leap in the development of human rights."[15] Moreover, "they have rid China of the label of 'The Sick Man of East Asia' and steered the country toward a civilized and healthy life of plenty and democratic freedom and away from chronic hunger, cold, and ignorance."[16] The white paper also emphasizes that "the Chinese government always respects the purposes and principles of the Charter of the United Nations for promoting and protecting human rights, supports the UN efforts in this regard and actively participates in the UN activities in the realm of human rights."[17]

Such claims, in the eyes of many INGOs and Western critics, emphasize stability of the entire society rather than the welfare of the individual. Therefore, INGOs and Western critics prefer to dismiss this Chinese argument, defending universal standards and calling on Beijing to take specific action, such as releasing a high-profile prisoner of conscience.[18] In this sense, they usually focus on civil and political rights and thus criticize China for its lack of criminal procedures, forced exile of dissidents, religious oppression, torturing of prisoners or forcing them into labor, and so on. The Chinese official press decries this as cultural imperialism and insists that China should be judged by its own traditions, not by foreign criteria.

Although most INGOs consider the rights of the individual sacred, China, along with many other Asian nations, looks at human rights at a more practical level, which includes such provisions as the right to life, freedom from starvation, shelter and clothing, and the rights to education and employment,

---

[14] Each year, the Information Office of the State Council issues "The Chinese White Paper on Human Rights," elaborating the achievements China scored in its human rights cause during the previous year.

[15] See http://www.china.org.cn/english/2001/Apr/10670.htm.

[16] Ibid. For example, the 14,000-word white paper issued in 2001, titled *Progress in China's Human Rights Cause in 2000*, argues that "In safeguarding and promoting human rights, although setbacks occurred, one indisputable basic fact is that after unremitting efforts over half a century, the poverty-stricken, weak and humiliated old China has become an independent New China in the early stage of prosperity, and the 1.25 billion Chinese people have become the masters of their own fates."

[17] Ibid. The Standing Committee of the 9th NPC ratified the International Covenant on Economic, Social and Cultural rights in February 2001. The white paper says this fully demonstrates the Chinese government's positive attitude toward carrying out international cooperation in human rights as well as China's firm determination and confidence in promoting and protecting human rights.

[18] Jeffrey N. Wasserstrom, "Judging China by Chinese Standards," *Christian Science Monitor* 89, no. 227 (October 20, 1997), 19.

and the means of self-support. Following the line of Beijing's argument, one would argue that under several major performance indicators,[19] China has done remarkably well in terms of economic reform since 1979.[20] For instance, with an annual growth rate of around 10 percent, China has quadrupled its gross domestic product in less than twenty years and is now, if we take the EU as a whole, the world's fourth largest economy.[21] The World Bank and International Monetary Fund have tried to use purchasing power parity (PPP) to recalculate the scale of China's economy, concluding that China would overtake Japan, becoming the second largest economy in the world.[22] Even if these numbers are questionable, INGOs still need to ask the following questions if they are serious about operating in China: to what degree are people willing to make compromises and sacrifices to their freedom to satisfy the need for economic growth? Can the Chinese regime enjoy any support from its people without granting them fundamental political rights? Moreover, INGOs need to think about the fact that when the Chinese people are confronted with the question of a trade-off between economic development and political democratization, nearly half of them chose economic development and only 20 percent believe democracy is more important.[23] Moreover, "democracy," in many Chinese people's minds, can refer to various things ranging from a more effective means "to resolving problems facing our country" to "certain adjustments" in the political system.[24] There is no evidence that people think of democracy as synonymous with liberty, in terms of fair and regular elections, competition for office, a constitutional guarantee of civil and political liberties, and civic participation.[25] Many would not clearly understand Schumpeter's definition of democratic "institutional arrangements."[26]

"The question of China and human rights," as argued in the chapter by Lindsnæs, Sano, and Thelle, is like a prism that "reflects the tension between the political arena of international negotiations and power balancing on one hand and the objective of finding a solution to people's real problems on the

---

[19] These criteria include growth rates of its domestic product (overall and per capita), industrial and agricultural output and retail sales, savings and investment ratios, acquisition of technological, financial, and marketing know-how, growth of external trade, foreign direct investment (FDI), foreign exchange reserves, and avoidance of excessive foreign debt.

[20] In economic reality, China's sensitivity and vulnerability to international actions, processes, and institutional arrangements are mixed and perhaps unique. The Chinese economy is technically backward and inefficient, but it is reasonably comprehensive.

[21] Charlotte Denny, "China Is No Threat to America–For Now," Guardian (April 8, 2002), http://www.guardian.co.uk/bush/story/0,7369,680495,00.html#article_continue (September 2003).

[22] The World Bank, China 2020: Development Challenges in the New Century (Washington, DC: 1997), 83.

[23] Ibid, 26.   [24] Ibid.

[25] Robert A. Dahl, Democracy and Its Critics (New Haven, CT: Yale University Press, 1989); On Democracy (New Haven, CT: Yale University Press, 1999).

[26] Joseph A. Schumpeter's, Capitalism, Socialism and Democracy (New York: Harper, 3rd ed., 1950).

other."[27] The interesting point here is this: the Chinese government now adopts an "engagement" policy toward INGOs but argues that any shortcomings in its rights record are due to the country's level of development as well as historical and cultural factors, and thus the best approach would be one that assists the country in its efforts to develop.[28] Several INGOs have chosen to work within the constraints of China's terms of engagement.

Has the strategy of engagement worked in China? What is the impact of the INGOs' work in China? It is clear that China relies on INGOs' natural and human resources (capital, skills, knowledge, as well as transnational networks) for its developmental programs. At a practical level, China's terms of engagement encourage "problem-solving" INGO programs while rejecting "interest group"-type activities.[29] As a result, INGOs are active in the areas of poverty alleviation, protection of women and children, and environmental protection. The only exception seems to be that some INGOs have in recent years also successfully persuaded the Chinese government to work on some joint research projects related to civil and political rights, such as programs on the protection of the rights of suspects and detainees and on legal and judicial trainings,[30] juvenile justice pilot projects,[31] and so on. Taking all these activities as a whole, I argue that the INGOs impact in China can be analyzed according to the following factors.

First, INGOs' presence in China has changed the Chinese mind-set. Now the Chinese government realizes that even if INGOs have their own ideals and charters, they are not necessarily "antigovernment" organizations.[32] The Chinese government has understood that most INGOs operate legally according to Chinese laws. They usually have their charters and rules, do not act at the behest

---

[27] Lindsnæs, Sano, and Thelle "Human Rights in Action. Supporting Human Rights Work in Authoritarian Countries," Chapter 6, this volume.

[28] For accounts of the policy shift and its origins, see "Human Rights in China," *From Principle to Pragmatism: Can "Dialogue" Improve China's Human Rights Situation?* (New York: HRIC, June 1998); and Ann Kent, "Human Rights: From Sanctions to Delegations to Dialogue," in *Re-Orienting Australia–China Relations: 1972 to the Present*, ed. Nicholas Thomas (Aldershot: Ashgate, 2004), 147–62.

[29] See Wu Zhongze, "The Current Situation of NGOs' Development in Our Country," Special Report by the NGO Research Center, Qinghua University, September 2002, 3.

[30] The Danish Institute of Human Rights engagement in China began in 1998 at the first round of the EU–China human rights dialogue, initiated by China in February. The first contacts resulted in agreement on a joint research project on protection of the rights of suspects and detainees, meaning prevention of the use of torture and ill treatment by the police in the pretrial phase. The project was completed in December 2001. See http://humanrights.dk/news/updateuk/all/Update-Chinaprogramme (September 2003).

[31] This global fund is funded by the UK Human Rights Project and administered by the UK Foreign Office; it was operational between 1998 and 2004. It is now being replaced by a grant-making facility to be called the Global Opportunities Fund.

[32] The term *fei zheng fu zu zhi* (nongovernmental organization) is confusing in Chinese. Sometimes it is translated as *fan zheng fu zu zhi*, or antigovernmental organization. Terrorist groups, underground organizations, and religious groups are rarely affiliated with, or supported by, INGOs.

of foreign governments, and usually have transparent accounting systems. Most important, they come to China not for the purpose of "overthrowing" the Chinese government but to offer human rights and humanitarian assistance. This is an important change in government thinking and thus has opened a window of opportunity for INGOs. For instance, in early 2004, the No. 1 Directory of the CCP had recognized the role played by INGOs in helping China to solve some social problems. In May 2004, the State Council invited some INGOs to participate in a conference on dealing with poverty issues.[33] Almost at the same time, China signed a mutual agreement with the International Red Cross and allowed it to open a Beijing office. This brought about a surge of similar applications by Amnesty International, World Vision, the Salvation Army, and other INGOs. These organizations were seen as civil groups or associations, not as "antigovernment" institutions.[34] Moreover, the Chinese government views them as important international forces that have shaped international norms and systems, thus making great contributions to society.

Second, INGOs in China have contributed to the growth of the country's local NGOs, and thus to the growth of Chinese civil society indirectly. In most advanced countries, NGOs are seen as the third branch of the political system, the first two being government and business. The activities of NGOs are also seen as important indicators of the maturity of civil society. In 2002, it is estimated that there were more than three million Chinese NGOs operating nationwide.[35] Some of them came into being because of the influence of INGOs in China. That is to say, INGOs in China were required to find cooperating partners, and their counterparts were Chinese local NGOs. The more INGOs came to China, the more local NGOs emerged. This has laid a foundation for the growth of Chinese NGOs in the reform era. Most NGOs are small social groups and have limited funds to operate. Many have turned to INGOs for help. Some American-based foundations, such as the Ford, Elizabeth Taylor, and the Bill and Melinda Gates foundations, have given generous support to Chinese NGOs and independent groups in the fight against AIDS. Among them, Ford helped the Chinese authorities establish a research network on AIDS studies in 1991, and thirty-four experts were working for the program.[36] Two Chinese NGOs were funded completely by INGOs: the Ai De Association in Nanjing, which focuses on poverty and special education and has an annual budget of about US $4–5 million, and the Min Cu Association in Beijing, funded by Germany,

[33] The conference was sponsored by the World Bank and opened on May 26 in Shanghai; the final document was named "Shanghai Consensus." *Renmin Daily*, May 25, 2004, 1.
[34] Zhao Liqing, "Non-governmental Organizations and Non-profit Organizations," available at www.cp.org.cn/jiuban/2233/ReadNews.asp?NewsID=1110&BigClassID=24&SmallClassID. (published July 8, 2003, accessed September 2003).
[35] Ji Jiangwei, "NGOs outside the Embassies," in *San lian sheng huo zhou kan*, No. 176 (January 14, 2002), http://www.lifeweek.com.cn/2002-12-30/000534378.html (September 2003).
[36] See http://www.chain.net.cn/article.php?articleID=2318.

Finland, and international religious groups with an annual budget of about US $1 million.[37] Another example is the European Union (EU) Human Rights Small Project Facility. On December 7, 2001, the EU held a press conference in Beijing and announced that as a result of an ongoing dialogue between the EU and China beginning in 1995, the project was fully supported by the Chinese government. It planned to fund 6.2 million RMB (yuan) a year for programs related to reducing use of the death penalty; workers' rights; policy issues; political participation in the policy-making process; free speech; economic, social, and cultural rights; and so forth.[38] According to one program coordinator, the EU Human Rights Small Project Facility had contacted 140 Chinese NGOs and encouraged them to apply for funding.

Third, the entry of INGOs has contributed to law-making activities in China. With the exception of some customary laws, all laws in the National People's Congress (NPC) are statute-based. Legislation in China can be considered in terms of three tiers: the Constitution and statutes as passed by the NPC and its Standing Committee of the National People's Congress (NPCSC), administrative rules and regulations as enacted by the State Council, and local laws enacted by the people's congresses of the provinces, municipalities, and autonomous regions.[39] China issued a temporary regulation in 1950 to manage domestic NGOs. In the reform era, the breadth and intensity of the new laws promulgated in China have been enormous and without precedent in its history. In 1988, China issued the Rules in Foundation Management (*Ji jin guan li ban fa*), followed by the Temporary Regulations for Social Group Registrations (*She hui tuan ti deng ji guan li tiao li*) and the Temporary Rules for Foreign Business Groups (*Wai guo shang hui guan li zan xing gui ding*) in 1989. Because of the growth of NGOs, the Temporary Regulations for Social Group Registrations were revised in 1998. The state council had also made more than fifty new regulations in the area of regulating operations of NGOs. The 2004 regulation could be considered a step forward for integrating an international element into new rules. It has classified NGOs into three categories: (1) those that can raise funds in China, (2) those that cannot raise funds, and (3) those foreign foundations that operate and are registered in China. The last one has opened windows of opportunity for INGOs and has made a contribution to the rise of a more liberalized China.

III. PATTERNS OF BEHAVIOR: CHINA'S STRATEGIES IN RESPONSE TO CRITICISM

Having explained the INGOs' presence and influence in China, let us consider the Chinese patterns of behavior in responding to international human rights

---

[37] Ji Jiangwei, "NGOs Outside the Embassies," in *San lian sheng huo zhou kan*, no. 176 (January 14, 2002), http://www.lifeweek.com.cn/2002-12-30/000534378.html (September 2003).

[38] Ibid.

[39] Thomas Chiu et al., *Legal Systems of the PRC*, 43.

criticism. China has formally signed two major international covenants[40] and quite a few international documents on human rights, but at the same time it has used various strategies in dealing with international criticism. These are demonstrated in the style of normative compliance and hard-bargaining activities. China has rejected international bullying by superpowers and emphasized that every country or region has its own way of putting human rights into practice.[41] In this sense, the Chinese government has used human rights as a tool against imperialism, and Beijing sees the human rights offensive as part of the Western, particularly American, drive for hegemony through ideological subversion of rival states.

U.S.–China relations can illustrate this point. On one hand, there is an "American liberal grand strategy" in the U.S. promotion of democracy abroad. That is to say, the United States has argued that international trade fosters economic growth, and promoting democracy and human rights abroad is a political process that shapes, constrains, and channels states' actions.[42] Dealing with these criticisms, the Chinese government was pressured to rally Third World support and point to the realpolitik concerns that seem to underlie U.S. intervention abroad. For example, China has criticized the United States for intervening in Bosnia-Herzegovina, Haiti, the Philippines, Russia, and other countries. These interventions have brought about economic and social disasters. China has also taken offensive and counteroffensive measures in criticizing the U.S. human rights record and pointed to the policy challenges of human rights advocates in the United States. China has pointed out in its "White Paper on American Human Rights Record" that "the United States, assuming the role of "a world judge of human rights," has distorted the impressions of human rights conditions in many countries and regions in the world, including China. The white paper also mentions how the United States has "accused [other nations] of human rights violations, all the while turning a blind eye to its own human rights–related problems." These double standards, which consistently feature in U.S. foreign policy, are fast waning that country's credibility for dealing out criticism.[43]

Here are a few statistics that China has used to counter the American critique:

It can be said that the United States has shown a poor record for safeguarding life, freedom, and personal safety. From 1977 to 1996, more than 400,000 Americans were murdered, almost seven times the number of Americans killed

[40] China signed the International Covenant on Civil and Political Rights (ICCPR) in 1998 and the International Covenant on Economic, Social and Cultural Rights (ICESCR) in 1997.
[41] Li Yunlong, "On the Universality and Particularity of Human Rights," available at http://www.humanrights-china.org/course/Basic2001101095515.htm (August 2003).
[42] G. John Ikenberry, "Why Export Democracy? The 'Hidden Grand Strategy' of American Foreign Policy," The Wilson Quarterly, vol. 23, no. 2 (spring 1999), 7–22.
[43] "Human Rights Record of the United States in 2001," published by the Information Office of the State Council of the People's Republic of China (March 12, 2002), available at http://english.peopledaily.com.cn/200203/11/eng20020311_91880.shtml (December 2002).

in the Vietnam War.[44] The number of registered weapon vendors in the country exceeds 100,000, which is more than the total number of overseas outlets of the fast-food giant McDonald's.[45]

There have been serious rights violations by law enforcement departments. The United States has the biggest prison population in the world. Prisons are overcrowded, and inmates are ill treated.[46]

The plight of the poor, hungry, and homeless is another key issue. It can be argued that the proportion of poor people is higher in the United States than in China.[47]

Worrying conditions for women and children is an important issue of social inequality in the United States[48]; it is also notorious for a deep-rooted history of racial discrimination that continues to shape social and political practices today.

America can be accused of wantonly infringing on the human rights of other countries: since the 1990s, the United States has used force overseas on more than forty occasions.[49]

Taking an anti-American stance and counterattacking using evidence of the U.S. human rights record does not come as a surprise. The question is whether the Chinese government takes the accusations it receives from the United States seriously. How sincere is the current Chinese line on human rights and social justice – meaning equitable distribution of wealth and opportunities – in China and elsewhere? Or is the issue simply that of development, to be followed by a gradual liberalization in the political sphere as legitimacy or policy effectiveness becomes linked to more vigorous pluralism?

The Chinese government's dilemma is that it has not yet demonstrated that free thought and speech, the establishment of mass organizations, and criticism of party leaders sharply contradict the rights of subsistence and development.[50] Moreover, its appeal to self-determination is not fully consistent. Beijing refuses to take criticism from the international community seriously, maintaining that "All peoples have the right of self-determination" and "by virtue of that right they freely determine their political status and freely pursue their economic, social and cultural development."[51] Yet China has joined other countries in condemning international abuses of human rights, such as the treatment of blacks in South Africa under apartheid.

---

[44] Ibid.

[45] Catharin E. Dalpino, "Human Rights in China," *Policy Brief*, no. 50 (June 1999), the Brookings Institution, available at http://taiwansecurity.org/IS/Dalpino-9906.htm (May 2003).

[46] "Human Rights Record of the United States in 2001," the white paper published by the Information Office of the State Council of the People's Republic of China (March 12, 2002), available at http://english.peopledaily.com.cn/200203/11/eng20020311_91880.shtml.

[47] Ibid.

[48] Susan Moller Okin, *Justice, Gender and the Family* (New York: Basic Books, 1991).

[49] "Human Rights Record of the United States in 2001," op cit.

[50] George Koo, "Human Rights," *Harvard International Review*, vol. 20, no. 3 (summer 1998), 68.

[51] Li Yunlong, "On the Universality and Particularity of Human Rights," in *Fazhi Daily*, December 8 1998, 3.

More recently, China has tried to acknowledge and join the international dialogue on human rights. The increased presence of INGOs in China implies that Chinese cooperative behavior can primarily be seen as a change in stance from seeing human rights as a tool of Western powers to consider human rights as an issue for international dialogue. In recent years, China has conducted dialogues on human rights at various levels with the United States, the EU, Canada, Australia, and many other Western countries. China has also taken an active part in international human rights activities, especially activities under the umbrella of the United Nations. For example, China has ratified eighteen international conventions on human rights and, by proceeding from its own conditions, incorporated into Chinese law the principles and criteria provided for in these conventions for the protection of human rights.[52]

Nonetheless, China is also firm in saying that China will adapt to certain international norms only if those norms are not defined or manipulated by the United States as tools for interfering with the domestic affairs of other countries. For example, when the United States issued its report on Chinese human rights, Jin Yongjian[53] argued that "the United Nations has never requested or authorized the United States to compile or release such report." In his view, "The United States has completely violated the UN Charter, principles and the gist of relevant international conferences and documents."[54] Other experts also responded with criticism. Dong Yunhu, vice president and secretary general of the China Society for the Study of Human Rights, noted that the United States always criticizes other countries and regions but turns a blind eye to its own human rights conditions. "Such practice has even provoked questions from its own people," Dong said, quoting Robert A. Seiple, the first U.S. ambassador-at-large for international religious freedom, by saying that the United States should include itself in the annual human rights report. He said that if the United States could not write its own report, it should invite other countries to do so.[55]

The analysis of the Chinese pattern of behavior shows that China took a "selective adaptation" method in dealing with international pressures. Here it is suggested that perception determines understanding about institutional arrangements and their origins and implications, concerning both one's own system and the system with which one is interacting. The conflicting view over human rights demonstrated that China, as well as some other developing nations, has used normative acceptance and hard bargaining as a coping strategy for balancing local regulatory imperatives with the requirements of compliance with international (largely Western) norms.

---

[52] Ibid.
[53] Jin Yongjian, former under-secretary-general of the United Nations, is the president of the UN Association of China.
[54] *People's Daily Online,* Saturday, March 9, 2002, available http://english.people.com.cn/200203/09/eng20020309_91767.shtml (May 2006).
[55] Ibid.

IV. IMPLICATIONS FOR HUMAN RIGHTS INGOs

In dealing with human rights in China, many Westerners have felt frustration and anxiety. The Chinese government perceives this as a growing uncertainty and lack of confidence about the future of Western civilization itself. It emphasizes that when assessing the Chinese political system's level of freedom, democracy, and individual rights, it is important to remember that the Chinese do not share the values and traditions of the West's Judeo-Christian heritage. Although this cultural pluralist outlook is not particularly controversial, the theoretical implication of inherent concern is more thought provoking. The concept of democracy can be muddled, controversial, and strongly normative. How one defines democracy affects how one analyzes such issues as transitions to democracy and democratic stability.

The Chinese case demonstrates that democracy can be easily conceptualized metaphorically as either a skyscraper or the weather. A skyscraper is easily recognizable. The weather always changes. So to what extent do we believe that there are many forms of democracy? If democracy has essentially only one form, it is considerably easier to decide which countries are moving toward its advanced form and which are not. If, on the other hand, there are numerous models of democratization, it becomes infinitely more difficult to identify countries that are even approaching democracy, let alone to promote it as a universal goal. Moreover, I think that reconsidering the merits of some authoritarian regimes, or posttotalitarian regimes, is crucial, because it is not only China that engages in selective noncompliance; many other countries face the same dilemma. Although the growth of the ethical impact of globalization may appear inevitable, it is by no means inevitable that governments in both China and other developing countries will merely adopt Western norms.

Still, the process of economic change in China has linked its people with the global community in a common search for justice. In the world today, the issue of human rights has already been institutionalized into the international community. As mentioned earlier, China agrees that human rights are an issue for international dialogue. For example, in 2001, China put forth a four-point proposal on attaining the common goal of promotion and protection of human rights at a meeting of the Third Committee of the 56th Session of the UN General Assembly.[56] The proposal includes "building up a peaceful and secure international environment, striving to narrow the gap of development among countries, attaching equal importance to the two categories of human rights and solving disputes over human rights issues among countries through dialogue and cooperation."[57] China's cooperative announcement provides a golden

---

[56] "China Puts Forth Proposal on Promotion, Protection of Human Rights," *People's Daily* (November 15, 2001), 2.
[57] Ibid.

opportunity for INGOs to further implement dialogue. In addition to sets of principles that would be accepted by China in a normative sense, there also exist some practical institutional arrangements for arriving at agreements in which China and INGOs can obtain equal opportunity to participate in the process of dialogue. These might lead to a consensus for common action in human rights development.

The practical methods for ensuring that China accepts and actually complies with international human rights norms should be constructed from both "structuralist" and "elite-centered" approaches. The structuralist approach requires the identification of the preconditions necessary for human rights dialogues. These may include certain institutional arrangements such as establishing forums, finding channels of contacts, and providing information exchange services. Such arrangements should contribute to a psychological orientation of accepting the principles or rules of dialogue. Moreover, the realm of human rights in China can be monitored more extensively. China's realization of its WTO obligations is already the subject of formal monitoring processes under WTO Trade Policy Review Mechanism and various member country initiatives, such as the U.S. Congressional Executive Commission on China. Continued examination of the processes of WTO-driven legal reforms in China is crucial in determining whether the evolving economic and legal reforms are attentive to human rights concerns.[58] For the "elite-centered" approach, I suggest that the role of an agency be addressed and formulated. Decision making plays a prominent role in making the dialogue work, especially in the earlier stages of development of any human rights promotions programs in China. For example, multilevel dialogues on human rights should be conducted and become platforms of mutual understanding and respect. Leading collective or individual institutions, theorists, or practitioners in China should be identified because they would share the responsibilities of making choices, managing cross-talks, and supervising the quality of the dialogues between the East and West.

I propose four tactics that the INGOs should take. The first strategy is that INGOs should have a more long-term vision, such as a five- or ten-year outlook. At the same time, they should lengthen the time horizon in assessing human rights progress in China. Progress over longer periods should be charted, mission program plans should be planned, and policy instruments for current conditions and opportunities should be well tailored. Such long-term outlooks would change the emphasis from threats to apply human rights sanctions to China to monitoring of its progress. In past years, the European Parliament has published many negative reports criticizing China. In April 2002, however, it released the paper, "European Parliament on an EU Strategy towards China," which positively reviews the development of Sino-European relations in the past few years

---

[58] Pitman B. Potter, "Are Human Rights on China's WTO Agenda?" (June 27, 2002), http://www.hrichina.org/public/contents/article?revision%5fid=2056&item%5fid=2055 (May 2006).

and makes favorable accounts of China's contributions to international affairs and its achievements in domestic areas. Giving emphasis to the great significance of developing the Sino–European cooperative partnership, the resolution makes some constructive suggestions on further strengthening the dialogue and expanding cooperation between the two sides in different fields in the future. China officially embraced and appreciated such an optimistic attitude.[59]

The second strategy is that INGOs should have a clear, substantive agenda. They should begin with goodwill and form a broader definition of human rights to engage their Chinese counterparts and encourage them to participate and cooperative more effectively. Political rights should be considered when informing the Chinese government that the widespread use of administrative detention does not conform with international human rights standards. Other suggestions might be the improvement of prison conditions, getting China to ratify UN treaties, and allowing UN and Red Cross human rights workers full access to prisons. Economic and social rights such as environmental protection, health care, women's rights, and so on should be placed near the top of the agenda.[60]

Some INGOs have already applied this cooperative strategy in dealing with China. Organizations such as the Ford Foundation and the Danish Institute for Human Rights (DIHR) are actively involved in human rights projects in China. For example, "the Ford Foundation has been establishing and developing grant-making activities in areas such as judicial reforms, legal aid, and constitutional law research. Such projects are explicitly designed to promote greater awareness and respect for individual rights and concern for the worst-off groups in society. Effective implementation of these projects is premised upon successful collaboration with government officials and institutions, notwithstanding appearances."[61] Human rights organizations working in China often choose to avoid politically sensitive issues such as labor rights, freedom of the press, and the political rights

---

[59] See http://english.people.com.cn/200204/18/eng20020418_94326.shtml (May 2006).

[60] For the first time ever in the history of the EU–China dialogue, at the May 1998 round, when the United Kingdom held the EU presidency, INGOs were involved. Amnesty International and the Council of Churches for Great Britain and Ireland participated in the meeting with the Chinese delegates. The Free Tibet Campaign and the June Fourth Support Group were on the INGO list submitted by the British government to the Chinese delegation, who refused to meet representatives of these two groups. The meeting was not public, and none of the participants have disclosed any information about it. Other INGOs were subsequently involved in the October 1998 dialogue session. Since then, most of them have decided, for their own reasons, to drop out of this process. Nevertheless, the question remains open. Participation of international, independent human rights organizations obviously gives rise to a problem of legitimacy: in the absence of independent human rights INGOs in China, who would be their counterparts? The United Kingdom, and the EU as a whole, should draw more systematically on the expertise that could be provided by China scholars and human rights organizations.

[61] Daniel A. Bell and Joseph H. Carens, "The Ethical Dilemmas of International Human Rights and Humanitarian NGOs: Reflections on a Dialogue between Practitioners and Theorists," *Human Rights Quarterly* 26, no. 2 (May 2004), 320–1.

of dissidents.[62] They might also decide to avoid politically sensitive places such as Tibet and Xinjiang.

The third strategy is that INGOs should consider establishing, through the UN channel, a comprehensive working body, which incorporates significant international resources and local representatives in China. The United Nations and its human rights mechanisms have a global mandate to monitor and promote human rights and have a unique legitimacy in doing so. The prestige of the United Nations in China remains high. Cooperating with the UN human rights mechanisms is crucial so that all countries engaged in a human rights dialogue with China build on and reinforce positive results generated by the work of UN procedures. For example, in May 2000, the UN Committee Against Torture (CAT) recommended that China eliminate all forms of administrative detention. This is a recommendation that should be taken up in every dialogue. It might increase its legitimacy by forging consensus in actual dialogue activities.

The last strategy is that, where possible, the human rights dialogue should also open a second track to include nongovernmental participants. China has expressed a willingness to conduct dialogues on human rights with INGOs in the past, although Beijing quite likely intended these as substitutes for government discussion. In any two-track activity, the United States should not insist on perfect symmetry. China will want to involve intellectuals and groups that are closer to the state than to their U.S. counterparts. A dialogue promoting links with citizens will help insulate the human rights discussion from the hazards of official bilateral politics. A policy that supports indigenous trends toward openness will give both Chinese and Americans a greater stake in human rights cooperation and harbors a far greater chance of success. In addition, it would be significant if China allowed independent social groups, scholars and lawyers, and other individuals to participate in the dialogue. To do this, the INGOs might need to encourage the Chinese government to engage in dialogue domestically as well as internationally.

CONCLUSION

The reciprocal impacts and interplay between China and the rest of the world in the field of human rights demonstrate that China represents both problems and solutions to world order. Because both China and the international system are experiencing profound transformations, the way in which the outside world responds to China is closely connected to the way China responds to the outside world.

The Chinese government has demonstrated extraordinary sensitivity to the debate on its human rights record. Over the last decade, it has shown progress and

---

[62] However, Daniel A. Bell and Joseph H. Carens observe that one organization – John Kamm's *Dui Hua* [Dialogue] Foundation – has had remarkable success in securing the release of dissidents from Chinese jails by engaging and cooperating with Chinese political authorities (ibid, 322–60).

resolve by signing international human rights treaties and opening up channels of dialogue. At the same time, however, it intentionally took a selective adaptive method in dealing with international criticism. The Chinese case reveals an ethical dilemma for INGOs: there is a pressing need to make a concerted lobbying effort that might integrate public monitoring of China's rights situation and the quiet diplomacy associated with dialogue. Change is inevitable; it is how it is brought about that makes the difference.

9 Defending Economic, Social, and Cultural Rights: Practical Issues Faced by an International Human Rights Organization

Kenneth Roth

Over the last decade, many have urged international human rights organizations to pay more attention to economic, social, and cultural (ESC) rights. I agree with this prescription, and for several years Human Rights Watch has been doing significant work in this realm.[1] Nonetheless, many who urge international groups to take on ESC rights have a fairly simplistic sense of how this is done. Human Rights Watch's experience has led me to believe that there are certain types of ESC rights issues for which our methodology works well and others for which it does not. Understanding this distinction is key, in my view, if an international human rights organization such as Human Rights Watch is to address ESC rights effectively. Other approaches may work for other types of human rights groups, but organizations such as Human Rights Watch that rely foremost on shaming to generate public pressure in defense of rights should remain attentive to this distinction.

During the Cold War, ESC rights tended to be debated in ideological terms. This was not only a matter of the West stressing civil and political rights while the Soviet bloc (in principle if not in practice) stressed ESC rights. Many in the West went so far as to deny the very legitimacy of ESC issues as rights. Aryeh Neier, the former head of Human Rights Watch and now president of the Open Society Institute, is perhaps the leading proponent of this view – most recently in his memoirs, *Taking Liberties*.[2] Certainly interesting philosophical debates can be had about whether the concept of human rights should embrace positive as well as negative rights.[3] Yet because consensus in such debates is probably unattainable,

---

[1] See Human Rights Watch, "Economic, Social and Cultural Rights," http://www.hrw.org/esc/. See also list of selected reports towards the end of this chapter.

[2] Aryeh Neier, *Taking Liberties: Four Decades in the Struggle for Rights* (Public Affairs, 2003), xxix–xxx.

[3] See Isaiah Berlin, *Four Essays on Liberty* (London and New York: Oxford University Press, 1969), 122–34, for more on the concepts on positive and negative freedom. See also Amartya Sen, *Development as Freedom* (New York: Anchor Books, 1999); Martha Nussbaum, *Women and Human Development: The Capabilities Approach* (New York: Cambridge University Press, 2000) (discussing this debate within a contemporary human rights framework).

the international human rights movement, in my view, has no choice but to rest on a positive-law justification for its work. That is, unless there are compelling reasons to deviate from human rights law, we must defend it largely as written if we are to retain legitimacy and effectiveness. That law, of course, codifies civil and political as well as ESC rights.[4]

That said, I must admit to finding the typical discussion of ESC rights rather sterile. I have been to countless conferences and debates in which international human rights organizations are advised to do more to protect ESC rights. Fair enough. Usually, though, the advice reduces to little more than sloganeering. People lack medical care; therefore, we should say that their right to health has been violated. People lack shelter; therefore, we should say that their right to housing has been violated. People are hungry; therefore, we should say that their right to food has been violated.

Such "analysis," of course, wholly ignores such key questions as the following: who is responsible for the impoverished state of a population? Is the government in question taking steps to progressively realize the relevant rights on the basis of available resources? What should the remedy be for any violation that is found? More to the point, for the purposes of this chapter, it also ignores the question of which issues can and cannot effectively be taken up by international human rights organizations that rely on shaming to generate public pressure. That is, for which kinds of ESC rights violations is the shaming methodology best suited for generating pressure on relevant actors to curb violations?

There are obviously various ways to promote ESC rights. One is simply to mobilize people to insist on respect for these rights. The language of rights can be a powerful organizing tool. But given that respect for ESC rights often requires the reallocation of resources, the people who have the clearest standing to insist on a particular allocation are usually the residents of the country in question. Outsiders such as international human rights organizations are certainly free to have a say in such matters, but when in all but the richest countries the fulfillment of one ESC right is often at the expense of another, outsiders' insistence on a particular trade-off has less legitimacy than that of the country's residents. Why should outsiders be listened to when they counsel, for example, that less be spent on health care and more on education – or even that less be spent on roads, bridges, or other infrastructure deemed important for long-term economic development and more on immediate needs?

I am aware that similar trade-offs of scarce resources can arise in the realm of civil and political rights. Building prisons or creating a judicial system can be expensive. My experience, however, has been that international human rights

---

[4] See UN General Assembly, *International Covenant on Civil and Political Rights*, Resolution 2200 (XXI), UN Doc. A/6316 (1966), 999 UNTS 171; UN General Assembly, *International Covenant on Economic, Social and Cultural Rights*, Resolution 2200 (XXI), UN Doc. A/6316 (1966), 993 UNTS 3 (hereinafter ICESCR); See also UN General Assembly, *Universal Declaration of Human Rights*, Resolution 217A (III), UN Doc. A/810 (1948), reprinted in *American Journal of International Law* 43 (1949): Supp. 127.

organizations implicitly recognize these trade-offs by avoiding recommendations that are excessively costly. For example, Human Rights Watch in its work on prison conditions routinely avoids recommending large infrastructure investments. Instead, we focus on improvements in the treatment of prisoners that would involve relatively inexpensive policy changes.[5] Similarly, our advocacy of due process in places such as Rwanda with weak and impoverished judicial systems implicitly takes account of the practical limitations facing the country, leading us to be more tolerant of prosecutorial compromises such as *gacaca* courts than we would be in a richer country.[6]

A second way to promote ESC rights is through litigation – or, of greater relevance to most countries, by promoting the legislation that would make it possible to enforce ESC rights in court. It is clearly in the interest of those who believe in ESC rights that these be codified in enforceable national law. Many countries have such laws in various forms – be they guarantees of a minimum level of income (minimum wage or welfare), food, housing, or health care – but too many countries do not. International human rights organizations might usefully press governments to adopt the legislation – the statutory rights – needed to make litigation a meaningful tool to enforce ESC rights. That procedural device still falls significantly short of actual implementation, however. When it comes to deciding which ESC rights should be implemented first, or which trade-offs among competing economic demands should be made, the advocacy of legislation does not give international human rights organizations any greater standing to address the concrete realization of ESC rights.

Similar shortcomings plague efforts by international human rights organizations to press governments to adopt national plans to progressively realize ESC rights on the basis of available resources.[7] Even though such plans would

---

[5] See Human Rights Watch, *Prison Conditions in South Africa* (New York: Human Rights Watch, 1994). Also available online at http://www.hrw.org/reports/1994/southafrica/; Human Rights Watch, *Out of Sight: Super-Maximum Security Confinement in the United States* (New York: Human Rights Watch, 2000). Also available online at http://www.hrw.org/reports/2000/supermax/; Human Rights Watch, *Prison Conditions in Japan* (New York: Human Rights Watch, 1995). Also available online at http://www.hrw.org/reports/pdfs/j/japan/japan953.pdf; Human Rights Watch, *Prison Conditions in Czechoslovakia* (New York: Human Rights Watch, 1989); Human Rights Watch, *Prison Conditions in Czechoslovakia: An Update* (New York: Human Rights Watch, 1991); Human Rights Watch, *Prison Conditions in Poland* (New York: Human Rights Watch, 1988); Human Rights Watch, *Prison Conditions in Poland: An Update* (New York: Human Rights Watch, 1991).

[6] See Human Rights Watch, "Rwanda: Elections May Speed Genocide Trials, but New System Lacks Guarantees of Rights" (October 4, 2001), available at http://www.hrw.org/press/2001/10/rwanda1004.htm.

[7] See UN General Assembly, *International Covenant on Economic, Social and Cultural Rights*, *supra* note 4, art. 2. "Each State Party to the present Covenant undertakes to take steps, individually and through international assistance and co-operation, especially economic and technical, to the maximum of its available resources, with a view to achieving progressively the full realization of the rights recognized in the present Covenant by all appropriate means, including particularly the adoption of legislative measures." See also UN Committee on Economic, Social and Cultural

facilitate enforcement through public shaming for failure to live up to the plan, the international human rights movement is poorly placed to insist on the specifics of the plan or the priorities or strategies for implementing it.

Another way to promote ESC rights is by providing technical assistance to governments. Many development organizations perform this service, and presumably international human rights organizations could as well. But as in the realm of civil and political rights, technical assistance works only when governments have the will to respect ESC rights but lack the means or know-how to do so. Technical assistance thus is ill suited to address the most egregious cases of ESC rights abuse – the area where, as in the civil and political rights realm, international human rights organizations would presumably want to focus. Indeed, the provision of technical assistance to a government that lacks a good-faith desire to respect rights can be counterproductive by providing a facade of conscientious striving that enables a government to deflect pressure to end abusive practices.[8]

In my view, the most productive way to address ESC rights for international human rights organizations like Human Rights Watch that use a shaming methodology is by building on the power of that methodology. The essence of that methodology, as I have suggested, is not the ability to mobilize people in the streets, to engage in litigation, to press for broad national plans, or to provide technical assistance. Rather, the core of the methodology is the ability to investigate, expose, and shame. Groups like Human Rights Watch are at our most effective when we can hold governmental (or, in some cases, nongovernmental) conduct up to a disapproving public. Of course, we do not have to wait passively for public morality to coalesce around a particular issue; we can do much to shape public views by exposing sympathetic cases of injustice and suggesting a compelling analysis for understanding them. In the end, the principal power of groups like Human Rights Watch is our ability to hold official conduct up to scrutiny and generate public outrage. The relevant public is best when it is a local one – that is, the public of the country in question. But surrogate publics can also be used if they have the power to shape the policies of a government or institution with influence over the officials in question, such as by conditioning international assistance or trade benefits, imposing sanctions, or pursuing prosecution.

Rights, Fifth Session, Annex III, General Comment No. 3 (1990) E/1991/23 (interpreting the meaning of the progressive-realization requirement).

[8] Leonard S. Rubenstein highlights another form of technical assistance that international human rights groups can perform: helping local or national groups better advocate respect for ESC rights. Leonard S. Rubenstein, "How International Human Rights Organizations Can Advance Economic, Social, and Cultural Rights: A Response to Kenneth Roth," *Human Rights Quarterly*, vol 26, no 4 (November 2004), 845-865. Such work is certainly useful, but it does not help to determine how international human rights groups that use a shaming methodology can best speak in their own voices in defense of ESC rights.

Although there are various forms of public outrage, only certain types are sufficiently targeted to shame officials into action. That is, the public might be outraged about a state of affairs – for example, poverty in a region – but have no idea whom to blame. Or it might feel that blame is dispersed among a wide variety of actors. Because in such cases of diffuse responsibility there is little if any stigma attached to any particular person, government, or institution, international human rights organizations that use shaming largely lack power to effect change. Similarly, stigma weakens even in the case of a single violator if the remedy to a violation – what the government should do to correct it – is unclear.

In my view, to shame a government effectively – to maximize the power of international human rights organizations like Human Rights Watch to embarrass a government into changing its policy – clarity is needed about three issues: violation, violator, and remedy. That is, we must be able to show persuasively that a particular state of affairs amounts to a violation of human rights standards, that a particular violator is principally or significantly responsible, and that there is a widely accepted remedy for the violation. If any of these three elements is missing, the capacity to shame is greatly diminished.

We tend to take these conditions for granted in the realm of civil and political rights because they usually coincide. For example, one can quibble about whether a particular form of mistreatment rises to the level of torture, but once a reasonable case is made that torture has occurred, it is fairly easy to determine the violator (the torturer as well as the governments or institutions that permit the torturer to operate with impunity) and the remedy (clear directions to stop torture, prosecution to back these up, and various prophylactic measures, such as ending incommunicado detention).

In the realm of ESC rights, the three preconditions for effective shaming tend to operate more independently. (For these purposes, I exclude the right to form labor unions and bargain collectively, because although codified in the International Covenant on Economic, Social, and Cultural Rights [ICESCR], this right functions more as a subset of the civil and political right to freedom of association.) I accept, for the sake of this argument, that indicia have been developed for subsistence levels of food, housing, medical care, education, and so on.[9] When steady progress is not being made toward realizing these levels on the basis of available resources, one might presumptively say that a "violation" has occurred.

[9] See *Maastricht Guidelines on Violations of Economic, Social and Cultural Rights*, adopted January 22–26, 1997, reprinted as "The Maastricht Guidelines on Violations of Economic, Social and Cultural Rights," *Human Rights Quarterly*, vol 20, no 3 (August 1998): 691–704; UN ESCOR, *The Limburg Principles on the Implementation of the International Covenant on Economic, Social and Cultural Rights*, Commission on Human Rights, 43rd Sess., Agenda Item 8, U.N. Doc. E/CN.4/1987/17/Annex (1987), reprinted as "The Limburg Principles on the Implementation of the International Covenant on Economic, Social and Cultural Rights," *Human Rights Quarterly* 9 (1987): 121–135; UN OHCHR, *Draft Guidelines: A Human Rights Approach to Poverty Reduction Strategies* (October 10, 2002).

But who is responsible for the violation, and what is the remedy? These answers flow less directly from the mere documentation of an ESC rights violation than they do in the civil and political rights realm. For example, does responsibility for a substandard public health system lie with the government (say, through its corruption or mismanagement) or with the international community (through its stinginess or indifference), and if the latter, which part of the international community? The answer is usually all of the above, which naturally reduces the potential to stigmatize any single actor.

Similar confusion surrounds discussions of appropriate remedies. The vigorously contested views about "structural adjustment" are illustrative. Is structural adjustment the cause of poverty, through its forced slashing of public investment in basic needs, or is it the solution, by laying the groundwork for economic development? Supporting evidence can be found on both sides of this debate. When the target of a shaming effort can marshal respectable arguments in its defense, shaming usually fails.

The lesson I draw from these observations is that when international human rights organizations that use a shaming methodology take on ESC rights, we should look for situations in which there is relative clarity about violation, violator, and remedy. That is not to say that other types of ESC abuses should be ignored, simply that a division of labor makes sense, with local or national groups using their special strengths to address ESC rights violations for which the shaming methodology of international human rights organizations is less suited.[10]

Broadly speaking, I would suggest that the nature of the violation, violator, and remedy is clearest when it is possible to identify arbitrary or discriminatory governmental conduct that causes or substantially contributes to an ESC rights violation. These three dimensions are less clear when the ESC shortcoming is largely a problem of distributive justice. That is, if all an international human rights organization can do is argue that more money be spent to uphold an ESC right – that a fixed economic pie be divided differently – our voice is relatively weak. Of course, we can argue that money should be diverted from less acute needs to the fulfillment of more pressing ESC rights, but there is little reason for a government to give our voice greater weight than domestic voices. On the other hand, if we can show that the government (or other relevant actor) is contributing to the ESC shortfall through arbitrary or discriminatory conduct, we are in a relatively powerful position to shame: we can show a violation (the rights shortfall), the violator (the government or other actor, through its arbitrary or discriminatory conduct), and the remedy (reversing that conduct).

What does this mean in practice? To illustrate, let us assume that we could show that a government was building medical clinics only in areas populated

[10] International human rights groups that do not rely on a shaming methodology might also productively address these ESC rights violations.

by ethnic groups that tended to vote for it, leaving other ethnic groups with substandard medical care. In such a case, an international human rights organization would be in a good position to argue that the disfavored ethnic groups' right to health care is being denied. This argument does not necessarily increase the resources being made available for health care, but it at least ensures a more equitable distribution. Because defenders of ESC rights should be concerned foremost with the worst-off segments of society, that redistribution would be an advance.

To cite another example, imagine a government that refuses to apply available resources for the benefit of its population's health. (South African President Thebo Mbeki's long refusal to allow donated nevirapine, or AZT, to be given to HIV-infected mothers to prevent mother-to-child transmission of the disease comes to mind.) A credible case can be made that such a government is acting arbitrarily – that it is not making a sincere effort to deploy available resources to realize progressively the ESC rights of its people. Again, by investigating and exposing this arbitrary conduct, an international human rights organization would have all the elements it needs to maximize the impact of its shaming methodology – a violation (the ESC shortcoming), a violator (the government acting arbitrarily), and the remedy (end the arbitrary conduct). Once more, there is no need to argue for more money to be spent or for a different allocation of available money (areas where there is little special power to the voice of international rights organizations), because in the case of arbitrary conduct, the money is available but is clearly being misspent.

To cite yet another example, Human Rights Watch investigated conditions facing child farm workers in the United States. Had we been forced to delve into details about the appropriate maximum level of danger or pesticide exposure or the appropriate number of working hours per day, we would have been in the amorphous realm of costs and benefits and thus lacked the clarity needed for effective shaming. We were able to show, however, that child farm workers stand virtually alone in being excluded from the laws regulating working conditions for children in the United States. In making this revelation, we were able to demonstrate that U.S. laws governing child farm workers were both arbitrary (the exception was written in an era when the family farm was predominant; it has little relevance to the agribusiness that typifies the field today) and discriminatory (most of the parents of today's farm-worker children are immigrants, politically an easy category to ignore).[11]

Education has been a productive area for this approach as well. For example, Human Rights Watch has been able to show that governments' failure to address violence against certain students (girls in South Africa, gays and lesbians in

[11] Human Rights Watch, *Fingers to the Bone: United States Failure to Protect Child Farmworkers* (New York: Human Rights Watch, 2000), 55–73. Also available online at http://www.hrw.org/reports/2000/frmwrkr/.

the United States) or bonded child labor (in India and Egypt) discriminatorily deprives these disfavored children of their right to education.[12]

If one accepts that international human rights organizations that rely on shaming are at our most powerful in the realm of ESC rights when we focus on discriminatory or arbitrary conduct rather than matters of purely distributive justice, this provides guidance for our ESC work. That is, an important part of our work should be to shape public opinion gradually so that it tends to see ESC rights issues not only in terms of distributive justice but also in terms of discriminatory or arbitrary conduct – or, to put it simply, as a matter of policy rather than resources. For example, governments' failure to provide universal free primary education would seem to be a classic case of distributive justice – there is not enough money to go around, so governments cannot provide education to all children. However, if one were to focus on the practice of funding education through school fees, one might argue that this is a discriminatory and arbitrary way of funding education because it has the foreseeable effect of excluding children from poor families. If this perspective can be promoted, it would transform the debate from one on which international human rights organizations have had little if any impact to one in which our ability to stigmatize and hence shape public policy on education would be much enhanced.

Human Rights Watch used a similar approach to highlight the neglect of "AIDS orphans" in Kenya. The provision of care for children without parents, though classically a state responsibility, is frequently limited by scarce resources. In Kenya, as in many African countries, the responsibility was typically delegated to, and accepted by, the extended family. Given the devastation caused by the AIDS crisis, however, extended families increasingly are unable to bear this burden, leaving many of these orphans destitute. By demonstrating that the classic state approach to the problem had become arbitrary (because it is no longer working in light of the AIDS pandemic) and discriminatory (because it falls on a group of people who are already stigmatized, AIDS-affected families), Human Rights Watch succeeded in generating significant pressure on the Kenyan government (and international organizations) to recognize and address the problem.[13]

---

[12] Human Rights Watch, *Hatred in the Hallways: Violence and Discrimination against Lesbian, Gay, Bisexual, and Transgender Students in U.S. Schools* (New York: Human Rights Watch, 2001), 3–7. Also available online at http://www.hrw.org/reports/2001/uslgbt/toc.htm; Human Rights Watch, "South Africa: Sexual Violence Rampant in Schools: Harassment and Rape Hampering Girls' Education" (March 27, 2001), available http://www.hrw.org/press/2001/03/sa-0327.htm; Human Rights Watch, *Underage and Unprotected: Child Labor in Egypt's Cotton Fields* (New York: Human Rights Watch, 2001), also available online at http://www.hrw.org/reports/2001/egypt/ Human Rights Watch, *The Small Hands of Slavery: Bonded Child Labor in India* (New York: Human Rights Watch, 1996), 14–19, also available online at http://www.hrw.org/reports/1996/India3.htm.

[13] Human Rights Watch, *In the Shadow of Death: HIV/AIDS and Children's Rights in Kenya* (New York: Human Rights Watch, 2001). Also available online at http://www.hrw.org/reports/2001/kenya/.

Similar efforts might be made to address issues of corruption. For example, if it can be shown that government officials are pocketing scarce public resources or wasting them on self-aggrandizing projects rather than meeting ESC needs, international human rights organizations can use our shaming capacity to enlarge the size of the economic pie available to fulfill ESC rights, without entering into more detailed discussions about how that pie should be divided to realize those rights. A good illustration is a Human Rights Watch report on Angola, in which we showed that the US $4 billion in state oil revenue that disappeared from Angolan government coffers from 1997 to 2002 roughly equaled the entire sum that the government spent on social programs during the same period – hardly a conscientious effort to progressively realize ESC rights on the basis of available resources.[14]

In making these observations, I recognize that there are certain realms in which international human rights organizations might be able to take on distributive justice questions more directly. If the issue is not how a foreign government divides a limited economic pie but how much money a Northern government or an international financial institution spends on international assistance for the realization of ESC rights, Northern-based international human rights organizations speak less as an outside voice and more as a domestic constituency. Even then, however, given our relative weakness at mobilizing large numbers of people at this stage in our evolution, pressure simply to spend more, rather than stigmatization over arbitrary or discriminatory spending, is less likely to resonate with decision makers.

It has been suggested that international human rights organizations might be in a stronger position to insist on more spending for ESC rights if we were to devote more resources to building large constituencies in the West.[15] That is, of course, true, but it begs the question of whether the tradeoffs involved would be wise, since even a relatively large organization such as Human Rights Watch has finite resources, so devoting more of them to constituency building would mean having fewer resources available for research and advocacy. It is far from clear that the tradeoff would be worthwhile.[16]

[14] Human Rights Watch, *Some Transparency, No Accountability: The Use of Oil Revenue in Angola and Its Impact on Human Rights* (New York: Human Rights Watch, 2004). Also available online at http://www.hrw.org/reports/2004/angola0104/.

[15] See Leonard S. Rubenstein, "How International Human Rights Organizations Can Advance Economic, Social, and Cultural Rights."

[16] For example, Amnesty International, with a global budget roughly six times that of Human Rights Watch, devotes an enormous percentage of its resources to public mobilization. Against that backdrop, it is unclear that anything Human Rights Watch or other international human rights groups could contribute would be more than a drop in the bucket. One prominent critic of the human rights movement suggested that international human rights groups should spend more resources sending representatives to "churches and shopping malls in the Midwest." David Rieff, "The Precarious Triumph of Human Rights," *New York Times Magazine* (August 8, 1999),

Still, the range of ESC rights violations that can be characterized as arbitrary or discriminatory and thus lend themselves to a shaming methodology is considerable. The following list of recent Human Rights Watch on ESC rights is illustrative:

- A report arguing that California's arbitrary restrictions on needle-exchange programs (facilitating the spread of HIV) impedes the right to health.[17] Ukraine was similarly criticized for the detrimental effect on the right to health (again, the spread of HIV) of its arbitrary decision, contradicting international health standards, not to allow the use of methadone as a heroin substitution therapy.[18]
- A report arguing that South Africa's ideological (and hence arbitrary) refusal to provide postexposure prophylactic drugs for victims of sexual violence impedes the right to health.[19]
- A report arguing that the arbitrary mistreatment of Russian conscripts violates the right to food and the right to health.[20]
- A report contending that Indonesia's discriminatory refusal to apply its labor code to domestic workers deprives them of basic labor rights.[21]
- A report arguing that rules requiring that people with criminal records in the United States be evicted from public housing is an arbitrary deprivation of the right to housing.[22]

---

37. Notably, he made no effort to argue that the payoff of such community outreach would be worth the cost of diminished research, reporting, press work, and targeted advocacy. Yet the trade-off is real. Given Amnesty's mobilizing role, and the enormous expectations on Human Rights Watch for research and advocacy, we have decided to build public pressure less through large constituency-building efforts than through the comparatively cost-effective use of the press and the Internet. Other strategies are certainly conceivable, but the burden is on proponents of greater attention to public organizing to explain why their approach would have more impact in light of the diminished organizational resources that, of necessity, would be available for other core aspects of our work.

[17] Human Rights Watch, *Injecting Reason: Human Rights and HIV Prevention for Injected Drug Users, California: A Case Study* (New York: Human Rights Watch, 2003). Also available online at http://www.hrw.org/reports/2003/usa0903/.

[18] Human Rights Watch letter to Prime Minister Julia Timoshenko, July 15, 2005, available online at http://hrw.org/english/docs/2005/07/20/ukrain11394.htm.

[19] Human Rights Watch, *Deadly Delay: South Africa's Efforts to Prevent HIV in Survivors of Sexual Violence* (New York: Human Rights Watch, 2004). Also available online at http://hrw.org/reports/2004/southafrica0304/.

[20] Human Rights Watch, *To Serve without Health? Inadequate Nutrition and Health Care in the Russian Armed Forces* (New York: Human Rights Watch, 2003). Also available online at http://www.hrw.org/reports/2003/russia1103/.

[21] Human Rights Watch, *Always on Call: Abuse and Exploitation of Child Domestic Workers in Indonesia* (New York: Human Rights Watch, 2005). Also available online at http://hrw.org/reports/2005/indonesia0605/.

[22] Human Rights Watch, *No Second Chance: People with Criminal Records Denied Access to Public Housing* (New York: Human Rights Watch, 2004). Also available online at http://hrw.org/reports/2004/usa1104/.

- A report arguing that Uganda's inadequate measures to address sexual and domestic violence, with resulting exposure of the victims to HIV, violates the right to health.[23]
- A report arguing that gross governmental negligence in the Chinese province of Hennan regarding the reinjection of blood into farmers violates the right to health.[24] Another report challenged China's arbitrary and discriminatory harassment of AIDS activists as undermining the right to health.[25]
- A report arguing that gender discrimination in Ukraine violates the right to work.[26]
- A report contending that Argentina's discriminatory and arbitrary restrictions on access to contraception and abortion threaten women's right to health.[27]
- A report arguing that abuses in India against sex workers, men who have sex with men, injection drug users, and HIV peer educators – a form of discrimination – violate the right to health.[28]
- A report arguing that gender discrimination in inheritance laws in Kenya violates, among other things, the right to housing.[29]
- Several reports criticizing unjustified and arbitrary impediments on children's right to education.[30]

To conclude, let me offer a hypothesis about the conduct of international human rights organizations working on ESC rights. It has been clear for many years that the movement would like to do more in the ESC rights realm. Yet despite repeated professions of interest, its work in this area remains limited. Part

[23] Human Rights Watch, *Just Die Quietly: Domestic Violence and Women's Vulnerability to HIV in Uganda* (New York: Human Rights Watch, 2003). Also available online at http://www.hrw.org/reports/2003/uganda0803/. See also Human Rights Watch, *Uganda: Domestic Relations Bill Would Save Lives,* available online at http://hrw.org/english/docs/2005/05/31/uganda11051.htm.
[24] Human Rights Watch, *Locked Doors: The Human Rights of People Living with HIV/AIDS in China* (New York: Human Rights Watch, 2003). Also available online at http://www.hrw.org/reports/2003/china0803/.
[25] Human Rights Watch, *Restrictions on AIDS Activists in China* (New York: Human Rights Watch, 2005). Also available online at http://hrw.org/reports/2005/china0605/.
[26] Human Rights Watch, *Women's Work: Discrimination against Women in the Ukrainian Labor Force* (New York: Human Rights Watch, 2003). Also available online at http://www.hrw.org/reports/02003/ukraine0803/.
[27] Human Rights Watch, *Argentina: Limits on Birth Control Threaten Human Rights* (New York: Human Rights Watch, 2005). Also available online at http://hrw.org/english/docs/2005/06/15/argent11093.htm.
[28] Human Rights Watch, *Epidemic of Abuse: Police Harassment of HIV/AIDS Outreach Workers in India* (New York: Human Rights Watch, 2002). Also available online at http://www.hrw.org/reports/2002/india2/.
[29] Human Rights Watch, *Double Standards: Women's Property Rights Violations in Kenya* (New York: Human Rights Watch, 2003). Also available online at http://www.hrw.org/reports/2003/kenya0303/.
[30] Human Rights Watch, "Children's Rights: Violence in Schools," available at http://www.hrw.org/children/schools.htm.

of the reason, of course, is expertise; the movement must staff itself somewhat differently to document shortfalls in such matters as health or housing than to record instances of torture or political imprisonment. But much of the reason, I suspect, is a sense of futility. International human rights activists see how little impact they have in taking on matters of pure distributive justice, so they have a hard time justifying devoting scarce institutional resources for such limited ends. Yet if we focus our attention on ESC rights policy that can fairly be characterized as arbitrary or discriminatory, our impact will be substantially larger. And there is nothing like success to breed emulation.

Thus, when outsiders ask international human rights organizations such as Human Rights Watch to expand our work on ESC rights, we should insist on a more sophisticated, and realistic, conversation than has been typical so far. It is not enough to document ESC shortcomings and to declare a rights violation. Rather, we should ask our interlocutors to help us identify shortcomings in ESC rights in which there is relative clarity about the nature of the violation, violator, and remedy, so that our shaming methodology will be most effective. As we succeed in broadening the number of governmental actions that can be seen in this way, we will go a long way toward enhancing the ESC work of the international human rights movement – work that, we all realize, is important in its own right and essential to our credibility.

Coincidentally, international development and humanitarian organizations are increasingly adopting the view that poverty and severe deprivation are less products of a lack of public goods than of officially promoted or tolerated policies of social exclusion. That insight meshes well with the approach I have outlined for promoting ESC rights. A lack of public goods tends to be a matter of distributive justice. But policies of social exclusion, in ESC rights terms, tend to have behind them a relatively clear violation, violator, and remedy. If development and humanitarian organizations indeed move in this direction, it portends useful partnerships with international human rights organizations such as Human Rights Watch that rely primarily on shaming methodologies.

10 Thinking through Social and Economic Rights[1]

Neera Chandhoke

The central questions that this chapter addresses are as follows: what is the conceptual status that human rights activism allots to social and economic rights, and what is the status that activism should allot to these rights, and why? These questions are significant because traditionally liberal democratic theory, which arguably inspires and sustains the activities of human rights INGOs, has been preoccupied with two sets of concerns: how to best safeguard human life and liberty. These concerns have been, throughout history, protected through codification of the right to life, the right to physical integrity, and the right to freedom. Correspondingly, because the best way of shielding these rights is to ensure the right to voice, or ensure the right to political participation and freedom of expression, political rights have emerged as concomitants of civil rights. Social and economic rights such as the right to livelihood, health, nutrition, and education, or the right *not* to eke out a living in conditions that prove highly detrimental to human dignity, have been, at least until recently, treated by liberal democratic theory and human rights INGOs much as poor cousins are treated in extended families – as hangers on at worst and as inconvenient necessities at best.

There was of course a time when the socialist tradition asserted the primacy of social and economic rights. That time passed when in the late 1980s communist states collapsed at the very moment civil societies in Eastern and Central Europe mobilized to demand civil and political rights. Today when we speak of human rights, it is civil and political rights that come to mind: the right not to be imprisoned without due cause, the right not to be tortured, the right not to be discriminated against, the right to freedom of expression and freedom of association, and the right to participate in the electoral system. The hegemony of liberal democratic theory is absolute; it has no rivals, at least in Western Europe and the

[1] I wish to thank Daniel Bell, Thomas Pogge, and Joe Carens for their helpful comments on an earlier version of this essay.

United States, which constitute power centers in the global moral and political economy. This hegemony is best exemplified in the political conditionalities that Western governments and donor agencies ritually attach to aid granted to Asian, African, and South American countries, it is best demonstrated in the foreign policy goals of Western governments, and it is best epitomized in the vocabulary of human rights organizations.

The consequences of the prioritization of civil and political rights over social and economic rights are not insignificant. For whereas the violation of a right – the violation of physical integrity through acts that torture and maim, for instance – fetches immediate international opprobrium and evokes strategies of "naming and shaming," the nonfulfillment of a right – say the right not to be hungry – is accorded a secondary status. In other words, *it is the violation of, and not the non-fulfillment of a right that has become important in the global discourse of rights.*[2] It is in connection to this that the United Nations (UN) Committee on Economic, Social, and Cultural Rights was to state regretfully in the Vienna World Conference of 1993 that

> The shocking reality . . . is that states and the international community as a whole continue to tolerate all too often breaches of economic, social, and cultural rights, which, if they occurred in relation to civil and political rights, would provoke expressions of horror and outrage and would lead to concerted calls for immediate remedial action. In effect, despite the rhetoric, violations of civil and political rights continue to be treated as though they were far more serious, and more patently intolerable than massive and direct denials of economic, social, and cultural rights.[3]

It is generally agreed that the Vienna Conference marked a significant turning point in global thinking on rights not only because it put economic, social, and cultural rights onto the agenda, but because it also emphasized the indivisibility and the interdependence of human rights. It is not as if the *recovery* of social and economic rights has not had considerable impact on international human rights organizations. The problem is deeper; human rights international non-governmental organizations (INGOs) continue to supervene social and economic rights onto civil and political rights. Social and economic rights are consequently denied the independent conceptual status that is due to them.

Understandably, human rights INGOs find it much easier to defend civil and political rights rather social and economic rights for the following reasons.[4] First, social and economic rights, it is argued, constitute 'manifesto' or 'aspiration rights', simply because they cannot be neatly pinned down through law or upheld judicially. Civil liberties or negative rights are easy to define and implement; social

---

[2] Strictly speaking, as I argue later, this amounts to nonfulfillment of an *obligation* that flows out of a rights claim.
[3] UN Doc E/C.12/1992/2, 83.
[4] Although social and economic rights are generally bracketed with cultural rights, in this chapter, I concentrate only on social and economic rights because cultural rights need a different kind of defense; they require a separate argument. I have argued for cultural rights in my *Beyond Secularism: The Rights of Religious Minorities* (New Delhi: OUP, 1999).

and economic rights are neither easily defined nor easily implemented. What is the degree of malnourishment, it is asked, which can be considered a violation of the right to nutrition? On the other hand, it is always possible to establish an individual's right not to be imprisoned without due cause.[5] Second, in a globalized, interdependent world where the power of governments over national resources has been drastically curtailed, which agency, it is asked, has the responsibility to uphold or implement these rights – governments, international institutions, global civil society, or the United Nations? Third, can governments be obliged to uphold social and economic rights even if they do not have the resources to do so? In that case, is the international community or, more precisely, the affluent West, obliged to furnish individual government with resources to implement social and economic rights?[6] Fourth, even as the discourse of human rights has been globalized through the activities of human rights INGOs, some of these organizations insist that it is neither proper nor practical for international bodies to pressure governments to provide their citizens with a decent standard of living. This would necessarily require a redistribution of resources, and this is a matter over which INGOs have no control. Whereas governments can always be pressured morally through naming and shaming not to torture dissidents or to release political prisoners, they cannot be compelled, even morally, by external agents to redistribute resources.[7] Fifth, even if governments are obligated to deliver basic amenities to their people and to marshal resources through, say, taxation to do so, will this not interfere with the property rights of other citizens?[8] Finally, social and economic rights – which accrue to only some sections of society – cannot be universal, and therefore they cannot be fundamental. Social and economic rights, it is argued, are not rights; they are merely a desirable state of affairs.

I wish to engage with precisely this kind of thinking by addressing the argument made by Kenneth Roth, executive director of Human Rights Watch [HRW], in his contribution to this volume (Chapter 9). I, let me hastily add, by no means wish to censure him or his organization. But I do wish to engage critically with his formulation on the nature of rights. This is admittedly a difficult prospect. For Roth, keeping the particular goals, the agenda, and the experiences of HRW as a constant referral, articulates his position on social and economic rights thoughtfully and carefully. His argument is practically foolproof. Moreover, the

---

[5] On this see, M. Cranston, "Human Rights, Real and Supposed' in *Political Theory and the Rights of Man*, D. D. Raphael (London: Macmillan, 1967), 43–52; also P. Alston and G. Quinn, "The Nature and Scope of States Parties Obligations under the ICESCR," *Human Rights Quarterly* 9 (1987), 157–229.

[6] Defenders of transnational justice would say yes. See, for example, Thomas Pogge's compelling argument in his *World Poverty and Human Rights* (Cambridge: Polity, 2002).

[7] This is the exact point made by Kenneth Roth, executive director of Human Rights Watch, in his chapter "Defending Economic, Social, and Cultural Rights: Practical Issues Faced by an International Human Rights Organization" (Chapter 9, this volume).

[8] This is of course the standard libertarian objection.

job of the external critic is not easy given that Roth at the outset dismisses such criticisms as impractical, utopian, and outside the limits of the methodology that HRW has charted for itself. I can still try to do so because I assume the following:

- Human rights are too important to be left to the judgment of one or the many organizations that have admirably taken on the task of defending them.
- The judgment of human rights groups is located within and is part of a larger moral community that is committed to rights.
- This moral community, engaged as it is in the task of charting out a fulfilling agenda of rights, is marked by informed debates on what it means to be human and what rights should accrue to the category of human.
- The human rights movement does not only consider itself an integral part of this community but is willing to learn from these debates to substantiate its own agenda.

My arguments in this chapter are built around the following presuppositions. First, the defense of particular human rights simultaneously articulates and validates these rights. These acts of validation serve, perhaps unintentionally, to downgrade other rights. This point may be important because given the political economy of the global order, human rights movements based in the West happen to exert an inordinate amount of influence on the way human rights movements based in the South do or do not privilege certain rights. Second, many countries in the world are characterized by such dire hunger, poverty, and homelessness that any talk of human rights that does not take these issues into account can be considered unfinished and inadequate. There may of course be a fine conceptual difference between a person dying as a result of intentional action by the state, such as torture, and a person dying because the state refuses to heed the problem of silent hunger that stalks many countries of the South. Yet both "intentional" and "unintentional" actions of the state lead to similar outcomes: loss of human life. Do not acts of commission as well as those of omission constitute violations of the basic right to life? Third, I assume that the state has obligations that are far deeper and far more morally compelling than those of nonintervention in the affairs of its citizens. These obligations lie in the realm of providing for its own people. I also assume that the legitimacy of states resides in their ability to provide the minimal conditions that allow citizens to live with some modicum of dignity.

I. INGOs AND HUMAN RIGHTS

Indisputably, much of the global discourse that accords a preeminent place to human rights in the political arrangements of societies has been heavily influenced by human rights INGOs. By placing a moral vision of how states *should* and *should not* treat their citizens squarely onto the center stage of the global agenda, these organizations have managed to ground the issue of what a morally desirable polity should look like. And by upholding an ethical canon that applies across nations and cultures, human rights INGOs have come to define and set the moral norms that ought to govern national and international orders. Moreover, compared to poorly funded and inadequately staffed human rights organizations in countries of the South, international human rights organizations possess somewhat awesome, high profiles. These organizations also happen to command the immediate attention of the international media. For these reasons and more, INGOs set the agenda for human rights.[9] The setting of agendas however inescapably involves the prioritization of human rights. It involves the fore-grounding of those particular rights that (a) human rights organizations consider worthy of defense, and (b) those which they find it possible to defend. Therefore, when Roth suggests that international organizations should concentrate on the defense of civil rights and leave economic and social rights, which demand redistribution of resources, to domestic human rights organizations, he just does not take cognizance of the power of INGOs to highlight some rights and underplay or even denote others.[10]

In sum, when human rights INGOs speak, the rest of us, particularly those of us who live in the South, listen. When these organizations certify that human rights are alive and kicking in our part of the world, we are reassured. And when human rights INGOs certify that violations of rights have taken place in a particular country at a particular time, the government of that country has reason to quake. And it should quake. This is not the issue at hand. The issue at hand is simply this: which human rights do human rights INGOs consider worthy of defense, and which human rights do they consider possible to defend? Or do they defend only those rights that these organizations find it possible to defend? This question is important given the great power of human rights INGOs over the setting of the human rights agenda and therefore over our collective lives. We have the right to know why they prioritize certain rights and why they relegate others to a secondary status.

Take HRW, one of the most influential of human rights INGOs. Although the organization had since its inception accepted that rights are indivisible, it had also exhibited considerable wariness when it came to social and economic rights. HRW had held that although survival, subsistence, and poverty can be considered subsets of civil and political rights, they were best thought of as assertions of a good.[11] In 1996, however, HRW abdicated its reluctance to uphold social and

---

[9] Neera Chandhoke, "The Limits of Global Civil Society," in eds. Marlies Glasius, Mary Kaldor, and Helmut Anheir, *Global Civil Society* (Oxford: Oxford University Press, 2002), 35–53.

[10] Roth suggests that since the demand for the implementation of social and economic rights demands the redistribution of resources, whereas domestic human rights organizations can by virtue of their location ask for such redistribution, INGOs are not in a position to do so.

[11] Human Rights Watch, *Indivisible Rights: The Relationship of Political and Civil Rights to Survival, Subsistence, and Poverty* (New York: Human Rights Watch, 1992).

economic rights and adopted a specific policy stance regarding these rights. It decided that henceforth it would investigate, document, and promote compliance with the International Convention on Economic, Social, and Cultural Rights (ICESCR). Its work in this area, the policy document stated, would, however, be limited to the following situations:

- Where the protection of an ICESCR [International Covenant on Civil and Political Rights] right "is necessary to remedy a substantial violation of an ICPPR right"
- Where "the violation of an ICESCR right is the direct and immediate product of a substantial violation of an ICPPR right"
- Where the violation was "a direct product of state action, whether by commission or omission"
- Where "the principle applied in articulating an ICESCR right is one of general applicability"
- Where "there is a clear, reasonable, and practical remedy that HRW can advocate to address the ICESCR violation"[12]

Yet despite the fact that HRW is committed to upholding social and economic rights, whether it can do so effectively is debatable. Does the methodology of the organization allow it to intervene effectively when social and economic rights are violated? Let me explicate. Kenneth Roth, outlining the strategy of his organization, suggests that HRW focuses on strategies of naming and shaming, that it documents violations of civil rights, builds popular pressure against such violations, and identifies the wrong, the wrongdoer, and the remedy. Here lies the rub. For whereas the identification of the violation, the violator, and the remedy is clear in cases of civil rights, it is not so clear in cases of violation of economic and social rights. "Broadly speaking . . . the violation, violator, and remedy are clearest when it is possible to identify arbitrary or discriminatory governmental conduct that causes or substantially contributes to an ESC [economic social and cultural] rights violation. . . . These three dimensions are less clear when the ESC shortcoming is largely a problem of distributive justice."[13]

In other words, HRW will only intervene if it can show that the government (or another relevant actor) is contributing to the ESC shortfall through arbitrary or discriminatory conduct or that the organization is in a relatively powerful position if it can identify a violation (the rights shortfall), the violator (the government or other actor through its arbitrary conduct), and suggest the remedy (reversing that conduct). The organization will *not* intervene, however, if the

---

[12] *Human Rights Watch's Proposed Interim Policy on Economic, Social, and Cultural Rights,* internal document, 30 September 1996. Cited in Makau Mutua, "Human Rights International NGOs. A Critical Evaluation," in *NGOs and Human Rights: Promise and Performance,* ed. Claude E. Welch (Philadelphia, University of Pennsylvania Press, 2000), 151–63, esp. 155–6.
[13] Kenneth Roth, Chapter 9, this volume.

relevant government has not distributed resources in such a manner that people can meet their basic needs. For argues Roth, even if HRW intervenes to demand redistribution of resources or demands redistributive justice, its voice is likely to be disregarded by governments.[14]

It is not as if HRW rejects either the idea of economic and social rights, or the worth of these rights.[15] Roth admits that these rights are worth defending, but their defense simply does not fall within the purview of the methodology adopted by HRW. As a result, the organization sees a violation of these rights as worth investigating only if such a violation *results from* or *will lead to* a violation of civil rights. For instance, if a government, suggests Roth, deliberately enables one ethnic group to access medical facilities simply because that group supports the government and if it denies such facilities to another ethnic group because it does not support the government, the said government can be accused of discrimination. The violation of the right to health (which is a social right) can thus be treated as a violation of the right not to be discriminated against (which is a civil right).

It is this position that I wish to investigate in this chapter. I want to argue that although social and political rights have been seen by substantial sections of the rights community as offshoots or as preconditions of civil and political rights, they occupy a conceptual, moral, and political ground that is coeval with civil and political rights simply because these rights are indispensable for human well-being. Therefore, one set of rights cannot be reduced to the other. Nor can one set of rights be justified on the conceptual plank of the other set. My discussion in the following section is accordingly organized around three principal themes.

First, the violation of a social and economic right can take place independently of the violation of a civil right. Second, we may be able to make a compelling case for seeing economic and social rights as equally important as civil rights and

---

[14] In a major way, the reluctance to call for redistribution of resources fits neatly into a conservative position – it even lapses into status-quoism. Naturally, governments are reluctant to engage in redistribution simply because this would eject protest from powerful sections of civil society. Therefore, even if the distribution of resources within a society is profoundly unjust, governments would rather work within this unjust system rather than make it more just. International organizations seem to feel the same. For instance, the ICESCR states that governments should take steps toward the progressive achievement of social and economic rights "according to available resources." HRW would rather call for the correction of an unjust system within the limits of the system itself and not seek to expand these limits through a call for redistribution of resources. But this is another line of critique, which I would rather not push to its natural conclusion, that is, that the HRW upholds an unjust global and national system. I would rather work within the frame of the discussion set by Kenneth Roth and critique it from its own presuppositions.

[15] Therefore, contrary to what Roth suggests in his response to my chapter, I do acknowledge that HRW has subscribed since 1996 to an expanded notion of rights. HRW, in Roth's own words, continues to maintain that it can oppose *"ESC rights violations that [are] closely related to civil and political rights violation. . . . we simply limited that enforcement to rights that were intimately related to our separate civil and political rights work,"* Kenneth Roth, "A Response to Neera Chandhoke," this volume, italics mine.

as standing on their own conceptual ground. Third, that the way we go about establishing this depends on what we think human rights are rights to, what human beings are entitled to, and what being human means.

II. THINKING THROUGH SOCIAL AND ECONOMIC RIGHTS

Roth's argument reiterates a well-known position in thinking on rights. For a long time, it has been held in the annals of liberal democratic theory that social and economic rights are justified because these rights accord meaning to civil rights. To offer a commonly cited example, a hungry human being cannot be a *free* human being. Freedom and the right to freedom are grounded in the ability to make choices – in the classical Hamlet-like option, to do or not to do. There is something in this, for whereas a person who possesses access to some resources can always opt to eat, fast, or diet, no such choice exists for the impoverished. They do not have the option to eat or not to eat. Social and economic rights, in other words, are important because they expand the realm of individual choice. Therefore, whereas civil rights are *core* rights, social and economic rights are seen as *preconditions* for the realization of these rights. Second, as Roth's example tells us, if the state deliberately makes health care available to some people and not to others, the core civil right not to be discriminated against is violated. This calls for action by human rights INGOs. This is the position to which HRW broadly subscribes.

Is it possible to conceive of a situation in which an economic and a social right can be violated even if a civil right has not been so violated? Does it then follow that it is possible to conceptualize social and economic rights on their own moral terrain?[16] Perhaps. Take the very case that Roth cites. A government builds health clinics only in areas populated by ethnic groups that tend to vote for it, relegating other groups to substandard medical care. In such a case, suggests Roth, an international human rights organization would be in a good position to argue that the disfavored ethnic group's right to health care is being denied.

Let us now attempt to rework this example. A government that prides itself on its neutrality and fairness builds health care facilities for all, in all the constituencies that fall within its jurisdiction. Each constituency is populated by different kinds of ethnic groups, some of which are in favor of the government, and others that have traditionally voted against it. Therefore, much as we may try, we can discern no discrimination or violation of rights in this case.

But in our world ruled as it is by the domination of the market, we can safely assume that these health care facilities are commercialized, or that they involve exchange transactions. Now on the face of it, we cannot criticize these arrangements. People have a right to health care, and the services for delivering

---

[16] Although there is a conceptual distinction between economic and social rights – the right to work is an economic right and the right to health is a social right – in this discussion I collapse the two.

health care have been set in place. There is no denial of any right that we can discern here. Yet we find that three-fourths of the population is not in a position to access these facilities. This is not because anyone has denied people health care but simply because the area is marked by chronic unemployment and poverty. In effect, this means that one-fourth of the population has access to health care and three-fourths of the population, denied as it is of access to health care, is vulnerable to every affliction, known and perhaps unknown.

Again at an obvious level, no discrimination has taken place, because health care, like membership to a luxurious health resort, is in theory available to everyone. When we take a deeper look at the issue at hand, however, we find another kind of discrimination that is at work here – perhaps a structural and therefore deeper discrimination than the one Roth detects in the example he offers. This discrimination has to do with income imbalances inasmuch as some people can afford health care and some cannot. What is important is that we can hold the state and society responsible for this discrimination. Or that the reason 75 percent of the people do not have access to health care has to do with factors *outside their control,* such as historically handed-down deprivation that accrues to skewed distribution of resources.[17] Their right to health care has been in effect neutralized not through deliberate *intentional* acts of the government, but through governmental *indifference* and *inaction,* through its refusal to correct income imbalances through social provisioning. In sum, discrimination results not from the *intentional violation* of a right, but from a *failure* to fulfill a social right – the right to health.

The question that immediately arises out of this proposition is the following: *why is the nonfulfillment of a right tantamount to a violation of a right?* To negotiate this question, we need to recollect one of the basic presuppositions of rights theories: when a right is claimed, the assertion of a claim places a compelling moral obligation on whomever the right is claimed against.[18] Rights, in other words, generate obligations. Generally speaking, the obligations that flow from

[17] I assume that society is only responsible for people who suffer deprivation for reasons that are outside their control – unjust distribution of resources, for instance. These reasons are not related to the individual; they are related to society. Society is, on the other hand, not responsible for human beings who have frittered away their resources. Thomas Pogge makes a similar argument in his contribution "Moral Priorities for International Human Rights NGOs," Chapter 12 of this volume.

[18] In the natural rights tradition, human beings possess rights by virtue of being human, and no other justification is needed for this assertion. The positivist legal tradition, on the other hand, as Daniel Bell has pointed out to me, holds that a right is a right only insofar as it is codified in law. I have some problem with this position, because it would assume that if a given state does not codify basic human rights, as authoritarian states wont do, basic human rights are not rights. The natural rights tradition, in contrast, gives human beings the power to both claim rights against the state and evaluate the kinds of rights that are codified. Consider that whereas a particular government may not recognize the right to freedom of speech in its statutes and its people may lose their freedom of expression, they do not, however, lose their right to the *right* to freedom of speech.

a rights claim are *agent-neutral* inasmuch as when I assert a right, others are obliged to fulfill it. Specifically, however, rights can only be claimed against those agents that *possess the capacity to meet the corresponding obligation that supervenes on the assertion of a right.* To phrase this point starkly, the state is responsible for discharging the obligations that are placed on it by rights claims.

We do not need any elaborate philosophical arguments to substantiate this claim at this point of our collective history. We expect that the democratic state is obliged to recognize, codify, implement, and protect fundamental human rights. This is by now a well-known proposition of modern democratic theory, a proposition that distinguishes democratic from nondemocratic states. More important, the proposition holds the status of a priority principle in political life inasmuch as the state is obliged to respect human rights even if it lacks the capacity to do anything else.

Now the state can honor rights claims in two ways. First, officials have to forbear from any action that may cause harm to individuals – for example, subjecting individuals to torture.[19] If the state fails to honor its first commitment or engages in any act that violates the life or liberty of its citizens, we can say with some certainty that the rights of these citizens have been violated. In this case, rights have been violated *intentionally* through an act of *commission.*

The second obligation of the state is positive; it has to protect citizens against any arbitrary action that may cause harm. Consider that the right to life is also violated if the state *fails to protect its citizens* against harmful acts carried out by other agents – criminals, for instance. If the state does not intervene, it fails to fulfill the obligation that supervenes on the individual's right to life. Failure to fulfill an obligation can in effect be interpreted as a violation of a right. The only difference is that in this case the government has violated a human right not through an act of commission but of omission.[20] The outcome of both deliberate violation and nonfulfillment of a right is, however, the same – loss of human life or harm to physical integrity. *Nonfulfillment of the obligation to protect individuals against actions that may cause them harm is arguably tantamount to a violation of the basic right not to be harmed.*

III. ESTABLISHING THE VALIDITY OF SOCIAL AND ECONOMIC RIGHTS

HRW maintains that intervention is only possible when a right has been violated intentionally, through an act of commission. Yet as we have seen, a right can

---

[19] The right not to be tortured or imprisoned without due cause applies both to citizens and noncitizens who reside in the area.

[20] In his contribution to this volume (Chapter 12), Thomas Pogge roughly substantiates this position. Philosophers, argues Pogge, call any moral reason not to cause harm to others a negative moral reason, or a negative duty. They call any moral reason or agent to prevent or mitigate harm others will have suffered a positive moral reason or positive duty.

also be violated if the government has not fulfilled the obligation that a rights claim has placed on it. Therefore, if a civil right is violated because the state has tortured an individual, it is also violated if the government does not protect the individual against torture. In the same way, if the government does not heed the obligation placed on it by the right to, say, health, nutrition, education, or shelter, nonfulfillment of an obligation can be considered to be a violation of a right.

But why, someone can ask at this point of the argument, are social and economic rights so important that the non-fulfillment of the obligation is tantamount to a violation of a right? Or why is a claim to the fulfillment of basic needs a right that possesses the same moral force as the right not to be arrested or tortured? Arguably, the import of these questions can only be comprehended if we manage to establish that the assertion of social and economic rights is such a morally compelling act that any failure to discharge the obligation that corresponds to these rights claims constitutes a violation of the right. It is only then that we can make a case that a violation of a social and economic right is of enough importance to warrant intervention by a human rights INGO.

Perhaps we can begin to negotiate this question by asking another that is logically antecedent to this one. Why are civil rights so important that they deserve in Rawlsian terms *lexical priority*? The usual answer that political theorists give to this question is the following: the fact that individuals are human entitles them to be treated in a particular way: with dignity. Conversely, human beings should not be treated in certain ways – they should not be tortured, imprisoned, maimed, raped, harassed, or subjected to any kind of humiliation and indignity.

Two foundational assumptions underlie the recognition of the importance of civil rights: (1) human beings are of value and (2) *all* human beings are of value. Equality and universality is built into the notion of human value. Of course, these two propositions – that human beings are of value and that all human beings, no matter how ordinary they may be, are of equal value cannot be empirically proved. Nor do we need to do so. These propositions are so self-evidently moral that those agents who do not believe that human beings are of value should be asked to prove their case. The onus of demonstrating this belief rests on them.

The moral and political implications of the proposition that human beings are of value are of some consequence. For what we in effect are stating is this: "This is how human beings have to be treated, this is their due; below this we cannot fall." Civil rights reiterate and reinscribe our commitment to the moral and political proposition that because human beings are of value, they will not be subjected to any kind of degrading treatment. This forms the basis of the right to life and the right to physical integrity.

But there is more to the justifications offered for civil rights. Human beings are of value because they are intentional, purposive agents who wish to make their lives worthwhile by pursuing their plans and entering into warm and rewarding relationships. In other words, human beings are capable of making their own histories even if they make these histories badly. Equally, human beings are capable of speaking back to history. Civil rights protect the right of people to make their own lives worthwhile with some degree of freedom.[21] Civil rights are therefore normally conceptualized as autonomy rights.

Let me illustrate this with an example. If a person wants to give up a rewarding teaching career at a university and spend her time writing what she hopes will be a best-selling novel, no one who is in a position to influence her future project – the state, university authorities, colleagues, friends, students, or family – can prevent her from doing so. They can persuade her, they can tell her that hers is a woolly-headed plan, but no one can force her to continue in a job in which her interest has waned. Our potential literary giant presumably has a very good reason for doing what she wants to do – making her life worthwhile.

Now consider that a person may be theoretically free to do whatever she thinks may make her life worthwhile – in this case, write a best seller. Yet she may not be able to do so for reasons other than lack of autonomy: she has never been to school or learned to read or write. After all, to write a potential best seller, one must possess a certain amount of literary competence, which is built up through access to education, to books (whether in the library or bookshops), participation in literary discussions and reading groups, or by simply being part of a community that appreciates reading and writing. Perhaps our budding literary giant cannot afford to do so, because she belongs to a poor family that has not been able to send her to school.

A story in one of India's weekly magazines may illustrate what I am trying to suggest.[22] A retired university professor noticed that whereas his domestic help performed her chores quickly and efficiently, her hands would linger with some care when it came to dusting his collection of books. It turned out that although she had never had a proper education, she did have a great love for books. The woman's employer, understanding and appreciating her hunger for books, not only allowed her to read literary masterpieces in Bengali in his collection but also gave her a pen and a notebook. Once she began to write, words poured out of her in a torrent. She wrote between chores; she wrote late at night; she wrote sitting on the floor; she wrote standing at the kitchen table. At the end of it, she had a novel *Aalo Andheri* (light and darkness), which when published went on to become a best seller. It is being talked of as India's answer to *The Diary of Anne Frank*. The novel is now being made into a play and a film and is being serialized in a literary magazine. This happened simply because an empathetic employer allowed his domestic help to read his books and because he gave her a notebook and a pencil to develop her talent for writing.

---

[21] We assume that human beings can make their lives in the way they want to, simply because they are both rational and moral. No one who did not have faith in the ability of human beings to make their own lives, or be self-determining, would recognize their right to do so.

[22] Sheela Reddy, "The Diary of Baby Haldar," *Outlook* (24 February 2003), 64.

The point I am trying to make should be clear by now: individuals require not only negative freedom to make their lives worthwhile; their basic needs must also be met to allow them to do so. The protagonist of this story had some education, and therefore when given the chance to access books, paper, and a pen, she could author a best-selling novel based on her life. But there are thousands of children in India who never get a chance to go to school and who consequently never get a chance to make their lives worthwhile. No one intentionally prevents them from doing so. The facilities are there for the asking – schools, libraries, bookstores, literary discussion groups, seminars, and public lectures. Yet these remain inaccessible simply because, historically, deprived individuals cannot access these goods.

In effect, a right is not simply a right, it is a right to something; it is a right to the conditions that make life worthwhile. The paradox of the classic formulation on rights – p [person] has an r [right] to g [goods] by virtue of h [being human] – is that the right may prove empty unless the rights holder is enabled to access g. For if she cannot access g, her right to live a life that she considers worthwhile is seriously compromised. It is only an empty right that decorates bookshelves laden with works of legal and political philosophy.

Therefore, if we stress only civil rights that serve to protect basic freedoms, we land up with moral minimalism. Civil rights are admittedly crucial, but we have to recognize that they do not touch other aspects of the existence of the human being whose freedoms are protected. That the freedom to make one's life worthwhile can be constrained in paralyzing and tangible ways through poverty, illiteracy, or ill health is more than evident. But the responsibility for poverty, ill health, and illiteracy, which constrain the ability to make our lives worthwhile, cannot be laid at the doors of individuals. The causes for these social harms are indisputably social, in the inequitable distribution of resources among citizens. Civil rights do not affect or challenge the unjust ways in which a society organizes its collective resources, however. These rights do not impact the way society treats its people in humiliating ways by forcing them to beg for goods that should be theirs by right. Defenders of civil rights either do not conceptualize or do not hold important that people's lives can be degraded if they suffer from want and deprivation. Undoubtedly, moral minimalism is important, but it is simply not enough to substantiate our commitment to human rights. Minimal moral codes do not define or protect the conditions that are necessary for human beings to live a life that can be termed as fully human.

In sum, if civil rights protect access to one kind of good – that is, freedom – social and economic rights protect access to another kind of good – that is, basic needs. Without civil rights that protect freedom, the right of human beings to make their life worthwhile is neutralized. Without social and economic rights, the right of human beings to make their life worthwhile is equally neutralized. Civil rights cannot give us the wherewithal needed to make our lives of value. Social and economic rights cannot give us the freedom needed to make our lives worthwhile. Conversely, it is possible to violate civil rights (through the nonfulfillment of an obligation that flows from those rights) even if social and economic rights are fulfilled. It is also possible to violate social and economic rights (through nonfulfillment of an obligation that flows from those rights) even if civil rights are fulfilled.

The two sets of rights are admittedly interdependent, but they are also relatively autonomous of each other. Recollect that erstwhile socialist societies gave to their citizens social and economic rights but not civil rights of freedom. Liberal capitalist societies give their citizens civil rights even as they roll back social and economic rights. In both societies, human beings suffer. Although the two sets of rights are equally important for human beings, the denial of even one of them harms the ability of human beings to make their lives of some worth.

Therefore, if we subscribe to moral minimalism, we end up with a paradox, for a right that may mean nothing for many people merely decorates constitutions and legal tomes. It does not affect me if I am deprived, it does not affect the way my society has organized itself, it does not touch my life, it does not enable me to realize my humanity, and it does not help me to make my life worthwhile. It is there and yet I cannot take advantage of it because I am not enabled to do so. Therefore, even though my right to do something has not been intentionally violated, that right does not carry any meaning for me for the obligation it places on the government has not been fulfilled.

I hope that by now it is clear why social and economic rights deserve the same status as civil rights. Social and economic rights are not always reducible to civil and political rights; they stand on their own conceptual ground as *enabling* rights. Accordingly, if rights are rights to the conditions that allow human beings to live lives that are of worth, social and economic rights are essential to human beings, for they enable them to access basic goods. It is true that civil rights protect the dignity of the human being, but this human being can be degraded and humiliated if she has to beg for the satisfaction of her basic needs. In sum, if social and economic rights are not conceptualized as enabling rights, if they are not seen as of equal importance as civil rights, we continue to engage in moral minimalism.

IV. REALIZING SOCIAL AND ECONOMIC RIGHTS

In substantive theories of enabling rights, social and economic rights are best actualized through a redistribution of resources in a society. This rests on the presupposition that everyone in that society has an equal prepolitical right to the collective resources of a community. If politics has been arranged in such a way that some people get far more shares of resources and other people have nothing, not even control over their labor power (think of bonded or slave labor), then socioeconomic rights both challenge and redress this unequal situation. Second, social and economic rights institutionalize a relational order in society. No one should be poor beyond belief, but no one should also be rich beyond belief, for that is fundamentally unjust, morally unacceptable, and politically undesirable.

Of course, no proponent of social and economic rights demands that everyone should get the same income. People have to be rewarded for their entrepreneurship, their skills, and their hard work. All that defenders of social and economic rights ask for is that all people should have the chance to exhibit their entrepreneurship, their skills, and their capacity for hard work. That is everyone should have a chance of accessing the goods – freedom as well as basic material needs – that are essential for them to make their lives worthwhile. If certain sections of society cannot access these goods, then the state must enable them to do so because the state is obliged to fulfill basic rights.

Redistribution of resources to make social and economic rights meaningful would be my preferred political position simply because I am located in a society in which the majority of people suffer from the double disadvantages of caste and class. I am not here to argue out my preferred political position but rather to engage with the political position that the HRW has adopted. HRW does not believe that it should intervene in the domestic affairs of societies in pursuit of distributive justice. It may have good reasons for this policy given its own mandate and goals. Therefore, putting aside for the moment dreams of a society in which no child goes to bed hungry or begs on the streets because she has been denied the advantages of schooling and a prospective job, I now concentrate on the framework proposed by HRW.

What are the social and economic rights that an international human rights organization can demand enforcement of in a realistic manner? The answer to moral minimalism is of course not moral maximalism. Therefore, we need to distinguish between *desirable* and *feasible* rights and, in the interest of political pragmatism, opt for the latter. A feasible version of social and economic rights would correspond to what are called basic rights that are minimally needed for human beings to live lives that are worthwhile. Below the level of basic needs to which human beings have a right, individuals lead lives that can best be thought of as subhuman. The rights to basic needs would thus include a right to nutrition, a right to shelter, a right to health, and a right to primary education. These rights, except the right to education, are subsistence goods that meet bare physical requirements, for education is basic to our understanding that there exists a world of possibilities to which every individual can aspire.

Ideally these rights should be provided for on a priority basis to every human being who suffers from want. Because, however, HRW is constrained from asking for the redistribution of resources to achieve this, let us add a second string to our bow. In a world where even international organizations have limited personnel and resources, HRW may need to contextualize its strategy and goals. In countries where massive violations of civil liberties take place, HRW should intervene in the cause of corrective justice. In other cases in which governments can afford to set up institutions to deliver services, where these governments have plenty of resources but still people go hungry or do not have adequate health care, HRW can intervene through strategies of naming and shaming. It does not have to demand redistribution even though it could in theory do so considering it does ask of governments that they treat their citizens decently.

Take the case of my own country, India. In recent years, the government has built up formidable food stocks, and yet the poor suffer from pervasive, stubborn, and invisible hunger that stalks every village and urban shantytown. About half of India's children are malnourished and a quarter are severely malnourished; 50 percent of Indian women suffer from anemia caused by lack of nourishment. This is happening at a time when the country stocks more than 24.4 million tons of food grains. This is far, far in excess of the customary stock maintained by the government, which is roughly 17 million tons.[23] The government does not know what to do with this food surplus; it would rather that rodents nibble at the stock of food grains than distribute it free of charge to the hungry. Ironically, even as the government of India spends vast sums of money in constructing storage bins for surplus food stocks, people starve in the midst of plenty. Food grains rot in granaries, but women and women-headed households, the elderly, the differentially abled, and the destitute suffer hunger and malnutrition, and perhaps death, simply because they do not have the money to buy food from the market. I would have expected that HRW focus on this paradox – death through starvation in a country where there is no lack of food. After all, death from hunger is a violation of a human right – the right to live a healthy life. HRW may regret that it cannot do this, but still choose to stick to its mandate.

Even as I respect this mandate and this methodology, I suggest to HRW that in such situations as we find India today, a human rights organization need not ask for redistribution of resources to lend assistance. What it can do is bring to the international community the empirical fact that a democratically elected government is supremely indifferent to its people's need for health care. One report on how India's people go hungry in a food-surplus state can do much to muster public opinion internationally and put moral pressure on the government. Indian human rights organizations have petitioned the nation's Supreme Court to mandate the right to food as a fundamental right and built up a campaign for this purpose, but INGOs have the kind of political clout that domestic organizations do not; they possess moral integrity, enjoy immense goodwill, and, above all, have visibility because they command immediate media attention. They certainly possess more resources than domestic, poorly organized and funded domestic organizations do. In sum, even within its self-imposed limits, HRW can surely intervene to demand that people not go hungry when there are stocks of food available for distribution (not redistribution), because ongoing malnutrition leads to death or at least to a life below the standards that we require for human beings.

---

[23] By 2007 food stocks in the country had depleted somewhat and the government imported food grain.

CONCLUSION

Within the framework of HRW's mandate, I have staked out three positions in the preceding sections. First, although social and economic rights make civil rights meaningful, they cannot be reduced to the latter all the time. Correspondingly, it is possible to consider that social and economic rights have been violated even if no civil right has been violated. Second, social and economic rights stand on their own conceptual ground because they enable human beings to access those goods that allow them to make their lives worthwhile. Third, it is possible to ask for the enforcement of social and economic rights without asking for redistributive justice. One is not required to accompany the other, although I must confess that in an ideal world they would.

In sum, social and economic rights are important to realize civil rights. More important, they stand on their own conceptual ground, as coeval with civil rights and not merely as conditions for the latter. For a violation of one set of rights – as suggested earlier – can be independent of the violation of the other. So, too, the enforcement of one can be independent of the enforcement of the other. If we collapse the two sets of rights into each other, we end up with either the tyranny of erstwhile socialist societies, which were ready to meet the basic needs of their people but which were by no means willing to give them fundamental civil rights or the tyranny of formal democracies like India that can ignore the empirical fact that 50 percent of its people are nonliterate, a majority of which are women, or that a majority of the people living miserable lives are willing to sell their children in exchange for what Marx called a "mess of pottage."

International documents and international human rights organizations are fond of employing the concept of indivisible rights, but it is only when social and economic rights begin to be conceptualized on their own terrain and not justified on conceptual grounds accorded to civil rights that we can begin to speak of the indivisibility of rights. Ideally, all human rights would need to be defended by human rights activists. All that is needed is expansion of political will, of a vision of what it means to be human, and of the idea of what it means to have a right. At the heart of the matter, I suspect, is the way that HRW conceptualizes the relationship of civil rights and social and economic rights and of the status it allots to social and economic rights.

I have suggested in this chapter that there are certain economic and social rights that every human being should possess to be truly human. I leave it to HRW to tell me whether this is practical and feasible; I think it is. I may be wrong; my suggestion that INGOs expand their agenda may be misplaced. I devoutly hope it is not.

Response to the Critique of Neera Chandhoke

Kenneth Roth

Neera Chandhoke takes issue with my conclusions in Chapter 9. Her argument is largely a handful of noncontroversial assertions. The only controversy in the chapter stems from Chandhoke's misreading of Human Rights Watch's policy on ESC rights and of my chapter.

According to Chandhoke's summary of her argument, she asserts that (1) economic and social rights cannot be reduced to civil and political rights, (2) economic and social rights enable people to access goods that are necessary for a worthwhile life, and (3) it is possible to enforce economic and social rights without asking for redistributive justice. I would not challenge any of these points.

However, Chandhoke goes on to critique my chapter based on a mischaracterization of Human Rights Watch's policy on ESC rights. She claims that INGOs in general "continue to supervene social and economic rights onto civil and political rights" and that Human Rights Watch "sees a violation of these [ESC] rights as worth investigating *only* if such a violation *results from* or *will lead to* a violation of civil rights" (emphasis in original). Those descriptions of Human Rights Watch's old policy have been, at the time of publication, inaccurate for three years. I have repeatedly pointed out to Chandhoke that her argument is built on a policy that is long out of date, but she persists as if the past is the present.

Under the superseded policy quoted in Chandhoke's chapter, Human Rights Watch would address ESC rights only if their violation were a direct product of a violation of civil and political rights or if their remedy were part of a remedy of a civil and political rights violation. However, Human Rights Watch abandoned that policy in April 2003. The current policy, which is prominently displayed on the ESC rights page of the Human Rights Watch Web site, http://www.hrw.org/esc, is the following:

HRW Policy on Economic, Social, and Cultural Rights
    Human Rights Watch considers that economic, social, and cultural rights are an integral part of the body of international human rights law, with the same character and standing as civil and political rights. We conduct research and advocacy on

economic, social, and cultural rights using the same methodology that we use with respect to civil and political rights and subject to the same criteria, namely, the ability to identify a rights violation, a violator, and a remedy to address the violation.

As a plain reading of this policy makes clear, the only constraint on Human Rights Watch's work in the area of ESC rights today is methodological. Our shaming methodology, regardless of the right involved, requires relative clarity as to violation, violator, and remedy. As explained in my earlier chapter, when these are clear, we are able to act effectively; when they are not, our methodology tends not to work because it is too easy for the target government to deflect criticism rather than face opprobrium.

As noted, in the case of ESC rights, these methodological requirements tend to be met when governmental conduct (or omission) can be characterized as arbitrary or discriminatory.[1] If we cannot show that governmental behavior is arbitrary or discriminatory and are left to argue simply that we would prefer a different distribution of resources, we tend to be ineffective. That is because, as an international organization addressing governments that are not our own, we have no special standing to contend, for example, that a government should be spending more on health care and less on education or more on roads to markets and less on housing.[2] These judgment calls do not lend themselves to the clarity of violation and remedy that are necessary for our shaming methodology to work. Because even a large organization such as Human Rights Watch has limited resources and moral capital, we try not to act in situations in which we know we will be ineffective. Nor should we.

In addition to ignoring Human Rights Watch's actual policy on ESC rights, Chandhoke misreads my chapter. She looks only at the part addressed to discriminatory government conduct and not at the part concerning arbitrary conduct. Insistence on discriminatory conduct alone could be dismissed as requiring a violation of civil and political rights – discrimination. The option of denouncing arbitrary conduct, however, allows Human Rights Watch to condemn a range of activities that have nothing to do with a violation of civil or political rights but instead reflect governmental conduct that lacks a conscientious effort to progressively realize ESC rights on the basis of available resources.

This dual approach to the enforcement of ESC rights – addressing either discriminatory or arbitrary conduct – hardly yields the null or sterile set of issues that Chandhoke suggests. As demonstrated in my chapter's sampling of Human

---

[1] Chandhoke claims that Human Rights Watch "maintains that intervention is only possible when a right has been violated intentionally, through an act of commission," but this is false. Governmental omission, quite obviously, can be arbitrary or discriminatory as well.

[2] As noted earlier, this dynamic is different when members of an international organization address their own government because then, as citizens of a state, they have as much right as anyone to advocate a particular redistribution of resources. Of course, even in the case of governments that are not our own, some wholly inappropriate allocations of resources can be effectively characterized as arbitrary, in which case our shaming methodology will work.

Rights Watch's recent work on ESC rights, this work has been rich and extensive – far more than many other organizations that tend to be vocal about the abstract need to enforce ESC rights but do relatively little to realize this commitment in practice. All of the projects mentioned in that chapter were pursued under Human Rights Watch's existing policy of focusing on arbitrary or discriminatory governmental action or inaction.

Chandhoke concludes by citing the case of India's hoarding of food surpluses. The Indian government, she claims, prefers to let its excess food rot than to give it to starving people. If true, this awful situation would indeed warrant intervention by Human Rights Watch. Chandhoke trumpets this fact as supposed proof that Human Rights Watch's current approach to ESC rights is too narrow – "moral minimalism", as she puts it. In fact, such withholding of food surpluses would be the epitome of the kind of arbitrary conduct on which a closer reading of this chapter would have made clear that Human Rights Watch *can* effectively intervene.

Apparently recognizing that this example hardly pushes the limits of what Human Rights Watch can do, Chandhoke also describes a situation in which people need health care but cannot afford it. She posits no governmental policy that causes this unfortunate situation other than the "*failure* to fulfill a social right – the right to health" (emphasis in original). "If the government does not heed the obligation placed on it by the right to, say, health," she claims, "non-fulfillment of an obligation can be considered a violation of a right".

Chandhoke thus apparently believes that the right to health is violated simply because some people do not have health care – an example of the approach to ESC rights that I described at the beginning of Chapter 9. One might indeed say that an injustice in this case has occurred, but despite the outrage at this fact that is justifiably felt at people lacking health care, it does not make a violation of the right to health unless the ICESCR is first rewritten. This is because, under the ICESCR, a violation occurs not simply when there is a deprivation of a specified right but only when the government is also not "tak[ing] steps" to secure that right "to the maximum of its available resources, with a view to achieving progressively the full realization" of the right (Article 2). If a government is not conscientiously taking such steps to progressively realize the right on the basis of available resources, its conduct might be shown to be arbitrary and thus subject to Human Rights Watch's policy on ESC rights. But if all that is shown is that the right is not fulfilled, only Chandhoke's wishful thinking yields a violation under the law as written. One might still argue for redistribution of wealth to rectify this injustice, but for the reasons explained in my chapter, the shaming methodology of organizations such as Human Rights Watch does not lend itself to pressing this issue successfully.

A Final Response to Kenneth Roth

Neera Chandhoke

Human rights have always proved to be a bit of a problem for political theory; recall Jeremy Bentham's famous dismissal of rights as nonsense – nonsense on stilts. The crisis in the discourse of rights, despite the widespread political accept-ability the issue commands, is today much deeper than at any point in history. Political theorists seem to be wracked with doubts and hesitations when it comes to negotiating either the foundations or the legitimization of human rights. This is primarily because of the impact of the postmodern spirit, which rejects con-cepts of an essentialized human nature and the idea that universal and standard norms can be imposed on people without regard for the cultural distinctiveness of their societies.

Defenders of human rights therefore have had to battle cultural relativism and communitarianism as well as allegations that rights are a product of Eurocen-tric experiences and imaginations and therefore are imperialistic. Defenders of human rights have in short had to tread rather warily when it comes to human rights. For these reasons, they have felt the need to take seriously attacks on human rights as well as alternative formulations on what it means to be human. Above all, defenders of human rights have found that they need to respect criticisms, alternatives, and suggestions, in concert with each other, if they are committed to building a culture of human rights.

Therefore, as I mentioned at the beginning of this chapter, human rights are too important to be left to the judgment of the organizations that have admirably taken on the task of defending them, that the judgment of human rights groups is located within and is part of a larger moral community that is committed to rights, and that this wider community, engaged as it is in the task of charting out a fulfilling agenda of rights, is marked by informed debates on what it means to be human and what rights should accrue to the category of human. In all this, I presumed that human rights activists not only consider themselves an integral part of this community but that they are willing to learn from these debates to substantiate their own agendas.

This really means that both theorists and practitioners of human rights should be willing to engage in dialogue. It may be of some interest to recollect the philosophical presuppositions that underlie the concept of dialogue – that human beings fashion their worlds and their words in and through interaction with each other.[1] Unless we talk to others and familiarize ourselves with other perspectives, other horizons of understanding, and other evaluations, we cannot possess informed judgments. In fact our own judgments may even degenerate into mere opinionated-ness and thoughtless assertiveness. Through the process of dialogue, we discover slowly but surely, however, areas of commonality with other members of the discursive community, areas that we were unaware of earlier. If these points of view prove complementary to ours, they will enrich and supplement our position. If they prove contrary to ours, they may compel us to rethink our position and perhaps accept that other arguments are much better than ours are. Alternatively, if we believe that other positions are flawed, we try to reason with and persuade the holders of these views.

Therefore, even though people may enter the discursive forum from radically divergent positions, the exchange of ideas can be so enriching and persuasive that the discursive community is able to generate some kind of consensus, however provisional, on the most vital aspects of collective and individual existence. Correspondingly, participants realize that what we call impartiality is not a "view from nowhere" but a matter of viewing the world from the perspective of other people. What is important is that through sustained interaction, we may find ourselves making the move from a purely self-regarding to an other-regarding perspective on grounds of reasonableness. Reasonableness consists of the following factors: the backing of arguments by reasons, a principled responsiveness to arguments, a willingness to accept criticisms and grant recognition to the better argument, and an equal readiness to correct mistakes.

The procedure generates some rather significant consequences. For one, even as we establish our readiness to listen seriously to other reasons, which through the process of dialogue prove to be simply more valid and appropriate, we establish that we respect others as free and equal partners in deliberation. Second, if we discuss all dimensions of an issue in a principled manner, we may be able to winnow out and defend desirable ideas and destroy undesirable ideas more effectively. Correspondingly, if we cannot generate consensus on a contested norm, we move toward the forging of a new norm.

This in turn implies that dialogue is an ongoing process. In any case, few contentious issues are ever resolved fully, and new uncertainties manage to appear regularly on the horizon, either blurring the edges of understanding or rendering them jagged. As a continuous process, dialogue regenerates, renegotiates, and

---

[1] I dealt with this in *The Conceits of Civil Society* (Delhi: Oxford University Press, 2003), Chapter 4, in some detail.

redrafts understanding. Therefore, decisions can never be final. In fact, to arrive at one final truth would be to proclaim closure on discussion. An ongoing dialogue, however, permits no final conclusion. It would be a poor hermeneuticist who thought he could have, or had to have, the last word, as Hans-Georg Gadamer suggested. It may sound paradoxical but truth is always subject to renegotiation. Dialogue is, consequently, a process rather than an end, with the process of inquiry – the *processual* – into the human condition being more important than *statis*. Certainly, it matters that a discussion community does or does not arrive at an agreement, but it matters more that the conditions and principles, that allow an ongoing discussion in the first instance are set in place.

It is for these reasons that I tried to engage with the formulations of one of the most important and influential human rights organisations – Human Rights Watch – in a critical but always a civil and respectful manner. Kenneth Roth, however, does not seem willing to consider the possibility of improving his methodology in response to critical input by otherwise like-minded thinkers. It is almost as if HRW refuses to listen to persons located within the very constituency that the organization works for and caters to. This saddens me, for it negates the notion of dialogue, thereby rendering both the practitioner and the theorist of human rights poorer in understanding and sympathy for each other.

11 Amnesty International and Economic, Social, and Cultural Rights

Curt Goering

In August 2001, Amnesty International (AI) adopted a new mission statement: "AI's mission is to undertake research and action focused on preventing and ending grave abuses of the rights to physical and mental integrity, freedom of conscience and expression, and freedom from discrimination, within the context of promoting all human rights." This new mission replaced AI's mandate[1]

---

[1] Prior to August 2001 AI's mandate stated: "AI works independently and impartially to promote respect for all the human rights set out in the Universal Declaration of Human Rights. The main focus of its campaigning is to:

free all prisoners of conscience. According to AI's Statute, these are people detained for their political, religious or other conscientiously held beliefs or because of their ethnic origin, sex, colour, language, national or social origin, economic status, birth or other status – who have not used or advocated violence;

ensure fair and prompt trials for all political prisoners;

abolish the death penalty, torture and other ill-treatment of prisoners;

end political killings and 'disappearances';

ensure that governments refrain from unlawful killings in armed conflict.

AI also works to:

oppose abuses by armed political groups such as the detention of prisoners of conscience, hostage-taking, torture and unlawful killings;

assist asylum-seekers who are at risk of being returned to a country where they might suffer violations of their fundamental human rights;

cooperate with other non-governmental organizations, the UN and regional inter-governmental organizations to further human rights;

ensure control of international military, security and police relations in order to protect human rights;

organize human rights education and awareness raising programs."

Adapted from Remarks of Curt Goering, Deputy Executive Director, Amnesty International USA at Carnegie Council Seminar, New York City, 15 Feb 2002.

that existed at the time, which concentrated on the area of civil and political rights.

My task here is to discuss some of the main factors driving the "remissioning" of the organization, to consider some of the key arguments that were articulated for and against the expanded focus during the lengthy organizational discussions that preceded the decision, and to reflect on some of the institutional steps the organization is taking to define its work as it seeks to address economic and social rights more prominently.

When I came to Amnesty in the 1980s, much of the human rights literature referred to economic, social, and cultural rights (ESCR) as "second-generation" rights. Of course, this traditional characterization clearly implied that "first-generation" rights – civil and political – were somehow more important and deserving of attention. The disclaimers in rhetoric and literature about complementarity, universality, and indivisibility of all rights notwithstanding, the actual practices of many human rights organizations in effect signaled to the world that the right to food, housing, basic education, health care, and so on were second-class rights and somehow less urgent and less important than the right to freedom of expression or association or the right to be free from torture. This terminology was of course also reflected in the discourse during the Cold War era when human rights often played out on the great ideological battlefield. Rather than reinforcing complementarity, some human rights groups, including AI, may well have contributed to sustaining that differentiation.

I. MANDATE DEVELOPMENT

In AI's case, although its work for more than forty years had been focused and relatively narrow, concentrating on documenting and generating public pressure to stop certain violations of civil and political rights, its history is, in fact, one of gradual incrementalism, that is, a cautious expansion of the boundaries of AI's work. The following illustrates in brief some of the major developments:

- From AI's inception in 1961 and throughout most of the 1960s, its primary concern was working for the release of prisoners of conscience – people imprisoned for the nonviolent expression of their beliefs or opinions. Those were relatively simple times organizationally.
- In the 1970s and 1980s, AI's work expanded to include essentially four concerns: working for the (1) release of prisoners of conscience and for (2) fair and prompt trials for political prisoners and opposing (3) torture and (4) the death penalty. During the period, AI interpreted house or town arrest, internal exile, to be a form of imprisonment, even though the "prisoners" were not strictly behind prison bars.

– In the 1980s and 1990s AI added extrajudicial executions and "disappearances" and began to consider work against other grave violations or measures of the right to physical and mental integrity, such as house or crop
destruction, among others.[2]

In terms of the perpetrators of human rights abuses, AI's focus for the first
thirty years was almost exclusively on violations by governments. Exceptions
to this were few and mostly restricted to situations in which nongovernmental
entities acquired attributes of government, such as exercising effective control of
a territory or population. But it was not until 1991 that AI decided to oppose
certain human rights abuses by political nongovernmental entities, such as armed
political groups.

Throughout the 1990s, AI tried to be more proactive in finding ways to stress
the indivisibility and universality of civil and political and economic, social,
and cultural rights and to counter attempts to delink them more aggressively.
For example, at the World Conference on Human Rights in Vienna in 1993,
AI, along with a broad coalition of human rights organizations, was active in
opposing the efforts by some governments to question and roll back the world
consensus regarding the universality of human rights. During this period, AI also
devoted more effort toward ratification of the ESCR covenant, launched internal
(to AI members) and external human rights education campaigns promoting
awareness of all the human rights set forth in the Universal Declaration of Human
Rights, and stepped up work on specific national or state legislation intended to
protect – with some result – a wider range of basic rights. For example, largely due
to local activist campaigns in recent years, the number of states without custodial
sexual misconduct legislation has been reduced from thirteen to one (Vermont)
in the United States. Another example is found in the legislation adopted by
some states prohibiting "profiling" – read, *discrimination* – on the basis of race
or national origin. Efforts by the U.S. government to downplay the significance
of some ESCR in the early 1990s – the opposition of the right to housing comes
to mind – were opposed by AI and others, in communications to the U.S.
government.

A next step in the incrementalist approach came in 1997 when AI began
to oppose abuses by nonstate actors. This encompassed further categories of
violators that were neither governments nor political nongovernmental entities,
but private actors. These abuses were not perpetrated directly by the state, but
a degree of governmental responsibility needed to be documented as a criterion

---

[2] Grave measures were defined as "The government and NGE [nongovernmental entity] practice
against targeted individuals which forms a pattern of military, police, administrative and/or
judicial persecution by means of arbitrary use of procedures and other forms of harassment
which gravely disrupt the targeted prison's daily life or his/her privacy, effectively barring him/her
from acting in public life." These were deemed a grave violation of the rights of every person
mentioned in Art. 1 of the Statute and were opposed by AI.

for getting involved. It was not immediately clear what contribution AI might be able to make in this sphere, so it opted to test the waters by embarking on pilot projects that would be carefully planned, implemented, and evaluated to determine what the implications might be for the organization's ongoing future work. Honor killings, trafficking of women, and killings by security forces hired by private land owners were some of the pilot projects undertaken.

As internal armed conflict in the 1990s increased, so did work against abuses that occurred in the context of armed conflict. For example, AI began to oppose indiscriminate attacks and to oppose the use of certain kinds of weapons that were inherently indiscriminate, such as landmines or, in some circumstances, cluster bombs. Of course, AI's legal and conceptual framework for this work was based on violations of international humanitarian law, instead of the human rights law doctrine on which AI's work had been based in the past.

These developments show that over the years, much of AI's work expanded from a prisoner-oriented focus to addressing larger human rights concerns. Many of the abuses took place outside prison walls. When the focus of AI's work was still relatively narrow, the organization was able to have at least the goal of applying the mandate areas consistently across all countries. In practice, however, resource limitations required that priorities be set. For instance, in some countries AI had to make practical choices to prioritize work against, say, torture and attach a lower research priority to "disappearances." As the boundaries of AI's work expanded and the range of abuses to monitor and act on became significantly wider, the dilemma became ever greater. For much of its history, AI's mandate defined the boundaries of its permissible work and acted as a kind of work regulator. If a particular type of abuse was not "in the mandate," it was not something AI's researchers spent time investigating. In practice, the mandate was seen by many as both the limits to AI's work and as the work that AI actually did. As the mandate expanded, many in the movement expected the actual work to expand as the boundaries did. It was, of course, impossible to meet this expectation fully.

II. SOME REASONS FOR ENLARGEMENT

Perhaps the most important factor in the argument to expand AI's work was that there was a strong moral and conceptual belief in most, if not virtually all, quarters of AI around the world, that ESCR needed to be recognized as basic rights to which every human being is entitled just as they are entitled to civil and political rights, and they needed to be fought for and defended equally as vigorously, much as Thomas W. Pogge (Chapter 12) articulates in his important contribution to this dialogue in this book. The argument was strong that INGOs, and perhaps particularly AI as the world's largest grassroots international human rights organization with an international membership in more than 100 countries, had a very important role to play not only in the promotion but also in the proactive defense and protection of ESCR, as Neera Chandhoke argues elsewhere in this volume

(Chapter 10). Many felt that AI, particularly with its ability to mobilize tens of thousands of individuals around the world to generate public pressure on relevant duty holders to fulfill and respect all human rights, had an indispensable role to play. That role included careful research and hard-hitting reports on ESCR violations for the purpose of mobilizing pressure and bringing to bear the full range of tactics AI used in trying to improve rights in the civil and political rights realm, including, among many others, making specific policy recommendations and developing litigation strategies. Many felt that, in principle, there was no inherent insurmountable reason that AI could not become an effective advocate of ESCR issues as well as of civil and political ones. Of course, appropriate methodologies would need to be developed and new expertise would have to be gained, but AI could learn from the scores of NGOs that were already engaged in effective approaches to ESCR work and over time be an effective advocate.

Also, by virtue of its incrementalist approach to expanding the boundaries of its work, there was a growing sense that although AI was a grassroots human rights movement comprising ordinary people from all walks of life, its mandate was becoming overly complicated and only truly understood by the mandate experts or lawyers. Which violations or abuses fell within the mandate and which did not? And why would AI, as the largest human rights organization of its kind, not address what many local human rights activists considered to be the most burning human rights issue in their country? The "outside the mandate" answer was not very satisfactory.

There were also questions about remaining relevant while still keeping our work coherent. Should we view human rights violations in a country only through AI's mandate lens or through the lens of the Universal Declaration of Human Rights and then make strategic decisions in setting priorities (as was, as noted earlier, already happening)? But what would this approach mean to the notion of a consistent approach to our work on countries? Was there a contradiction among consistency, coherency, and relevancy? And how do we explain the worldwide nature of our work if the focus was, say, trafficking in women or children in Thailand, and our priority in Russia was, say, torture?

If that were not enough, during the 1990s, AI sought specific ways to "promote" all the rights in the Universal Declaration. It developed policies to guide its "promotional" work in the ESCR area. It encouraged public awareness raising and educational activities on the full range of civil, political, social, economic, and cultural rights; reporting, comment, and analysis on the context in which the violations and abuses against which AI campaigns take place; and adoption of standards and practices in the governmental, intergovernmental, nongovernmental, and business and financial spheres that advance respect for human rights concepts and principles. In practice, however, there was immense confusion about the distinctions drawn between, on the one hand, the civil and political human rights abuses we opposed and campaigned to stop and, on the other, the ESCR we "promoted."

In the day-to-day work, the mandate boundaries were simply impractical. One example cited was the Sudan, where in 1994 the government engaged in massive displacement of local populations and destruction of their crops and food reserves. It was difficult to explain why AI researched as human rights violations the shooting and torture of a few victims and actively campaigned against such violations, while the manufactured starvation of thousands of people was treated as background that explained the context of abuses but not an issue AI members were asked to campaign against.

Another example came from Afghanistan. The warring factions opposed to the government in 1996 imposed a total road blockade on Kabul. AI denounced the indiscriminate killings from the daily bombings but said little about the starvation resulting from the blockade. As one of my colleagues wrote, "We were seen to be suddenly irrelevant and our inaction at a time when everyone else was shouting left a scar on our work on Afghanistan and on Amnesty's credibility for that matter, for a very long time. We still hear echoes of AI having no interest in the real suffering of the people."[3]

Supporters of expansion into ESCR argued that AI's statements about the universal and indivisible nature of all human rights ring hollow if the organization does not actively campaign on and offer policy recommendations to address ESCR or if it relegates ESCR issues to background information in its reports.

Another colleague noted that AI criticizes governments, corporations, and others for selectivity and exceptionalism. Yet, it was argued, AI itself is selective when it does not research, document, and campaign against certain whole categories of human rights violations.

As an international human rights organization, AI has taken important steps over the past several years to become a truly multicultural organization. Yet the focus of its work – the selection of which categories of human rights violations to actively research and campaign against – reflected, some felt, a Northern bias or preference for work, civil, and political rights instead of ESCR. Many people and NGOs in the Global South and a growing number in the North felt that AI's narrow mandate with its limited serious work on violations of ESCR was a barrier to inclusion of people whose views on this issue differed from the prevailing "Northern consensus." Importantly to an organization that strived to be truly international, the civil and political focus was also seen as a barrier to development of AI's structure and membership in the South. This was seen to undermine AI's credibility in general with important audiences.

Some in the movement also argued that AI's focus carried a bias toward male concerns. Some noted that women's experience of human rights is often different from men's: property rights and reproductive rights and the rights to health, education, and nutrition were some of the areas mentioned. In addition, by maintaining the distinction, AI limited its opportunities for cooperation with

[3] Example cited is from an undated internal AI memo.

other civil society and human rights groups at a time when coalition work was becoming ever more critical in advancing a human rights agenda.

Given that AI has a worldwide and growing membership in more than 100 countries in every region of the world, which it plans to increase further (and which ESCR work might enable to expand quickly), it was argued that AI's local membership, as citizens and constituents, might be particularly well placed to be engaging their government in specific questions of ESCR, including budget priorities and spending questions. Rather than hearing a voice from an international headquarters based in London, a government would not be so easily able to dismiss as "outside interference" indigenous advocacy on ESCR issues organized by local AI members in a particular country. AI's international network could stand in solidarity with and strengthen local efforts.

There were also voices from other parts of the human rights movement urging broadening the scope of its work: Said one, "AI is regarded worldwide as a voice for human rights. Due to its size and prominence it is a trendsetter for the broader human rights movement. It is very damaging that this voice should continue to speak strongly for only a portion of human rights, especially ten years after the Cold War removed the ideological reasons for the split in human rights. That is not to say that AI cannot focus on certain rights if that is more effective, but it also needs to have room for concrete support of indivisibility within its mandate."[4]

These were some of the main arguments made by the proponents of expanding into ESCR areas.

III. CONCERNS ABOUT AN EXPANDED MISSION

Main concerns of the expanded approach raised a number of concerns to many in the AI movement. Some were specific to AI; others mirrored various questions other experts raised. Some of the main concerns are reflected in the following:

- From its inception, AI understood that to be effective in its work, it needed to maintain a clear and limited focus. Resources are always scarce – as Kenneth Roth also notes in his chapter (Chapter 9) – and one organization should not try to take on too much. Otherwise, it will diffuse its efforts to the point where it might compromise effectiveness. That is why until this point, AI kept a relatively narrow mandate and did not try to address other areas of civil and political rights.
- Many felt that there was still so much work to be done in the areas AI was already working on that any additional capacity it might achieve should be focused on fighting political imprisonment, torture, and so on. At a minimum, it should not de-prioritize these areas to take on new ones.

---

[4] Excerpted from an internal AI discussion paper (POL August 8, 2000), "Mandate Review 1997–2001, Economic, Social and Cultural Rights (August 2000), 5.

- Over AI's forty years of work on specific civil and political rights, it had established a reputation and an identity as an organization working on those specific issues. Some felt that it was important to maintain this identity. Many individuals and organizations understood the limitations of AI's role and related to this identity, and it was important that AI not build expectations that it could not fulfill.

- One of AI's strengths was that its worldwide membership agreed (more or less) on the mandate areas as they had been developed and incorporated into AI's ongoing work. Although members from various countries in all regions of the world, encompassing many religions (or none) might differ on political or economic issues, they were united in standing behind AI's work in the areas of the existing mandate. Broadening that in ESCR issues would challenge the unity and cohesion of the movement, it was argued, which would lead to decreased effectiveness if the AI movement did not speak with one voice.

- In AI's years of work on certain civil and political issues, it had built up expertise in these areas. AI had no expertise in the area of ESCR, so why should the organization try to address issues with which it had no experience, especially when there was still so much to do in existing mandated areas.

- Some argued that AI should only take on certain areas of work in which there was a clear universal consensus. They argued such was mostly the case when it came to the work against torture, imprisonment for the peaceful expression of one's opinions, extrajudicial executions, and so on (although less so on the death penalty, for example), but this consensus broke down over many issues relating to ESCR.

- Since its inception, AI had prided itself on consistency, credibility, and impartiality in its work. With a limited and focused mandate, it was argued, AI was able to apply that mandate to each country. If AI dealt with "disappearances" in one country, its mandate stated that it would also address that violation in the next. The consistent application of the mandate across countries was an important factor in establishing AI's credibility and impartiality. If AI were to use different criteria now in determining which issues in a country it would focus on and if priority issues varied from one country to another, AI would be susceptible to charges of partiality, which would be more difficult to refute.

- Some argued that ESCR were not easily justiciable, as were civil and political rights. Some argued that the concept itself as applied to ESCR was too complex and needed clarification, not to mention how it would be applied in practice. Some understood civil and political rights (such a legal remedies – habeas corpus, for example) to be immediately realizeable, whereas ESCR could only be progressively realized (through public policies, for example).

- Some maintained that entering the ESCR arena would inevitably lead AI into domestic debates about spending priorities and allocations in national budgets for ESCR related issues, and questioned, as Kenneth Roth seems to in his chapter (Chapter 9), the appropriateness, wisdom, and utility of an international human rights organization playing this role, particularly if the resources required are large. Although it is recognized that, in effect, AI and other human rights groups already did that in their civil and political rights advocacy – implementing recommendations for prison condition or justice system improvements also involve sometimes substantial resource allocations – some felt AI had a less legitimate role doing so on ESCR issues.
- Some in AI were apprehensive that a shift to ESCR might result in AI's professional staff having greater, and perhaps undue, influence in determining organizational priorities at the expense of membership involvement. Given that AI is a worldwide grassroots membership organization, the implications for AI's decision making in certain areas were, for some, worrisome.
- Finally, there was concern in some quarters that expanding the areas of AI's potential research and action might lead to extensive and protracted internal debates over priorities and the allocation of resources. Instead of maximizing energies spent on stopping human rights abuses, more time would be spent in internal debate.

These concerns were not, of course, without response from proponents of change. It is important to note that as this debate unfolded, there seemed to be a general recognition and acknowledgment among AI's members that the positions taken and concerns voiced by advocates of one position or the other were both valid. The difference was the importance attached to the concern or how the concern could be addressed. Again, it is important to emphasize that almost all participating in the debate agreed that ESCR needed to be recognized as basic rights just like civil and political rights and needed to be defended just as vigorously.

IV. AI's 2001 INTERNATIONAL COUNCIL MEETING

This great debate culminated in an international meeting in Dakar, Senegal, in August 2001. There had been intense internal discussion to varying degrees among literally hundreds of thousands of AI members in scores of countries. Group meetings, annual meetings, and special meetings in all corners of the world discussed what the future of AI should look like. There were major divisions within and between AI national branches. The debates were grueling and often heated. Individuals felt passionate about their positions. Friendships were tested. Ideological camps emerged: the full (or fuller) spectrum versus the incrementalists versus the more traditionalist approach. Emotions ran high. Perhaps there were even some instances of verbal abuse!

Eventually, most agreed that AI needed to further change to address more kinds of violations. The questions then became "change to what" and "how fast." Essentially the discussion narrowed to whether AI should adopt what was called a "full spectrum approach" – in which the entire UDHR – that is, any or all the articles in the UDHR – could be an object of AI's research and campaigning or whether the organization should expand to provide more range and flexibility while still focusing on a subset of all human rights. It also became clear that a decision on the scope could not be separated from larger questions about decision making in the movement. Who would decide what AI would work on country by country? The individual country researchers? The International Board? What were the appropriate decision-making structures for these kinds of issues in a grassroots international democratic movement?

After days of discussion, the delegates found a position acceptable to all, at least for the next four years. AI agreed to alter its statute to say that its work is "focused on preventing and ending grave abuses of the rights to physical and mental integrity, freedom of conscience and expression, and freedom from discrimination, within the context of promoting all human rights." At the same time, the organization would, over the next four years, prepare for a decision in 2005 on whether the statute should be further expanded to oppose grave abuses of all human rights.

The foundation was thus laid for AI, conceptually, to be able to respond to a much broader range of human rights concerns than under the previous mandate parameters. AI will now be less constrained by the rigidities of the previous mandate while enabled to campaign against some abuses of ESCR. The decision should also provide AI the opportunity to be more effective by having the ability to focus on the main human rights concerns in different countries, whether civil or political or economic, social, or cultural.

AI recognizes that although a decision has been made, the way forward is still far from clear. AI needs to determine methodically how it can best contribute to and move forward in the new areas of work to which it is committed.

At the time of this writing, there are major discussions underway about building AI's capacity in ESCR. These will involve, among other topics, education and training for staff and volunteer activists and acquiring expertise in the new areas. (My own section, Amnesty International USA, made ESCR capacity building one of its highest institutional priorities for the immediate future.) There is in AI a recognition that the development of substantive ESCR program work will require forging genuine partnerships with organizations already doing ESCR work and that developing strategy collectively in the areas of reporting-monitoring and campaigning-lobbying will be essential.

As a first step, AI has formed an international ESCR working group comprising experts from the organization as well as from outside it to develop options for AI's work in this area. Early examples of possible starting points include the areas of discrimination: limited access to health of housing or education for migrant workers. Another might be policies of persecution aimed at jeopardizing the very existence of ethnic groups, such as crop destruction. An example of a violation of the right to physical and mental integrity in which AI might be more active could be the denial of treatment to people living with HIV/AIDS. Of course, operationalizing the concepts of interdependence and indivisibility of all human rights will be the crucial test.

There is some concern about the risk of AI duplicating what others are doing in the field of ESCR. Said one leader working in this field, "There is not just risk, there is certainty. Not all duplication is bad, but a lot is, not just for wasted resources but more importantly for provoking tensions between groups, especially since AI is a newcomer to this field and must tread carefully not to dominate discourse and eventually practice."[5] To ensure that such tension is minimal, AI will need to consult and coordinate very closely with a broad range of NGOs already working in the field.[6]

In conclusion, it is important to stress again that an integrated human rights approach means we recognize and act on the firmly held belief that people have a right to food, to clean water, and to a safe and adequate place to live as much as they are entitled to the right to express their opinions peacefully or practice their religion; the right of a woman to have access to credit is as much of and as

---

[5] Ibid, 6.

[6] As noted in various internal papers written to guide AI's internal debate, AI is committed in moving ahead to learning from and partnering with the regional and international NGOs that have been pioneering ESCR and that have made enormous contributions in advancing the work – Organizations such as the Coalition on Housing Rights and Evictions (COHRE) and Habitat International Coalition (HIC), as well as Foodfirst Information and Action Network (FIAN) and the American Association for the Advancement of Science (AAAS) have all been actively involved in, among many others, international standard-setting mechanisms with regard to the right to adequate housing, food, and health, respectively. The Center for Economic and Social Rights (CESR) is involved in several projects in several countries in Latin America and the Middle East and was the first INGO to document, based of firsthand fieldwork, the impact of international sanctions of ESCR. Forum Asia, together with the International Human Rights Internship Program, has launched several initiatives to provide training tools for human rights activists working in the field of ESCR. The International Commission of Jurists (ICJ), in cooperation with the Urban Morgan Institute and the Center for Human Rights of the Faculty of Law of Maastricht University, was responsible for producing guidelines on violations of ESCR (Maastricht Guidelines). There are, of course, many others. AI will also need to build on progress made in recent years by INGOs, particularly in the field of standard setting (the United Nations [UN] Committee on Economic, Social and Cultural Rights; the Sub-Commission on Prevention of Discrimination and Protection of Minorities; as well as committees dealing with rights of specific sectors [women and children's rights]). Other UN agencies are integrating a human rights approach in their work, as is the case of the World Health Organization and the UN Development Program.

important a right as her right to be free from violence in the home; children have a right to education and basic health care as much as they have a right not to be sentenced to death; indigenous communities have a right to live and work on their ancestral lands as much as they have the right to be free from extrajudicial slaughter.

In making this decision to embrace a new mission, AI has taken a concrete step toward putting teeth into its commitment that ESCR are rights every bit as essential as political and civil rights. Putting into practice the concepts of interdependence and indivisibility of all human rights and developing AI's capacity to contribute appropriately will be absolutely critical next steps as AI collaborates and partners with others in addressing the many challenges ahead.

CONCLUSION: UPDATE (AUGUST 2005)

Since Amnesty International revised its mission in 2001 and opened the door to integrate work on ESCR, the organization has been developing a long-term strategy for work related to such rights, including launching pilot research projects, issuing campaigning actions, and building the foundation for a global campaign in the field. Some individual AI country sections have made ESCR "capacity building" an organizational priority and have been building staff and volunteer activist capacity to work in this area.

AI's International Secretariat has produced reports addressing ESCR issues (available at AI's Web site) on forced evictions and housing rights in Angola, Israel/Occupied Territories [OT], and Swaziland; right to food in North Korea and Zimbabwe; right to work in Israel/OT; forced labor in Myanmar; right to health in Democratic Republic of Congo and Rwanda; mental health discrimination in Bulgaria and Romania; HIV/AIDS and human rights including the right to health in southern Africa; right to education of minorities in Croatia; minority rights in Kosovo/Serbia Montenegro and Myanmar; ESCR of refugees in Lebanon; and ESC rights abuses by corporate actors in Bhopal, India. Each of these reports has been accompanied by action strategies that provide recommended actions and guidance for activists working on these issues. In addition, there have been some initiatives taken on the right to water (in connection with the World Water Forum), and substantial attention has been devoted to the Optional Protocol to the International Covenant on ESCR.

To assist with capacity building, specialized advisory bodies were created in some sections. In Amnesty International USA, for example, to guide planning and strategy development and implementation, an ESCR Advisory Committee was formed with members available for consultations with staff, volunteer leadership, and activism at the grassroots level. That committee works closely with a staff interdepartmental working group that was established to help coordinate the integration and mainstreaming of ESC rights within the organization.

Among the resources that have been created are a video, "Human Needs, Human Rights," intended as a tool for members to use to understand the thinking behind the evolution of AI's mission and to build their knowledge of the global movement for ESC rights; and a book, *Human Rights for Human Dignity: A Primer on Economic, Social and Cultural Rights.*

AI has also recently started planning a long-term global campaign on ESCR. Although the specific theme has yet to be determined, the campaign will be designed to promote legitimacy of ESCR; highlight the indivisibility and interdependence of rights; complement the efforts of others working in this field; address the responsibilities of a wide range of actors, including governments, nonstate actors, corporations, international financial institutions, and intergovernmental organizations; focus on marginalized people; and be informed by a strong gender perspective. In addition, further issue- and country-specific projects relating to ESCR are being incorporated into the organization's next two-year operational plan.

In preparation for AI's International Council Meeting in August 2005, an evaluation of its ESC country work so far was undertaken. The experience indicated that many within the organization felt AI can undertake effective campaigning against specific ESCR violations in much the same way it has sought to do in other areas. This includes meticulous and accurate research documenting violations, carefully analyzing the information from a human rights framework, and selecting appropriate targets for action. Positive legislative changes in Angola and Bulgaria were cited among examples in which AI campaigning may have contributed to positive measures.

It was also noted that AI's work on ESCR is often seen as a natural extension or outgrowth of previous work, such as closures in the Israeli Occupied Territories or forced evictions in Angola. The broader approach has also allowed a more integrated strategy and gives greater meaning to the understanding that rights are indivisible and therefore reflecting more holistically the actual experience of particular marginalized peoples.

At the same time, there are new challenges in research methodology. When has a governmental obligation been breached, and what even constitutes a human rights violation? How should AI undertake budgetary analysis? There is an ongoing need for training and development of greater expertise among staff as well as to draw on a broader range of professionals as research delegations travel to countries to assess a broader range of human rights issues. There also appears to be ongoing questions in some quarters of AI's membership about whether the organization is spreading itself too thin and whether this might have an impact on its effectiveness.

The importance of working in partnership with other organizations – recognized during the debates leading to the new mission – has been seen as vital to AI's efforts. For example, AI has partnered on housing, mental disabilities, and food security issues with local NGOs in a variety of countries; collaborating appropriately has been extremely important.

Policy issues that the organization needs to consider carefully have also emerged, including debt relief, international trade agreements, property rights, and aid conditionality. For example, the prohibition on using food as a tool to exert political or economic pressure necessitated careful thought in formulating recommendations for action to the international community.

12 Moral Priorities for International Human Rights NGOs[1]

Thomas Pogge

We inhabit this world with large numbers of people who are very badly off through no fault of their own. The statistics are overwhelming: some 850 million human beings are chronically undernourished, 1,037 million lack access to safe water, and 2,747 million lack access to improved sanitation.[2] About 2,000 million lack access to essential drugs.[3] Roughly 1,000 million have no adequate shelter and 2,000 million lack electricity.[4] Some 799 million adults are illiterate[5] and 250 million children between ages five and fourteen do wage work outside their household – often under harsh or cruel conditions: as soldiers, prostitutes, or domestic servants, or in agriculture, construction, textile, or carpet production.[6] Some 2,735 million people, 44 percent of humankind, are reported to be living below the World Bank's US $2/day international poverty line.[7] Roughly one-third of all

[1] Many thanks to Daniel Bell, Joe Carens, Neera Chandhoke, Nir Eyal, Lakshmi Jacota, John Kleinig, Terry MacDonald, Frank Miller, Kimberley Perez, Jen Rubenstein, and Robert Wachbroit for many good and some truly excellent written criticisms and suggestions. I am grateful also for the helpful comments I received at the Hong Kong conference and at subsequent presentations at the Institute for Politics, Philosophy, and Public Policy of the University of Maryland and at the Department of Clinical Bioethics of the National Institute of Health, which has also been my intellectual home during the completion of this essay.
[2] United Nations Development Programme (UNDP) 2005, 24 and 44.
[3] See http://www.fic.nih.gov/about/summary.html.
[4] UNDP 1998, 49.   [5] See http://www.uis.unesco.org.
[6] The United Nations International Labor Organization (ILO) reports that "some 250 million children between the ages of 5 and 14 are working in developing countries – 120 million full time, 130 million part time" (http://www.ilo.org/public/english/standards/ipec/simpoc/stats/4stt.htm). Of these, 170.5 million children are involved in hazardous work and 8.4 million in the "unconditionally worst" forms of child labor, which involve slavery; forced or bonded labor; forced recruitment for use in armed conflict, forced prostitution, or pornography; or the production or trafficking of illegal drugs (ILO 2002: 9, 11, 17, 18).
[7] Chen and Ravallion 2004, 153. (Ravallion and Chen have managed the World Bank's income poverty assessments for well over a decade. These latest data are for 2001.) The US $2/day line is defined in terms of annual consumption expenditure that has the same purchasing power as US $785.76 had in the United States in 1993 (ibid, 147). By this standard, U.S. residents would be counted as poor in 2006 only if their consumption expenditure for the entire year fell

human deaths, 18 million annually or 50,000 each day, are due to poverty-related causes, readily preventable through better nutrition, safe drinking water, cheap hydration packs, vaccines, antibiotics, and other medicines.[8] People of color, females, and the very young are heavily overrepresented among the global poor and hence also among those suffering the staggering effects of severe poverty.[9]

The people appearing in these statistics live in distant, underdeveloped countries. Some of us in the rich countries care about and seek to improve their circumstances. But it is difficult to do this on one's own. So we cooperate with others. We can do this politically, trying to get our governments and corporations to do less harm and more good in poor countries. We can also do this by supporting international nongovernmental organizations (INGOs) that offer to pool money we give them and to make such funds effective toward human rights, development, and humanitarian goals.

Not enough of us act in either of these ways. A full-fledged effort to eradicate severe poverty and its attendant medical and educational deficits worldwide might cost some US $300 billion annually – at least initially; the cost would fall off dramatically in future years.[10] This amount of US $300 billion is affordable, even if it came from just the twenty-four high-income Organization of Economic Cooperation and Development (OECD) countries containing merely 14.5 percent of the world's population. The gross national incomes of these countries sum to US $30,760 billion,[11] so a mere 1 percent of this would suffice. But US $300 billion annually is a huge amount relative to the US $13 billion the rich countries actually spend each year to protect the global poor: about US $7 billion are given by the citizens of the rich countries through INGOs,[12] and about US $5.7 billion are provided by rich-country governments in official development assistance (ODA) for basic social services.[13]

---

below US $1,100 (http://www.bls.gov/cpi/home.htm). It is likely that flaws in the World Bank's methodology cause it to understate the world poverty problem (Reddy and Pogge 2006).

[8] In 2002, there were about 57 million human deaths. The main causes highly correlated with poverty were (with death tolls in thousands): diarrhea (1,798) and malnutrition (485), perinatal (2,462) and maternal conditions (510), childhood diseases (1,124 – mainly measles), tuberculosis (1,566), malaria (1,272), meningitis (173), hepatitis (157), tropical diseases (129), respiratory infections (3,963 – mainly pneumonia), HIV/AIDS (2,777), and sexually transmitted diseases (180) (World Health Organization 2004, 120–5).

[9] Children under age five account for about 60% or 10.6 million of the annual death toll from poverty-related causes (United Nations Children's Fund 2005, inside front cover). The overrepresentation of females is documented in UNDP 2003 (310–30) and UN Research Institute for Social Development 2005.

[10] Pogge 2002a, chapter 8.   [11] World Bank 2005, 292–3.

[12] UNDP 2003, 290.

[13] Cf. http://millenniumindicators.un.org/unsd/mi/mi_series_results.asp? rowId=592, giving figures for 2003. This US $5.7 billion is about 8 percent of all ODA, which was US $69 billion in 2003 (www.oecd.org/dataoecd/19/52/34352584.pdf). I do not use the higher figure, because the large remainder of ODA is spent strategically: on "friendly" ruling elites or on subsidizing

Seeing how much human deprivation there is and how little money to reduce it, INGOs face difficult moral decisions about how to spend the funds they collect. In this chapter, I examine some of the more central moral issues from the perspective of an INGO.

I adopt this perspective, rather than that of contributors, on the assumption that the INGO defines the terms of the relationship. This need not always be so. Very rich persons can create their own foundation (such as the Bill and Melinda Gates Foundation) and dictate its conduct and policies. In such a case, it is the contributors who face difficult moral decisions of the kind to be examined here. I focus on the inverse case of an INGO that receives many small contributions meant to protect people abroad from serious harm. How should it spend such funds? This question points to an awesome responsibility because, in the world as it is, any decisions it makes are likely to affect many lives severely. To put it bluntly, an INGO must often make decisions that will certainly lead to many deaths because spending one's limited funds on trying to protect some is tantamount to leaving others to their fate.

Small contributors also face such awesome choices when they decide where to send contributions. Some INGOs are wasteful and corrupt, and contributions to them may then prevent no serious harm at all. And even when I am pretty sure that my contribution to one INGO will enable it to prevent deaths, it is clear that there are other INGOs of whom the same is true. Different INGOs prevent different deaths. By contributing to one rather than another, I am, then, indirectly deciding who will live and who will die. Obviously, spreading my contribution over all effective INGOs is no solution, because each will then receive much less than if I had given my whole contribution to it alone.

Most small contributors lack the time and dedication to study carefully where their contributions are going. To some extent, this is a good thing, a further gain from pooling. Just as it is disproportionately costly (in time, money, and effort) for small contributors to deliver their contributions personally to people

exporters in the "donor" countries. As USAID proclaims with disarming frankness: "The principal beneficiary of America's foreign assistance programs has always been the United States. Close to 80 percent of the U.S. Agency for International Development's (USAID's) contracts and grants go directly to American firms. Foreign assistance programs have helped create major markets for agricultural goods, created new markets for American industrial exports and meant hundreds of thousands of jobs for Americans" (recently removed from the USAID Web site). These priorities are evident also when one looks where ODA goes: Though India has more poor people than any other country, ODA going to India is only US $0.90 annually per citizen, and ODA going to China US $1.00. The corresponding figures are US $24.20 for Cyprus, US $24.50 for Hungary, US $25.80 for the Czech Republic, US $33.60 for Slovenia, US $52.70 for Bahrain, and US $65.80 for Israel (UNDP 2005, 280–1), whose gross national incomes *per capita* are thirteen to twenty-nine times that of India (World Bank 2005, 292–3, 300). Still even their citizens get much less in foreign aid than is allocated to the owners of cows in Europe and Japan, who are subsidized at (respectively) US $900 and US $2,700 annually per cow to the great detriment of farmers in poor countries. See World Bank chief economist Nicholas Stern's speech "Cutting Agricultural Subsidies" (available at globalenvision.org/library/6/309).

in need, so it is also disproportionately costly for them to think through which priorities should govern the use of these funds. Most contributors giving money to an INGO do so with a triple trust: We trust that this INGO has developed carefully formulated moral priorities governing how the collected money should be spent. We trust that this INGO has procured the information and inventive talent it needs to implement the priorities well through the funding of specific projects. And we trust that this INGO is funding the chosen projects efficiently. To be sure, contributors can "check up" on their INGO in various ways. A large element of trust nonetheless remains that most contributors cannot eliminate at reasonable cost.

The trust of contributors saddles INGO staff with a second, still awesome responsibility: they must not let their contributors down by setting the wrong moral priorities, by funding infeasible or counterproductive projects, or by frittering money away through carelessness and corruption. This responsibility cannot be discharged by ensuring that contributors never learn that their trust has been abused and their funds wasted. As a contributor, I care about averting serious harm. To be sure, I feel better believing that my contribution has succeeded than believing it has failed. Still, my objective is to avert serious harm – not merely to believe that I have done so. Whether an INGO lives up to its contributors' trust depends, then, solely on whether it *actually* makes their contributions effective through morally important projects.

Of course, it is desirable that when an INGO succeeds in this way, its contributors should believe or know this. One main reason this is desirable is that these contributors will then continue giving to the successful INGO. However, there is nothing desirable about contributors *falsely* believing that they are supporting a successful INGO and continuing to contribute on the basis of this belief. In fact, it is hard to think of anything more despicable than an INGO with a policy of hiding its violations of its contributors' triple trust through misrepresentations. Such an INGO prevents contributions from serving their intended purpose and thus lets down both its contributors and their intended beneficiaries. (Some INGOs do exactly that.) Such an INGO in effect steals money from those in mortal danger from hunger, disease, and violence who would receive more protection if the INGO lived up to the trust of its contributors – or if it at least did not hide its violation of their trust, thus giving its contributors a chance to direct their contributions elsewhere.

Fortunately, the two responsibilities largely coincide in content. An INGO that fulfills its triple task well does no wrong either to its contributors or to the poor and oppressed abroad – even though it can protect only a small fraction of the latter.

The remainder of this chapter offers some thoughts on the first task of INGOs, the task of developing moral priorities governing how the entrusted money should be spent. These thoughts, for the most part, fall short of clear-cut answers. They merely try to assemble the more important moral considerations that must inform any full-blown answer to the question of moral priorities. In investigating this question, let us bear two thoughts in mind: reflections on the first task are not wholly separable from the other two; predictions about what an INGO can do and how cost-effectively it can do it are relevant to what moral priorities it should set. Further, an INGO is not merely an actor in its own right but is also an agent and trustee for its contributors; it must then reflect not merely on its own moral responsibilities but also on its contributors' moral responsibilities, which these contributors entrust it with discharging.

I. FOUR BASIC COUNTERS

Let us begin with four moral considerations that may seem obvious but still need clarification.

> (A) Other things (including cost) being equal, it is morally more important to protect a person from greater serious harm than from lesser.

The key concept in this proposition is that of serious harm. In the present context, I propose to define *harm* as shortfalls persons suffer in their health, civic status (civil and political rights, respect within their community), or standard of living relative to the ordinary needs and requirements of human beings. This rough definition has three noteworthy features: (1) It is sufficientarian in its suggestion of some threshold of minimal sufficiency to which shortfalls are relative. Those living at or above this threshold suffer no *serious* harm at all. To save words, I use *harm* in the sense of *serious harm* from now on. (2) By focusing on the basic needs of persons, the definition takes account of the decreasing marginal significance of resources (such as medical care, civil rights, education, and money). (3) The definition recognizes as harms any shortfalls, irrespective of cause. Thus, severe poverty is harm regardless of whether it is due to a drought, a person's social status as a bonded laborer, or her own earlier recklessness. Harm caused in the last way is morally less important; the "other things being equal" clause allows for this.

To illustrate the first two features, suppose that some planned INGO project in India would add 50 rupees per month to someone's income. Feature (1) suggests that this addition may be morally insignificant because the relevant person's standard of living is already minimally adequate. She is suffering no harm from poverty as it is, and the project thus would not protect her from harm (although it may, of course, so protect others). Feature (2) suggests that greater income deficits constitute *disproportionately* greater harm. Thus, an Indian subsisting on 100 rupees per month below a minimally adequate standard of living is, other things being equal, suffering *more* than twice the harm of someone living only 50 rupees below. Thus, an extra Rs. 50/month for someone living Rs. 100/month below a minimally adequate standard of living protects her from greater harm than it would if she lived only Rs. 50/month below minimal sufficiency. Put in general terms, incremental resources generally are morally more important the less its recipients have. What matters morally is not the project's impact on persons' resources but its impact on their standard of living, on their ability to meet their basic human needs.

The further specification of Proposition (A) confronts three main questions. One is what should count as harm and what weight should be attached to harm of different types. The development and defense of a suitable harm metric is evidently a complex task. I bypass this task here for reasons of space and because there is already a large and sophisticated literature about the metric in terms of which we are to assess how badly off persons are.[14]

Another question is to what extent *effects* should be taken into account. When a child suffers severe malnutrition, her mental and physical development is stunted, and this imposes additional harm on her throughout her life. Here it seems clear that the effects should count: preventing that child's malnutrition also prevents her suffering this later harm. The focus should be, then, on the overall harm reduction accomplished for the child's life as a whole.

But if the effects are counted in this way, then protecting those with greater life expectancy will often be morally more important than protecting those with lesser life expectancy. Even life-saving efforts, it would seem, should then generally be focused on younger people insofar as death would impose on them a greater loss. Although widely accepted within the medical profession, these implications may seem problematic to some who are also attracted to the view that the whole future of any one person has the same moral import as the whole future of any other person, regardless of how much time each is expected to have left to live.

The last question concerns disagreements between those threatened by harm and those seeking to protect them (INGOs and their contributors) about what is to count as harm and how to count it. A woman may believe that cliterodectomy is normal and necessary, no more harmful than the extraction of a rotten tooth, or that the subordination of women in the household and in the public sphere is holy and good. We may believe that women are harmed by their subordination and also by being indoctrinated to believe that this subordination is not harmful to them. If so, do we have moral reason to protect that woman from harm she does not recognize as such? A man may believe that he would suffer much greater harm by failing to fulfill an expensive religious duty than by being undernourished. We may believe the opposite. If so, do we have more moral reason to enable him to fulfill his supposed religious duty or to enable him to provide for his food needs?

---

[14] Cf. especially Sen 1995, 1999, Dworkin 2000 (reprinting "What Is Equality? Part I: Equality of Welfare" [1981] and "What Is Equality? Part II: Equality of Resources" [1981]), Rawls 1982, Cohen 1989, Nussbaum and Sen 1993, and Pogge 2002b.

Would it not be paternalistic to impose our own notion of harm on those whom
we are seeking to protect?

> (B) Other things (including cost) being equal, it is morally more important to
> protect persons from harm the more such harm they would otherwise be suffering.

Given how I have conceived harm – in terms of the ordinary needs and requirements of human beings – (B) is independent of (A) in that the decreasing marginal
significance of resources is already incorporated into the conception of harm. This
conception already takes account of the fact that extra income of Rs. 30/month
has as much of an impact on the standard of living of the typical extremely poor
Indian as, say, Rs. 50/month of extra income has on the standard of living of the
typical merely poor Indian. Proposition (B) thus holds that – quite apart from
taking account of the decreasing marginal significance of resources – we should
prioritize the worse-off (defined in terms of harm).

The point is straightforward in cases where the decreasing marginal significance of resources plays no role. Thus, consider an INGO that supplies poor
households with a smart fuel-efficient stove that greatly reduces hazardous indoor
air pollution and time spent gathering firewood. With nowhere near enough
stoves for all poor households, the INGO must choose whether to supply the
stoves to one rural area inhabited by extremely poor people or to another inhabited by merely poor people. People in both groups would realize equal harm
reductions (gains in life expectancy, health, etc.), and even the merely poor people could never afford to buy such a stove on their own. Even though the two
groups thus do not differ in terms of achievable harm reduction, Proposition (B)
directs the INGO to decide in favor of the extremely poor.

One might fix this point terminologically by drawing a distinction between
the *magnitude* and the *moral value,* or *moral importance,* of any harm reduction.
Although an extra Rs. 30/month (a smart stove) is no more significant to a typical
extremely poor person than an extra Rs. 50/month (a smart stove) is to a merely
poor one (the harm reductions achieved are the same), the former gain is still
morally more important than the latter (the harm reduction it achieves is of
greater moral value).

Proposition (B) holds then that the harm reduction achieved for one person
may be both *smaller* and yet also *morally more valuable* than the harm reduction
achieved for another. This can happen when the former person is exposed to
greater overall harm than the latter. Insofar as scarce resources force INGOs
to choose between such achievements, (B) directs them to prefer a smaller but
morally more valuable harm reduction for one person over a larger but less
valuable harm reduction for another. Equivalently, I will say that INGOs should
aim for the greater *harm protection,* defined as reflecting the moral importance
(moral value) of harm reductions rather than their magnitude.

The moral priority for the worse-off expressed in (B) reflects the widely
accepted Pigou-Dalton condition, common ground between egalitarian and

prioritarian moral conceptions.[15] This condition holds that if one distributive pattern, D_1, relative to another, D_2, involves an increase in harm suffered by a worse-off person and an equal decrease in harm suffered by a better-off person, then D_1 is inferior to D_2. Egalitarians accept this condition, because inequality rises when the well-being of a better-off person improves and that of a worse-off person declines (both by the same increment). Prioritarians accept the Pigou-Dalton condition because they attach greater moral importance to gains and losses at lower levels than to equal gains and losses at higher levels of well-being.

The further specification of Proposition (B) confronts three main questions, roughly parallel to those encountered in the specification of (A). One is about how the moral value of a harm reduction depends on how badly off its beneficiary is.[16] An elegant partial solution is to employ the same harm metric developed in the specification of Proposition (A) for this purpose: INGOs should aim to achieve as much harm reduction as possible for those exposed to the greatest harm. This is only a partial solution, because its two maximands must still be integrated with each other, so that one can decide in a principled way between a greater harm reduction for someone exposed to less harm and a lesser harm reduction for someone exposed greater harm. Integration is the task of specifying the moral importance of any harm reduction an INGO project might achieve for some particular person as a function of (a) the magnitude of this harm reduction and (b) the level of overall harm suffered by the person to be protected.

Here is a simple formula that illustrates this integration based on a single metric of harm (shortfall from minimal sufficiency):

$$V_{Pi} \sim (H_{0i} - H_{Pi})^*(H_{0i} + H_{Pi})$$

In this formula, H_{0i} stands for the harm individual i suffers if the INGO does not affect her situation.[17] H_{Pi} stands for the harm i suffers if project P is implemented. Thus, $(H_{0i} - H_{Pi})$ represents the harm reduction (or increase) project P entails for individual i. $(H_{0i} + H_{Pi})$ represents the average weight to be attached to harm reductions over the range from H_{0i} to H_{Pi}.[18] Finally, V_{Pi} signifies the harm protection that project P achieves for individual i, that is, the moral value of the harm reduction (or increase) P entails for i. As required by (A), this moral value increases with any increase in the first factor ($H_{0i} - H_{Pi}$): the harm reduction P achieves for i. As required by (B), this moral value increases with any increase in the second factor ($H_{0i} + H_{Pi}$): i's overall harm level. My illustrative formula accommodates both factors symmetrically by positing that harm protection is simply their product.

---

[15] See Broome 2002.   [16] Cf. Broome 2002 and Parfit 2000.
[17] The symbol 0 (zero) is used to indicate that this is the baseline or null case.
[18] This average is, of course, $(H_{0i} + H_{Pi})/2$. But we may drop the constant denominator 2 for simplicity. Doing so just doubles the numerical value of all harm protections and so does not affect comparisons among them.

Let us generalize this formula so we can accommodate the factors asymmetrically, giving more weight to one than to the other. This may be done through exponents. Because we want the sum of the moral values of several smaller harm reductions for i to equal the moral value of an equivalent larger harm reduction for i, the weight adjustment should be accomplished by attaching an exponent only to the second factor. Attaching to it an exponential constant $e > 1$ gives more weight to i's overall harm level than to the magnitude of the harm reduction P achieves for i. Attaching to it a constant exponent $0 < e < 1$ gives more weight to the magnitude of the harm reduction P achieves for i than to i's overall harm level.

If we choose an exponent $e \neq 1$, the average weight to be attached to harm reductions in the range from H_{0i} to H_{Pi} is not proportional to the sum of H_{0i} and H_{Pi}. It takes some integral calculus to work it out, but the resulting general formula is simple:

$$V_{Pi} \sim H_{0i}^{(e+1)} - H_{Pi}^{(e+1)}$$

It is easily seen that $e = 1$ is the special case displayed earlier in which both factors are symmetrically accommodated and are given equal weight.[19] Further, $e = 0$ is the limiting case where the overall harm level is disregarded, given no weight at all. This would negate Proposition (B), rendering harm protection (the moral value of harm reduction) simply proportional to harm reduction. Plausible values for e would seem to fall between 0 and 1, but there is much room for reasonable disagreement within this range about how strongly the worse-off should be prioritized. Different INGOs will fix e at different levels. Each particular INGO, however, can meaningfully compare candidate projects only if it fixes e at one unique level, using the same constant e for assessing the impact of all its candidate projects on the individuals they affect.

A further question faced in the specification of Proposition (B) is how much of persons' lives we should consider for determining how badly off they are. At one extreme, one might attend to their present situation only; at the other, one could take into account their entire past and estimated future, their life as a whole. According to the latter view, the fact that people have, years ago, suffered through a horrible drought would strengthen one's reasons to combat malaria among them rather than elsewhere. According to the former view, only harms suffered by these people now are relevant. One could take an even narrower view by confining attention to harm of the type to be reduced. Thus, in combating malaria, one could say that, other things being equal, resources should be focused on those who suffer most *from this disease* while leaving out of account any other

---

[19] Multiplying out, $(H_{0i} - H_{Pi}) * (H_{0i} + H_{Pi}) = H_{0i}^2 - H_{Pi}^2$. I use the $\sim$ sign, *proportional to*, to emphasize that V_{Pi} results calculated by using different values for e are *not* comparable. Thus, INGOs fixing e at different levels are disagreeing not about the moral value of particular projects or harm reductions but about the (cardinal) ordering of such projects or harm reductions – about their moral importance relative to one another.

harm they may also, even concurrently, be exposed to – such as being homeless, orphaned, illiterate, maimed, or socially excluded as a despised minority.

The last question once again concerns disagreements, between those threatened by harm and those seeking to protect them, about how badly off persons are. We may believe that the worst off in some society are the women and girls in extremely poor families who, because they have to eat only what is left after their menfolk have eaten, are suffering severe malnutrition. But most members of that society may be agreed that the worst off among them are any men who are too poor to fulfill some expensive religious duty. Again, it may seem paternalistic to insist that our efforts to protect people must be guided by *our* notions of harm rather than their own.

> (C) Other things (including cost) being equal, it is morally more important to achieve some given harm protection for more persons than for fewer. Here aggregate harm protection is a linear function of the number of persons protected. Generally, the moral value of several harm reductions is the sum of their moral values.

Proposition (C) makes three progressively stronger claims. Its first and weakest claim is ordinal: Other things being equal, if $n > m$, then achieving some harm protection for n persons has more moral value than achieving the same harm protection for m persons. The second, stronger claim is cardinal: Other things being equal, achieving some harm protection for n persons has n/m times as much moral value than achieving the same harm protection for m persons. The third, strongest claim extends this additive aggregation of moral values to nonequivalent harm protections.

The weakest claim has been challenged by philosophers,[20] and defended.[21] The steps from it to the two stronger claims have not been explicitly discussed by philosophers – although their defense is sometimes implicit in the defense of the weaker claim. On the whole, I believe, the defenders have been successful in showing, against Taurek's radical doubts that "the numbers count." But I will not here revisit this debate.

Accepting the strongest claim of Proposition (C) leads to another simple formula:

$$V_P = \sum^i (V_{Pi})$$

The moral value or importance of a project is the sum of the moral values of the harm reductions this project achieves for the individuals it affects.

Taking the three propositions together yields the following principle:

> (ABC) Other things (including cost) being equal, INGOs should choose among candidate projects according to the moral value (harm protection) each project would realize, which is the sum of the moral values of the harm reductions (and increases) it would bring about for the individual persons it affects.

---

[20] Cf. especially Taurek 1977.
[21] Cf. especially Parfit 1978; Kamm 1993, chaps. 5–7; and Scanlon 1998, 230–41.

We can make this principle somewhat more specific by integrating the factor of cost. If the overall cost of projects can be expressed on a one-dimensional scale (in currency units, say), then it is rather straightforward that

> (D) Other things (including harm protection) being equal, an INGO should choose cheaper candidate projects over more expensive ones. More specifically, the choice-worthiness of candidate projects is inversely proportional to their cost.

This is motivated by the thought that any INGO's resources are scarce relative to the morally important projects it might undertake. Any INGO should prefer to implement cheaper projects because it can then achieve more of what is morally important.

Proposition (D) yields one more simple formula, equating the choice-worthiness (W) of a candidate project with its cost-effectiveness, that is, with its overall moral value (harm protection) divided by its overall cost:

$$W_P = V_P / C_P$$

or, fully spelled out:

$$W_P \sim \Sigma^i \left(H_{0i}^{(e+1)} - H_{Pi}^{(e+1)} \right) / C_P$$

Taking all four propositions together, the moral principle governing INGO conduct can then, in first approximation, be formulated as follows:

> (ABCD) Other things being equal, an INGO should choose among candidate projects on the basis of the cost-effectiveness of each project, defined as its moral value divided by its cost. Here a project's moral value is the harm protection it achieves, that is, the sum of the moral values of the harm reductions (and increases) this project would bring about for the individual persons it affects.

This principle is underspecified in various ways – with regard to its notion of harm as well as with regard to its "other things being equal" clause. I devote most of the remainder of this chapter to the exploration of this clause, that is, to the question, what other factors may come into play to affect the balance of reasons bearing on the ranking of candidate projects. My exploration cannot be even nearly exhaustive, but I hope it makes a decent start.

II. DISTRIBUTIVE FAIRNESS

One significant factor that may render other things unequal is the factor of distributive fairness. At the first conference,[22] I learned that many INGO managers are strongly committed to a particular ideal of fairness across countries: they think it unfair to spend more resources on protecting people in some countries than on protecting people in other countries merely because resources can be

---

[22] At the Carnegie Council on Ethics and International Affairs in New York, 15–16 February 2002.

employed more cost-effectively in the former than in the latter. They believe that so long as resources can achieve *some* harm protection in a country, a fair share thereof should be allocated to this country even if the same resources could achieve much more elsewhere.[23]

This commitment to distributive fairness among those who are working on harm reduction abroad manifests itself in the real world. INGOs and other relevant (governmental and intergovernmental) agencies would work very differently if they did not have this commitment. They would then concentrate the limited funds available for this purpose on locales that offer the most favorable environments for the cost-effective reduction of severe poverty. According to Collier and Dollar, these countries are, in order, Ethiopia, Uganda, and India.[24]

Employing a somewhat crude methodology, Collier and Dollar assess the cost-effectiveness of the current allocation of ODA. Finding that on a poverty-efficient allocation two-thirds of all aid would go to India,[25] which has vastly more poor people and is also currently much more neglected than other countries,[26] they remove India from the picture on the ground that any increase in ODA to India is politically impossible. They then estimate that, even with India (and apparently also Bangladesh) so excluded, a poverty-efficient reallocation of aid among the remaining countries would reduce the average cost of lifelong poverty protection from US $2,650 to US $1,387 per person and would thus make it possible to save 19.1 million rather than only 10 million people from poverty.[27] Such a

---

[23] I speak of a *particular* ideal of fairness across countries because there are alternatives. One obvious, and to me less disagreeable, alternative would hold that poverty itself, not resources for protecting people against poverty, ought to be fairly distributed across countries. This ideal would encourage INGOs to devote their resources toward equalizing the extent (incidence and depth) of severe poverty. At least initially, they would then *concentrate* their resources on eradicating poverty in the countries where poverty is now most severe and extensive.

[24] Collier and Dollar 2002, 1488. Even if their analysis were entirely sound, I would not want its conclusions to be unthinkingly extended to guide INGO priorities. One reason is that Collier and Dollar do not accept the combination of propositions I have developed in the preceding section. In particular, they focus on poverty narrowly understood as income poverty rather than on harm more broadly conceived. The three countries they single out may not, then, offer the most favorable environment in the sense of (ABCD). See also n. 30 to this chapter.

[25] Ibid, 1490.

[26] At least on a per capita basis. In this respect, China and India are now at the very bottom of international concern (cf. n. 12), figuring even below Iran and Myanmar. Depending on the conception of fairness or nondiscrimination endorsed, one might argue that the present resource allocation is not unfair to China and India because, in total, they do relatively well, ranking seventh and fourteenth, respectively, in ODA inflows (UNDP 2005, 280–2).

[27] Collier and Dollar, 2002, 1497. Were India and Bangladesh included in the reallocation exercise, the feasible gain would be even more dramatic. The authors define poverty in terms of the World Bank's US $2/day international poverty line (cf. n. 6). Assuming a global aid budget (including India) of US $28 billion (ibid, 1490), they take account of a much larger fraction of ODA than I have done and do not attempt to differentiate among types of ODA (cf. n. 12). It is possible that the annual US $12.7 billion (US $5.7 billion in governmental ODA for basic social services plus US $7 billion from citizen donations) now actually expended on international poverty eradication is

reallocation would completely exclude several dozen poor countries where aid is inefficient and would raise aid to other countries where the cost of lasting protection from poverty is as low as US $600 (Ethiopia) or US $1,000 (Uganda) per person.[28]

Why is it more efficient to concentrate funds in a few countries? Collier and Dollar stress two factors: efficiency tends to be higher in countries with better government policies or a higher incidence of poverty (or both). The countries they list score highly on both counts. There are six further factors worth adding to theirs:

- Favoring countries with good policies improves *long-term* cost-effectiveness as well by providing incentives toward such policies. Even expenditures narrowly focused on poverty eradication tend to benefit a country's political elite indirectly by providing foreign exchange and by stimulating domestic demand and hence economic activity. Governments therefore have some interest in attracting such expenditures to their country. This interest remains inert if aid keeps coming irrespective of how corrupt or inept a government may be. Insofar as international aid is dependably concentrated on well-governed countries, however, this interest encourages good government.
- Cost-effectiveness is improved by excluding countries where the government's control is precarious. In such countries, project achievements are threatened by contending political factions and criminal gangs, who may extort side payments and misappropriate INGO resources and then use such gains to fund destructive activities (buying arms or recruiting fighters).
- Projects are cheaper to implement in countries where prices, compared at market exchange rates are lower. INGOs operating in poor countries, hiring staff and buying resources locally, can multiply the value of money they raise in rich countries. This advantage is the greater the more the purchasing power parity (PPP) of national currency to the US-Dollar diverges from its market exchange rate.[29]

---

better spent in two senses: that it eradicates poverty at a substantially lower average cost per person and that its cost-effectiveness does not underperform by as large a percentage that of a poverty-efficient allocation. The data from Collier and Dollar are at best illustrative of the priorities reflected in current INGO allocations to harm protection projects.

[28] Ibid, 1488 and 1490. The authors suggest that the marginal efficiency of funds is monotonically decreasing in each country. On this assumption, a poverty-efficient allocation is one that focuses funds on the countries where marginal efficiency of funds is highest. As aid reduces poverty in these countries, its marginal efficiency declines. This will gradually enlarge the set of countries included in the poverty-efficient allocation. Given the magnitude of the poverty problem in India alone, however, this enlargement might happen slowly, at least if we hold fixed the small amount the world is currently spending on international poverty eradication.

[29] Here the comparison must be made in terms of appropriate PPPs. The World Bank, in its poverty assessment exercises, uses general consumption PPPs, which weight all commodities in proportion to their share in international consumption expenditure. This is obviously not a plausible guide to assessing the standard of living of very poor households that must concentrate their

- Cost-effectiveness is improved by favoring areas where many poor people live in geographic proximity. Here stationary projects (e.g., schools and wells) can serve more poor people, and mobile projects (e.g., vaccination programs) can reach people at lower cost. Moreover, multiplier effects of INGO activities may here be stronger and more focused on the poor. (Narrowly conceived, multiplier effects arise when poor people spend additional income in ways that benefit other poor people. More broadly, one might also include cultural and inspirational effects: the example of some people escaping poverty with the help of an INGO project is likely to give encouragement and guidance to other poor people.)
- Concentrating resources on a few countries is more cost-effective because of synergies and economies of scale. Synergies occur when different projects in the same area contribute to one another's success. Economies of scale are realized, for instance, by saving on the overhead costs involved in building and maintaining a presence in a country.[30]
- The poorer the poorest are in some country, the cheaper it is to protect them from harm. This is a consequence of the decreasing marginal significance of resources (Proposition (A)) and is reinforced by the greater moral importance of improvements for the worse-off (Proposition (B)). This reason does not apply, of course, if one defines the goal (with Collier and Dollar) as reduction of the poverty gap relative to some poverty line.

Reflection on these further points suggests that Collier and Dollar are surely right: the existing allocation of funds for harm reduction efforts is highly inefficient, and concentrating on a few countries would greatly increase what these funds achieve by way of poverty eradication. Although there is much to dispute in their rough calculations,[31] they do provide a real-world context for discussing the

---

expenditures on a very narrow subset of these commodities, which often are not as much cheaper in poor countries as general consumption PPPs would suggest (cf. Reddy and Pogge 2006). For analogous reasons, general consumption PPPs may be a poor guide to the cost of the specific goods and services needed in the implementation of an INGO project.

[30] There may be countervailing reasons to favor a larger number of smaller projects over a smaller number of larger ones. For example, the former strategy may produce more clear-cut successes that inspire, educate, and are helpful in raising new funds.

[31] Collier and Dollar abstract away the heterogeneity of conditions within countries, thus disregarding that there may be excellent opportunities for poverty eradication in countries that, under their poverty-efficient allocation, would receive no funds at all. They exclude this possibility by making the simplifying assumption that aid is distribution-neutral, raising by the same percentage all incomes in the recipient country. The authors also work with a one-year time horizon. Yet use of a longer (indefinite) time horizon may yield further efficiencies. An obvious example is that of projects (e.g., in education) that involve a large time lag between cost incurred and moral value realized. A less obvious example is that of "windows of opportunity": When the cost of protecting people in some area is rising rapidly, then it may be cost-effective to protect them now, even if there are people elsewhere who could now be protected more cheaply. Conversely, it may not be cost-effective to protect those who can now be protected most cheaply when the cost of protecting them is rapidly falling.

proposed distributive fairness constraint: is it morally more important to protect an additional 9.1 million people from a life in poverty by concentrating our efforts on where we can be most cost-effective – or is it morally more important to allocate scarce resources fairly across all countries in which persons face the prospect of lifelong poverty?

It seems obvious to me that we should here decide against the proposed distributive fairness constraint and in favor of protecting more people. I recognize that if we concentrate on a few countries, then we will do nothing to protect many very badly off people who, through no fault of their own, live elsewhere. But if we spread our efforts fairly over all poor countries, then we will do nothing to protect even more people who are just as badly off and just as free of fault in their fate. *Any* conceivable allocation of available resources will leave many people exposed to a life of severe deprivation – people who ought to be protected. If we cannot fully protect everyone from such harm, then we should at least achieve as much as possible.

To make this choice more concrete, imagine an INGO that, with its limited resources, can either build two wells in Ethiopia, providing safe drinking water to 5,000, or else build one well in Chad, providing safe drinking water to 1,000. The former project would protect many more people, but the latter would achieve a fairer distribution of INGO resources across countries because other funds have already been allocated to projects in Ethiopia. If we choose the former project, we can justify to the 1,000 Chadians our neglect of their plight: "We do not have the resources to protect all those as badly off as you are. We must choose where to concentrate our efforts. We have chosen to focus on Ethiopia, because we can protect the most persons there. Had we chosen to protect you instead, we would have protected a much smaller number." But how could we justify to the 5,000 Ethiopians our neglect of their plight, if we choose the latter project? How could we explain to them that we find protecting them less important than protecting 1,000 Chadians who are no worse off than they are?

We would say that these funds should go to a project in Chad because other funds have already been allocated to projects in Ethiopia whereas no funds have yet been allocated anywhere in Chad. But is this a good reason? Our interlocutors can respond: "The projects elsewhere in Ethiopia do nothing to protect *us*. So why should they affect the decision? We happen to live in the same country as people now protected by other projects. Why should this count against us? Why are we so much less worthy of protection than we would be if our province were a separate country?"

Let me pose this challenge somewhat more formally by invoking an idea that philosophers call *universality* and economists refer to as the *anonymity condition*: in the moral assessment of conduct and social institutions, their impact on any person matters equally, irrespective of who this person is.[32] Thus, when some

---

[32] There are obvious complications here concerning special ties, which may be generative (like the special duty to keep some particular promise, which is derivative on the universal duty to keep

group of very badly off persons is threatened by some harm, we have equally strong reasons to protect these people, irrespective of their race, nationality, gender, religion, and other morally arbitrary features.[33] For example, protecting 1,000 very poor Ethiopians from harm has the same moral importance as protecting 1,000 equally poor Chadians from equally serious harm. If this weak premise is accepted, a problematic case involving *competing* claims of *disjoint* groups can be transformed into a much less problematic case involving *noncompeting* claims of *fully overlapping* groups: It is evidently *more* important, morally, to protect 5,000 very poor Ethiopians from harm than to protect only every fifth member of this group, a proper subset of 1,000 very poor Ethiopians. Pursuant to the anonymity condition, however, protecting 1,000 very poor Ethiopians from harm has the *same* moral importance as protecting 1,000 equally poor Chadians from equally serious harm. Therefore, by substitution, it is more important, morally, to protect 5,000 very poor Ethiopians from harm than to afford equivalent harm protection to 1,000 equally poor Chadians.

This argument from the anonymity condition shows how the effort to achieve fairness across countries may come at the expense of achieving fairness across their individual inhabitants: by spreading our efforts fairly across all poor countries, we are giving much greater weight to the protection of some persons than to the protection of others. We may be giving five times greater weight to protecting Chadians than to protecting Ethiopians from harm, in my example. (The estimates in Collier and Dollar suggest that some implied weight ratios are actually even higher than 5:1.)

To complement this somewhat abstract reasoning, consider a more concrete hypothetical emergency rescue on the high seas. A large cruise ship has sunk in very cold waters, and we are trying to save some of the scattered survivors by pulling them aboard our smaller vessel before they die in the icy waters. The passengers and crew of the cruise ship are nationals of many countries. If we simply try to save as many as possible, these countries would not be fairly represented among the rescued (e.g., in proportion to their share of the cruise ship's population or according to whatever standard the advocates of a distributive fairness constraint care to specify). May we aim for fair representation of countries, then,

---

one's promises) or nongenerative (like the special duty to show substantial concern for one's parents). These complexities can be left aside for now (but are discussed in the final section of part III of this chapter) on the empirically plausible assumption that they do not introduce any asymmetry between how we – the managers and supporters of INGOs – are related to very poor people in different foreign countries.

[33] There may be features of persons not screened out by the anonymity condition: We may have more reason to protect young people than to protect old people, for example, but this sort of discrimination is not genuinely discriminatory because it favors everyone in one stage of his or her life. We may have less reason to protect undeserving people (such as the defeated Hutu genocidaires in Rwanda), but this sort of discrimination is not problematic provided if desert is understood in a plausible way so that everyone can live up to it. Again, I can here leave aside these factors on the empirically plausible assumption that the worst-off in different poor countries do not systematically differ with regard to them.

even if this would make our rescue efforts less cost-effective and would thus lead to our saving fewer people? If the answer is negative, why must not INGOs, too, display fairness across individuals – giving equal weight to the interests of each and hence protecting as many as possible – at the expense of fairness across countries?

So the insistence on distributive fairness across countries stands in tension with common commitments to the equal worth of all human beings, to the idea that we should treat all *persons* with equal concern irrespective of their nationality.

The advocates of distributive fairness across countries also face another problem: what about groups defined in terms of features other than nationality? If the allocation of resources must be fair across *countries,* must it then not also be fair across provinces, across counties, across religious denominations, across generations, between the sexes, between rural and urban populations, and so forth? Affirmative answers add ever more – possibly inconsistent – fairness constraints, each of which will tend to reduce the cost-effectiveness of our harm protection efforts. Negative answers provoke the charge of inconsistency: what is so special about nationality? Why should we have to treat nationalities fairly, but not the other groupings mentioned?

To illustrate, consider an INGO that is funding the construction of deep wells providing access to safe drinking water. The INGO has nowhere near enough money to fund wells wherever clean water is urgently needed. If it follows the policy of protecting as many as possible, then it will fund wells in larger towns where the availability of safe water will protect more people from waterborne diseases. But this may seem unfair toward those who, merely because they happen to live far from any such town, have no chance of benefiting. (It is obviously not feasible for all such people to move near one of the wells.)

Yet if it seems unfair to concentrate limited funds on protecting as many people as possible, what is the alternative? Should one run a lottery over all persons who lack safe drinking water? Lowering cost-effectiveness, such a lottery would give villagers some chance. But they would still be disadvantaged because, with fewer inhabitants, villages would be less likely than towns to win a well. Isn't this still unfair?

There is a way of achieving genuine fairness in the sense of equalizing chances among all individual persons threatened by harm. This involves running a lottery over all the villages and towns lacking a supply of safe drinking water. But this third strategy would lead to most of the wells being built in villages where they protect only a few people. Thus, although the third strategy achieves more fairness than the second (involving a lottery over all endangered persons), it also lowers cost-effectiveness even further.[34]

---

[34] Making the example more concrete, assume there are twenty-four villages for every town and that a well built in a village provides safe water to 150 people whereas a well built in a town provides safe water to 1,800. On these assumptions, the first strategy of funding wells only in

The last two paragraphs show that the concern for fairness across groups can exact a very high price in terms of cost-effectiveness. But we should also attend to the other concern: that such fairness at the group level has no moral significance. Suppose you are an INGO officer at headquarters and receive a call from a field operative requesting authorization for funds to build seven wells in different towns. In response to your query, the operative tells you that there are dozens of similar towns just as much in need of a well. You tell her that she cannot just pick seven towns, if there are so many others. She is to run a lottery over all the needy towns and then to fund wells in the winning ones. She follows your instructions. Have you achieved a morally significant gain? You may say that by insisting on the lottery, you have, in addition to bringing safe water to thousands, also brought a *chance* of safe water to millions more. But does this matter? Did these millions really, unknowingly, derive any benefit from the chance they had between your phone call and the conclusion of the lottery? If not, is there some other way in which this lottery has morally improved the world?

One may think that to be morally significant, the chance for protection must be made known to those who have it. To achieve this, you can instruct your local operative to send a sound truck around the candidate towns to announce that seven of them, chosen by lot, will soon have a deep well. Better make that six, because now the funds must also cover this announcement. Is there any moral gain in the knowledge shared by millions of people in the losing towns that, with better luck, they might have won access to safe drinking water?

I see no reasons for answering any of these questions in the affirmative. This may be due to my lack of imagination. In advance of being shown such a reason, I can only conclude that the concern for supposed fairness has no moral weight and must be set aside in deference to the very weighty concern to maximize the harm protection we achieve. If we are equally concerned with all human beings who, as things are, have no access to safe drinking water, then we should disregard distributive fairness constraints on (ABCD) and discriminate (under the empirical conditions stipulated above) in favor of towns and against villages. Through no fault of their own, many villagers will not then gain access to safe water. This discrimination is justifiable as minimizing the number of persons who must be left without access. There is no injustice in this discrimination – although there is surely horrendous injustice in the fact that, in a world so affluent in aggregate, 1,037 million human beings remain exposed to waterborne diseases.

---

towns will protect 1,800 people per well built but will give only townspeople any chance of protection. The second strategy, involving a lottery over persons, will result in two-thirds of the wells being built in villages and one-third in towns. Wells will then protect 700 people on average, and townspeople will have a twelve times greater chance of protection than villagers do. The third strategy, involving a lottery over villages and towns, will result in 96 percent of the wells being built in villages. Wells will then protect only 216 people on average, but villagers and townspeople will have equal chances of protection.

The arguments presented seem to me sufficient to defeat any distributive fairness constraints on (ABCD). Before drawing any definite conclusions, however, let us consider two special cases that are more problematic.

Imagine an acute famine emergency. An INGO is bringing in food, but, given its limited resources, it cannot ensure everyone's survival. No one can survive on a fair share of the available food. So, if some are to survive, the INGO must distribute its limited food supply selectively. But how to do the selecting? Consider two options. The INGO might select hungry persons at random up to the point where their minimal food requirements equal the available food supply. Alternatively, the INGO might opt for selection rules that maximize the expected number of survivors. Such rules would, in general terms, favor those whose minimal food requirements are smallest. They would, in particular, favor persons with more efficient metabolisms, children over adults, and women over men. How should the INGO staff proceed in such a horrifying situation?

In response to such questions, it is sometimes said that the INGO staff "should not play God." I find this idea unhelpful because I cannot see what is supposed to follow from it. The decision about which distribution rule to use is ineluctably ours. The situation imposes this awesome choice on us, and we cannot evade the responsibility: even if we run a lottery and even if we flee the scene leaving desperate people to fight over the food we leave behind, we are still making a decision that determines who will live and who will die. We *must* face the question: how do we distribute the food?

Facing this question, I think we ought to apply optimizing selection rules to the situation. We ought to protect twenty men and sixty-five women, for example, if doing so enables eighty-five people to survive instead of the eighty that would survive if we chose to protect equal numbers of men and women.[35]

This general rejection of distributive fairness constraints seems least plausible in cases when the fact that some people are harder to protect is a result of injustice suffered by these very people. Thus, consider once more the decision faced by the INGO constructing wells to ensure access to safe drinking water. Modifying the initial case, suppose this INGO operates in a country where the members of some despised minority religion are barred from living in urban areas (where their beliefs might set a "bad" example) and are thus forced to inhabit isolated rural areas. In this context, one may well be inclined to reject the

---

[35] The optimal rules must be designed with regard to empirical complexities that are too obvious and too tangential to merit full discussion: if *only* children receive food, then they will all be orphaned and will have no surviving adults to take care of them when the emergency passes. If only female adults receive food, then they will all be widowed and the whole group will suffer a severe demographic imbalance. Even when such complexities are fully taken into account, it will still be possible to increase the expected number of survivors considerably by departing from a random distribution. Reference to such empirical complexities does not, therefore, enable us to avoid the hard question. (And it bears stressing: such horrific life-and-death choices are commonplace in the work of INGOs dealing with food emergencies.)

optimizing policy because it would, in effect, systematically aggravate the unjust disadvantage imposed on the members of the minority religion.

To see how much support this case can give to the idea of distributive fairness constraints, we must carefully strip away at least two impurities. The case as described may evoke the thought that the members of the religious minority, suffering disdain and discrimination, are really worse off than the urban dwellers who would gain access to safe drinking water if the wells were built there. Insofar as this is true, propositions (A) and (B) already provide countervailing reasons that may tip the scales in favor of constructing the wells in minority areas. The case as described may also evoke the thought that those urban dwellers share in the disdain of, and collaborate in the discrimination against, the religious minority. This consideration might shift the balance of reasons against them, but for reasons of desert (cf. n. 32) that have nothing to do with distributive fairness. To present the case as supporting distributive fairness constraints, let us then construct it by envisioning another equally despised religious minority, this one living in urban ghettos – a minority that is just as badly off as but does not share the widespread disdain of the first religious minority. Should our INGO here follow the optimizing policy and construct wells in the urban ghettos (where they will protect many members of the second minority) or should our INGO construct wells also in rural areas (where they will protect members of the first minority) even if this substantially reduces the overall number of people gaining access to safe drinking water? In the case so described, I do not find it difficult to endorse, for all the reasons discussed earlier, the first option at the expense of the suggested fairness constraints.

I do not believe that the arguments I have presented settle the matter conclusively. But they do convince me, for now, that the proposed ideals of distributive fairness should not constrain the straightforward application of (ABCD). The "other things being equal" clause in this principle should not be read as permitting departures from cost-effectiveness for the sake of achieving an equalization of chances among needy individuals or a proportionate distribution of harm reduction efforts across countries or other collectivities.

III. FURTHER CONSIDERATIONS

Without any claims to completeness, this section addresses six additional issues relevant to the proper specification of (ABCD).

Extinction and Diversity

(ABCD) conceives the moral value of any project in individualistic terms: as the sum of the moral values of the harm reductions (and increases) this project would bring about for the individual persons it affects. It may thereby leave out significant moral concerns. Suppose, for instance, that the cost-effective allocation of funds would exclude a certain region (the Amazon, say) in which certain nations or cultures are threatened with extinction. One may well think that when the last members of such a nation are killed or forced out of their ancestral lands, the moral loss is greater than the harm suffered by these individuals.

One may invoke the value of diversity to explain these intuitions in a way that fits the individualist paradigm: all human beings lose when the biological and cultural diversity of humankind is diminished. But it is hard to establish that this loss to individuals can shift the balance of reasons away from, say, saving the lives of 5,000 starving Ethiopians toward saving the lives of 500 Amazon natives.[36] Thus, it would seem that to accommodate those intuitions, normative individualism would have to be relaxed somewhat to make room for the realization that not every morally serious loss is harm suffered by individual human beings. The demise or demoralization of a nation with its own culture (language, religion, shared way of life) can be a serious loss in itself, over and above any harm this event involves for the nation's last members.

Risk and Uncertainty

Projects may differ in terms of how much visibility they afford. With some projects, moral value and cost are clearly predictable, but with other projects there are significant risks or even uncertainties. Let me briefly outline the latter distinction. A decision involves risk insofar as the decision maker does not know what will happen but can make reliable assumptions about the possible outcomes and their probabilities. A decision involves uncertainty insofar as the decision maker cannot make reliable assumptions about the probabilities associated with various outcomes or even about what the possible outcomes are. The distinction between decisions under risk and decisions under uncertainty is scalar – a matter of degree. For instance, one may know the value ("payoff") of one possible outcome and that its probability is between 40 and 45 percent and the value of another outcome and that its probability is between 35 and 50 percent but be ignorant of what would happen if neither of these outcomes came about. In this case, there is some uncertainty associated with the first two outcomes (their exact likelihood is unknown) and much uncertainty about other possible outcomes because their exact probabilities and even their values are unknown.

(Throughout, I have in mind the probabilities it makes sense to assign to various outcomes on the basis of the evidence available to decision makers. That they

---

[36] In presenting such cases, one should occasionally attach the reminder that although particular INGOs do face horrific choices of this sort, the world at large does not. The rich countries could eradicate life-threatening poverty worldwide at a cost barely noticeable to their citizens (see text preceding n. 12). Their policies and design of the world economy perpetuate the catastrophe of world poverty and thus the context in which INGOs have such horrifying choices forced on them.

must work with probabilities need not be due to a genuine indeterminacy in the physical world. Even if a slot machine is a wholly deterministic device, players lack access to the information that would allow them to predict its behavior and can therefore reason only probabilistically. Similarly, even if the universe is wholly deterministic, INGOs cannot fully predict the consequences of their decisions and must therefore reason probabilistically. This raises the question of how much effort an INGO should divert to acquiring more information and to monitoring the impact and side effects of its activities. The general answer is that an INGO should make its decisions about how much to spend on what information in such a way as to maximize its expected long-run cost-effectiveness. In this regard, INGOs could reap much greater benefits than they currently do from cooperating with one another and other agencies. Such cooperation could be organized by INGOs themselves or by third parties. The latter possibility is exemplified in the Netherlands, where the government has acted as catalyst through the Directorate General for International Cooperation and the Netherlands Development Organization.[37])

To cope with risk, the standard method would estimate the moral value of a chancy project as its *probability-weighted expected moral value*. Insofar as the realized value of a project depends on chancy factors, different outcomes are possible. In this case, one estimates for each outcome its probability and the moral value the project would then realize. The probability-weighted expected moral value of the project is then calculated as the sum of these products (probability times conditional value).

Likewise for risks regarding cost: here one estimates the cost of a chancy project as its *probability-weighted expected cost*. Insofar as a project's cost depends on chancy factors, different outcomes are possible. In this case, one estimates for each outcome its probability and what the project would then cost. The probability-weighted expected cost of the project is then calculated as the sum of these products (probability times conditional cost).

A chancy project's cost-effectiveness (*ex ante*) is then estimated as before: by dividing its (probability-weighted expected) moral value by its (probability-weighted expected) cost.[38]

---

[37] For a brief account, see Bendix 1996 and the OECD Development and Cooperation Review of the Netherlands (http://www.oecd.org/document/47/0,2340,en_2649_201185_1883887_1_1_1_1,00.html).

[38] The cost-effectiveness *ex ante* of a project must *not* be equated with its probability-weighted average cost-effectiveness *ex post*. This is easily seen by example. Consider the choice between two types of projects. Each project of type A cures 30 children for each US $10 spent; such projects thus have a cost-effectiveness score of 3. Each project of type B has a 50 percent chance of curing 25 children at a cost of US $25 and a 50 percent chance of curing 27 children at a cost of US $1. The average *ex post* cost-effectiveness score of type-B projects is 50% * 1 + 50% * 27 = 14. This large number suggests that type-B projects are greatly superior and ought to be chosen. But this

Is this a morally plausible way to assess chancy projects? Is it plausible, for instance, to assign equal moral value to (i) a 10 percent chance of saving 1,000 lives and (ii) a 100 percent chance of saving 100 lives? Egalitarians may respond that (i) should be preferred because it spreads survival prospects more evenly. Although this is true in a sense, I find the *ex ante* sense in which it is true morally irrelevant: in the long run, both strategies save equal numbers of lives. And the fact that, under (i), many additional people were the objects of failed harm protection attempts – this fact is of no value to these people. What other moral value could it have?[39]

Others think that (ii) should be preferred. They may feel that, taking a gamble, (i) expresses disrespect for human life – a feeling I find hard to understand. Or, familiar with financial markets, they may feel that some risk premium should be levied on (i). In the financial world, such a risk premium is deemed appropriate because of the decreasing marginal utility of money. But there is no decreasing marginal value of human lives saved.[40]

Lacking compelling reasons for departing, in either direction, from an equal assignment of moral value, I conclude, then, regarding decision making under risk, that the cost-effectiveness of a chancy project should be understood to be its cost-effectiveness *ex ante*, calculated by dividing its probability-weighted expected moral value by its probability-weighted expected cost.

Coping with uncertainty is considerably harder. Some theorists have argued that uncertainty calls for a conservative response, one that gives great weight to the worst conceivable outcome.[41] The most conservative strategy here is the so-called maximin rule. "Maximin" is short for the Latin "*maxi*mum *mini*morum," meaning highest minimum. The maximin rule instructs agents to choose the option that is associated with the best worst-case scenario. But this rule seems plainly too conservative here. To see this, consider a case like this: An INGO has a truck with perishable food in a region where starvation is widespread. The food is enough to protect up to 800 people from premature death (keeping them alive until harvest time, say). One option is to drive the food to a township in the

---

suggestion is mistaken. Funds ought to be spent on type-A projects. The *ex ante* cost-effectiveness score of type-B projects is actually only 2: repeatedly implementing type-B projects, we will cure 26 children per project on average and will pay US $13 per project on average.

[39] This brief response is obviously closely related to the thought more elaborately developed in the two paragraphs following n. 33.

[40] There may be effects on accretive contributions (to be discussed in the next subsection): funding chancy projects, an INGO may risk going broke before scoring its first success. Or, even if its survival chances are undiminished, less in new contributions may be triggered by saving 1,000 lives through one successful and nine failed attempts than would be triggered by saving 1,000 lives through ten successful sure-thing projects. If either of these were a fact, it would speak in favor of (ii). But this point is irrelevant here, because we have implicitly assumed that cost is equal. The question here at issue concerns only the *ex ante* moral value of chancy projects.

[41] For example, Rawls 1999, 132–5, who cites Fellner 1965, 142–4.

East, where it would certainly protect 200 people from imminent starvation. The other option is to drive it West, where the food may save 800 people in a larger town. Although it is known that the township in the East is reachable by truck, information about whether the town in the West can be so reached is unavailable. Trying the route West will consume the available fuel and, should the truck not get through, the food will protect no one.

In this sort of case, I think one should reason as follows: If the town in the West is reachable, then going west would save 600 more starving people than going east. If the town in the West is not reachable, then going east would save 200 more people than going West would. Given the uncertainty, these two conditionals are symmetrically placed. There is only one factor that can break the symmetry: the larger number of people protected. Therefore, the truck should proceed toward the town in the West.

In the real world, the uncertainty about probabilities is typically less total than in this example. Some rough estimates are normally possible concerning the likelihoods of some of the outcomes. In the real world, however, there are often other sources of uncertainty because agents may not even have a complete understanding of all possible outcomes. Each of the two projects in the example might be helped or hindered in myriad ways, and it is impossible to anticipate all these possibilities, let alone to attach rough probabilities to them. Still, the overall principle that should guide INGOs in coping with risk and uncertainty is clear enough. An INGO should incorporate risk and uncertainty into its decision making in such a way as to maximize its expected long-run cost-effectiveness. More generally:

> (ABCD*) Other things being equal, an INGO should govern its decision making about candidate projects by such rules and procedures as are expected to maximize its long-run cost-effectiveness, defined as the expected aggregate moral value of the projects it undertakes divided by the expected aggregate cost of these projects. Here aggregate moral value, or harm protection, is the sum of the moral values of the harm reductions (and increases) these projects bring about for the individual persons they affect.

Fundraising

The projects an INGO undertakes have a feedback effect on its fundraising success. And this INGO may then face complex choices between intrinsically more cost-effective projects on one hand and more donor-enticing projects on the other.

Consider the decision between two projects, each of which would cost US $2 million to implement. Project G has an estimated moral value of 9,000, whereas Project H has an estimated moral value of only 3,000. (Project G might save 9,000 children from death by starvation, for instance, whereas Project H would save only 3,000 children from such a death.) One might then say that Project G's *intrinsic cost-effectiveness* (9,000/US $2m, score of 4,500) is three times as great as the intrinsic cost-effectiveness of Project H (3,000/US $2m, score of 1,500).

However, Project H would be conducted in a current "hotspot" and therefore would draw a lot more media attention. This in turn would trigger extra contributions, which would reduce the "true" cost of Project H, or so one might think. Suppose the fund-raising experts predict that Project H would raise incoming contributions by US $1.5 million, whereas Project G – conducted in some remote location – would raise incoming contributions by only US $200,000. If this is the situation, then one might say that the "true" cost-effectiveness of Project G is 9,000/US $1.8m, score of 5,000, and that "true" cost-effectiveness of Project H is 3,000/US $0.5m, score of 6,000.

Which of the two methods of assessing the cost and cost-effectiveness of projects – intrinsic versus "true" – is correct? The answer, I believe, is *neither*. Focusing on intrinsic cost-effectiveness – perhaps on the ground that the concern with fund-raising is profane or that the responsibility for how much money is received by an INGO rests solely with its potential contributors – unacceptably ignores the gain in harm protection that additional funds would make possible.

To appreciate why focusing on "true" cost-effectiveness is likewise unacceptable, one needs to draw a further distinction with regard to the additional contributions that projects may trigger. One needs to distinguish between additional contributions that constitute merely a redirection from one INGO to another and additional contributions that increase the sum total of funds received by all relevant INGOs. To mark this distinction, let us say that an INGO's projects may attract both *substitutional* and *accretive* contributions. In the former case, one INGO is substituted for another as recipient of part of the overall pool of relevant contributions. In the latter case, this whole pool is enlarged.

This distinction may be unfamiliar because it has little significance in the business world, where talk of cost-effectiveness has its main home. When deciding whether to run an advertising campaign, a firm will assess the cost of the campaign against its expected benefits in terms of additional business and earnings. In considering these benefits, the firm need not care whether it is benefiting by taking business away from its competitors or by increasing overall demand. If anything, it will slightly prefer taking business away from competitors because this will have a greater impact on its market share[42] and will also weaken its competitors in absolute terms. Firms pursue different goals that put them in

[42] Suppose that the firm in question starts out from a baseline of 45 percent market share and that the advertising campaign would increase its business by two-ninths. Then, if the increase comes at the expense of its competitors, its market share will rise to $(45 + 10)/100 = 55$ percent. If the increase comes from new business, the firm's market share will rise to only $(45 + 10)/(100 + 10) = 50$ percent.

competition with one another.[43] A firm has no reason to want its peers to be successful and effective in the pursuit of their goals.

The distinction has great significance, however, in the INGO world, where many INGOs pursue the *same* goals *in an agent-neutral sense.* Many INGOs, for instance, seek to protect children from hunger and malnutrition. Each such INGO has vastly more moral reason to be concerned that children be protected than it has reason to be concerned that such protection be provided by *itself* rather than by one of its peers.

To illustrate the point, consider two INGOs with such a common goal and assume that $INGO_1$ tends to favor projects like G, whereas $INGO_2$ tends to favor projects like H. Insofar as the pool of contributions is fixed, the result will be that the cost-effectiveness of the two INGOs, considered as a team, will decline. This is so because the diverse project policies of the two organizations will divert contributions from $INGO_1$ to $INGO_2$. This has the effect that more and more of the projects they initiate will be type-H projects initiated by $INGO_2$, rather than type-G projects initiated by $INGO_1$. By diverting funding from $INGO_1$ to itself, $INGO_2$ is reducing the cost-effectiveness of these contributions by two-thirds (because type-G projects are three times as cost-effective as type-H projects).

Seeing how its funding is drying up, $INGO_1$ can follow $INGO_2$'s example by likewise switching its activities toward projects of type H. Doing so may help $INGO_1$ stem the decline in its funding. But it will also accelerate the overall drift from type-G to type-H projects. In the end – whether $INGO_1$ makes the switch or not – the money raised by the two INGOs will go to projects of type H rather than to projects of type G. Further, on the assumption of a fixed pool of contributions, this is a disaster, rendering these contributions much less cost-effective in terms of harm protection than they would be if devoted to projects of type G.[44]

Insofar as high-profile projects will bring in contributions that would not otherwise have been made, the shift to type-H projects may be desirable, as is illustrated by the "true" cost-effectiveness calculation conducted earlier. A key to deciding between projects G and H is then an empirical estimate about the extent to which new funds raised through projects G and H are substitutional or accretive.

The correct way of calculating the cost and cost-effectiveness of projects takes account of new funds, which the candidate projects would attract, only insofar as these are accretive. To illustrate with the numerical example provided earlier, the

---

[43] To be sure, there is a sense in which firms pursue the same goal: profit maximization. But this goal is understood in agent-relative, not in agent-neutral terms: Each firm aims to maximize *its own* profits. There is an ineliminable indexical (pronoun referenced to the agent) in the statement of the goal that firms pursue.

[44] For the claim that something like this is actually happening, pursuant to what he calls the "humanitarian Gresham's Law," see de Waal 1998, 138–43.

following are the *correct* cost-effectiveness scores of the two projects for various assumptions about what percentage of new money raised is accretive:

Percentage of new funds that are accretive	Cost-effectiveness of project G	Cost-effectiveness of project H
100	5,000	6,000
90	4,945	4,615
80	4,891	3,750
70	4,839	3,158
60	4,787	2,727
50	4,737	2,400
40	4,688	2,143
30	4,639	1,935
20	4,592	1,765
10	4,545	1,622
0	4,500	1,500

In our numerical example, then, INGOs should choose type-H projects over type-G projects only if the new funds the former would raise are almost entirely accretive. This on the assumption that an INGO should care about harm and harm protection in general – not just about the harm protection it itself achieves.

This discussion of fund-raising illustrates a somewhat more general point. An INGO can pursue an *agent-relative* goal, defined in terms of the moral value *it* realizes, or the corresponding *agent-neutral* goal, defined in terms of the moral value *all INGOs together* realize. As the example has shown, pursuit of the former goal may well detract from achievement of the latter by worsening the allocation of funds within and among INGOs.

In addition, pursuit of the agent-relative goal is also *directly collectively self-defeating:*[45] each INGO does worse, even in terms of this goal, if all INGOs successfully pursue it than it would do if all INGOs successfully pursued the agent-neutral goal instead. An INGO seeking to maximize the moral value it itself realizes will favor type-H projects over type-G projects. Others must follow suit or be driven out of the business of harm protection. Once all INGOs focus their resources on type-H projects, however, each will realize less moral value than it would realize if all INGOs focused their resources on type-G projects.

Because the agent-neutral goal is morally more plausible and because the agent-relative goal is directly collectively self-defeating, INGOs ought to be committed to the agent-neutral goal and should therefore understand *cost* in (ABCD*) in the sense of *correct cost*.

---

[45] See Parfit 1984, chap. 4. This is analogous to how the goal of doing what is best for oneself is directly collectively self-defeating in prisoners'-dilemma type situations: if each prisoner does what is best for himself, each will do worse than he would have done had they both chosen what is best for the pair of them.

But what should any *one* INGO do if other INGOs are "defecting" to the agent-relative goal? Should it stick to the agent-neutral goal, accepting the consequent reduction in its funding? Should it likewise defect, accepting the consequent reduction in global INGO effectiveness? Or should it try to raise the issue with other INGOs and the contributing public?

Deontological Concerns: Discriminating Contributors

My discussion thus far of moral priorities for INGOs has resulted in a broadly consequentialist conception. To be sure, this conception is not consequentialist in the traditional sense. It does not instruct us simply to maximize the good, defined as harm reduction, but instead gives greater weight to protecting from harm those who are worse off (Proposition (B)). Some theorists hold that this prioritarian element suffices to render a moral conception recognizably deontological.[46] In my view, however, a conception that instructs us to maximize some *weighted* aggregate (weighted in favor of the worse-off, in this case) is still broadly consequentialist – it merely conceives morally relevant consequences a little differently. This is a terminological squabble among philosophers that need not detain us. I mention it only to flag that I now discuss more significantly deontological concerns.

Thus far, I have argued that INGOs ought to focus their resources on the projects that are most cost-effective. This claim implies that INGOs ought to discriminate in favor of badly off people who can be cheaply protected from harm and thus against badly off people whom it would be expensive to protect. I have accepted this implication as plausible: such discrimination is not morally offensive in any way insofar as it is driven entirely by the concern to protect as many badly off people as possible (Proposition (C)).

But now consider this complication. Suppose the affluent people giving money to INGOs are mostly white and somewhat racist: projects that protect from harm badly off white people elicit much greater gains in accretive contributions per dollar expended than alternative projects that protect from harm equally badly off persons of color. (Judging by the public responses to the crises in Rwanda and Kosovo, this supposition is anything but unrealistic.) To illustrate the difficulty,

---

[46] Rawls is an example. He holds that "deontological theories are defined as non-teleological ones" (Rawls 1999, 26). He also defines teleological theories as ones that hold that "the good is defined independently from the right, and then the right is defined as that which maximizes the good" (ibid, 22f.). He then classifies his own theory as deontological on the ground that it "does not interpret the right as maximizing the good" (ibid, 26). Rawls's theory does not instruct us to choose the public criterion of justice that maximizes higher-order interest fulfillment nor to design society's basic structure so as to maximize citizens' social primary goods. Instead, this theory gives greater weight to the worst-off (to optimizing the lowest level of higher-order interest fulfillment) and to the least advantaged (to optimizing the smallest shares of social primary goods). On Rawls's understanding, then, my view on INGO priorities as developed thus far would already qualify as deontological.

consider the choice between two projects. Project K is targeted at badly off whites and Project L is targeted at badly off blacks. Ignoring feedback effects on fund-raising, Project L is considerably more cost-effective (in the intrinsic sense). Because Project K would produce much greater gains in accretive contributions, however, Project K is considerably more cost-effective on (what I have argued is) the correct understanding of cost-effectiveness. Given all that has been said thus far, then, the INGO ought to implement type-K projects over type-L projects. Is this plausible?

One may be tempted to try to avoid this hard question by pointing out, cor-rectly, that the attitudes of affluent people are subject to change. An INGO might engage in a publicity campaign designed to foster sentiments of identification and solidarity also with badly off people of color. This is true enough, but it does not answer the difficulty. Any such publicity campaign diverts funds that could have been expended on harm protection projects. To be sure, this diversion can be justified: when it would increase the harm protection all INGOs achieve in the long run, for instance, by increasing the willingness to support type-L projects, by winning accretive contributions through improved INGO reputation, and by reducing the sense of exclusion and humiliation among poor blacks abroad. Still, such diversion would often be unjustified. Therefore, if correct cost-effectiveness is what matters, then an INGO faced with a situation like the one described often ought to leave the racist attitudes of its contributors alone and focus its resources on projects of type K. Does this show that the focus on correct cost-effectiveness needs to be modified?

There are essentially five responses to this difficulty. The first argues that there is nothing morally wrong with contributor racism or, more generally, with con-tributors directing their harm reduction efforts toward projects of their choice. It is *their* money, after all, and just as they may freely decide what movies to watch or whom to go out with, so they are equally free, morally, to decide which good causes to support. I disagree with this first response on two counts. As the next subsection brings out, I believe that, in the world as it is, our moral reasons to support efforts at harm protection are not exclusively positive (in the sense of positive duties). Rather, our contributions are morally required by more stringent duties arising from our material involvement in the production of harm. Moreover, even if we had only positive moral reasons to contribute to INGOs, it would still be morally odious to favor some badly off people merely because of their skin color. The stronger such favoritism, the more offensive it is morally. It would be offensive, in my view, if someone gave preference to a charity that provides dental braces to white children abroad over a charity that provides life-saving vaccinations to black children abroad – indicating that he deems it morally more important for white children to have straight teeth than for as many black children to survive.

The second response argues that contributor racism is indeed regrettable but that there is nothing morally questionable about an INGO taking account of such contributor racism as an empirical fact in its effort to optimize its harm protection strategy. Again, I cannot share this response. To be sure, the INGO is intending to do the best it can toward realizing moral value and has no sympathy for the racism of its contributors. Still, it implements this racism, and this is morally offensive even when done in the service of a good cause.

The third response argues that it is indeed morally offensive for an INGO to implement contributor racism but that this significant reason for favoring type-L projects is usually overwhelmed in our world by the great moral importance of achieving harm protection. The reason against allowing oneself to implement racism can then be permitted to tip the scale only when competing projects are, as far as can be estimated, close in cost-effectiveness correctly assessed. If one project is much superior in this respect, like Project L is superior to Project K, then the superior project ought to be chosen, albeit with a sense that one is thereby participating in a wrong done to those whom Project K would have protected. I find this the most plausible response.

The fourth response argues that the concerns of combating racist attitudes among contributors and of not allowing oneself to become an instrument of racism have enough weight to affect the balance of moral reasons even with many early deaths at stake on the other side. This moral reason must then be traded off against the others. Thus, it may well be that we ought to save ten black children from death by starvation, even if focusing on white children would have generated accretive contributions that would have enabled us to save more to stand up for the principle that all children matter equally. This response also strikes me as having some appeal, although I do not know how one can answer the question how many extra deaths this "standing up for principle" can justify. What is the correct exchange rate between racism spurned and additional lives saved? As this exchange rate is increased so that standing up for principle becomes really costly in terms of harm protection, this response quickly becomes implausible to me.

The fifth response, in absolutist-deontological fashion, gives overriding priority to the antiracist principle. When it comes to factors such as sex and skin color, we must simply ignore accretive contributions and focus solely on the *intrinsic* cost-effectiveness of projects. If this diminishes, even greatly, the harm protection we can achieve, then we must simply accept this diminution. In view of the huge difference our choice of harm protection strategy makes in terms of severe human suffering, I find this response unacceptable. The final subsection implicitly undermines one main source of its appeal: the deontological idea that one should not wrong some people to help others. Whatever the merits of this idea (it is implausible when understood as an absolute constraint), its relevance in this world is severely limited because most of what we, through INGOs, do to protect people in the poor countries is morally required from us not merely under the label of help or positive duty but also as mitigation of wrongs from which we profit and in the production of which we participate.[47]

---

[47] See Pogge 2005a.

Deontological Concerns: Local Participation

My broadly consequentialist approach to the question of INGO priorities can be criticized for ignoring the values of consultation, dialogue, and democracy: INGOs should not operate dictatorially according to some rigid algorithm. They should instead cooperate with local partner organizations and also give those whom they seek to protect a voice and a role in the planning and execution of their work. This objection is, I believe, less significant than it appears at first.

Given the current mismatch between total INGO resources and the vast scale of severe deprivations, INGOs face vital choices about where to operate. This kind of primary decision *cannot* be made in consultation with local partners and the deprived themselves because their identities cannot be known in advance of the decision. Further, it is simply infeasible to involve potential partners and potential beneficiaries from all poor regions in such primary decision making (which is not to deny that many INGOs would do well to recruit more managers and staff from poor countries). INGOs must decide on their own where to operate, and my (ABCD*) principle is relevant then by sketching how they can approach such decisions.

Once an INGO has chosen project locations, it should indeed generally consult with local partners and with the deprived in planning and executing its projects. Such dialogue usually has great instrumental value, rendering the INGO more effective in the pursuit of its objectives. But such a dialogue may also, of course, reexamine these objectives themselves. Local groups may, for instance, challenge an INGO's commitment to the (ABCD*) principle.

Such dialogue about the ultimate ends an INGO ought to be pursuing is not an end in itself, not an instance of pure procedural justice (so that any agreement freely struck is as good as any other, regardless of content). Rather, the main point of such a dialogue is to determine how the resources the INGO holds in trust ought to be deployed. The (ABCD*) principle and all the considerations adduced in support of its features contribute to answering this question. This contribution is subject to refutation or modification *by argument* (from local stakeholders or indeed from anyone else). But it is not subject to refutation or modification by baldly stated opposing convictions or preferences. The question of *which moral priorities are sound* is not reducible to the question which moral priorities are declared, however sincerely, to be sound by this or that group.

When differences about ultimate values persist in the dialogue, the INGO must in the end decide by itself how to proceed (giving due weight to disagreement as an indicator of possible error as well as a hindrance to effective project realization). The INGO has control of the resources. If it decides to hand these over to some local groups or to allow itself to be outvoted, it still bears responsibility for this decision and for its consequences on how effectively the resources are deployed. There may well be reasons for an INGO to defer to local convictions and preferences about appropriate priorities for the sake of smoother project realization or even at the cost of accepting (the risk of) small losses in cost-effectiveness. Seeing how much is at stake, however, it is hard to see how these reasons could justify more than small departures from the (ABCD*) principle.

Deontological Concerns: Material Involvement

The discussion so far suggests a broadly consequentialist approach, roughly: the greater the harm protection we can achieve, the more reason we have to achieve it. This suggestion is fine so long as other things are presumed to be equal. One pivotal factor that may not be equal, however, is how we, the INGO and its contributors, are causally related to the harm in question.

The relevance of this thought is clearest with regard to harms that an INGO project itself would or might cause. Harm causally dependent on an agent's conduct may be sorted into two broad categories according to whether the agent will have been materially involved in causing it. Philosophers typically call any moral reason not to cause (or to participate in causing) harm to others a *negative* moral reason or, if this reason is strong, a *negative duty*. Correspondingly, they call any moral reason an agent has to prevent or to mitigate harm others will have suffered a *positive* moral reason or *positive duty*.[48] Here moral duties, or duties for short, are moral reasons of some minimum weight or *stringency*. Being a subset of reasons for action, duties are *pro tanto*: they count for or against certain courses of action, but they may not be decisive when there are weighty countervailing reasons. It may turn out that what an agent ought to do, all things considered, violates some of her duties.

It is widely believed that, holding constant what is at stake for the agent and for those affected by her conduct, negative moral reasons are stronger than positive moral reasons. We can get a sense of the relative weight of moral reasons

---

[48] I do not believe that this distinction can plausibly be specified in purely empirical terms. To get a sense of the difficulty, imagine Bob in danger of drowning far out at sea. Jill is nearby with her boat. She sees Bob struggling in the water but sails away. There are different ways of describing this case. On one description, Jill failed to act so as to rescue Bob, and her conduct thus constitutes an omission. On another description, Jill did not remain passive but rather actively caused the boat to sail away from Bob, thereby making it impossible for him to reach it. Those who believe the first description to be the morally significant one will say that Jill was not materially involved in causing Bob's death; Bob would have died even if Jill had not been on the scene at all, and so she did not harm him. Those who see the second description as the morally significant one will say that Jill was materially involved in causing Bob's death; Bob would not have died if Jill had not sailed her boat away from him, and so she did harm him. I think the decision between these two accounts must be made on moral grounds. There is no purely scientific way of sorting all the different possible ways in which an agent might behave (move her body) into those that constitute passive omissions with regard to a certain situation and those that constitute active interferences. For a good discussion of this issue, see Bennett 1995.

by reflecting on situations in which moral reasons conflict with one another or with nonmoral reasons for action. Reflections of the first kind may ponder straightforward conflicts between positive and negative moral reasons, such as a situation in which an agent can save three children from being killed only by killing two others. The widely affirmed impermissibility of such an action shows that, at least when killings are at stake, negative moral reasons (not to kill) are more stringent than their positive counterparts (to prevent killings). Reflections of the second kind involve pairs of situations in which the greater stringency of negative moral reasons affects the permissibility of a given trade-off. For example, it is widely judged that it is impermissible for an agent to save her own hand by killing a child and yet permissible for an agent to fail to rescue a child from being killed when such rescue would involve the loss of her own hand. This pair of judgments shows that negative moral reasons are, here as well, judged to be more stringent than their positive counterparts.

There is no agreement about *how much* greater weight negative moral reasons have than positive ones. Views on this question, by ethicists and others, fall along a spectrum that ranges from a consequentialist to a deontological extreme. Extreme consequentialists hold that the weight of the moral reason to reduce some future harm (holding fixed the cost to the agent) is strictly proportional to the moral disvalue of this harm, regardless of the agent's causal relation thereto. Extreme deontologists hold that the stringency of negative moral reasons, relative to positive moral reasons and other reasons for action, is infinite: if there is a duty not to lie to innocent persons, then agents must not lie to the innocent even when doing so is the only way to save the planet. Both extreme views are highly implausible and widely rejected.

Rejection of the extreme consequentialist view requires elaboration of (ABCD*). We cannot treat harm that an INGO project brings about on a par with the harm reduction it achieves. For example, a project that saves the lives of 100 children but also kills five others is ordinarily judged – if not altogether impermissible, at least much less choice-worthy than a project that, saving the lives of ninety-five children, only reduces harm.

I say "ordinarily" because this judgment is in an interesting way conditional on available information. The judgment applies when the five children whom the project would kill can be identified in advance. But it does not apply when these five children cannot be identified in advance and are also expected to benefit from the project. This case is exemplified by many vaccination projects. It is permissible to vaccinate a town's children against a disease that would otherwise kill 100 of them prematurely, even if it is known in advance that five children will be killed by the vaccination itself – *provided* this project does not raise any child's expected (*ex ante*) risk of premature death above what it would be in the absence of the vaccination project. If this proviso is met, the project can be justified *to each child* as reducing, or at least not increasing, his or her expected harm (risk of premature death). The vaccination project can then be assessed by its aggregate impact: the reduction in the number of child deaths by ninety-five.

Projects may lie between these poles: It may be unknowable in advance who exactly will be harmed by the project yet knowable that there is a net increase in expected harm for some specific individuals. For example, we may be in a position to know that certain children, because of their physical constitution, are more likely to be killed than to be saved by being included in some vaccination project. Because it increases their premature death risk, this vaccination cannot be justified to them. Generally, such children should then be excluded. In special cases, when excluding them would greatly reduce the aggregate harm protection achieved by the project, these children may nonetheless be included – but only if the moral value of the expected increase in harm imposed on them is *greatly* outweighed by the expected moral value of the additional harm reduction achieved for the rest of the population. Again, any harm an INGO would itself bring about must be assigned greater weight in this INGO's deliberations.

It is often foreseeable that candidate INGO projects would cause harm to innocent people. It may be foreseeable, for example, that warring factions will rob some of the resources we might dispatch into some volatile region and will then use them to inflict further violence. By fuelling the fighting, these projects would thus cause harm. In such cases, the unmodified (ABCD*) may still be a plausible guiding principle, provided the available evidence does not allow us to identify any persons for whom the project's expected moral value is negative. But often we do have such evidence. We know which armed group is able and disposed to loot our resources, and we know who its intended victims are. In such cases, the ordinary cost-effectiveness reasons against choosing this project (cf. Section 2) are enhanced by negative moral reasons not to add to the (risk of) harm suffered by such potential victims.

We have distinguished and discussed positive moral reasons to prevent or to mitigate harm and more stringent negative reasons not to cause and not to be materially involved in causing harm. There is a third *intermediate* category: moral reasons to prevent or to mitigate harm that one otherwise will have caused or have participated in causing. Such reasons are, I believe, of intermediate stringency (holding fixed what is at stake for the agent and for those affected by her conduct). This can be shown by assessing their stringency against nonmoral reasons for action, against conventional positive moral reasons, and then against conventional negative moral reasons. Let me do this with examples of possible future harm that, if the agent does not actively intervene, will be caused by her past conduct.

An agent is not ordinarily thought to be required to sacrifice her own hand to save an innocent stranger. Imagine a situation in which this stranger is in mortal danger due to the agent's own prior conduct, however. Here the agent may be required to sacrifice her own hand to save the stranger – certainly if she knew or should have known at the time of her earlier conduct that it would put the stranger in mortal danger. Assessed against nonmoral reasons for action, the stringency of intermediate moral reasons is then between that of positive and that of negative moral reasons.

Drunk, a driver has run over two children on a pedestrian crosswalk. These children will survive only if they receive expensive operations. They will receive these operations only if the driver offers to pay for them. The driver has enough money to do this but only barely so. He could instead spend this money on three other children who would also die without his intervention. In response to this sort of case most would judge that the driver ought to save the lives of the two children he has run over so as to spare them future harm (premature death) that he himself would be the cause of. This suggests that intermediate moral reasons are more stringent than ordinary positive moral reasons – although less decisively so, I would think, than negative moral reasons are.

Assessed against ordinary negative moral reasons, intermediate moral reasons look less stringent. Most would judge it impermissible for an agent to kill two children where this is the only way of saving three others from a mortal danger arising from her prior misdeed. Still, the fact that the mortal danger to the three children arose from her prior conduct clearly increases the weight of her moral reasons to protect them and thus makes a difference to what trade-offs against negative duties are permissible.

Intermediate moral reasons can be relevant to INGO work in special cases in which INGO staff have – wrongfully, negligently, or even innocently – set in motion a train of events that threatens to harm innocent people. In such cases, the INGO's moral reason to protect them from these harms is more stringent than it would be if this INGO had not been materially involved in causing this threat.

Intermediate moral reasons may have much wider relevance, however. I have argued in the introduction that an INGO is not merely an actor in its own right but also an agent and trustee for its contributors, entrusted with fulfilling *their* moral responsibilities. As citizens of rich and powerful countries, we may well have been (and still be) participating in causing much of the harm that INGOs are working to reduce. At least our governments would seem to be so involved. Some of these governments have, for example, promoted the exportation of landmines and "small arms" into volatile regions of Africa and Asia where they are foreseeably used to maim and kill millions of innocent civilians. Some have encouraged and supported wars, civil wars, and coups whose devastating effects are continuing to harm many. Some have themselves employed large quantities of defoliants (Agent Orange), napalm, cluster bombs, and depleted uranium, the aftereffects of which (birth defects, burn wounds, internal injuries, cancer) are still being suffered in various countries. Many rich-country governments have cooperated in imposing unfair international rules of trade, finance, and intellectual property, thereby making extreme poverty and all its attendant evils much worse than they would have been under a minimally just global economic order.[49]

Insofar as governments of rich and powerful countries participate in causing harm, most of their citizens, on whose political and economic support they depend, are likewise implicated in these harms. To be sure, we often cannot, even in cooperation with like-minded others, prevent all the harmful policies of our governments. We typically can avert some of the harm these policies would otherwise bring about, however. Insofar as we share responsibility for harmful policies pursued by our government, we have an intermediate moral duty to avert our share of the harm these policies would otherwise cause.[50] This duty may be even more stringent and also more demanding when we are also profiting from the harmful policies our government is pursuing in our name.

It may seem that these thoughts about intermediate moral duties make our moral situation rather messy. How can an individual citizen in a rich country possibly determine which impending harms suffered worldwide are ones that she would be materially involved in causing? How can she determine her share of the responsibility for each such harm? How can she determine, for each such harm, the identity of those who would share responsibility with her as well as the precise share of the burden that each of these people ought to bear to avert this harm? And how can she effectively contribute minuscule fractions of a cent to the millions of people she would otherwise be co-responsible for harming?

Fortunately, these unmanageable complexities can be largely avoided.[51] The massive harm in today's highly interdependent world cannot be neatly sorted into harm that the government and citizens of some rich country are, and harm they are not, materially involved in causing. To be sure, it is often clear of specific harm that it falls into the former class. Yet there is not much specific harm that clearly falls into the latter class. Even when people are harmed by clear-cut natural disasters, such as an earthquake or a long-standing congenital defect, social factors are heavily involved in causing the resulting harms. Thus, earthquakes of given magnitude cause vastly more harm among the poor than among the rich because of differences in the quality of buildings. Similarly, congenital blindness harms poor persons in poor countries much more than affluent citizens of rich countries who have vastly superior opportunities to compensate for their lack of sight. Where harvests fail, food is imported for the affluent while the poor starve or die. Among the affluent, diseases are wiped out or cured, while they continue to

---

[49] All this is argued in Pogge 2002a, 2005b.

[50] For some citizens, this share may be zero. This is true most obviously of children and often also of many who are themselves severely victimized by harmful government policies. It may further hold for those who, being underprivileged, socially excluded, or disabled, afford no significant support (e.g., through the tax system) to government policies. Intermediate moral duties may also be outweighed when compliance would prevent the fulfillment of other, weightier duties or impose great hardship on the agent.

[51] See Pogge 2005a, 78 ff.

decimate the poor, some 12.5 million of whom are dying each year from diarrhea, perinatal and maternal conditions, measles, tuberculosis, malaria, pneumonia, meningitis, hepatitis, and other tropical diseases.[52]

The persistence of severe poverty in many poor countries, in turn, is partly due to the design of the global institutional order that foreseeably (re)produces vastly more poverty than would be reasonably avoidable. Had the rich countries pursued a different path of globalization in the last fifteen years, the problem of severe poverty would be a fraction of its present size. Insofar as we citizens of rich countries (through our governments) participate in, or profit from, the imposition of this unjust order, we are materially involved in a large majority of all the harm human beings are suffering worldwide. INGOs and their contributors therefore rarely face actual hard choices between morally *less* valuable harm reductions that we have *intermediate* moral reasons to achieve and morally *more* valuable harm reductions that we have only *positive* moral reason to achieve.

Only a small fraction of the citizens of the rich countries are willing to contribute to averting such harm. Their contributions are nowhere near sufficient to avert all the harm that the citizens of the rich countries have intermediate moral duties to avert. In the context of this grievous injustice, we should, for the most part, direct our grossly insufficient contributions for maximum effect: toward the most cost-effective harm protection projects. Reflection on intermediate moral duties thus greatly increases the strength of our moral reasons to achieve cost-effective harm protection without justifying significant departures from (ABCD*).

CONCLUSION

The discussions we have had about this chapter indicate that most readers will sharply disagree with my conclusions. Fortunately, they also suggest that we all have a great deal to learn from a careful elaboration of, and engagement with, this view.

BIBLIOGRAPHY

Bendix, Paul J. "Exemplary in Concept and Reach: The Development Policy of the Netherlands." *Development and Cooperation* 3 (1996): 24–26. Available at http://www.euforic.org/dandc/96e_ben.htm.
Bennett, Jonathan. *The Act Itself.* Oxford, England: Oxford University Press, 1995.
Broome, John. "Equality versus Priority: A Useful Distinction." 2002. Available at http://aran_univ-pau.fr/ee/page3.html.

---

[52] These diseases account for 22 percent of the annual human death toll. See WHO 2004, 120–5 (Annex Table 2).

Chen, Shaohua, and Martin Ravallion. "How Have the World's Poorest Fared since the Early 1980s?" *World Bank Research Observer* 19 (2004): 141–69. Available at wbro.oupjournals.org/cgi/content/abstract/19/2/141.

Cohen, G. A. "On the Currency of Egalitarian Justice." *Ethics* 99 (1989): 906–44.

Collier, Paul, and David Dollar. "Aid Allocation and Poverty Reduction." *European Economic Review* 46 (2002): 1475–500.

de Waal, Alex. *Famine Crimes: Politics and the Disaster Relief Industry in Africa.* Bloomington: Indiana University Press, 1998.

Dworkin, Ronald. *Sovereign Virtue.* Cambridge, MA: Harvard University Press, 2000.

Fellner, William. *Probability and Profit.* Homewood, IL: R. D. Irwin, 1965.

Kamm, Frances. *Morality, Mortality I.* Oxford, England: Oxford University Press, 1993.

International Labor Organization. *A Future without Child Labour.* 2002. Available at http://www.ilo.org/dyn/declaris/DECLARATIONWEB.INDEXPAGE.

Nussbaum, Martha and Amartya Sen, eds. *The Quality of Life.* Oxford: Clarendon Press, 1993.

Parfit, Derek. "Innumerate Ethics." *Philosophy and Public Affairs* 7 (1978): 285–301.

Parfit, Derek. *Reasons and Persons.* Oxford, England: Oxford University Press, 1984.

Parfit, Derek. "Equality or Priority" [1995]. In *The Ideal of Equality,* eds. Matthew Clayton and Andrew Williams. Houndmills, England: Macmillan, 2000.

Pogge, Thomas. *World Poverty and Human Rights: Cosmopolitan Responsibilities and Reforms.* Cambridge, England: Polity Press, 2002a.

Pogge, Thomas. "Can the Capability Approach be Justified?" *Philosophical Topics 30,* no. 2 (2002b): 167–228.

Pogge, Thomas. "Severe Poverty as a Violation of Negative Duties." *Ethics and International Affairs* 19 (2005a): 55–84.

Pogge, Thomas. "Recognized and Violated by International Law: The Human Rights of the Global Poor." *Leiden International Law Journal* 18, no. 4 (2005b): 717–45.

Rawls, John. "Social Unity and Primary Goods." In *Utilitarianism and Beyond,* eds. Amartya K. Sen and Bernard Williams. Cambridge, England: Cambridge University Press, 1982.

Rawls, John. *A Theory of Justice.* Cambridge, MA: Harvard University Press, 1999 [1971].

Reddy, Sanjay, and Thomas Pogge. "How *Not* to Count the Poor." In *Measuring Global Poverty,* eds. Sudhir Anand and Joseph Stiglitz. Oxford: Oxford University Press, 2006. Available: http://www.socialanalysis.org.

Scanlon, Thomas M. *What We Owe to Each Other.* Cambridge, MA: Harvard University Press, 1998.

Sen, Amartya K. *Inequality Reexamined.* 2d ed. Cambridge, MA: Harvard University Press, 1995 [1992].

Sen, Amartya K. "Equality of What?" [1980]. In *Choice, Welfare and Measurement.* Cambridge, MA: Harvard University Press, 1999.

Taurek, John. "Should the Numbers Count?" *Philosophy and Public Affairs* 6 (1977): 293–316.

United Nations Children's Fund. *The State of the World's Children 2005.* New York: UNICEF, 2005. Available at http://www.unicef.org/sowc05/english.

United Nations Development Programme. *Human Development Report 1998.* New York: Oxford University Press, 1998.

United Nations Development Programme. *Human Development Report 2003.* New York: Oxford University Press, 2003. Available at www.undp.org/hdr2003.

United Nations Development Programme. *Human Development Report 2005*. New York: Author, 2005. Available at hdr.undp.org/reports/global/2005.

United Nations Research Institute for Social Development. *Gender Equality: Striving for Justice in an Unequal World*. Geneva: UNRISD/UN Publications, 2005. Available at: http://www.unrisd.org.

World Bank. *World Development Report 2006*. New York: Oxford University Press, 2005.

(World Health Organization. *The World Health Report 2004*. Geneva: WHO Publications, 2004. Available: http://www.who.int/whr/2004.

13 The Problem of Doing Good in a World That Isn't: Reflections on the Ethical Challenges Facing INGOs

Joseph H. Carens

One great virtue of bringing together moral theorists and representatives from international nongovernmental organizations (INGOs) in a project like this one is that each group can potentially learn from engagement with the other. Moral theorists are trained to think carefully about the ways in which moral claims can be advanced and defended, to distinguish good arguments from bad ones, to clarify terms, to identify presuppositions, to examine the relationships between various elements in a moral position, to expose contradictions and inconsistencies, and to present accounts of moral views that are coherent. So people working in INGOs might gain by engaging with the kinds of abstract and systematic thinking that are the theorist's stock in trade. This could help those in INGOs to reflect more deeply about the underlying moral principles that they want to guide their actions and about whether the courses their organizations pursue really live up to their own principles.

Moral theorists have much to gain as well by engaging with people from INGOs. In contrast to organizations like corporations and political parties for whom ethical considerations normally function only as constraints on the pursuit of the organization's primary goals (if ethical considerations play any role at all), INGOs like the ones connected to this project have ethical concerns as their primary goals. Whatever the specific formulation of their mission – social justice, human rights, and so on – their raison d'être is the promotion of some moral good. Thus moral theorists might learn by paying attention to the kinds of ethical challenges that people in INGOs encounter as they do their organizational work. The issues that INGOs face in trying to do good may reveal moral problems that have been neglected in philosophical debates and their practices may contain solutions to those problems that would be excluded from, or at least obscured by, academic moral theories. By engaging reflectively with the experiences of those in INGOs, moral theorists might find ways to modify and improve their moral theories.

Some of the benefits that I have just outlined will be apparent from reading the chapters in this volume, but I want to explore the potential for even further gains. In particular, I use the chapter by Thomas Pogge (Chapter 12) to show both how philosophers could learn more from the experiences of those in INGOs and how those in INGOs could learn more from philosophers. Because I am myself a moral theorist, I will concentrate especially on what moral theorists can learn by engaging more fully with the experiences of INGOs.

Pogge is one of the best moral and political philosophers in the world, perhaps the leading expert in the study of global justice. His chapter is an excellent example of what a first-rate philosophical paper in the field looks like. It is characterized by the depth of analysis, sophisticated philosophical reasoning, and clarity that have distinguished his work. For that reason his chapter can be a valuable resource for those working in INGOs. In the last part of my essay I try to illustrate this point by showing how INGO participants in this project would gain if they confronted some of the challenges Pogge poses. On the other hand, Pogge's chapter nowhere directly engages with the real world of INGOs as presented in the chapters in this volume and in the verbal contributions of participants at the conference. In the bulk of this chapter, I argue that this approach has significant intellectual costs.

Like most moral philosophers, Pogge prefers hypothetical examples to real ones. I counted fifteen examples in his paper, all of them hypothetical. At one point, Pogge introduces a hypothetical to "strip away...impurities" from a (hypothetical) case previously introduced. This quest for an example that isolates one moral issue for consideration resembles in some ways the scientist's approach in conducting controlled experiments in the laboratory. It is a quest for basic knowledge. I do not mean to dismiss such efforts. On the contrary, both in science and in moral philosophy, this sort of quest is immensely valuable. But it is commonplace to find that things that work in the laboratory do not work outside it. This can be a function of environmental interactions or even of the predictable behavior of human beings who do not always use things as directed. In any event, this means that we have to see how something works in practice outside the lab before we recommend it for general use. I wonder if there may be a moral equivalent of this phenomenon, so that some moral principles that appear to make sense on the basis of hypothetical examples would prove morally disastrous if used as guides for action in real life. Whatever the merits of that speculation, I argue in the next few sections that Pogge's reluctance to turn his mind to the actual experiences of INGOs has led him to make at least one important mistake in his moral analysis and to construct some parts of his discussion in a way that fails to come to grips with the moral concerns of those in INGOs even when he addresses topics that seem relevant.

I. WHAT SHOULD INGOs DO?

Pogge says that the purpose of his chapter is to examine some of the moral issues faced by INGOs that receive "many small contributions meant to protect people from abroad from serious harm" in deciding how to spend the money they collect.

He argues that such INGOs have a responsibility both to the poor and oppressed abroad whom they are trying to help and to the contributors on whose behalf they act to set appropriate priorities, to choose effective projects, and to spend money efficiently. These seem like innocuous general claims. I assume that the INGOs that participated in this project and receive many small contributions – groups such as Amnesty International, Human Rights Watch (HRW), Médecins Sans Frontières (MSF), Habitat for Humanity, and Oxfam Canada – would accept them. They all see themselves as trying to protect people from abroad from serious harm, and they would all agree that they have a responsibility to the people they are trying to protect and to their contributors not to set bad priorities or to fund projects that do not work or to waste money. Yet several pages later Pogge has moved by a few small steps to the claim that INGOs should concentrate all (or almost all) of their efforts on the reduction of severe poverty in three states, or, at most, in several. Admittedly, Pogge presents this position only as an inference that follows from his principle, given certain plausible empirical claims, not as an independent principle of action. Nevertheless, the prescription is radically at odds with the actual behavior of most INGOs, including the ones I have just mentioned.

What should we make of this conflict? One possibility is that the INGOs have simply not thought through the implications of their own moral commitments as carefully as Pogge, and that they should follow his advice and change their practices accordingly. I do not want to dismiss this possibility entirely. Indeed, I will show later why INGOs could gain from coming to terms with Pogge's challenge. But I want to start by considering the possibility that INGOs have good reasons for what they do. The question is why people in INGOs see the moral challenge of setting priorities and spending their funds so differently from the way Pogge constructs it and what moral theorists might learn from starting from the perspectives of those in INGOs.

Let me begin by showing why Pogge's own analysis creates a conundrum that he fails to recognize and that severely hampers his program. Pogge emphasizes that INGOs are not simply independent moral agents. They are, in a certain sense, trustees for the people whose contributions they receive and they have a duty to carry out the moral responsibilities of their contributors. However, Pogge also offers his own account of the moral principle that ought to guide INGOs in setting their priorities. So here is the problem. What if the contributors' own views of their moral responsibilities – the ones they want the INGOs to carry out – lead to different priorities from the ones that flow from Pogge's principle? Should the INGOs adopt Pogge's priorities or those of their contributors?

To sharpen the dilemma here, I want to assume – contrary to our experience at the workshops – that the INGOs (and here, of course, we must mean those people with the authority to act in the name of the INGOs) are entirely convinced by Pogge's argument. I also want to assume that the contributors cannot be so convinced – a more plausible assumption empirically, even if the

INGOs were to circulate Pogge's chapter (or a popularized summary of it) to their contributors.

First, as a practical matter, if an INGO were to pursue a course that its contributors regarded as significantly different from the one that they had given money to support, the INGO would lose its contributors and soon would have no funds to spend. This has moral relevance, even on Pogge's account, because the amount of harm reduction that organizations can achieve depends in part on how much money they can raise, so that it is appropriate for them to take into account the fund-raising effects of alternative courses of action.[1]

In addition to negative fund-raising effects, INGOs have a second moral reason not to follow Pogge's prescription. The people running the INGOs are not morally free to follow their own moral views (by hypothesis here, Pogge's principle) and to disregard those of their contributors, precisely because of the trustee relationship between INGOs and contributors to which Pogge has drawn our attention. So Pogge's argument that INGOs should follow his harm reduction principle in establishing their priorities conflicts both with his own consequentialism and with his account of the moral relationship between INGOs and their contributors.[2]

The reason Pogge does not notice the problems posed for his position by potential conflicts between the moral views of the INGOs and the moral views of contributors is that he assumes contributors do not have enough knowledge to make any judgments about what the priorities of the INGOs ought to be.[3] He can make this assumption only because he does not consciously consider the actual relationships between real INGOs and their contributors. Real INGOs are not generic units for serious harm reduction nor do they solicit funds from their contributors on that basis. They do not start with a blank slate in setting their priorities. They are organizations with particular histories and commitments that determine the kinds of activities in which they engage. When they seek contributions, they describe all this.

---

[1] I leave aside here the important nuances in Pogge's account regarding what kinds of fund-raising effects are appropriately taken into account.

[2] One could perhaps rescue Pogge's argument from conflict with his consequentialism by noting that the latter can incorporate the negative fund-raising effects of following Pogge's principle as a relevant moral consideration. This preserves the formal consistency of Pogge's position at the expense of the critical perspective that the principles are designed to provide.

[3] I am assuming here that Pogge is referring to the challenge of acquiring detailed knowledge about the actual activities of INGOs and about alternative projects and their consequences when he says that it would be "disproportionately costly [for small] contributors to think through which priorities should govern the use of these funds." This is, I think, the most natural interpretation of his argument. But Pogge's own analysis, which does propose guidelines for the priorities that INGOs ought to adopt, does not depend on any claims about what INGOs actually do. So he might mean that ordinary contributors would find it costly to think through the philosophical issues. This raises an interesting set of questions about the relationship between academic philosophy on one hand and moral knowledge and moral judgment on the other, but I will not pursue those questions here.

When we ask ourselves what INGOs ought to do and how they ought to spend their money, we are likely to be led astray if we start with abstract moral principles from which we try to deduce general guidelines for the priorities of all INGOs. It is wiser to begin by reflecting (critically) on what real INGOs do and how they justify this to themselves and to others. If we take this approach, the difficulties that plague Pogge's analysis will be greatly reduced. Further, if we notice that there is a wide range of INGOs with quite different missions and priorities and we ask ourselves whether this is something to be applauded or deplored from a moral perspective, we may find our attention drawn to the moral relevance of moral disagreement. We arrive in the end at a much more pluralistic moral universe than the one Pogge presupposes.

How do actual INGOs set their priorities? The chapter in this volume on Habitat for Humanity by Steven Weir gives us a glimpse of how one INGO has done this. Habitat emerged from the moral vision (and organizational skills) of a few people who saw housing as a crucial human need (later articulated also as a fundamental human right) and who felt their Christian moral commitments obliged them to try to meet this need and right for those who lacked adequate housing. So housing for the poor (in the context of overall community development) was established as Habitat's basic priority. When Habitat solicits funds from contributors, it does so precisely by explaining this organizational mission. It seems likely that its appeals will be particularly effective to those who share the Christian commitments of its founders and their interpretation of those commitments. Thus, the question of how Habitat ought to spend its money is not entirely open-ended for either the organization or its contributors.

A similar story could be told about the history and mission of each of the other INGOs that I mentioned earlier. Amnesty International and HRW are human rights organizations, much of whose work involves criticism of existing institutions and practices. Like Habitat, MSF is concerned with meeting a specific basic need – in its case, health – but MSF tends to be more focused on the immediate needs created by crises and Habitat more on long-term development. Oxfam Canada says in its 2002 annual report that its mission is to "build lasting solutions to global poverty and injustice." This description perhaps comes the closest to Pogge's own conception of what the priorities of INGOs ought to be, although Oxfam in fact engages in a much wider array of activities and locations than Pogge's analysis seems to recommend.

Pogge emphasizes how little ordinary contributors can be expected to know about how their money is used and how much they have to trust that the INGOs are using it wisely. This is fair enough, but by not looking at actual cases, he is led to overstate the contributors' ignorance. Most contributors would certainly be able to learn enough from conventional fund-raising materials to distinguish among the basic orientations of these five INGOs. They already have clear priorities. So there is no danger in practice of a deep disconnection between the moral views of the contributors and those of the organization regarding the priorities that should govern how the organization spends its money. People only contribute if they share the organization's basic moral views and established priorities.

I do not mean to suggest that INGOs are rigidly locked into whatever conception of their mission and description of their activities is contained in their latest fund-raising brochures. As the chapters in this volume indicate, INGOs often go through a process of critical self-examination that leads to an evolution in their priorities and practices. Thus, we see that Amnesty and, to some extent, HRW have moved to incorporate economic, social, and cultural rights more fully into their mission and their programs as a result of internal and external criticism of the moral problems posed by an exclusive focus on civil and political rights. (And, as the chapters in this volume reveal, that debate continues.) Oxfam has evolved from an organization concerned primarily with famine relief to one concerned more (although not exclusively) with long-term development, and it has shifted its underlying rationale from one based on charity to one based on justice. These sorts of changes usually have a close connection to the original, specific mission of the INGO, however, and INGOs tell their contributors about such changes (as they should) and invite contributors to participate in the debates surrounding the changes, as the earlier examples indicate. If contributors think the organization's new approach no longer reflects their moral views, they can shift their donations to an organization that better fits those views.

II. WHAT MORAL STANDARD SHOULD WE USE?

One objection to the analysis so far is that it offers no independent critical perspective on what INGOs do. The fund-raising dynamic ensures a fit between what the contributors think and what the organization does, but what if both the contributors and the organization are wrong? In responding to this question, we must consider a prior one about the moral standard that we should use in assessing the activities of INGOs. Pogge's analysis seems implicitly to presuppose that there is a single clear, correct standard for measuring INGO activities and that anything that falls short of that standard is morally wrong, deserving to be condemned because the INGO has then allowed people to suffer severe harm that it could have prevented. This is a perfectionist standard, and I think it is both a moral and an intellectual mistake to adopt it. What is needed instead is an approach that incorporates some recognition of the plurality of moral views and of the legitimacy of moral disagreement without succumbing to relativism. It should assign appropriate moral responsibilities to INGOs but ones that it is possible to meet.

In trying to identify an appropriate moral standard for assessing INGOs, we might start once more by asking ourselves what human rights and humanitarian INGOs do and why. In this case, the striking fact is that INGOs generally refrain from criticizing one another openly, even though, as organizations, many of them are deeply engaged in social criticism. It is plausible to suppose that many of those in any given INGO feel the problems they are tackling are the ones that are the most crucial and that their approach is the most fruitful. This is why they are working for that particular INGO. Still, one INGO rarely asserts openly its moral superiority in relation to other INGOs.

Why this restraint? (In explaining this phenomenon, I am on less certain ground than in describing it. I rely on impressions gathered from the conference and from other sources, not on systematic study, although it would be instructive for someone to investigate this more fully.) Some of the restraint is doubtless a matter of good organizational politics, a reluctance to start a war in which one may be exposed to return fire. I think this mutual forbearance has a more principled basis, however. Above all, it lies in the recognition that there are many ways of doing good in the world, and all of them deserve respect.

In the first place, many people from INGOs recognize the need for a variety of approaches to the kinds of problems they are addressing, and they think that no one organization can simultaneously employ all the approaches that are needed in an effective way. For example, although many participants at the conference were skeptical about Ken Roth's insistence that human rights INGOs should focus primarily on a naming and shaming methodology and should restrict their aspirations in the area of economic, social, and cultural rights accordingly, many did agree that there are tensions between public criticism of governments and constructive operational engagement with them on shared projects. Further, many agreed that one way to address these tensions without abandoning the advantages of either approach is to have a division of labor between organizations.[4]

A second reason INGOs do not judge others may be a sense of intellectual modesty on the part of at least some INGO members. They recognize they cannot be certain that their own priorities are the best or that they are making the best judgments about how to implement these priorities. Having others pursuing similar but slightly different concerns in similar but somewhat different ways can be an important source of knowledge and an important form of experimentation.

In a related vein, INGOs can see that they are not simply or even primarily competing with other INGOs. Whatever the differences in their priorities, they are all concerned with a broad set of similar moral concerns: problems of human rights, severe poverty, and global injustice. It is usually not other INGOs that pose direct obstacles to an INGO's efforts to achieve its objectives but governments, corporations, organized interest groups, and the underlying social structures that such organizations maintain and protect. This means that people in one INGO can respect what those in others are trying to do, even if they believe that their own organization's approach is better.

To be sure, INGOs do often compete with one another for contributions, but even there the main sources of competition for resources are probably not other INGOs but cultural institutions like universities and museums and domestic

---

[4] See, for example, the chapter by Lindsnæs, Sano, and Thelle in this volume (Chapter 6).

charities of one kind or another. Even within the INGO sector itself, where there is undoubtedly competition for funds, it is difficult to know how much fund-raising is competitive and how much additive (to use Pogge's terms). As I noted earlier, contributors are apt to be motivated by the sense of a match between their moral views and those of the organization. In the absence of such a match, they may simply not give at all, and so having more INGOs improves the chances of some satisfactory match. Having more INGOs soliciting funds may also increase the awareness of the importance of supporting these sorts of activities, whereas criticism of one INGO by another may have the effect of damaging the credibility of all.

For these and perhaps other reasons, there is a fair amount of solidarity within the INGO sector, at least in terms of restraint from mutual criticism. This restraint is not absolute, however. For example, the discussion of the pornography of poverty in the chapter by Betty Plewes and Rieky Stuart (Chapter 1) is a clear criticism of the fund-raising techniques of other INGOs, even though the organizations are not actually mentioned by name. Prior sharp criticisms of the actual activities (not just the fund-raising techniques) of the same child sponsorship INGOs had persuaded most of them to change their focus from a single child or family to the entire local community. To push the point further with an imaginary example (just to show that I am not always opposed to the use of hypotheticals), if an INGO equivalent of the Ku Klux Klan, openly promoting racial intolerance as its goal, were to emerge, there can be no doubt that most other INGOs would publicly and sharply criticize the fundamental purpose of such an organization. Moreover, in such a case, the fact that the contributors shared the racist goals of the organization would not provide a moral justification for its activities.

How might we characterize the moral standard for judging the priorities of INGOs that is reflected in the actual behavior of INGOs themselves, and how does it differ from the one Pogge proposes? In the first place, it is a sufficientarian standard, to adopt Pogge's phrase, but in a way that differs from Pogge's. It is sufficientarian in the sense that it sets a minimum threshold for the justification of the activities of INGOs. Not all activities of INGOs are morally justifiable, but any that rise above the threshold are. Whatever priorities they reflect, they fall within the range of the morally permissible.

It does not follow, however, from the fact that various activities are morally permissible that we must view them all as equally morally valuable. For example, I agree with Pogge that the most urgent moral task is to reduce the harms caused by severe poverty. For that reason, I regard the work of INGOs that focus on severe poverty as more important than the work of INGOs that concentrate on promoting civil and political human rights.[5] This does not mean, however, that I see the work of human rights INGOs that do not focus on severe poverty as

---

[5] I am assuming here that promoting civil and political rights is not the most effective way to reduce severe poverty in the long run.

unimportant or, worse still, as morally unacceptable. The work they do is also immensely valuable, just less so, in my view, than the work that some other INGOs do.

One important difference between the approach I am advocating here (following INGO practices) and Pogge's approach is that I draw a distinction between doing wrong and not doing as much good as one can. In Pogge's scheme that distinction collapses. INGOs that do not do as much good as they can are responsible for the harm that they could have prevented if they had acted differently, simply because they could have done better. Early on in his chapter he says, "To put it bluntly, an INGO must often make decisions that will certainly lead to many deaths because spending one's limited funds on trying to protect some is tantamount to leaving others to their fate." Soon afterward, he makes clear that he is holding the contributors to the same standards: "By contributing to one [INGO] rather than another, I am, then, indirectly deciding who will live and who will die." This is an unreasonably high standard of moral responsibility, one that makes the best the enemy of the good.

Pogge does not draw out the implications of his approach for evaluating the activities of actual contributors or actual INGOs, but it follows from his analysis, it seems to me, that every organization that does not follow his principle deserves moral censure and every contributor who gives money to such organizations likewise deserves moral censure. Although Pogge's concept of serious harm includes any "shortfalls persons suffer in their health, civic status . . . , or standard of living relative to the ordinary needs and requirements of human beings," all of the (hypothetical) examples of serious harm reduction that he mentions in discussing how INGOs ought to act are ones linked to the reduction of severe poverty. It seems to follow that an organization that spends some (or all) of its resources promoting, say, gender equality or the rights of gays and lesbians (in contexts where these are not intimately linked to severe poverty) has not brought about as much serious harm reduction as it might and is thereby responsible for letting people die from severe poverty; thus, such organizations are not worthy of support from contributors. This would clearly apply to most (if not all) actual INGOs.

As a critical perspective on INGOs, this is too critical. It is one thing to argue, for example, that human rights INGOs ought to pay more attention to economic, social, and cultural rights (as a number of contributors to this volume do), but quite another to claim that the work human rights organizations do in promoting civil and political rights is of no moral value or does not deserve our moral respect. The critics in this volume generally do not make that much stronger sort of claim. By establishing a perfectionist standard that no actual organization meets, Pogge's approach makes it harder to distinguish morally between organizations that are doing good and ones that are causing harm. They are all on a continuum of moral failure with some simply failing more than others. It is far more appropriate to recognize that most INGOs are doing good and deserve recognition for that, even while acknowledging that some do more good than others and all have room for improvement. This still leaves open the possibility that some INGOs do more harm than good and deserve censure for that.[6]

A further reason for adopting a more tolerant standard for judging INGOs than Pogge's flows from a recognition of the inevitability and legitimacy of moral disagreement. Over many years of doing political philosophy, I have noticed that people sometimes – to be honest, frequently – do not find themselves persuaded by one or another of my positions, even when I have supported them with what I think are carefully reasoned, well thought-out arguments. Often enough the people who disagree with me are people whose intelligence and moral judgment I respect (like, say, Thomas Pogge). We agree on many things but disagree on a few. It does not usually lead me to think worse of the people who disagree with me. Often my response is simply to think that reasonable people disagree on certain issues. Similarly, in assessing the moral value of what INGOs do, I find I differ with others. As I indicated earlier, I share Pogge's view that the most important moral task is to reduce the serious harms caused by severe poverty, and so, as a contributor, I primarily support organizations like Oxfam that make this their focus. But I recognize that others have different views of the relative moral importance of INGO activities. I see no reason to criticize them for contributing to, say, Amnesty rather than Oxfam.[7] There is a range of reasonable disagreement about the relative moral importance of different INGO activities and, within this range, it is appropriate simply to respect the judgments of others. (This does not preclude trying to persuade others to change their views.) Again, the practice of INGOs in their relationships with one another fits better with this sense that there is a range of reasonable disagreement about priorities than with Pogge's single-minded approach.

III. COMPARING ALTERNATIVE STRATEGIES

I want to show now how Pogge's contribution is limited by the fact that he starts from philosophers' puzzles rather than from the concerns of INGOs and by the fact that he uses a rhetoric that is biased toward the use of quantification and calculation.

Pogge says he is designing a moral principle to govern the conduct of INGOs, but his principle is implicitly designed primarily to answer one sort of question: which people should be helped among the many who need it or, to put this in a slightly different way, what is the relative moral value of different sorts of harm

---

[6] There are in fact some critics who claim that human rights and development INGOs generally do more harm than good, but this is an extreme and relatively rare position.

[7] The ones who deserve criticism are the ones who do not contribute at all or who do not contribute enough. The latter category is one that arguably includes most of us in rich societies. But to criticize people for not contributing (enough) is not the same as to criticize INGOs for what they do or contributors for choosing one organization rather than another.

protection? There are potentially competing considerations here (e.g., between helping as many people as possible and helping the worst off, between preventing a very serious harm for a few people and a smaller but still serious harm for many), and Pogge's discussion is designed to help us sort out those considerations with a great deal of analytical precision. But how important is this question for INGOs in setting priorities within the framework of their basic organizational missions? Does Pogge's analytical precision provide helpful guidance for real decisions, or does it risk leading decision makers astray?

Let us start again with the experiences of people from INGOs. What do they see as the most difficult problems they face in trying to set priorities within the context of their organizational missions? In a paper presented at an earlier workshop but not published in this volume, Rieky Stuart described some of the difficult choices Oxfam has faced in deciding how to spend its money. For example, in promoting long-term development, Oxfam has to decide how much of its resources to devote to policy advocacy, how much to institution building at the local level abroad, and how much to specific development projects. There are advantages and disadvantages to each of these approaches. As Pogge points out, public policies, especially (although not exclusively) the policies of governments and institutions in the North, are the biggest obstacle to the reduction of severe poverty. So the potential payoff in harm reduction from changing such policies is enormous. The likelihood of Oxfam having an impact on the major public policies that are creating problems (e.g., domestic agricultural subsidies, trade restrictions) is relatively small, however. At the other end, specific development projects have immediate benefits in terms of harm reductions, but these benefits are tiny compared with the overall problem being addressed (again for reasons that are clear from Pogge's analysis). Finally, institution building at the local level appears to be somewhere between the other two approaches both in terms of its potential impact and in terms of the likelihood of success.

Now consider these strategic alternatives in light of what Pogge proposes as a moral principle to govern INGO conduct:

> (ABCD) Other things being equal, an INGO should choose among candidate projects on the basis of the cost-effectiveness of each project, defined as its moral value divided by its cost. Here a project's moral value is the harm protection it achieves, that is, the sum of the moral values of the harm reductions (and increases) this project would bring about for the individual persons it affects.

The first point to note is that Pogge talks about projects rather than strategies, although he is trying to devise a principle to guide spending choices. As Stuart's paper shows, the most fundamental choices are often about basic strategies rather than particular projects.

Would Pogge's principle be helpful to an INGO like Oxfam in thinking about which strategies to adopt? I am not confident that it would. Pogge's careful discussion of how to calculate the moral value of harm protection (the A, B, and

C of his ABCD) is almost entirely irrelevant to the choice Oxfam has to make among the three strategic alternatives identified here. All three approaches are ways of pursuing the organization's mission of building lasting solutions to global poverty and injustice (which, as I noted earlier, is quite close to Pogge's concern with harm protection), but deciding how many resources to devote to each approach is mainly a question of trying to assess the relative overall effectiveness of these alternative strategies for the reduction of severe poverty. Answering that question has little to do with fine distinctions between the seriousness of various kinds of harms or with differences between the people who would be helped by one approach rather than another.

This kind of strategic choice is characterized by a much higher degree of uncertainty than Pogge allows for. Pogge takes up the question of risk and uncertainty in the latter half of his chapter, but he downplays the importance of uncertainty. He argues that risk can be taken into account by assigning appropriate probability weights to the harm reduction to be achieved and the costs to be incurred. So it is actually expected moral value and expected costs that should guide decisions, and INGOs should aim to maximize their "expected long-run cost effectiveness" in generating morally valuable harm protections. Leave aside the economistic language for a moment. What I think at least some of the people in INGOs are saying is that they do not have enough information about the likelihood of various outcomes to make use of this sort of prescription. To return to the Oxfam example, a small upward change in the probability assigned to the likelihood of success in changing major public policies would have a huge impact on the weight to be assigned to that alternative because the policies are so consequential. But the numbers assigned to such probability estimates are bound to have a high degree of arbitrariness to them. Although no one can doubt the wisdom of a general prescription that says do more good rather than less, other things being equal, it is often impossible to tell what will do more good. As I read Stuart, Oxfam has engaged in frequent internal debates about these alternative strategies, and the primary focus of these debates has been on what will do the most good. It has not been possible to for people in Oxfam to reach a consensus on a single strategy not because people within Oxfam disagree about what the good is but because they disagree about the effectiveness of the different strategies. In practice, Oxfam has decided to pursue all of the strategies simultaneously, with the balance shifting from time to time in response to changing circumstances. Some within Oxfam find this a frustrating refusal to make a choice, but Stuart says that the dominant view within Oxfam is wary of "either-or" approaches. Her claim seems to be that there are good arguments for pursuing each of these approaches, and enough uncertainty about outcomes to justify a mixed set of approaches both within one organization like Oxfam and among different INGOs.[8] Pogge's discussion of risk

---

[8] The contribution by Plewes and Stuart (Chapter 1 in this volume) adds the argument that there is a positive interactive effect between the various approaches that would be lost if only one were adopted.

and uncertainty suggests that he might be one of those within Oxfam urging the organization to commit itself to a single approach based on its best guess about what is likely to be most effective, but I see no compelling argument for the moral superiority of this view.

Finally, there is a danger to the language that Pogge deploys in his elaboration and analysis of his proposed principle. In most of the chapter, one gets the impression that Pogge thinks we would know exactly what we ought to do if we could just plug the right numbers into the formulas he provides. Pogge does not actually say that it will be easy to gather the data that would be required to change his formulas from useful devices for clarifying abstract relationships into operational guides to action, but readers could certainly be forgiven for imagining that he thinks this is the case. Whether it is his intention or not, Pogge's approach here fits rhetorically with a trend in the wider environment to demand that INGOs come up with measurable results, with proof that they are actually doing good and that the money allocated to them is being well spent. Now, no one can object in principle to the idea that INGOs ought to be accountable for how they spend the money they receive, but it is all too easy to slide from this sound general principle to the use of criteria of success that bias the choice of what activities INGOs engage in. In her paper on Oxfam, Stuart notes that it is easier to measure things such as inoculations and wells than the development of local institutions and social capacities. She is clearly worried that an emphasis on "results" will undermine long-term, capacity-building approaches for which the ultimate benefits may be greater in the long run. Mona Younis's contribution on the Mertz-Gilmore Foundation (Chapter 2, this volume) expresses a similar concern about the difficulty in measuring the effects of capacity-building efforts and the dangers of placing too much emphasis on measurable results.

I should note that the last part of Pogge's chapter, which talks about possible deontological constraints on a consequentialist approach, deploys language that is more tentative and makes no effort to construct formulas. I think those sections are more likely to guide the judgments of those in INGOs in helpful ways than the earlier ones, although even there Pogge's analysis would have been richer if he had engaged with actual examples of deontological concerns rather than hypothetical ones. The chapter by Weir on Habitat for Humanity (Chapter 3) contains a number of useful illustrations of the problem in its discussion of the tensions the organization sometimes experiences between achieving success in involving the local community in its house-building and community development projects and Habitat's own commitment to gender equality and nondiscrimination on the basis of religion and ethnicity. It would be instructive to learn whether Pogge regards these compromises and trade-offs as reasonable and why.

IV. PROJECT SELECTION

Even if the preceding critique of Pogge is valid, his principle could still provide guidance to INGOs on how to set priorities in spending their money on specific projects, given their basic organizational mission and their strategic choices. For example, a human rights organization like such as Amnesty International could use his principle to help decide which were the most urgent human rights problems, an INGO like Habitat could use the principle to set priorities for its housing projects, and so on. Indeed, it seems likely from the particular (hypothetical) examples he uses that Pogge really has project selection rather than choice of organizational mission or basic strategy in mind throughout his discussion.

To avoid some of the difficulties I identified earlier and to bring out more sharply the challenge Pogge poses, we might reconstruct his claims as follows. INGOs should not rest content with doing some good.[9] If they have a choice between two projects, and one does more good than the other, given their organizational mission and strategy and assuming other things are equal between the projects, they should choose the project that does more good. This means, at a minimum, that they have to say how they go about selecting the projects they fund and why this way of selecting projects is justifiable in terms of this general obligation to do more good rather than less. All this should be suitably qualified by caveats regarding the costs of acquiring information, the inevitability of limited knowledge, and so on.

Restated in this way, Pogge's principle seems fairly modest and unobjectionable, but his analysis reveals that one concrete implication is that the geographic location of projects should be solely determined by the question of where the organization can do the most good. This poses an important challenge to INGOs even if we assume the more flexible definition of doing good that I have advocated. Most INGOs work in many countries, and the reaction to Pogge's chapter suggests that they would resist contracting the geographic scope of their efforts on the grounds that they would be more effective if they did so. But why? They may be correct in their resistance to Pogge, but his challenge shows why it is important for them to articulate the reasons for this resistance.

There is surprisingly little in the various papers that people from INGOs have written in connection with this project that explores why they choose to fund one project rather than another, and especially why they choose to locate a project in one country rather than another. I assume that every INGO has more potentially worthy recipients of the funds at its disposal for projects abroad than it has funds. How does the organization decide which ones to fund? Younis's chapter on the Mertz-Gilmore Foundation mentions the various criteria that it used to fund organizations when it was running an international human rights program but does not say how it selected among the applicants who met the basic criteria and why. How does Oxfam decide where it will work? Stuart's paper on Oxfam

---

[9] Note that this prescription is perfectly compatible with the view that INGOs should not normally criticize other INGOs whose activities pass some minimal moral threshold because here it is a question of what stance the organization takes toward its own work rather than the work of others.

did not say. How does Habitat choose its locations? Weir's chapter does not say. How does Amnesty select its projects? Goering's chapter does not tell us. I do not mean to suggest that these authors were ducking the question. Those of us organizing the workshops did not think to ask them to address it, but Pogge's paper makes it clear why it is important for them to do so. Do INGOs give any thought to the relative moral claims of people in various locations for assistance? If not, why not? If so, what moral considerations do they take into account? These are important questions, and Pogge's challenge frames them effectively.

At one point Pogge argues that INGOs committed to the reduction of severe poverty should concentrate all of their funds on a few countries because in that way they will help many more people in dire need. Pogge is clearly well aware that his recommendations on the location of antipoverty projects go against the grain of ordinary moral views. That is why he has a long section arguing that such a norm does not violate any reasonable view of distributive justice, indeed that it is those who insist on spreading the poverty reduction efforts among different countries that are acting in a discriminatory and unjust manner and wasting resources that could have helped more people. There may well be good reasons for not following Pogge's recommendations here, but it is surely incumbent on INGOs to try to provide those reasons. Pogge's strong formulation makes the challenge harder to avoid. The most powerful part of Pogge's critique seems to me to be the claim that people in India are getting far less than their fair share of antipoverty resources even on a per capita basis. Pogge is pressing people to think whether they have been discriminating against people in India (unconsciously and inadvertently) because Indians live in a large country. Although people in INGOs may not want to adopt Pogge's maximizing criteria, they will almost certainly not want to defend a criterion for the distribution of resources that treats all states equally regardless of size. It would be instructive to learn whether they think there is a deep, principled reason for the choices they make or whether it is a response to fund-raising or other imperatives.

One final point about Pogge's challenge. Societies that face fundamental divisions along ethnic or religious lines often attract the attention of INGOs (Northern Ireland, Israel, Sri Lanka). Pogge seems to be arguing that it is a moral mistake for INGOs whose primary mission is to reduce poverty or provide housing for the very poor to become involved in contexts like this because these sorts of societal divisions make it much more difficult to accomplish their goals. Weir's discussion of Habitat's involvement in Fiji, Sri Lanka, and Northern Ireland is instructive in this regard. Why has Habitat chosen these countries for its efforts? Have they taken into account the increased difficulties of achieving their basic goals in such environments? Are they weighing the likelihood of their involvement contributing to a solution to these basic societal divisions against the problems it will pose for their efforts at building housing and promoting community development? In effect, Pogge is arguing for a kind of triage system that distinguishes places with serious but treatable problems from those who are so badly off that they cannot be helped and those whose problems are not serious enough to justify their receiving scarce resources. Whatever the organization's mission and strategy, it will have to consider the possibility of these sorts of trade-offs. If an INGO wants to resist making this sort of judgment, it should say why.

In sum, although Pogge's chapter would be better in various ways if it engaged more fully with the experiences of INGOs, it still poses a number of important moral challenges that INGOs would do well to address.

Respect and Disagreement: A Response to Joseph Carens

Thomas Pogge

Insofar as Carens disagrees with my views, readers can weigh up the arguments and decide for themselves. Still, it may be useful to flag briefly the points where I believe he misreads my chapter. I care little who is at fault for these misunderstandings. My concern is just to get my views across and to avoid appearing as a stereotypical philosopher – dictatorial, dogmatic, perfectionist, uncompromising, and blind to the rich nuances and complexities of the real world. There are four points, in particular, that I want to set straight.

First, Carens objects that, as shown by my frequent use of hypothetical examples, I start "from philosophers' puzzles rather than from the concerns of INGOs."[1] But my entire essay grew out of my reaction to Rieky Stuart's presentation at our first conference in New York. Stuart said then that some of the hardest choices she has had to face in her work for Oxfam had been about abandoning a project when it becomes apparent that it does more harm than good. (One example she gave involved food supplies being captured by armed groups and then being sold for weapons.) I responded that surely even a project that does more good than harm should be abandoned when a lot more net good can be achieved with the same resources elsewhere. This response provoked all but universal condemnation from the INGO representatives, which, in turn, with the debate that followed, inspired me to write the chapter under discussion.

My main reason for using hypotheticals was that, like Carens, I found that "there is surprisingly little in the various papers that people from INGOs have written in connection with this project that explores why they choose to fund one project rather than another."[2] A further reason is that I sought to focus my discussion on assessing the moral relevance of specific considerations, especially those concerning equity across groups (defined by nationality, location, rural–urban, and so on). This is better done with a hypothetical decision, in which other things can be stipulated to be equal, than with an actual decision, in which many other factors must be taken into account. I have tried nonetheless to be

---

[1] Joseph H. Carens herein.　　　　　　　　[2] Ibid.

responsive to the actual experience of INGOs by constructing cases that illustrate what I had learned are the main divergences of actual INGO practice from my proposed principle of cost-effective harm protection (ABCD*).

Second, Carens writes that I want all INGOs to concentrate on poverty eradication in three specific states, thus creating a dreary monoculture.[3] My central claim is, rather, that INGOs ought to spend their resources so as to achieve as much harm protection as possible by aiming, as it were, for the lowest-hanging fruits. It is possible that the most cost-effective way to spend INGO resources today would focus them on poverty eradication projects in three specific countries. If so, however, this is a consequence of the long-standing neglect of cost-effectiveness INGOs have heretofore practiced. If INGO resources, or a substantial subset of them, were focused on cost-effective harm protection, then as exceptionally cost-effective projects are accomplished, a broader range of diverse projects would soon come to be top priorities by (ABCD*). Systematically harvesting apples from the bottom up would eliminate the lowest outliers and soon get to the point where there are many apples roughly equally difficult to reach.

The monoculture worry is alleviated by two further considerations. Even if all INGOs followed (ABCD*), they would specify the open parameters of this principle differently. In particular, there would be reasonable differences among them with regard to the three main specification questions that Proposition (B) leaves open with regard to making judgments about how badly off people are. There would be reasonable differences with regard to the three main specification questions that Proposition (A) leaves open concerning the metric in terms of which to measure expected improvements. There would also be reasonable differences with regard to the weights to be attached to these two considerations, that is, with regard to the value to be assigned to the exponent e. By asking INGOs to develop a cost-effective strategy that is consistent in its own terms and by proposing a general schema for developing such a strategy, I have not suggested that all INGOs should specify this general schema in the same way.

The other consideration alleviating the monoculture worry is that the information available to make comparative judgments of cost-effectiveness is incomplete and imperfect, rendering judgments about the long-term impact of alternative projects highly speculative.[4] This informational deficit, which cannot be fully overcome, further broadens the range of diverse projects that can reasonably be judged consistent with (ABCD*), including experimental projects that can indeed be an important source of new knowledge.[5]

(ABCD*) is nowhere near strong enough to permit a precise ranking of all possible INGO projects and thereby to require all INGOs to choose from a narrow set of possible projects. Nor is (ABCD*) so weak that it enables INGOs to justify

---

[3] Ibid.

[4] This fact is adduced by Carens himself.

[5] Carens speculates that I would favor projects with effects that are more predictable or more easily measurable, but there is no basis for such a bias in (ABCD*).

pretty much any project they like, as Carens also, and inconsistently, suggests.[6] This suggestion may have some truth with regard to any one project viewed in isolation. An INGO must justify its projects *together*, however, as designed according to a single plausible strategy. It must not, for example, specify the open parameters of (ABCD*) in one way to justify a project choice in one country and then specify the same parameters in another way to justify a project choice in some other country. To be sure, an INGO may have reason to revise its specifications of the open parameters, but between revisions, the specific strategy in place greatly reduces the possible projects that can be chosen – although many of these candidate projects may remain open to some other INGO that has reasonably adopted a different specification of (ABCD*).

Third, Carens suggests that I want dictatorially to substitute my own judgment for the diverse judgments of INGO workers and contributors and that I am calling on INGO staff to follow my moral views while disregarding those of their contributors. Both suggestions are incorrect; I address them in this order.

In the context of a discussion among equals, I am articulating my best judgment about how we ought to spend the resources we control. My hope is that INGO staff and contributors[7] will reflect on my arguments – be convinced by them or show me how I have gone wrong. They should follow the moral judgment they reach after due reflection even if it differs from mine. This advice is not in tension with my essay, so long as a clear distinction is made between the substance and procedure of decision making. My essay addresses substance only: what are the correct moral priorities that we all, INGO staff included, should urge INGOs to adopt and to follow in regard to the resources at their disposal? A strong view about substance implies nothing about procedure. One can be strongly opposed to a policy of some country, one's own or another, and still insist that this dispute should be settled by majority rule.[8] Similarly, I can sharply criticize an INGO's present spending priorities and still accept that the staff and contributors of this INGO should follow their own best judgment when, on reflection, they regard mine as morally mistaken. Nothing I have written conflicts with Carens' view that "there is a range of reasonable disagreement about the relative moral importance of different INGO activities and, within this range, it is appropriate simply to respect the judgment of others. (This does not preclude trying to persuade others to change their views.)"[9] Relative to my proposal, such disagreements could be either internal, concerning the specification of my notion of harm protection for instance, or external, disputing (ABCD*) by assigning great independent moral weight to group equity considerations, say, or to geographic dispersal or the continuation of existing projects.

---

[6] Ibid.
[7] Pace Carens, I have not claimed, and do not believe, that "contributors do not have enough knowledge to make any judgments about what the priorities of the INGOs ought to be" (ibid).
[8] Wollheim 1962.   [9] Carens op cit.

We should shift our contributions to INGOs that prioritize projects according to a consistent strategy derived through a specification of (ABCD*), and we should seek to influence these and other INGOs to reform themselves in this direction – so I have argued. Carens objects that, applied to INGO staff, this "analysis creates a conundrum that he fails to recognize and that severely hampers his program."[10] The conundrum is that (ABCD*), if found convincing by an INGO's staff but not by its contributors, would lead the former to disregard their trusteeship duties. I do not think (ABCD*) has this implication. Suppose the staff of an INGO devoted to the rights of non-poor gays and lesbians[11] came to be convinced of (ABCD*). This principle would guide them to seek to adjust the priorities of their INGO in light of its actual and potential contributors' moral views, so as to achieve the greatest possible gain in harm protection. Given Carens's stipulation that the contributors cannot be convinced, the optimal adjustment would not be a dramatic reorientation toward the eradication of severe poverty, because this would lead to huge declines in funds raised. The optimal adjustment might more plausibly involve a refocusing on the rights and well-being of very poor gays and lesbians. With such an adjustment, the loss in funding would likely be small enough to be greatly outweighed by the gain in cost-effectiveness. By stipulation, the adjustment would be unwelcome to the contributors but, if clearly explained in the INGO's publications and Web site, it would not violate any trusteeship duties. To violate such duties, the INGO's staff would have to conceal the adjustment in spending priorities from its contributors – an option that is morally problematic as well as highly unrealistic.

Fourth, Carens presents me as a perfectionist and intolerant by branding as wrongdoers those INGO workers and contributors who are avoidably failing to maximize the cost-effectiveness of their harm-protection efforts. Carens offers two quotes from me to show that I put forward "an unreasonably high standard of moral responsibility, one that makes the best the enemy of the good."[12] The quoted sentences do not put forward any normative standard at all, however, but merely state a *fact* about *all* INGO expenditures, cost-effective or not: "an INGO must often make decisions that will certainly lead to many deaths because spending one's limited funds on trying to protect some is tantamount to leaving others to their fate."[13] This point is made at the beginning of my chapter, where I address not yet the moral responsibilities of INGOs, but their causal impact.[14] The point is made to show that INGO priorities pose an important moral question, one we better take seriously.

---

[10] Ibid.   [11] This example is suggested by Carens, ibid.

[12] Ibid.   [13] Ibid.

[14] In our world, where millions live on the brink of death from poverty-related causes, this point holds for many other agents as well – for governments, major corporations, and affluent individuals, for example. Directly or indirectly, their decisions often affect who will live and who will die.

Carens proposes that we "draw a distinction between doing wrong and not doing as much good as one can."[15] Following this proposal, we would not say that someone is acting wrongly when she is deliberately doing less good than she can. Consider an INGO field worker who saves five children from a painful diarrhea death when she evidently could, with equal resources and effort, save ten. Is she doing nothing wrong? To be sure, it is good that she works for an INGO and it is of immense moral value that she is saving five children. But that she intentionally leaves five others to die is hardly a minor matter that we should refrain from criticizing her for. Contrary to Carens, I continue to believe that INGO workers who deliberately do less good than they can are typically acting wrongly and are subject to legitimate moral criticism.[16]

The fourth point must be kept distinct from the third. There is reasonable disagreement about what the moral priorities of INGOs should be; and when an INGO worker acts in a way that evidently fails to maximize harm protection, this will generally be because she conscientiously judges that (contrary to my view) this is what she ought to do. She may sincerely believe that she ought to save five children in the countryside in preference to ten in the city, say. If her judgment is mistaken and mine correct, then, with five lives at stake, her conduct is wrong. Yet following her best moral judgment reached after due reflection, she may have acted well. If so, she merits *respectful* criticism. And my essay was written in this spirit: as a *respectful* critique of prevalent INGO priorities and practice.

My willingness to criticize where others do not may be related to my seeing INGOs not primarily as venues for "helping"[17] but as instruments for undoing a fraction of the vast harms the affluent countries are inflicting on the poor and marginalized in the so-called developing world. Were we not implicated in, and profiting from, the horrendous deprivations of those distant strangers, then it might be morally acceptable, perhaps, that we help *whom* we like *as* we like, even if we could prevent more suffering by helping others or in other ways. But we *are* so implicated, through the frequently unjust foreign policies of our governments and the unjust global rules they impose worldwide, and we are also profiting substantially from such injustice.[18] The work of INGOs should thus not be seen as reflecting our generous effort, pursuant to a merely positive "duty of assistance,"[19] to give some of what we legitimately own to the less fortunate.

---

[15] Ibid.

[16] The word *wrong* must here, of course, be understood in the *ex ante* sense. We should not criticize INGO workers if merely, with the benefit of hindsight, we see that they could have prevented more harm by acting differently. Moral criticism is appropriate only when such workers could or should have known *at the time of acting* that another course of conduct would have prevented more harm.

[17] Ibid.

[18] This case is made at length in Pogge 2002a, 2005a, 2005b.

[19] Cf. Rawls 1999.

Rather, it should be regarded as reflecting our all-too-insufficient efforts to direct some of our unjustly large share of resources toward mitigating, pursuant to a far weightier intermediate duty, the great harms we are also continually contributing to. On this basis, I reject then the common thought of citizens in the affluent countries that "this is *my* hard-earned money, and I am morally free to spend it on any good cause I like, or none"; and similarly the thought by INGO staff that "this is *our* INGO, and we are morally free to raise money for any cause we like and spend it as we deem fit."

INGOs control but a minuscule fraction of the global social product – about one fortieth of 1 percent.[20] Vastly more – perhaps one full percent[21] – would be needed to eradicate most severe deprivations (unfulfilled human rights) world-wide. Still, these INGO resources are of great importance because they are explicitly intended to be spent according to moral criteria. It is very good that the question of how to specify such criteria has been a main focus of our discussions. I have tried to contribute to this discussion by arguing, as forcefully as I could, for one particular answer. I am not convinced that this answer is entirely correct. Indeed, I am sure that it will prove inadequate in various ways and will need to be modified accordingly. Still, I believe it is useful to put forward one clear and coherent answer that can serve as a first approximation and focal point for critical discussion; and the thoughtful responses from Carens and many other participants confirm this belief. It is good that we have initiated and sustained this discussion – mainly because it may, in due course, bear fruit for the world's poor and oppressed.

BIBLIOGRAPHY

Pogge, Thomas. *World Poverty and Human Rights: Cosmopolitan Responsibilities and Reforms.* Cambridge: Polity Press, 2002.
Pogge, Thomas. "Severe Poverty as a Violation of Negative Duties." *Ethics and International Affairs* 19, no. 1 (2005): 55–84.
Pogge, Thomas. "Recognized and Violated by International Law: The Human Rights of the Global Poor." *Leiden International Law Journal* 18, no. 4 (2005): 717–45.
Rawls, John. *The Law of Peoples – With "The Idea of Public Reason Revisited."* Cambridge, MA: Harvard University Press, 1999.
United Nations Development Programme. *Human Development Report 2003.* New York: Oxford University Press, 2003. Available at http://www.undp.org/hdr2003>.
Wollheim, Richard. "A Paradox in the Theory of Democracy," in *Philosophy, Politics and Society*, eds. Peter Laslett and W. G. Runciman, 2d series (Oxford: Oxford University Press, 1962).

---

[20] Or 0.03 percent of the aggregate gross national incomes of the Organization of Economic Cooperation and Development countries (United Nations Development Programme 2003, 290).
[21] Cf. Pogge 2005b, 744 with n. 65.

INGOs as Collective Mobilization of Transnational Solidarity: Implications for Human Rights Work at the United Nations[1]

Jean-Marc Coicaud

We have seen throughout this book that while international nongovernmental organizations (INGOs) have gained importance, they have come to be confronted with a number of ethical challenges.[2] This has been reinforced by the fact that INGOs work in areas which are often contentious and in countries which do not necessarily welcome their initiatives. Against this background, the book has concentrated on the ethical challenges encountered by INGOs in the course of their human rights work on the ground. These challenges have been discussed within the framework of three sets of issues.

There is, first, the question of Northern INGOs and Southern aid recipients, namely, the impact that inequality of power has on the agenda setting, ownership of policies, implementation, and financing of Southern NGOs. Second, there is the issue of the relations between INGOs and governments, with the challenges that the former face when they work in countries and with states that restrict their activities. A third question is the role of INGOs in the defense of economic rights and whether the challenge of dealing with global poverty should take priority over other human rights concerns.

---

[1] This chapter is based partly on research done by Joanna Godrecka, for which I am thankful. I also thank Jibecke Jönsson and my coeditor Daniel Bell for their comments.

[2] At the most basic level NGOs can be defined as autonomous legal entities that are not (in principle) instruments of governments and are nonprofit, that is, not distributing revenue as income to owners. INGOs are structured internationally and at heart work transnationally. Both NGOs and INGOs are expected to serve a public or community purpose. As such, they embody a double commitment: first, a commitment to freedom and personal initiative, to the idea that people have the right to act on their own initiative to improve the quality of their own lives or the lives of people they care about; and second is an emphasis on solidarity, on the idea that people have responsibility not only to themselves but also to their fellow humans. On this refer to Lester M. Salamon, S. Wojciech Sokolowski, and Regina List, *Global Civil Society: An Overview* (Baltimore, MD: Johns Hopkins University, Institute for Policy Studies and Center for Civil Society Studies, 2003), 1. In this conclusion the term *INGO* signifies those organizations defined and exemplified throughout the chapters of this book, whereas *NGOs* is used in its more generic sense. For a more detailed definition, see the Introduction of this book, in particular footnote 2.

The goal is for INGOs to address challenges in a successful manner. If the ethical dilemmas encountered by INGOs during the course of their human rights work on the ground are challenging, the dilemmas they face in the diplomatic and political settings, in the United Nations (UN) context in particular, are equally trying. To reflect and find out more about the latter, the UN University organized a brainstorming session in August 2005 that brought together INGOs representatives at the UN, as well as a small number of academics.[3] The INGOs attending were identified based on two criteria: those who are contributors to the book and those who on an everyday basis deal with themes tackled in the book. Two important themes emerged at this brainstorming session: (1) the need to specify what accounts for the growing importance of INGOs in human rights work and (2) the need to specify the distinctive challenges experienced by INGOs during the course of the human rights work at the UN and to suggest possible ways of dealing with those challenges. The aim of this chapter is to shed light on both of those themes.

This chapter proceeds in four steps. First, it indicates the strong connection between the progressive aspects of international life and INGOs, their emergence, development and agenda. Second, it examines the reasons accounting for the fact that this connection is likely to grow in the coming years and, with it, the role of INGOs. Third, it identifies the dilemmas and challenges that INGOs encounter during the course of their human rights work at the UN. Fourth, and finally, the chapter makes a number of recommendations as a way to improve the impact of INGOs and their relations with the UN and its member states.

I. INGOs AND THE PROGRESSIVE ASPECTS OF NATIONAL AND INTERNATIONAL POLITICS

Although often referred to as a phenomenon of our time, INGOs have been around for a long time, dating back to the nineteenth century. It is generally

---

[3] Participants included John Ambler, senior vice president of programs, Oxfam America; Robert Arsenault, president, International League for Human Rights; Widney Brown, (then) deputy director of programs, Human Rights Watch; David Cingranelli, professor of political science, Binghamton University, SUNY; Allison Cohen, international human rights officer; Jacob Blaustein, Institute for the Advancement of Human Rights; Sakiko Fukuda-Parr, research fellow, Belfer Center for Science and International Affairs, John F. Kennedy School of Government, Harvard University; Niel Hicks, director, international programmes, Human Rights First; John L. Hirsch, senior fellow/interim director of Africa program, International Peace Academy; Sharon Hom, executive director, Human Rights in China; Richard Jordan, chief executive officer, World Harmony Foundation; Shulamith Koenig, director, People's Movement for Human Rights Education; William R. Pace, executive director, World Federalist Movement; and Kevin Sullivan, director of advocacy, Habitat for Humanity. The United Nations University thanks the participants for their contributions. Convening the discussions were Jean-Marc Coicaud, United Nations University, New York, and Daniel Bell, Tsinghua University, Beijing.

considered that the earliest INGO is the antislavery mobilization, formed as the British and Foreign Anti-Slavery Society in 1839, although there was a transitional social movement against slavery much earlier. The International Committee of the Red Cross (ICRC) was founded by Henri Dunant in 1864. By 1874, there were thirty two registered INGOs, and this number had increased to 1,083 by 1914. INGOs grew steadily after World War II.[4]

In the past thirty years, INGOs have come to be granted a special importance, with a significant acceleration since the early 1990s. In terms of numbers, notice for example that around one quarter of the 13,000 INGOs existing by 2001 were created after 1990. Moreover, membership by individuals or national bodies of INGOs has increased even faster: well over a third of the membership of INGOs joined after 1990.[5] The ability that INGOs have acquired to shape the international agenda since the early 1990s, through advocacy and raising awareness and calling for state actors to change their ways, has been equally impressive. In this regard, their power was first visible at the Earth Summit in Rio in 1992, where about 2,400 representatives of the nongovernmental sector, by highlighting issues of global concern and stirring up proceedings in general, practically hijacked the event. Another major impact was the INGO-launched campaign to pressure governments to draft a treaty to ban the production, stockpiling, and export of landmines. The campaign proved so effective that the treaty to ban landmines was signed in 1997.

In addition, the nongovernmental sector has become an economic force to reckon with. According to a study by the Johns Hopkins Comparative Nonprofit Sector Project, by the late 1990s it had become, in the thirty-five countries on which the study is based, a considerable economic force, accounting for a significant share of national expenditures and employment. It had aggregate expenditures of US $1.3 trillion.[6] Moreover, the share of INGOs in development aid flows has increased significantly in the past fifteen years or so. While in the 1990s official aid flows declined overall, both directly (bilateral and multilateral) and indirectly via INGOs, INGOs aid flows augmented. In particular, through private donations, including individual, foundation, and corporate contributions at the international level, echoing the rapid growth in wealth creation in the 1990s, it more than doubled, from US $4.5 billion to $10.7 billion. This underscores the significant expansion of INGOs in the changing development field of the 1990s and the major private mobilization effort they represent.[7] Finally, in the

[4] Lester M. Salamon, S. Wojciech Sokolowski, and Regina List, *Global Civil Society*, op cit., 4.
[5] Helmut Anheier, Marlies Glasius, and Mary Kaldor (eds.), *Global Civil Society 2001* (Oxford, New York: Oxford University Press, 2001), 4.
[6] Lester M. Salamon, S. Wojciech Sokolowski, and Regina List, *Global Civil Society*, op cit., 13.
[7] Mary Kaldor, Helmut Anheier, and Marlies Glasius, "Global Civil Society in an Era of Regressive Globalization," in *Global Civil Society Yearbook 2003*, eds. Mary Kaldor, Helmut Anheier, and Marlies Glasius (Oxford, New York: Oxford University Press, 2003), 11–12.

1990s, INGOs became much more interconnected both to each other and to international institutions such as the UN and World Bank. Thus, not only did the global range of INGO presence grow during the 1990s, the networks linking these organizations became thicker as well.[8]

* * *

The importance that INGOs have come to acquire in recent years is a phenomenon that has to be understood in connection with the evolution of governance, at the national and international level. To a large extent, this evolution is in itself linked to a number of democratization trends that have taken place worldwide, within and among borders. This connection between INGOs, the evolution of governance and democratization, has been at work in four major ways with interdependent relations.

First, there is the role of INGOs vis-à-vis the state in terms of governance. Traditionally, state institutions have had a relative monopoly of voice and action on how society is and ought to be run. Sure, in democratic societies, elections helped to express the opinion of the people and took it into account. But in between the public (state) and economic (private) sectors in their various forms, there was not much room for organizations with the aim to pursue some type of public good. In contrast, in the past three decades or so, the nongovernmental sector has come to question the dominance of the state. In doing so, NGOs have come to be active participants and even one of the defining elements of a democratic society. The contemporary challenge of the state by NGOs was particularly significant in the 1970s in the context of authoritarian politics in Central Europe and Latin America. Elsewhere, in Western developed countries, in Northern America and Europe, nongovernmental organizations developed as full-fledged collective social actors, able not only to counterbalance the state agenda on issues of public concern but also to fill the policy gaps left by mainstream institutions as the welfare state retreated because of the pressure of globalization. In the aftermath of the Cold War, the nongovernmental sector, continuing to expand in its role vis-à-vis governments, became an increasingly familiar feature of the political landscape. This is illustrated by the growing activities of civil society in Central Asia and the Balkans, where INGOs in particular contribute to the relative democratization of societies and make up for the shortcomings of national and international bureaucracies.

Human rights is another element that connects INGOs with governance and democratization (or democracy). Historically, the nongovernmental sector has indeed given much attention to human rights issues. To guarantee that norms of

---

[8] David Held, Anthony McGrew, David Goldblatt, and Jonathan Perraton (eds.), *Global Transformations: Politics, Economics and Culture* (Stanford, CA: Stanford University Press, 1999), 21–27. See also the tables 22 a–e on transborder NGOs networks in Marlies Glasius, Mary Kaldor, and Helmut Anheier, *Global Civil Society Yearbook 2002* (Oxford, New York: Oxford University Press, 2002), 342–51.

human rights are taken seriously and implemented as much as possible has been of central concern of the nongovernmental agenda. As such, INGOs have worked hard to advance human rights throughout the UN system. An important mile- stone was the role played by INGOs in the context of the World Conference on Human Rights, held in Vienna, Austria, in June 1993. Working with like-minded delegations from member states, INGOs contributed to achieve a number of significant results, including the creation of a UN high commissioner for human rights with a rather sizable office to support the role. As we have seen in this book, the tendency has been for INGOs working in the field of human rights to concentrate on the defense of civil and political rights. Among the historically most prominent INGOs are those that have made such defense their mission. Amnesty International, formed in London 1961, and Human Rights Watch, established in 1978 as Helsinki Watch to monitor the compliance of Soviet bloc countries with the human rights provisions of the landmark Helsinki Accords, top the list.[9] Yet today, INGOs are increasingly moving into the field of economic, social, and cultural rights.[10] This orientation calls for them to go beyond a crisis situation and tackle the long-term and more "intangible" violations associated with lack of, and unequal, development. Oxfam, for example, gradually came to believe that it was not enough to relieve the immediate suffering of those caught up in a famine situation and that it was equally or more important to address the underlying social and economic conditions that rise to situations in which people found themselves in desperate need for food. It is not an easy task, but there is nevertheless no turning back. In addition to the fact that non- governmental organizations are now opening their work to economic, social, and cultural rights,[11] new international nongovernmental actors tend to make development issues (including public health) their focus of choice, as illustrated by the international contribution of the Bill and Melinda Gates Foundation to prevent illness caused by malnutrition and to improve maternal and child health.

A third element connecting INGOs, governance, and democratization is the development of a greater sense of international responsibility and solidarity in the context of humanitarian crises. Embedded in and expressed and conveyed by international human rights and humanitarian norms, this sense of international solidarity and responsibility was given much impetus in the 1970s and 1980s by the INGOs' response to humanitarian emergencies including famines and wars. In this regard, Médecins sans Frontières, founded by Bernard Kouchner in 1971, involved in the alleviation of numerous disasters in the 1970s and

---

[9] On Amnesty International and Human Rights Watch, see, for example, chapters 1–4 in Claude E. Welch, Jr. (ed.), *NGOs and Human Rights. Promise and Performance* (Philadelphia: University of Pennsylvania Press, 2001).

[10] To this we should add that environmental rights are also given growing attention by NGOs.

[11] That is the case of Amnesty International and Human Rights Watch. See Chapters 9 and 11 of this book for an account of their evolving mandates.

1980s (earthquakes, wars, floods, massacres, hurricanes), did much to raise public consciousness of suffering in faraway places. It is, however, the end of the Cold War that provided a major opportunity to expand concerns for victims of humanitarian disasters, in particular, calling for an end to the principle of nonintervention as an absolute priority over humanitarian considerations. The relaxation of global strategic competition between the Communist bloc and the West and the multiplication of local conflicts affecting civilians first and foremost led INGOs to play a key role in putting humanitarian issues on the map, beginning with the question of humanitarian intervention. Ultimately, their operational work and advocacy efforts contributed to the norm of intervention becoming more accepted in the 1990s, and to its recognition under the term *responsibility to protect* on the occasion of the UN World Summit in September 2005.[12]

Finally, it is the issue of globalization that accounts for the link among INGOs, governance, and democratization. After all, globalization, or partial globalization (depending on the term one uses[13]), is not a straightforward engine of democratization and better governance. Although supporters of liberalism often underline the connection among globalization, democratization, and good governance, globalization also has negative side effects. In this context, the fact that opposing the pathologies of globalization has become a key aspect of INGOs' work makes them a valuable contributor to a more democratic globalization. As such, INGOs turn out to be the beneficiaries of world openness, a factor contributing to globalization, and a critic of its shortcomings. Trade and financial policies, and their social consequences, have been a particular concern for anticapitalist-oriented INGOs. What came to be known as the "battle of Seattle" epitomized the ability of INGOs to challenge the "Washington consensus."[14] By organizing massive protests on the occasion of a ministerial meeting of the World Trade Organization in Seattle at the end of November 1999, INGOs contested the mainstream policies of the financial international organizations and their main member state supporters, contributing to the launching of movements that around the world seek alternatives to the discourse and practice of economic liberalism.[15]

---

[12] Refer to *2005 World Summit Outcome* (New York: United Nations, 20 September 2005), A/60/L.1, section "Responsibility to Protect Populations from Genocide, War Crimes, Ethnic Cleansing and Crimes against Humanity," paragraphs 138–140.

[13] See Robert O. Keohane, *Power and Governance in a Partially Globalized World* (London: Routledge, 2002).

[14] Joseph E. Stigliz, *Globalization and Its Discontents* (New York: Norton, 2003).

[15] On these issues, refer for instance to Mario Pianta, "Parallel Summits of Global Civil Society," in *Global Civil Society 2001*, eds. Helmut Anheier, Marlies Glasius, and Mary Kaldor, op cit.; and Yahia Said and Meghnad Desai, "Trade and Global Civil Society: The Anti-Capitalist Movement Revisited," in *Global Civil Society Yearbook 2003*, eds. Mary Kaldor, Helmut Anheier, and Marlies Glasius, op cit.

II. INGOs AND THE SHAPING OF FUTURE GOVERNANCE

The significant role that the nongovernmental sector has in national and international politics is only destined to grow stronger in the coming years. The reasons for this are multifold. Six of them deserve to be underlined. They concern the counterbalance function of nongovernmental organizations, the type of collective mobilization that they constitute, their attractiveness for young people, the importance that women have in INGOs, the alliance between new technologies and nongovernmental organizations, and the increasing presence of INGOs in non-Western countries.

What about, first, the counterbalancing role that INGOs play vis-à-vis mainstream politics? I mentioned earlier that the nongovernmental sector is part of a democratization process. This does not mean that the political establishment, with its institutions and leaders, is always willing to allow democratization to unfold. As a matter of fact, at the national (in nondemocratic but also in democratic regimes) and international (be it in the multilateral context or not) levels, wide participation from civil society, transparency, and accountability still tend to be resisted rather than truly embraced. Compared with political realism, abiding by the principles of participation, transparency, and accountability remains in a distant second place, too often being a matter of lip service rather than a "natural" urge of those in charge. Yet as individuals increasingly identify with democratic values and norms, the pressure that nongovernmental organizations exercise in favor of these principles will be needed more and more in the future. They will be key in helping political decision makers and institutions not to lose sight of the fact that fulfilling their responsibilities toward society and its people is a central condition of their legitimacy.

It is also because INGOs are now more or less alone in the field of collective mobilization that their role could turn more important in the coming years. In the past, beyond the differences existing among countries – developed and developing, democratic and nondemocratic, liberal and socialist – trade unions were a social and political force that could not be disregarded. It was not possible to ignore their power of attraction and capacity to challenge the establishment. This force started to decline in the 1980s. The 1990s and 2000s, far from changing the trend, only deepened it. Sure, "proletarization" and factories spread in a number of developing countries during the last two decades, particularly in China. But de-industrialization, combined with new forms of employment and new types of workers, especially through a shift to the finance, services, information, entertainment, and tourism industries, undermined the traditional base of trade unions. Compared with the blue-collar membership and left-wing focus on labor, social, and political conditions of trade unions, the more middle-class and educated staff of nongovernmental organizations, and their relatively abstract (to some extent socially and politically disembodied) concerns for individual rights, led INGOs to emerge as more adapted to and equipped for the ongoing changes. The commitment of the nongovernmental sector to progressive liberal values, while creating some overlap and compatibility with the dominating neo-liberalism, put them in a better position to mount a challenge (of course, within limits). This will remain the case for the foreseeable future. Although since around 2000 there have been signs of reemergence of labor solidarity, the fact that it is taking place, as part of the anticapitalist movement, more within the framework (in spirit and structure) of the INGOs than in the one of traditional trade unionism, encourages this speculation.[16]

The strong relationship between INGOs and the younger generation, particularly young university graduates, is another factor indicating that their importance is likely to increase.[17] The goals and working modalities of INGOs contribute to explaining this relationship. There is a community of value between INGOs and the young. The desire to improve the world and the living conditions of people at the center of the progressive agenda of INGOs resonates with young people who are often idealist. In addition, unlike traditional workplaces (in the public and private sectors) structured around hierarchy, seniority, and process, NGOs welcome the skills and the initiative and result-driven approach that the most dynamic and public good-minded graduates have. Less positively, the difficulty to find employment in mainstream national and international organizations (either because the positions are few and competitive or because, following bad economic conditions or an introduction to "flexible" working conditions, employment opportunities are reduced while the number of students grows) also make nongovernmental sector attractive. This helps overlook the uncertainty regarding long-term career prospects that is still, at least for those with a low level of institutionalization, the mark of NGOs.

Compared with private corporations, governments, or international organizations, INGOs tend not to be at the high end of power ranking. This reality cannot, however, mitigate the importance that women occupy in the leadership and workforce of INGOs. More than in any mainstream workplace and despite all the progress made, INGOs make the most out of the increasing number of educated women. They also make the most out of the internationally oriented

---

[16] For an interesting perspective on trade unions and NGOs, see, for example, Dan Gallin, "Trade Unions and NGOs: A Necessary Partnership for Social Development," in *Global Policy Forum* (January 2001). Available at http://www.globalpolicy.org/ngos/role/globalact/business/2001/0101tu.htm. Refer also to Peter Waterman and Jill Timms, "Trade Union Internationalism and a Global Civil Society in the Making," in *Global Civil Society Yearbook 2004/5*, eds. Helmut Anheier, Marlies Glasius, and Mary Kaldor (London: Sage, 2004), 192–3.

[17] Increasingly, INGOs are created with a focus on youth, especially in developing regions, such as Alliance Towards Harnessing Global Opportunity (ATHGO International), aiming to inspire future generations of international professionals to become decision makers and diplomats with skills and vision to cope with the changes and challenges of the twenty-first century. For more information, see http://www.athgo.org.

expertise acquired by women to break away from traditional roles.[18] Take, for example, linguistic skills. In countries where women have access to education but little opportunities for careers, their often more developed command of English allows them to create professional opportunities that are out of reach for men who remain captives of their secured paths.[19] This is another element that puts NGOs on the map for the future. Openness to women gives INGOs a social and professional edge that will be built on.

The link between INGOs and new technologies is a fifth factor. Nongovernmental activity tends to mobilize across borders. This is especially important for developing and transitional countries. In this regard, technology is one of the main ways of communication that allows cross-border mobilization, in particular, when physical movement can be difficult because of either political or monetary impediments. Here, obviously, youth holds a somewhat natural advantage, since young people are more likely to be able to use technology to make civil society as active and vibrant as possible.

Sixth, there is the increasing presence of INGOs in non-Western countries. Within certain limitations imposed by the obvious forces of less freedom of expression and mobilization, non-Western states have indeed seen a growth and expansion of their own nongovernmental sector. For these organizations to pursue their goals and activities in a meaningful manner, despite the challenges they face on an everyday basis, they tend to organize across state borders. The example of Eastern Europe, before but also after the fall of the Soviet Union, is prominent in this context. This comes in addition to the growing presence of Western INGOs in non-Western regions.

III. THE ETHICAL DILEMMAS OF INGOs AT THE UNITED NATIONS

The connection among INGOs, governance, and democratization at the national and international level and the fact that INGOs are, for the reasons mentioned earlier, today and tomorrow's social fabric of collective mobilization, do not mean that they are "in the clear." Parallel to their gained importance and visibility is the greater scrutiny under which they are operating – a scrutiny that frequently leads observers of INGOs to question their representativity and mechanisms of

---

[18] On women and NGOs, consult, for instance, Mark M. Gray, Miki Caul Kittilson, and Wayne Sandholtz, "Women and Globalization: A Study of 180 Countries, 1975–2000," in *International Organization* (Cambridge, MA: MIT Press, 2006).

[19] In Japan, internationally trained women can at times turn the limitations that society imposes on them into sources of professional opportunities for the benefit of nongovernmental organizations, foreign corporations working in Japan, and international organizations. This is possible because Japanese women have equal access to education and because the wealth of Japanese society makes education abroad (in particular, in English-speaking countries) affordable. Nevertheless, this state of affairs does not amount to an entirely rosy picture. Refer to Karen Kelsky, *Women on the Verge: Japanese Women, Western Dreams* (Durham, NC: Duke University Press, 2001).

accountability as well as other shortcomings. This is essential considering the place that INGOs, in addition to their current significance, are poised to have in the future.

Before turning in the final section of the chapter to recommendations for how to handle dilemmas, let us review the challenges INGOs encounter at UN headquarters. In this perspective, the first thing to underline is that they take place within the framework of four characteristics: (1) the institutional guidelines of UN–NGO interactions; (2) the evolving nature of UN activities and how this affects the nongovernmental sector's work; (3) the agenda of NGOs and how they relate to the UN; and (4) resulting from this state of affairs, the need to balance ethical priorities and political considerations in making choices meant to have a maximum positive impact and minimum downsides.

(1) The UN and nongovernmental organizations have been working together at UN headquarters since the early days.[20] While from 1946 to 1950 NGOs participation rights were acquired on a piecemeal basis, the developing practice was codified by the Economic and Social Council (ECOSOC) Resolution 288 X (B) of 27 February 1950. The resolution granted INGOs with a consultative status to matters falling within the competence of the ECOSOC with respect to international economic, social, cultural, educational, and health matters and to questions of human rights.[21] Consultations were meant, on one hand, to enable the council or one of its bodies to secure expert information or advice and, on the other hand, to allow organizations that represent important elements of public opinion to express their views.[22] They entailed three main levels: attendance at meetings of the Economic and Social Council and its committees,[23] access to the UN Secretariat and its public information resources,[24] and accreditation to UN conferences and other onetime events.[25] Since then, two other resolutions have been adopted regarding arrangements for consultations with NGOs. Resolution 1296 of 23 May 1968 did not bring much change. Slightly different was Resolution 1996/31, adopted on 25 July 1996, as an outcome of the review of the practice that followed the UN conference on environment and development at Rio. Although the consultative status of nongovernmental organizations was not modified, a significant political change was introduced: the presumption that an NGO must be international was deleted, and it became routine to grant

---

[20] See Article 71 of the Charter of the United Nations: "The Economic and Social Council may make suitable arrangements for consultation with non-governmental organizations which are concerned with matters within its competence" (New York: the United Nations, Department of Public Information, September 1993).

[21] Paragraph 2 of section B of the resolution concerning "Arrangements for Consultation with Non-Governmental Organizations," February 27, 1950.

[22] See Article 14 of Resolution 288 X (B), February 7, 1950.

[23] See Parts IV, V, and VI of Resolution 288 X (B).

[24] Part IX of Resolution 288 X (B).   [25] Part VII of Resolution 288 X (B).

consultative status to "national" nongovernmental organizations.[26] This contributed to a significant increase in the number of NGOs accredited to the UN. Between 1996 and 2003, there was an exponential growth of nongovernmental organizations, many of them national NGOs, applying for consultative status, with the number of those acquiring it increasing from 744 in 1992 to 2,350 in 2003 and a mounting backlog of applications waiting for review by the Economic and Social Council's (ECOSOC) committee on NGOs.

(2) What has also helped to shape the relationship between the UN and the nongovernmental sector at UN headquarters as it currently stands, and consequently the framework in which INGOs face dilemmas, is the evolution of the UN activities since the 1990s. In this regard, increased UN involvement in international economic, social, cultural, educational, and health matters and in questions of human rights and humanitarian affairs has had a significant impact. In augmenting the occasions of overlap and interaction between the UN and nongovernmental organizations with consultative status, this trend has contributed to influence the work of the nongovernmental sector at UN headquarters. Three developments have played a particular role here. First, is the fact that, with the UN's increasing involvement in peacekeeping, it came to address human rights and humanitarian issues and economic, social, health, and related matters more frequently (with, for instance, a variety of measures taken to prevent the eruption of conflicts, humanitarian assistance dispositions adopted during wars, and peace-building initiatives launched in the aftermath of conflicts). Because these questions echoed nongovernmental organizations concerns, this orientation affected INGOs working in the intergovernmental setting. Second, a similar effect is related to the renewed interest of the international community in development issues, not simply in the context of the reconstruction demands in postconflict situations but also regarding the continued shortcomings of development in Africa and the unwelcome economic, social, and cultural effects of globalization. Considering the historical and ever more heated engagement of INGO's in these matters, this evolution was destined to trigger a response from their work at UN headquarters. Third, the same can be said of the growing commitment since the 1990s of the international community to democratization and democracy requirements. The nongovernmental sector has adjusted to this state of affairs, conjointly supporting it and challenging its limitations to encourage a deepening of UN efforts in favor of democratic rights.

(3) A third element influencing the framework in which INGOs' dilemmas unfold in their work at and interactions with UN headquarters is the agenda and activities of INGOs themselves in the late twentieth and early twenty-first centuries. In this perspective, it is significant that although INGOs invest resources and effort in the advancement of progressive values in international law,

[26] Refer to ECOSOC Resolution 1996/31, 25 July 1996.

especially in connection with human rights, such investment is more about ensuring the best possible implementation of the norms in place than about creating new ones. The fact that the major normative areas of the various aspects of human life in a social environment tend now to be covered and addressed by international law explains this orientation. Surely this has an impact on how INGOs work at UN headquarters. As a complement to the hands-on activities of INGOs on the ground, it is mainly about making sure that member states and the UN take seriously the norms to which they are committed. The wide use and high effectiveness of "shadow reports,"[27] called on to check whether states comply with their agreed-on obligation in the context of international human rights treaties and conventions (e.g., by bringing attention to neglected and politically sensitive issues), has to be seen in this light. Such focus on implementation can also mean pressing for a progressive interpretation of human rights norms, as was the case for the "responsibility to protect" or for the establishment of institutions designed to help implementation of human rights, shown, for example, by the support of INGOs to the International Criminal Court (ICC).

(4) It is against this background that the need to balance ethical priorities and political considerations to make choices with a maximum positive impact and minimum downside takes on particular importance in the context of the work of INGOs at the UN headquarters. In their relations with the UN and its member states, nongovernmental organizations have to be both ethical and politically savvy. The two sides of the equation, and finding an equilibrium between them, are equally critical to ensure the effectiveness of INGOs. Because the UN and its member states are key partners in INGOs' ability to make a difference, INGOs must be pragmatic, factoring in their often realist approach to international life. But because ethical commitment is the central part of their legitimacy, INGOs must make it an essential dimension of their deliberations, decisions, and actions. When they succeed in this enterprise, INGOs, without being decision makers per se and formally in a position to negotiate policies in and with the UN, can have a real influence. This does not mean that, in the process, INGOs stop having to deal with dilemmas. Because the hiatus, and therefore the tension, between the demands of ethics and the demands of politics remains, dilemmas cannot be disposed. At most, they can be endured, calling for seeking to identify and implement opportunities in the midst of constraints.

In the multilateral environment, these dilemmas fall into two main categories: dilemmas of ends and dilemmas of means. Although coming in forms and shapes characteristic of the politics of UN headquarters, they are not entirely foreign to those encountered in the field. This does not come as a surprise. After all, the dichotomy between the field and headquarters is to some extent artificial, if

---

[27] Shadow reports are a method for nongovernmental organizations to supplement or present alternative information to the periodic government reports that state parties are required to submit under treaties.

simply because in both cases, the goals pursued by the nongovernmental sector are similar.[28]

Balancing the Ethical Ends of INGOs with the Multilateral Politics of UN Headquarters

The dilemmas of ends that INGOs face in the course of their interaction with the UN concern two issues in particular: long-term versus short-term objectives and INGOs' views on human rights violations versus those of the victims.

Long-term versus short-term objectives – The dilemma between long-term versus short-term goals is twofold: how to assess the benefits of a long-term strategy compared with the ones of a short-term approach and how to avoid allowing the pursuit of one to undermine the other. This twofold dilemma, which distances INGOs from the ideal situation in which, far from being part of an either-or logic, long-term and short-term approaches are complementary and even reinforce each other, is especially significant at UN headquarters. This is true because diplomatic work at UN headquarters is often geared toward long-term changes that are at odds with short-term results. Dealing with diplomats at the UN can be a dilemma when the choice between voicing a controversial truth and nurturing an important dialogue has to be made. The pursuit of a long-term success on one issue can limit the ability to comment on another. At times, it might even be necessary to have some secrecy in the short term to maintain more long-term work to which much time and energy has been dedicated. Because this encourages INGOs to invest in the long term, it also exposes them to use resources with little expectation of immediate achievement and with uncertain outcomes down the road. INGOs try to address this predicament in two ways: by spreading, or distributing, as much of their resources as possible (time, financial, and human resources) between the long and short term, and by going for what they can win quickly, even if it is not ideal, while not forgetting entirely the long term.

INGOs' views on human rights violations versus those of the victims – The hiatus that can exist between what nongovernmental organizations and victims see as human right priorities is the source of another quandary. Once again, the dilemma is twofold: when the views of INGOs and victims fail to coincide, how is it possible to balance the trade-offs between what nongovernmental organizations do and what is most important for victims? Rights and needs that are considered to be of great importance in one society are not necessarily viewed as such in

---

[28] The dichotomy between the field and headquarters is also relative because the field of someone is the headquarters of someone else, and vice versa, and because the development of the Internet connects fields but also widens fields of activity, as the strategy adopted by Human Rights in China in its advocacy work confirms.

another. Issues such as homophobia[29] and maltreatment of women might not be highest on the priority list in environments where the pressing needs concern pure survival both in terms of nourishment and security. Also, how is it possible to ensure that when INGOs focus on human rights violations that are, for one reason or another, attention grabbing at the UN, and consequently are more likely to attract funding, political mileage, and possibly results, they do not overlook issues that are less visible or offer less traction but are equally important? In this regard, the fact that the nongovernmental organizations' agenda on human rights at times aligns with the UN's, including its Security Council, rather than serving all victims equally, tends to reproduce the biased attention of the international community.

INGOs' Dilemmas of Means in the Multilateral Environment

The dilemmas of means, that is, modalities of action, that INGOs have to deal with in the UN context come particularly to the fore in relation to five issues: forming coalitions versus acting alone, aligned participation versus critical engagement, the independence versus dependence of INGOs, the pros and cons of "naming and shaming," and power location versus institution location.

The quandary of the INGOs' coalition approach – For INGOs, entering into a coalition amounts to weighing the benefits of maintaining institutional integrity versus the benefits of mobilizing as widely as possible in the service of change. On one hand, coalitions allow INGOs to gain strength, put forward more diverse voices, and even attract greater funding. In this regard, despite the fact that focusing on one issue can limit addressing other questions, the benefits of coalitions are easier to achieve when the matter at hand is clear-cut and relatively uncontroversial, for example, regarding issues such as landmines and child soldiers. On the other hand, INGO coalitions have their downsides. In particular, they may end up restricting much of INGOs' independence and the ability to put forward their own agendas. There are often substantial differences within large INGOs – differences which are only magnified when working with others; for example, Oxfam Belgium favors boycotting Israeli goods whereas Oxfam USA is against this policy. Because independence, including holding on to their views, is an essential aspect of the fabric of INGOs, the leverage that they gain in coalescing does not always compensate for what is lost in the glossing over of their specificities. This may explain why INGOs tend to be eager to preserve their respective approach on issues, even after they join a coalition. Obviously, this state of affairs makes such coalitions fragile.

Aligned participation versus critical engagement – Another dilemma of means entails having to choose between the benefits and downsides of a muted participation to UN activities versus those of critical engagement. When it comes

---

[29] This is notably something that Human Rights Watch came to discover in South Africa.

to muted participation, it takes a variety of forms – for example, agreeing to participate in UN forums on the conditions imposed by governments that participants will not criticize them; agreeing not to use publicly information coming from diplomats; and agreeing not to disclose shortcomings or corruption among the UN and its member states' institutions and actors. What is pursued here by INGOs, through seeking to establish continuous working relationships in the UN framework, is changing the system from within. The downsides of this attitude, which amounts to having nongovernmental organizations deprive themselves of speaking out on sensitive issues, are also the upsides of a critical engagement approach. In complying with UN demands, INGOs run the risk of failing in their commitment to truth, as well as in their commitment to the democratization of the norms, institutions, and practices of governance. In their desire to be recognized as partners, let alone as insiders, nongovernmental organizations blur the line between them and the status quo, which, in principle, they have vowed to challenge for the sake of improving social reality.[30]

Independence versus dependence of nongovernmental organizations – Closely related to both the quandary of INGOs' coalition approach and aligned participation and critical engagement, the imperative for INGOs to be independent accounts for another dilemma. Independence is so important for INGOs that it is an indication of their credibility and legitimacy, yet INGOs are constantly in a situation of dependency. As a matter of fact, they cannot avoid it, not only because they rely to some extent on governments for funding but also because they frequently need the cooperation of the UN and its member states to advance their causes. How, then, to balance the imperative, and advantages, of independence with the reality of dependence? In other words, how much dependence can be endured without undermining the credibility of INGOs and their ability to make a difference?

The pros and cons of naming and shaming – The trade-off associated with naming and shaming is a fourth dilemma with which INGOs are confronted at the UN. Naming and shaming is a method that can be effective. For instance, describing Guantanamo Bay prison as a gulag allowed Amnesty International to bring attention to the conditions of detainees at the prison. Also, because in the UN system the settings where naming and shaming are pursued are separate from the ones in which capacity-building and development take place, the former does not have to jeopardize the latter, therefore making it possible to engineer a win–win situation (on the naming and shaming and on the capacity-building and development fronts). This being said, naming and shaming can also be counterproductive. It is prone to alienate governments at a time when their cooperation would be useful. This is, for example, the case in China, where the

---

[30] This situation brings to mind the similar case of journalists, who must often trade critical reporting for access to information.

politics of embarrassment, so to speak, can backfire because of the nationalism of the government and of its ordinary citizens.[31]

Power location versus institution location – The plurality of UN locations and the power imbalance existing among them create another dilemma for INGOs. This is particularly significant in the context of human rights. The fact that the power in the UN system is largely located in New York whereas its human rights institutions are mainly based in Geneva is something that is generally presented as a contributing factor to the relative weakness of the human rights agenda. The problem was compounded by the dysfunctional character of the UN Human Rights Commission – a situation that has led a number of human rights INGOs to somewhat reduce their representation in Geneva. Thus, the need for INGOs to balance their presence in Geneva with their exercising of pressure in New York (with the advantage of power proximity).

Ultimately, the dilemmas of ends and means, representing a sample of the ethical and political challenges encountered by INGOs at the UN, are more than a testimony of the challenges confronting them. They indicate as well that the multilateral environment is important enough to make confronting these difficult issues worthwhile.[32]

IV. THE WAY FORWARD: CONCLUDING RECOMMENDATIONS FOR THE FUTURE

In recent years, a number of UN panels have been organized, both inside and outside the UN framework, on the relations between nongovernmental organizations, the UN, and its member states.[33] The main aims of these panels have been twofold: first, to take stock of the present situation and, second, explore the ways through which NGOs, the UN, and member states could become better partners, for their respective benefits as well as for those of global governance in general.

Regarding the first point, it is interesting to note the concerns raised by a background paper prepared for the Secretary-General's Panel of Eminent Persons on

[31] Something with which Human Rights in China, for example, is confronted on a regular basis.
[32] Incidentally, this is why NGOs do not hesitate, whenever possible, to invest resources in training human rights activists to deal with UN mechanisms.
[33] See, for instance, the report of the secretary-general, *Views of Member States, Members of The Specialized Agencies, Observers, Intergovernmental and Non-Governmental Organizations from all Regions on the Report of the Secretary-General on Arrangements and Practices for the Interaction Of Non-Governmental Organizations in all Activities of the United Nations System* (New York: United Nations, 8 September 1999), A/54/329; *Report of the UN Civil Society Outreach Symposium*, sponsored by the Stanley Foundation and cosponsored by the World Federation of United Nations Associations (New York: Arden Conference Center, Harriman, 30 May–1 June 2001); *Multi-Stakeholder Partnerships and UN-Civil Society Relationships*, Collection of Materials from the Multi-Stakeholder Workshop on Partnerships and UN-Civil Society Relationships (New York: Pocantico, February 2004); *We the Peoples: Civil Society, the UN and Global Governance* (New York: United Nations, June 2004).

United Nations Relations with Civil Society listed on behalf of member states, the UN Secretariat, and nongovernmental organizations.[34] When it comes to member states, the presence of civil society in the United Nations is presented as characterized by a dichotomy: willingness of member states to allow participation on the one hand, and their desire to keep it firmly under control on the other. Concerning the UN Secretariat and its management, the importance of adopting a trilateral relationship including governments in their dialogue with civil society and vice versa is stressed, where feasible, to avoid the erosion of the UN's legitimacy in the eyes of NGOs and the broader public. However, the rapid growth of NGOs in numbers and demands is also seen as problematic. For instance, UN management finds it increasingly difficult to verify the bona fides of organizations seeking accreditation to ECOSOC or to major meetings. This issue tends to become more and more politicized now that divisions exist between the European Union and the United States over global governance and that parallel divisions have emerged within the South, leading to the fact that there is no longer a straightforward North–South divide. As for NGOs, if they welcome the access that they now have to the UN and its components, they are also frustrated that their greater proximity to deliberations continues to translate into little, or too slow, substantial change in international agreements or what is done on the ground.[35]

To if not overcome then at least remedy these concerns and dilemmas that they create, the report of the Panel of Eminent Persons on UN-Civil Society Relationships, published in June 2004, issued a number of recommendations, thirty to be exact.[36] The first twenty-three recommendations dealt with substantive suggestions to improve relations and the last seven last explored concrete modalities to ensure their implementation. Among these recommendations were the following:

On the convening role of the United Nations and the need to foster multiconstituency processes, the report recommended:

> *Proposal 1.* In exercising its convening power, the United Nations should emphasize the inclusion of all constituencies relevant to the issue, recognize that the key actors are different for different issues and foster multi-stakeholder partnerships to pioneer solutions and empower a range of global policy networks to innovate and build momentum on policy options. Member States need opportunities for collective decision-making, but they should signal their preparedness to engage other actors in deliberative processes.

---

[34] "UN System and Civil Society – An Inventory and Analysis of Practices, Background Paper for the Secretary-General's Panel of Eminent Persons on United Nations Relations with Civil Society" (New York: United Nations, May 2003). Available at http://www.un-ngls.org/UNreform.htm.

[35] Ibid, section IV, "Reviewing the Relationship."

[36] *We the Peoples: Civil Society, the UN and Global Governance*, op cit.

Proposal 2. The United Nations should embrace an array of forums, each designed to achieve a specific outcome, with participation determined accordingly. The cycle of global debate on an issue should include: interactive high-level round tables to survey the framework of issues; Global conferences to define norms and targets; Multi-stakeholder partnerships to put the new norms and targets into practice; Multi-stakeholder hearings to monitor compliance, review experience and revise strategies.

Proposal 5. The Secretariat should foster multi-constituency processes as new conduits for discussion of United Nations priorities, redirecting resources now used for single-constituency forums covering multiple issues. The Secretariat, together with other relevant bodies of the United Nations system, should convene public hearings to review progress in meeting globally agreed commitments. . . .

Proposal 6. The General Assembly should permit the carefully planned participation of actors besides central Governments in its processes. In particular, the Assembly should regularly invite contributions to its committees and special sessions by those offering high-quality independent input.[37]

On investing more in partnerships:

Proposal 7. In order to mainstream partnerships, the Secretary-General should, with the approval of Member States and donor support: . . . Ensure systematic learning from partnership efforts by creating a multi-stakeholder Partnership Assessment Forum that includes United Nations staff, Governments, civil society organizations and others. Provide training in partnership development to Governments, civil society and other constituencies, as well as to United Nations staff. Periodically review the effectiveness of those efforts.[38]

On strengthening the Security Council and the role for civil society:

Proposal 12. Security Council members should further strengthen their dialogue with civil society, with the support of the Secretary-General by:

- Improving the planning and effectiveness of the Arria formula[39] meetings by lengthening lead times and covering travel costs to increase the participation of actors from the field. United Nations country staff should assist in identifying civil society interlocutors.
- Ensuring that Security Council field missions meet regularly with appropriate local civil society leaders, international humanitarian NGOs and perhaps others, such as business leaders. United Nations Headquarters and field staff should facilitate the meetings.
- Installing an experimental series of Security Council seminars to discuss issues of emerging importance to the Council. Serviced by the Secretariat, these would

[37] Ibid, 15–16.   [38] Ibid, 16–17.
[39] The Arria Formula, named after Ambassador Diego Arria of Venezuela who devised it in 1992, is an information arrangement that allows the UN Security Council to be briefed about international peace and security issues by invited parties.

include presentations by civil society and other constituencies as well as United Nations specialists, such as special rapporteurs.

- Convening independent commissions of inquiry after Council-mandated operations. A global public policy committee connecting national foreign affairs committees could serve as such a commission.[40]

On streamlining and depoliticizing accreditation and access:

Proposal 19. The United Nations should realign accreditation with its original purpose, namely, it should be an agreement between civil society actors and Member States based on the applicants' expertise, competence and skills. To achieve this, and to widen the access of civil society organizations beyond Economic and Social Council forums, Member States should agree to merge the current procedures at United Nations Headquarters for the Council, the Department of Public Information and conferences and their follow-up into a single United Nations accreditation process, with responsibility for accreditation assumed by an existing committee of the General Assembly.[41]

As for what these proposals mean for staff, resources, and management, the report suggests:

Proposal 26. The Secretary-General should make redressing North-South imbalances a priority in enhancing United Nations–civil society relations. He should enlist donor support for enhancing the capacity of the United Nations to identify and work with local actors, establishing a fund to build Southern civil society capacity to participate and ensuring that country-level engagement feeds into the global deliberative processes.

Proposal 27. The United Nations should establish a fund to enhance the capacity of civil society in developing countries to engage in United Nations processes and partnerships.[42]

Ultimately, the secretary-general is asked to provide global leadership:

Proposal 29. The Secretary-General should use his capacity as chairman of the United Nations system coordination mechanism to encourage all agencies, including the Bretton Woods institutions, to enhance their engagement with civil society and other actors and to cooperate with one another across the system to promote this aim, with periodic progress reviews.[43]

As a whole, these recommendations called for more transparency, accountability, effectiveness, and shared partnership on all sides. Following up on this, the 2005 World Summit Outcome document, published in September 2005,

---

[40] *We the Peoples: Civil Society, the UN and Global Governance*, 19.
[41] Ibid, 21.   [42] Ibid, 23–4.
[43] Ibid, 24.

underlined the importance of the relations among NGOs, the United Nations, and member states.[44] Throughout these recommendations, as well as agreements of the United Nations in general, a vagueness that will come to influence the ways in which INGOs work at the UN and beyond cannot be overlooked. Although this lack of clarity grants INGOs a certain leeway for them to define their role and activities, it might also make for something of a challenge, or even a dilemma, of its own.[45]

* * *

INGOs expressed concerns on certain aspects of the 2004 Report of the Panel of Eminent Persons on UN-Civil Society Relationships. Amnesty International, for example, indicated that it felt uncomfortable with the emphasis that the report put on broadening the participation of civil society and other actors in the UN processes, among them, the private sector and parliamentarians.[46] The World Federalist Movement had similar concerns.[47] But even those INGOs that expressed concern joined the great majority of organizations in giving their support to the panel's efforts. The World Federation of United Nations Associations (WFUNA) was one of those that reacted positively. Among other things, it endorsed the four main principles underlying the proposed paradigm shift in the way the UN functions, that is, that the UN needs to become an outward-looking organization; embrace a plurality of constituencies; connect

[44] See *2005 World Summit Outcome*, op cit., paragraph 172: "We welcome the positive contributions of the private sector and civil society, including non-governmental organizations, in the promotion and implementation of development and human rights programmes and stress the importance of their continued engagement with Governments, the United Nations and other international organizations in these key areas," p. 39.

[45] See how multilateral negotiations and diplomacy leads to vagueness of policy recommendations; Jean-Marc Coicaud, *Beyond the National Interest* (Washington, DC: United States Institute of Peace, 2006), in particular, chapter 2.

[46] Letter from Yvonne Terlingen, Amnesty International representative at the United Nations, addressed to the UN Deputy Secretary-General, Ms. Louise Fréchette, dated 31 August 2004, reference UN/NYt/093/04.

[47] See the letter of William R. Pace, executive director, World Federalist Movement (WFM), to the UN secretary-general and the deputy secretary-general: "we are concerned with the Panel's emphasis on the participation of other actors such as the business sector without outlining a framework for the rules of engagement for these actors. We do not object to the access and participation of for-profit organizations but we find it crucial that legitimate rules of engagement are established for these actors.. . . We have some concerns regarding the need for more inclusiveness in consulting with parliamentary associations. WFM has had a parliamentary dimension to our organization throughout its six decades and while we welcome the emergent role of the Inter-Parliamentary Union with the General Assembly, we have substantive recommendations on how to improve this relationship," dated 24 August 2004. Refer to http://www.un-ngls.org/.

the local with the global; and help strengthen democracy in the twenty-first century.[48]

In a modest way, and along similar policy lines, the participants in the workshop that the United Nations University organized in August 2005 on NGOs at the UN came up with additional suggestions.

At the most general level, what continues to be important is to ease the fears of governments regarding sovereignty issues. Because states tend to view the rising role of INGOs as part of the hollowing out of their power, it is critical to convey the message that INGOs are not about diminishing the role of the state but about reinforcing, more or less directly, its democratic dimension and its ability to perform its responsibilities.[49] This could be of particular relevance in the context of the regulation of multinational corporation activities, a question that will not be possible to address systematically in the future unless there is a high level of trust and cooperation between member states and INGOs.

In institutional terms, a better coordination among UN agencies focusing on specific issues and INGOs working on similar matters would also help to maximize what are, in the end, insufficient resources with which to tackle the major ills of the world, especially in the various areas of development. Considering how much there is to do, it does not make much sense to allow competition and overlap among UN agencies and INGOs. Looking for divisions of labor and complementarity based on their respective strengths, both at the agenda and implementation level, would be a better option.

In the field of human rights, reporting mechanisms open to civil society such as shadow reports could make more efficient and credible the activity of the UN and, more precisely, feed into the establishment and functioning of the foreseen UN Human Rights Council. Also in the domain of reporting, one of the participants in the workshop, David Cingranelli, professor of political science at Binghamton University, emphasized the importance of having the heads of the central offices of human rights INGOs issue annual human rights reports, separating the function of reporting on the human rights practices of governments around the world from the function of remedying human rights abuses.[50]

Regarding those INGOs that issue annual reports, Cingranelli made the two following points:

---

[48] See the WFUNA response to the Report on Civil Society Relations with the UN, http://www.un-ngls.org/.

[49] As Russia is trying to implement laws that severely limit the activity of INGOs within its borders, concerns are being raised in regard to the undermining of years of efforts toward democratization. See, for example, Marie Jégo, "La Douma place les ONG sous le strict contrôle de l'Etat russe," *Le Monde*, 25 November 2005.

[50] The following suggestions are based on a memo that Professor Cingranelli sent to the editors of this volume, in connection with the third workshop in New York.

First, activist scholars and policy makers need a human rights report that better reflects the range of human rights recognized in the Universal Declaration of
Human Rights. Existing annual reports by Amnesty International and Human
Rights Watch that strongly emphasize civil and political rights are not objective
because they are selective. They also are not fair to countries that are weak in
this area but have strong points in their efforts to protect other types of human
rights. The best way to convince the rest of the world that Amnesty International and Human Rights Watch are now more concerned about an "integrated
human rights approach"[51] is to change the content of the most visible publications these organizations produce. Alternatively, they could produce new
publications that serve the new function while keeping the existing reports as is.
Presenting a fuller picture of each country's strengths and weaknesses through
reporting would strike a balance between the shaming tactic and the constructive engagement approach preferred by some who work for human rights in
the field.[52]

Second, Cingranelli suggests that the new report could take the form of a
Human Rights Report Card similar to what the Center on Democratic Performance at Binghamton University has developed.[53] A truly comprehensive, discursive human rights report would be too long to be useful. The U.S. Department
of State *Country Reports on Human Rights Practices* is more comprehensive than
existing INGO reports, but it does not report on government performance on
many economic and social rights dimensions. Still, it runs more than 1,000 pages
annually. A more discursive report might accompany the summary report card
to provide details justifying the grade assigned.

CONCLUSION

INGOs have become a key form of collective mobilization, replacing traditional
forms of collective bargaining, especially unions. The long-term meaning and
impact of this profound transformation are still unclear. At a time when the values
and mechanisms of social solidarity in developed countries are under attack and
the solidarity needs of developing countries vis-à-vis the international realm and
its internationalist actors are ever more important, it remains to be seen whether
INGOs will be able to fill up the gap.

What is certain is that whatever happens, INGOs will continue to face the
dilemmas that we explore in this book. Their commitment to a progressive
agenda at home and abroad is destined to encounter tensions, if not clash, with
the realities of political life, forcing INGOs to compromise and to pursue ideals
in the midst of constraints. This is not a unique situation. After all, any actor,

[51] As referred to earlier in this book by Curt Goering (Chapter 11).
[52] David Cingranelli's memo.
[53] See http://cdp.binghamton.edu/reportcard.htm.

or any institution for that matter, eager to improve people's living conditions, whatever the field of intervention, is destined to face this state of affairs. The real test of fortitude and integrity is to not allow expedience to take over the pursuit of the good, but to balance the two. For when expedience overshadows the persistent, and quite admirable, quest for the good, this amounts to nothing less than, echoing La Fontaine, "lâcher la proie pour l'ombre."[54]

---

[54] Free translation of this French idiom reads: Letting go of the prey for the shadow.

Index